WITHDRAWN

FEAR OF INTIMACY

FEAR OF INTIMACY

ROBERT W. FIRESTONE AND **JOYCE CATLETT**

AMERICAN PSYCHOLOGICAL ASSOCIATION
Washington, DC

144085

Copyright © 1999 by the American Psychological Association. All rights reserved. Except as permitted under the United States Copyright Act of 1976, no part of this publication may be reproduced or distributed in any form or by any means, or stored in a database or retrieval system, without the prior written permission of the publisher.

First printing October 1999
Second printing March 2000
Third printing September 2000

Published by
American Psychological Association
750 First Street, NE
Washington, DC 20002

Copies may be ordered from
APA Order Department
P.O. Box 92984
Washington, DC 20090-2984

In the U.K., Europe, Africa, and the Middle East, copies may be ordered from
American Psychological Association
3 Henrietta Street
Covent Garden, London
WC2E 8LU England

Typeset in Goudy by EPS Group Inc., Easton, MD

Printer: Automated Graphic Systems, Inc., White Plains, MD
Cover Designer: DRI Consulting, Chevy Chase, MD
Technical/Production Editor: Anne Woodworth

Library of Congress Cataloging-in-Publication Data
Firestone, Robert.
    Fear of intimacy / Robert W. Firestone, Joyce Catlett.—1st ed.
      p. cm.
    Includes bibliographical references and index.
    ISBN 1-55798-605-3 (cloth: acid-free paper)
    ISBN 1-55798-720-3 (pbk: acid-free paper)
    1. Intimacy (Psychology) 1. Catlett, Joyce. II. Title.
BF575.I5F57 1999
158.2—dc21   99-34381
                                            CIP

British Library Cataloguing-in-Publication Data
A CIP record is available from the British Library.

Printed in the United States of America

CONTENTS

ACKNOWLEDGMENTS

We express appreciation to Tamsen Firestone and Jo Barrington for their inspirational efforts in editing the manuscript. We are also grateful to Anne Baker, who worked closely with us to complete the final draft. Special thanks to the Glendon Association for their ongoing support and dedication, in particular to Ann Doucette-Gates, PhD, Lisa Firestone, PhD, Ana Perez, Irma Catlett, Jerome Nathan, PhD, and Jina Carvalho, for helping with the manuscript and for disseminating a growing body of written and filmed works.

We also thank Margaret Schlegel, acquisitions editor at APA Books for asking us to submit a manuscript that would reflect the development of theory and methodology in the years since *The Fantasy Bond* was published. Our appreciation goes to Judy Nemes, development editor, for her valuable suggestions regarding editorial and organizational changes.

We express our gratitude to the men and women whose stories gave life to the ideas and concepts described in this work. We acknowledge their courage, openness, and honesty in revealing their personal truths and appreciate their ongoing participation in the longitudinal study and the expanding body of knowledge about the fantasy bond, the voice process, and other important concepts. They have been strongly motivated to share their insights so that other individuals and couples might benefit from their experiences.

The names, places, and other identifying facts contained herein have been fictionalized, and no similarity to any persons, living or dead, is intended. In some instances, certain names in the filmed material were not fictionalized—as these individuals specifically requested that their names remain unchanged—and first names were retained.

PREFACE

This is a book about love: its possibility, its rarity, our longing for love, and our fear of it. In working with individuals from a wide range of clinical and nonclinical populations over the past 43 years, I have found that most people are involved in personal relationships characterized by emotional hunger, desperation, and an intense need for fusion, which seriously interfere with their developing genuine love, respect, and concern for each other. Indeed, most people seem drawn toward being deceptive about their motives, distort the motives of the other, and are compelled to act out defensively. They are both frightened of and tend to withdraw from intimacy. Why?

I have sought answers to this puzzle by studying various populations over the years. My principal focus for the past 21 years has been on a relatively stable group of high-functioning individuals who, motivated by a deep interest in psychology and their own personal development, formed an experimental social milieu and became involved in a multigenerational study of couples and families. I refer to this group as the reference population.[1] As noted above, this is not the exclusive source of the ideas about love and intimacy we present here (I spent 22 years in the practice of individual and group psychotherapy), but it is perhaps the most important.

This unusual psychological laboratory evolved from a small group of professional associates and long-standing friends and eventually came to

---

This preface was written by the first author, Robert W. Firestone, PhD, who originated the theoretical concepts and developed the therapeutic methodology elucidated throughout this book. He also served as the facilitator in the couples' discussion groups described in several chapters. The second author, Joyce Catlett, MA, collaborated in the writing process, organized case material, referenced the concepts, and established the place of the theory in the professional literature. She coproduced with filmmaker Geoff Parr the video documentaries from which much of the illustrative case material in the book was excerpted and transcribed. The reader can assume when encountering the use of first person (I, my) that the author or speaker is Dr. Firestone, and that instances of the first person plural (we) and plural possessive (our) refer to Dr. Firestone and his colleague, Joyce Catlett, unless otherwise indicated.

include about 100 people. As these people revealed their inner lives in their ongoing discussions, I was also provided with an opportunity to observe the external manifestations of their personal interactions with friends and relatives. Their sustained interest in exposing their thoughts and feelings established an environment of open communication, creating an extraordinary psychological laboratory that offered me a new vantage point from which to view "normal" individuals in their everyday interactions with their spouses and children. I had access to material not typically seen or heard by psychotherapists working with couples and families within the confines of the 50-minute hour in the office. The discoveries I made during this long-term study of three generations of individuals has contributed significantly to my understanding of the myriad ways people defend themselves in their intimate associations. To provide the reader with the historical background of this reference population as well as with the earlier sources of my findings, this volume opens with background about when I initially became involved in psychotherapy in a specialized environment.

HISTORY

Beginnings

My career as a psychotherapist and researcher began in 1954, when I worked with psychotic patients with Dr. John Rosen, who at that time had achieved recognition for his contributions to the psychological treatment of schizophrenia. J. N. Rosen (1953) conducted psychotherapy in a noninstitutional atmosphere with very disturbed patients whose days were spent in close association with their therapists. The wealth of information about the patients gathered in this setting left a lasting impression on me. In this residential treatment center, I first experienced, on a 24-hour basis, the full range of psychopathology and its behavioral manifestations.

My wife and I lived in a house with two of these patients. My colleague, Jack Rosberg, and I provided psychotherapy to the patients with schizophrenia and offered our services to patients in several of the other residences. These patients were severely regressed, and some exhibited violent behaviors that required physical restriction to protect them and us. Within several months, in these unusual and anxiety-provoking surroundings, I learned far more about these people than I could have learned in years of treating them in a traditional hospital environment. At the same time, I was participating with several of the other therapists in a small therapy group in which we discussed our work as well as issues in our own development. The total immersion in the process of conducting psychotherapy by living with these patients led to exciting discoveries, which I shared with my colleagues.

My main focus was on the means by which patients who were severely damaged in their self-esteem attempted to defend themselves. I observed that in the historical development of schizophrenic patients, their primary defense was a retreat from relationships into a fantasy process. When things got too rough for these people, they became progressively more reliant on fantasy processes, which functioned as a drug might, deadening their anxiety. The more they were addicted, the more they became dysfunctional, and the worse things got. This addiction to fantasy was comparable to syndromes of chemical dependency: They were involved in a downward spiral that essentially destroyed their lives.

I was stimulated by my growing insight, and my time was consumed with the problem of tracking down the mystery of mental disorder. I was concerned with understanding patients' breakdown and retreat from personal relationships. In what way did fantasy compensate for the extensive damage to the egos of these hurt individuals? How did it come to be preferred over real gratification, and how and why did it work to establish a kind of maladaptive equilibrium? Upon returning to graduate school following my work with Dr. Rosen, I proposed answers to these questions and consolidated my hypotheses about schizophrenia in a doctoral dissertation, *A Concept of the Schizophrenic Process* (Firestone, 1957).

After graduating from the PhD program in clinical psychology in 1957, I began the private practice of psychotherapy in Los Angeles, where I applied my theoretical understanding of the schizophrenic process to a wide range of mental and emotional problems in less disturbed patients and developed a comprehensive theory of neurosis. With these patients, I was able to trace the thread that established the connection among painful experiences in early life, present-day unhappiness, and problems in interpersonal relationships. This process of discovery was more complicated in my office practice. I found that unconscious material was not as accessible and that internal conflicts were masked to a greater extent in "normal" or neurotic individuals. Although the schizophrenic patients expressed their conflicts on the surface symbolically in symptoms and productions that I was able to decode, the neurotic patients tended to obscure the core issues by elaborate psychological defenses.

Later, the experience of using an intensive feeling release therapy with approximately 200 patients provided me with clarity and insight into the dynamics of defense formation (Firestone, 1985). The techniques elicited deeply repressed feelings and reawakened emotional pain that had its primary source in early interpersonal relationships within the family complex. After reexperiencing this pain, the patient generally developed powerful intellectual insights and was able to understand the meaning of his or her present-day neurotic symptoms and behaviors. The material that was uncovered verified, in a straightforward manner, basic hypotheses about the unconscious and the organization of human behavior. In working with patients in this therapy, I found that many of my original concepts regarding schizophrenia and the neuroses were validated by the productions of patients who interpreted their own material and integrated it without assistance from the therapist.*

The Early Discussion Group

Over the next decade, I continued to meet with my associates and friends to discuss the ideas I was developing. As I expanded my investigations and elaborated my concepts of defense formation, my colleagues recognized that the theory had obvious ramifications for themselves as well as for their patients. They were quick to relate the concept of "self-mothering" or "self-parenting" to developments in their own lives.[2] It became clear how fantasies of fusion, omnipotent fantasies, and pseudoindependent attitudes damaged their personal relationships.

In 1969, I started a group therapy project with several selected patients from my psychotherapy practice. The personal growth, openness, and honesty of the members of this group were impressive. When I told my colleagues and friends about the results achieved in the therapy group, they were fascinated and asked about the possibility of starting a discussion group to meet on a regular basis, where they could share their ideas and feelings. I responded by saying that I was willing to become involved in their discussions as a consultant or participant–observer;[3] however, I would not function in the capacity of a psychotherapist or in any way assume responsibility for their mental health. These people, who were mostly professionals themselves (several were licensed psychologists), wanted to work on an equal basis with me in developing a deeper understanding of themselves and their relationships.

The Adolescent Discussion Group

In 1972, a serious problem arose involving my children and the adolescents of some of my associates and friends. Our teenagers, who were 13 to 15 years old at the time, were exposed to a drug culture in the neighborhood, and several had begun experimenting with dangerous drugs. We learned that some of the children's friends and classmates had overdosed. My associates and I were concerned and decided to provide the young people with an opportunity to meet together in a weekly discussion group to try to avert a negative outcome. We asked one of the fathers, who

---

*Feeling release therapy uses techniques similar in many respects to those of Arthur Janov's (1970) primal therapy, as described in The Primal Scream. Basically, we encouraged patients to breathe deeply and make sounds when they exhaled. This technique alone brought out powerful expression of affect, which was followed by insights, both emotional and intellectual, regarding the connection between the original suppressed feelings and present-day behavior.

interestingly enough was not a psychologist but had a natural rapport with the teenagers, to lead this discussion group.

The adolescents met and began to talk about their thoughts and feelings, their alienation from their parents, and their emerging sexuality and competitiveness. The discussion group did succeed in its goal: The young people soon gave up their involvement in drugs and the problems and dishonesty associated with that lifestyle. After several months of talking among themselves, the teenagers asked their parents to join their talks. In these discussions, the right of each youngster to speak out and say his or her perceptions and feelings was protected: Parents were not permitted to interrupt their children or to try to talk them out of their opinions or feelings. The democratic exchange of perceptions and sincere expression of feelings gradually dissolved the boundaries between the generations, and the adolescents and their parents related on a more equal basis.

In 1973, these parents (representing some seven families) pooled their resources and purchased a partially completed 80-foot wooden schooner that eventually became a vehicle for these young people to further develop themselves. My friends and I began training the teenagers so that they would be capable of handling the boat on their own. After 2 years of planning, rebuilding, and outfitting the boat, the 11 teenagers from the discussion group set sail on a circumnavigation of the world. Their parents joined them at several points on the 17-month voyage, whenever they could leave work. During numerous storms in the Indian Ocean and mid-Pacific, the tradition of talking together openly proved invaluable to the young people.

The open forum for communication that continued to develop during and after the voyage was a step beyond a town-hall democracy in that it included the expression of emotions as well as ideas and differing opinions. This stands in contrast to most formal gatherings or meetings in our society. Democratic forums do allow people the freedom to speak out and argue widely divergent views, yet open expression of feeling, especially sad feelings and tears, is often deemed unacceptable and perceived as a sign of weakness.

LATER DEVELOPMENTS

After a number of years of talking together, participants in the adult's discussion group suggested holding a series of weekend meetings away from the city. I agreed, because I felt that the experience of prolonged communication would break down defensive barriers and allow people to reach a deeper understanding of themselves. During these weekends, many individuals expressed deep feelings and developed insight into painful events they had endured while growing up. As each person told his or her story and others identified in some way with the painful childhood memories, I was struck by the commonality of people's experiences. Important questions came to the foreground: Why was there so much unhappiness and pain in close relationships? Was despair inherent in the human condition?

At one point, I realized that I was pleased with the manner in which I was conducting the meeting. I thought to myself, "I'm a good facilitator." Suddenly I realized that my sense of worth was attached to performance, and I felt a pervasive sadness. I knew that I valued others for simply being human. Why not feel that for myself? A single thought became louder and louder: "I am a person." "I am a person." It was difficult to find words to describe the depth of emotion I experienced as I shared my feelings and thoughts with the others. The thought "I am a person" implied that it was not my performance that mattered; I was a human being and deserved to be treated as such. My sadness also had to do with the feeling of being seen for who I was. To people who were not seen or were misunderstood as children, the experience of being seen as a person can be very moving, tantamount to a spiritual experience.

The participants in the early discussion group gradually began to change habitual modes of living and abandoned some of the deadening routines and painkillers that had been limiting their development.[4] In their discussions, they attempted to be straightforward and honest in talking about their relationships, their sexuality, and their friendships. Their conversations were characterized by an implicit morality based on an understanding of what had injured them in their formative years and by an effort to remove unnecessary barriers against communication.

In 1979, I was hired by this group of people on a full-time basis to develop my ideas, to elaborate on my theoretical position, and to continue consulting with them in discussions and business meetings. Again, I made it clear that I would not contract to do any psychotherapy. I would not assume any responsibility for the well-being of the people involved but would just pursue my own creative work. The offer appealed to me because of the opportunity it provided for participating with and observing people at close quarters in a residential setting. At the same time, I would be able to maintain my friendships and professional associations. Thus, in spite of some initial feelings of trepidation about leaving my extensive psychotherapy practice, I committed myself to the project.

I recognized that, in an important sense, I was being forced to renounce my work as a psychotherapist because it precluded my becoming more aware of and understanding of people in this new context. The practice of psychotherapy actually conflicted with the path I had chosen to pursue in my own research. My goals were to educate, investigate, gather data, and develop my knowledge of people in their relationships over an extended period of time rather than to be limited by time constraints of the therapy session and the other restrictions inherent in psychotherapeutic practice.* On a personal level, the situation seemed to be the most fulfilling part of my life: It was a place where I could further develop an understanding of myself and my relationships with family and friends and have a lifestyle of honesty and open communication.

Indeed, this study has taken a long time. Some 20 years later, most of these individuals are still friends. They have succeeded in the many ventures they have undertaken and have found a better, more satisfying way of life. During this time I experienced firsthand the activation of defense systems in couples and families, the consequent loneliness and alienation people experience when locked into these systems, and the liberation and fulfillment of vital human needs for intimacy when individuals feel safe enough to suspend their defensive postures, relate openly and honestly, and give and accept love. This book represents the insights gained during this extended period of research. They are offered to the reader in the same spirit of generosity and openness that the research participants extended to me.

ENDNOTES

[1] Figures were compiled in 1980 with respect to the participants' ages, sex, occupation, number of children, income level, and so forth. At that time, the average age for the entire population was 30.3 years; the youngest member was 4 weeks old and the oldest, 63 years old. Almost half the population, 40 individuals, were between the ages of 26 and 40, so this was a relatively "youthful" group. When the children who were under 15 years of age were excluded, the average age of the adults was 34.8 years.

There was a total of 45 females and 43 males over age 15, and 13 children between the ages of 4 weeks and 14 years. (Since 1980, 21 more children have been born into this circle of friends, and virtually all the adults have taken an interest in the children and their development and well-being.) In 1980, 44 men and women were married, 20 were cohabitating, and there were 24 single adults over age 15. Of the 24 singles, 11 were divorced, and 13 had never been married. The adults comprised almost equally Christians and Jews. There were 2 Hispanics, 1 African American, and the remainder were Caucasians. Although not traditionally religious (the majority did not practice a formal religion), they had strong humanistic values. There were 2 lawyers, 1 physician, 4 psychologists, 2 engineers, 1 teacher, 2 commercial artists, 10

---

*In 1982, The Glendon Association was established by my colleagues to support this type of research. It disseminates books, articles, and video documentaries and conducts continuing education workshops based on the concepts and findings that were uncovered during the longitudinal study of couples and families.

salespeople, 11 people in management positions, 2 bookkeepers, 1 real-estate broker, 4 interior designers, 4 project managers, 2 carpenters, 5 computer programmers, 1 technician, 1 film producer, 10 secretaries and clericals, 1 jewelry designer, 1 chiropractor, 1 author, 1 child-care specialist, 1 purchasing agent, 3 customer service representatives, and 3 administrative assistants.

[2] My hypothesis that fantasy gratification partially fulfills the child's needs and reduces tension under conditions of deprivation was a key element in my concept of *self-mothering*. If adequate parenting, particularly mothering, is unavailable, the child attempts to parent him- or herself in his or her imagination. He or she forms a fantasy of connection (fantasy bond) with the mother and becomes, in effect, his or her own mother. The individual then basically treats him- or herself as an object, much as he or she was responded to by the incorporated parental figure.

My conceptualization of the schizophrenic process does not deny or minimize other influences on the child. Biological tendencies, inherited temperamental differences, and physiological predispositions combine with personal environmental influences to form unique and complex phenomena (Chess & Thomas, 1987). In some cases, somatic aspects clearly outweigh environmental factors in the etiology of psychological disturbance. "However, in most cases, the impact of psychological elements on the child's development in all probability exceeds the influence of innate predispositions" (Firestone, 1990b, p. xv).

[3] See Leonard Krasner's (1988) discussion "On Being a Participant-Observer."

[4] During this same period of time (1976–1979), many of the adults entered into business together. Several of the younger people, upon their return from the voyage, became involved and quickly rose to leadership positions. These businesses flourished and led to outstanding financial success, which was beneficial to all concerned. The unusual energy generated by candid discussions between management and employees played a significant part in this success.

FEAR OF INTIMACY

INTRODUCTION

The absolute value of love makes life worth while, and so makes Man's
strange and difficult situation acceptable. Love cannot save life from
death; but it can fulfill life's purpose.

Arnold Toynbee (1969, p. 24)

For centuries, authors and playwrights have been aware of the fear
and distrust of love that prohibit men and women from freely accepting
affection, respect, and compassion in their lives. An unavoidable truth
about human beings is that very often the beloved is compelled to punish
the lover who appreciates and acknowledges his or her positive qualities.
The fact that lovers see their loved ones in ways that they do *not* see
themselves threatens their defense systems, interrupts negative fantasies
about themselves, and disrupts psychological equilibrium. People stubbornly hold on to their negative self-attitudes and are resistant to being
seen differently in many aspects of their lives. They usually will not allow
the reality of being loved to affect their basic defensive structure. The
average person is unaware that he or she is living out a negative destiny
according to his or her past programming, preserving his or her familiar
identity, and, in the process, pushing love away. On an unconscious level,
many people sense that if they did not push love away, the whole world,
as they have experienced it, would be shattered and they would not know
who they were.

People internalize both positive and negative attitudes they experience during the developmental process. Positive attitudes are assimilated
into the self-system while growing up, whereas negative attitudes are retained as an alienated, nonintegrated part of the personality. As a result,

these negative attitudes or fantasies make up a crucial part of people's feelings toward themselves. These critical self-attitudes are resistant to change because by the time they become adults, most people have already formed a significant defensive apparatus, incorporated a somewhat harsh view of themselves, and achieved a psychological equilibrium compatible with this negative fantasy structure.

This core identity is more extensive than the *provisional identity*, or the identity handed to the child in the family system. Chapter 3 elaborates on this provisional identity, in which the child is dubbed the "bright one," the "beautiful one," the "bad one," or the "troublemaker." Negative fantasies and core beliefs about oneself exist on a deep level with powerful affects. A hurt individual's negative identity is related to a core feeling of shame—an inner feeling of being basically bad, unlovable, or deficient in a way that appears to the individual impossible to correct. In the developmental process, virtually every child idealizes his or her parents at his or her own expense as part of a psychological survival mechanism. This idealization process is inextricably tied to the individual maintaining an image of being bad or deficient.

Punishing the beloved to preserve a negative fantasy of who one is represents a basic dynamic in personal relationships and is more common than anyone would like to believe. Just as parents often suffer from a compulsion to act out on their children the same abuses they endured during childhood, men and women feel driven to act in ways that hurt those closest to them, pushing love away, and thereby, maintaining their defenses. Part of the problem is that the defensive apparatus is triggered without conscious awareness. In other words, when men and women begin to feel a minimal level of anxiety, they start to make the defensive adaptation before they are fully conscious of what they are adapting to.

It is actually painful on an emotional level to see oneself as more or better than one thought oneself to be in the past. Challenging this negative identity is anxiety-provoking. Most people don't feel the full anxiety directly. If they did, they could identify it. They would think, "It really scared me when I realized that he or she really loved me, or when I got that special raise or promotion." When their core identity is disturbed by positive events, people tend to react with suspicion and paranoia. They will fight to the death if they are seen in too positive a light by someone whom they love and admire. If the lover persists and survives the testing stage, progress is possible.

A number of fiction writers have described this seeming paradox, notably Carson McCullers (1940) in *The Heart Is a Lonely Hunter*. Her book emphasizes an important truth—that we are negatively predisposed toward those who tempt us to lower our defenses and inadvertently expose us once again to potential pain or rejection. "Basically, most people have considerable anger, albeit unconscious, toward a person whom they feel is responsible for 'luring' them into a less defended position" (Firestone, 1988, pp. 264–265). Often they work on the other person to get him or her to reflect their negative fantasy or identity back to them. In many couples, both partners eventually manage to induce the other to manifest negative behavior or attitudes that reflect the way they perceive themselves.

Contrary to stated goals, people often react indifferently or adversely to positive approval, recognition, and love, yet latch on to indications that support their negative identity. They have no problem believing critical feedback that corresponds to their negative fantasies in spite of the pain it causes them. It is comparatively easy to integrate rejection and failure because these are harmonious with the process of self-attack, whereas the intrusion of having positive reactions directed toward them is disruptive. Instead of feeling the full excitement of personal success and vocational achievement, people often choose confirmation of their negative thoughts and attitudes, opting for a situation that offers safety, certainty, and a dead-ened, unfeeling state that allays their anxiety. In many relationships, people maintain a fantasy or illusion of love and connectedness while their be-havioral manifestations and those of their partner are often devoid of af-fection, tenderness, or respect.

The fear of intimacy is not solely a fear of being close to another person, but also is based on existential fears. Being close to another in a loving relationship makes one aware that life is precious, but must even-tually be surrendered. If we embrace life, we must also face death's inevi-tability. Because of existential fears, most people avoid being original, being a real self. Occasionally, a rare individual does not conform to childhood conditioning processes, refuses traditional solutions, and develops into a genuine, feeling individual, realizing his or her potential as a human being. However, most people achieve little individuation and separation from their original programming. To the extent that they are blindly following the course laid out by their parents, family members, and society, they are not really living their own lives.

There are forces—both familial and societal—that support the ide-alization of family, reinforce people's negative views of themselves, and keep them moving in the direction of their conventionally programmed destiny. Compliance with this programming diminishes people's lives. In-dividuals in effect perform for others and are more concerned with image than the actuality of their experience and the gratification of their needs and values. Generally, they remain unaware of this state of affairs and play the game out to the end, punishing anyone who challenges their defensive posture.

Early emotional programming is "hard-wired" into children during the first 2 or 3 years, and it takes dynamite, so to speak, to blast free and to allow for the possibility of growth to take place. In my study of resistance, I have come to believe firmly that people can change and be different, they can accomplish wonders, and they can modify even serious psychopathology, but only if they are willing to register information that is painful and accompanied by powerful negative affects.

The ultimate resistance to change is based on the fact that primal fears interfere with taking the essential risks involved in self-actualization and autonomy. When people take a chance and move toward progressive individuation, they experience pain and fear. If they challenge the fear and keep moving ahead, they can eventually overcome it. If they retreat from the anxiety involved in growth and the development of more positive relationships, they tend to develop habit patterns that are inhibiting and destructive, and they become even more fearful. If people refuse to take a chance on love and retreat into inward, self-protective behaviors, they inadvertently punish those who love and respect them.

Therapists must be aware of people's fear of positive movement and help them to challenge themselves and take the essential risks involved in goal-directed behavior. They must be fully aware of the limitations imposed by psychological defenses to help individuals suffer through their anxiety and increase their tolerance for love. Although there is no guarantee that the patient will choose to "go for broke," the good therapist will maintain an intellectual and emotional climate that is ideally conducive to helping people expand their lives. This is best achieved in a therapeutic relationship characterized by mutual honesty, trust, and a lack of defensiveness on the therapist's part. In this atmosphere, men and women can continually challenge their core resistance and come to accept increased love and fulfillment in their lives.

This book was written in part to help therapists gain an empathic understanding of the defenses and resistances to intimacy that they encounter in their work so that they may work compassionately to help couples and families give up restrictive ways of relating and embrace more authentic ways of loving. As with my previous books, especially *The Fantasy Bond*, this volume is also accessible to educated lay persons who will find the vivid case examples both evocative and instructive in understanding themselves and their relationships.

INITIAL FINDINGS FROM THE PSYCHOLOGICAL LABORATORY

It seems that what is now stimulating, reenergizing, and moving this group of people is the insight into the nature of relationships as they constitute connections and dependencies and manipulation, versus equalities, freedoms, and responsibilities.

Stuart Boyd (1982)*

I have described in detail in the preface the genesis of my work and how I came to be involved in a research project involving couples and families that spanned over 20 years. The decision to devote myself to this longitudinal study has been rewarding in acquiring an accumulated body of knowledge about relationships between men and women, couples, and families—knowledge that is presented for the first time in this volume. The most interesting finding revealed in this laboratory was the fact that people who are exposed to a better life are refractory to it because it threatens core psychological defenses. The truth seems to be that people are afraid to realize their dreams. In this long-term study, intolerance of affection, real acknowledgment, and tenderness was particularly notable in close relationships. Although the friendships deepened and endured, intimate relationships between couples and families were the most resistant to further development.

Another important and related phenomenon was observed in people's tendencies to maintain basic negative attitudes about themselves and cynical views of others. In spite of their progress, they still tended to hold on to many of the same defenses they had observed in their parents. My associates and I found that these negative views of self and distrust of others are controlled by a process that we refer to as a "voice," a systematized pattern of negative thoughts and attitudes accompanied by angry affect (Firestone, 1988, 1997a). This voice process subsequently became the object of an extended study and investigation. In examining the sources of this voice, we discovered that it is part of a self-parenting, inward protective posture that, to varying degrees, prevents individuals from finding gratification in their most significant relationships. Thus, in spite of the fact that the men and women in this reference population were able to develop themselves personally and achieve success in their careers and friendships, they still experienced a certain level of pain in their intimate relationships.

It is important to note that despite these difficulties, over the years most of the people have deepened their insights about resistance and have significantly increased their knowledge of self. As a result, to varying degrees, they have learned to accept more affection and love in their closest associations and are less conflicted and distressed than before. For example, men and women, instead of blaming each other for their troubles, have come to recognize the effects their own pain and anxiety have on the

---

*This quote is taken from a written commentary by Stuart Boyd (1982), psychologist and former tutor at St. John's College in Santa Fe, New Mexico, who visited my colleagues and friends and observed their interactions and activities for a 3-month period. He summarized his findings in the form of an anthropological essay about the psychological laboratory.

relationship. Partners who are separated or divorced have tended to remain friends, in contrast to the acrimony that characterizes most divorces in society. In a number of instances, men and women who separated during a difficult phase in their relationship have reunited. Their maturity, understanding, and increased capacity for giving and accepting love can be contrasted with their earlier struggles to remain close.

Our focus on this reference population is not to suggest that people should attempt to live in the same manner as the members of the social group or that these experiences are generally available; it is that important aspects of what was learned during this longitudinal study can be adapted to a wide range of circumstances. Breaking into inward, defensive patterns, living more sociably, and learning to be more honest are all courses of action open to individuals in their everyday lives. Similarly, challenging and relinquishing addictive habit patterns are necessary parts of any effective therapy.

Over the past 4 decades, I have traced the psychodynamics of relationships, ranging from the total breakdown in relating exhibited by schizophrenic patients who are terrified of intimacy and react angrily to virtually all personal intrusion, to the partial breakdown in the relationships of less disturbed individuals who misuse each other in an attempt to alleviate psychological pain and existential dread. Manifestations of the breakdown in relating that occurs in its most extreme form in the schizophrenic process can be observed in the less extreme but nonetheless maladaptive patterns manifested by "normal" individuals.

The end product of the schizophrenic regression is a form of psychological equilibrium at the expense of interpersonal relationships. Schizophrenic individuals literally shut people out of their lives, become their own mothers and fathers, psychologically, and are pseudo-independent. In neurotic or "normal" individuals, the various aspects of self (parent and child) are less fragmented than in the psychotic patient, and there is more ego integration. However, these people, like their disturbed counterparts, tend to seek gratification through an imagined fusion (fantasy bond) with their partners at the cost of genuine intimacy in their relationships. Conceptualizing relationships as existing on a continuum, ranging from a total disruption in relating in schizophrenia, to a partial breakdown in relating in less disturbed individuals, to healthy relating that approaches the ideal of love, provides the essential groundwork for understanding why many relationships fail. This book illuminates the psychodynamics operating within relationships and explains the basic causality underlying the fear of intimacy.

In chapter 2, my colleague Joyce Catlett and I offer a conceptual model of relationships that (a) provides the basis for assessing the level of defensiveness of each partner, and (b) offers a direction for treatment and intervention within a couple therapy setting. We also describe positive child-rearing methods that lead to a strong sense of self and are less likely to cause an individual to adopt self-protective, inward patterns that actively interfere with the happiness and satisfaction people could enjoy in later life (Firestone, 1990b).

We have found that the key issues in conflicted couples and the corresponding breakdown in relationships are not the time-worn explanations customarily given for failures in relating: the "wrong choice" of partner, economic hardship, religious differences, problems with in-laws, breakdown of church and family, sexual incompatibility, and many others; but an intolerance of intimacy that is based on negative attitudes toward self and others and the deeply embedded inward patterns of psychological defenses manifested by the partners. Both parties' essential fear of aloneness, vulnerability, abandonment, rejection, and potential loss are serious factors at the core of marital and family distress.

When a strong defense system is activated, as it tends to be when there is anxiety and emotional deprivation in the developmental years, there is an overriding need to hold on to and protect that system of defenses. In other words, once a fantasy bond or imagined connection is formed in early childhood, people are reluctant to take a chance again on real gratification from another person in an intimate relationship, even though they are tempted to do so. Their fears ultimately drive them to reenact their parents' defensive style of interaction, stereotypes about the opposite sex, and prescriptions for living. The process of reverting to outmoded defense patterns interferes with the establishment of secure and satisfying intimate relationships characterized by feelings of humanity, compassion, and equality.

Indeed, people are faced with a basic dilemma: They must choose between investing in relationships and remaining vulnerable to possible loss and rejection, or attempting to protect themselves by retreating to an inward, defensive posture. The dilemma is analogous to the one facing all human beings: the choice between fully investing in life despite its temporal nature, or accommodating to death, and defending against death anxiety by limiting one's gratifications and denying one's enthusiasm for life.

ORGANIZATION

Part I of the book sets forth the foundations of our theoretical model for understanding why relationships fail. The chapters describe the basic concepts of the fantasy bond and voice process, examine psychological and societal factors that contribute to people's fear of intimacy, argue for a concern with human rights in interpersonal relationships, and delineate characteristics of a prototypical ideal couple and family relationship. Part

II provides an analysis of the psychodynamics underlying individuals' defensive behaviors that lead to relationship distress. Chapters 10 and 11 present a fresh perspective on commonly accepted stereotypes about men and women, their origins, and their destructive effects on relationships and give examples that contradict stereotypic attitudes. Part III demonstrates the application of voice therapy methodology in interventions with couples, with illustrative transcribed material from our couples' discussion groups. The final chapter describes personality characteristics of the "good" therapist, dimensions of an effective therapeutic alliance, and a number of misconceptions regarding transference and countertransference.

The book includes endnotes that refer to the work of other theorists supportive of my theoretical model (Firestone, 1984, 1985, 1988, 1997a). In the endnotes, we cite the writings of psychoanalytic and object relations theorists and those dealing with family systems theory, the rapidly expanding body of research on attachment theory, and conjectures from a relatively new field of study, that is, evolutionary psychology. We include selected works of social theorists regarding issues of power and individual rights within society and cite various interpretations of findings from gender studies regarding differences between men and women.

Fear of Intimacy expands the concepts of the fantasy bond and the voice process and applies them to personal relationships of all varieties. The current work explains how defensive processes limit one's capability to sustain meaningful relationships. It is both philosophical and pragmatic, contains specific material pertaining to disturbances in interpersonal relationships, and elucidates the present-day theory regarding this important aspect of life.

I

FOUNDATIONS

1

THE CHALLENGE OF INTIMATE RELATIONSHIPS

The affirmation of one's own life, happiness, growth, freedom, is rooted in one's capacity to love, i.e., in care, respect, responsibility and knowledge.
Erich Fromm (1947, p. 130)

Interpersonal relationships are the ultimate source of happiness or misery; love has the potential to generate intense pleasure and fulfillment or produce considerable pain and suffering. Our basic sense of self is formed originally in a relationship constellation that predisposes our attitudes toward ourselves, others, and the world at large. Our feelings about life are developed in the context of a close attachment with a parent, parents, or other significant people in the early years. Research studies have shown that these early attachments create feelings of wholeness and security or states of anxiety and insecurity that can persist for a lifetime (Ainsworth, 1989; Bowlby, 1988; Fonagy, 1998; Fonagy et al., 1995; Main, Kaplan, & Cassidy, 1985). Although other issues in life cause us concern—crime, poverty, war, the existential issues of aloneness and death—we seem to experience the most distress and turmoil in relation to the difficulties we encounter in our personal interactions. Indeed, dissatisfaction or rejection in a relationship is perhaps the most common reason people enter psychotherapy.

The ideal combination of loving companionship and sexual contact in a long lasting relationship is conducive to good mental and physical health and is an essential goal for most people. In our opinion, love is the one force that is capable of easing existential despair and the endemic pain of the human condition. We feel that to develop emotionally as well as

13

spiritually, one needs to learn how to love, to continue to search for love throughout life, and to remain positive, not become cynical or despairing when love fails. We feel a sense of kinship with R. D. Laing's (1976) statement:

> The main fact of life for me is love or its absence. Whether life is worth living depends for me on whether there is love in life. Without a sense of it, or even the memory . . . of it, I think I would lose heart completely. (p. vii)

VIEWS OF RELATIONSHIPS

In my study of human relationships, I have not only been fortunate enough to draw upon the personal experiences of numerous clients in psychotherapy and close observations of people in everyday life, but I have also been exposed to the honest disclosures of the group of men and women in the reference population described in the Preface. These people have provided my colleagues and me with access to their innermost thoughts about relationships as well as with a unique opportunity to study the dynamics of their interpersonal interactions. In this chapter, we summarize the opinions about relationships offered by participants in a recent series of videotaped seminars. The information revealed may be controversial and at times contradict certain commonly held attitudes about love and sex in the culture at large.

Men and women's views about relationships expressed in these seminars fell into the following categories: (a) Relationships are central in affecting a person's life; (b) relationships are generally unstable; (c) there is a good deal of dishonesty in relationships; (d) relationships are often based on emotional hunger and desperation; (e) few long-term relationships are made up of high-level choices; (f) high-level choices can be made for negative as well as positive reasons; (g) people tend to confuse sex with love; and (h) people feel they are failures unless they succeed in finding mates.

Relationships Are Central in Affecting a Person's Life

When asked to state one fact they believed to be most characteristic of relationships, the participants responded as follows:

"Relationships are a really important part of people's lives."
"I think they're confusing."
"I think they take up a lot of people's thoughts."
"They can be the greatest thing in someone's life and they can be the worst thing."
"I look forward so much to starting a relationship or to being close

with someone, and then once I'm involved with them, I don't feel good."

"I think relationships bring a lot of joy and a lot of pain."

Relationships are ambiguous emotional investments because they are just as likely to foster pain and grief as joy and pleasure. In the initial phases, couple relationships are usually characterized by mutual feelings of sexual attraction, friendship, and love; yet more often than not, as the relationship unfolds, these feelings fade and are replaced by routinized interactions, indifference, and at times, outright hostility.

Overall, there was a general consensus among these men and women about the importance of intimate relationships in their lives. They indicated that relationships were worth struggling for because of the potential gratification of being close to someone in a tender, sensitive, respectful manner.

Relationships Are Generally Unstable

The participants agreed that most relationships are tenuous at best:

"Relationships are exciting and desirable, but they don't usually last."
"It seems like they start out very exciting and very romantic, usually, but that tends to fade out."
"People just move from one relationship to another and they become very cynical towards themselves as they get older."

These opinions tend to be supported by recent surveys showing that younger people in the United States who are marrying for the first time face roughly a 40% to 50% chance of divorcing in their lifetime (U.S. Bureau of the Census, 1992).[1] This negative prognosis for relationships and marriage has created disillusionment and cynical attitudes in many people. For example, Carolyn, a 35-year-old divorcee, revealed a pessimistic outlook regarding her prospects for finding happiness and satisfaction in another relationship:

When I was younger, I felt more like relationships were an adventure. Now that I've been through different relationships, if I enter into a new relationship, it doesn't feel as exciting. I feel scared, because I don't know what the outcome will be and I don't have a good track record. I don't go into it thinking it's going to be all fun at all. I know it's going to get complicated.

Social factors contributing to unstable relationships are varied. Over the past 3 decades, the high mobility of families as well as the increased number of women in the workplace have affected the longevity of marriages (Shiono & Quinn, 1994). In addition, individuals change, grow, and develop at different rates. It would be naive to expect, for example, that two people who meet and marry in their early twenties will develop at the same rate or retain the interests they originally shared for the next 25 years.[2]

A number of anthropologists (Daly & Wilson, 1983; Ford & Beach, 1951) found that relationships are unstable in terms of mating patterns in every culture and throughout every era of history. They noted that many societies practice some form of polygamy or serial monogamy (one mate at a time in a series of successive relationships).[3] In the United States, serial monogamy is becoming increasingly common (44% of those who marry will divorce, 26% will remarry, and 16% will redivorce; Shiono & Quinn, 1994). This trend of divorcing and remarrying has potentially negative consequences for future generations because often children are left behind to be raised by one spouse as the other moves on to a new relationship (Wallerstein & Blakeslee, 1989; Wallerstein & Kelly, 1980). This disruption of family life has contributed to the psychological distress, behavioral problems, and drug use so prevalent among children and adolescents in our culture. For example, 8.8% of children living with formerly married mothers received help for emotional or behavioral problems in the preceding year, as compared with only 2.7% of children living with both biological parents (Dawson, 1991).

On the other hand, although love is a vital force in life, we must also make the distinction that love is not essential for physical survival. Furthermore, the fact that relationships are changeable or unstable need not be tragic, nor should this reality breed cynicism and despair. When one has a sense of being whole and integrated, the disruption of an important relationship, although painful, is not experienced as overwhelming or annihilating. When a person is developing in his or her capacity to love and accept love, his or her relationships will tend to become more desirable and increasingly satisfactory over a period of time. However, when people feel insecure, they will cling desperately to any relationship, no matter what negative consequences are involved, thereby limiting their own development.

When people use relationships to compensate for perceived deficits in their personalities, rejection will be experienced as catastrophic. Reacting as though it were "life threatening" introduces an element of emotional melodrama based on primal feelings from the past. The realization that few real events in adult life impose the same type of threat attached to emotional abuses in childhood is liberating. In separating appropriate adult feeling reactions from the surplus emotionality based on primal feelings, a person can become much stronger in facing life. With this in mind, he or she will be freer to invest emotionally in being close to another person, despite the possibility of loss or rejection. A person's sense of well-being and overall emotional health is enhanced when he or she continues to seek love and closeness and remains vulnerable rather than seeking protection by becoming cynical or indifferent. Cynicism invariably leads to depression and alienation, both from oneself and from others.

There Is a Good Deal of Dishonesty in Relationships

The deceptions and manipulations of couples in love are obvious and familiar to observers; however, most people are not aware of the extent to which they are dishonest with their partners. Duplicity exists in many areas within a relationship, including sexuality, money, preferences, opinions, and feelings. People are reluctant to reveal their lies and manipulations to their mates for fear of losing the relationship. In addition, a good deal of self-deception is necessary to alleviate feelings of guilt that accompany one's deception of one's partner. Self-deception facilitates deception of the other. The probability of successfully deceiving one's partner is dependent on the extent to which one truly believes one's own lies.

Participants in the discussions revealed some of their duplicities and strategies in a straightforward manner:

Carl: I think relationships are probably the hardest place to be honest. You can be honest in a lot of other areas of your life, but in your relationship, it's very difficult to stay honest. You need to see yourself honestly to be honest in a relationship with another person, because if you don't, then the other person is afraid to be honest with you. If you're lying to yourself in some way, then the other person is going to be afraid of challenging that in you.

Andrea: People lie in some really big ways. They lie about having sexual relationships with other people; that's just out and out dishonest, but there are all kinds of levels of subtlety. There's even a book about it now, to tell you how to manipulate a man so you can get him. Everything in that book is based on dishonesty.*

Mark: There are all kinds of manipulations between men and women to get what they want from the other person. Women acting like they're not interested so that the man becomes more attentive; men doing the same thing. I've heard women talk about this. They plan it. They don't want to appear too interested. She doesn't want the man to know

---

*As another example, in a recent afternoon talk show on the subject of deception in marriage, several participants revealed how they lied to each other (faking orgasms, getting pregnant surreptitiously, sneaking money from a mate's wallet, and other secrets and hidden agendas). The talk show host and audience applauded these ploys and declared them clever and humorous, while the guest psychologists (a husband and wife team) interpreted deception as necessary for maintaining marital harmony. One man in the audience who protested, saying he thought that lies and deceit invalidated any sense of meaning in a relationship, was booed by the audience and his opinion was summarily dismissed by the psychologists.

how interested she really is. But she's very interested, and she doesn't want to give too much away in the beginning.

Donald: I think that people are dishonest in order to hold on to each other instead of taking the risk of being honest and saying their own perceptions about themselves and about the other person. They change it around in order to hold on.

Mark: I think the deception starts early in the courtship process where the man or the woman might try to appear more wealthy, look better. They put on their absolute best appearance when they meet the person. They might even borrow a friend's car and allude to it as their car. They want to put their best foot forward, actually more than put their best foot forward, they'll put their best friend's car forward. (Laughter.) Maybe the man or the woman had a terrible past, was in jail, but he [she] doesn't say it. Or she had a very promiscuous background and she deceives her boyfriend during the courtship. I really believe that there are a lot of lies, a lot of deception, a lot of omissions, and that it continues throughout the relationship.

Natalie: When I first started my relationship with you [husband], I was deceitful in the sense that I told you that I had only been with five other men when I had been with many more—but it was so that you would still choose me.

Later in the same discussion, several women described how they deceived men by pretending to be less intelligent or competent than they actually were, while some men admitted that they preferred the build-up over honesty:

Andrea: I used to act as though a man were way more interesting than I thought he was. I would act like whatever he was saying was just so fascinating and brilliant, and I'd never disagree, never state my opinions strongly if they were different than his. But I was taught that well in my family.

Carolyn: One thing a woman will do is act like the man is funnier than he is, laughing harder than she would laugh at a joke that's not that funny. Another thing I noticed was that in other relationships I've had, as soon as I noticed differences between me and the man I was with, I wouldn't want to make a point of that and would just kind of go along and act like we were the same, had the same outlook.

Donald: The women I've pursued in the past were women who were flattering instead of honest, even though I do really value honesty and frankness in women. The women I was involved with would build me up and pretend that I was more important to them than I was.

Marjorie: Playing up to the man is the other side to it. Women act not as smart, not as capable, not as intelligent as they really might be. To build up a man, you have to act less than him.

Evolutionary psychologists have offered various explanations regarding the pervasiveness of deception and duplicity between sexual partners. They conjecture that in the environment of evolutionary adaptedness (EEA; Bowlby, 1982), encompassing a time period of approximately 2 million years, deception in certain ways offered a selective advantage in terms of gene survival (Wright, 1994).[4] Subsequently, as a significant element in the process of natural selection,[5] specific mechanisms of concealment and deception might well have spread and become a common characteristic in modern man. For example, during the courtship phase, a man might conceal the fact that he has other sexual relationships because it does not make him as appealing as a stable provider or caretaker of children. As a married man, he would conceal the fact that he has extramarital relationships. Through this deception, he could hold onto his mate and yet be free to distribute his genes among a larger number of females, thereby obtaining a genetic advantage. Similarly, an "unfaithful" woman might be selecting better genes in sexual encounters with other (stronger or healthier) males outside of her pair bond. Deception regarding her extramarital activities helps her sustain her primary relationship and insures her mate's assistance in caring for her offspring. In this manner, patterns of deception may be selected over more morally acceptable traits.

Although evolutionary theorists have identified instinctive responses or tendencies related to the perpetuation of genes, human beings are not necessarily passive victims of these inclinations. Becoming aware of these patterns, instead of forecasting a negative prognosis, may actually help people develop more freedom and integrity.

A number of other explanations have been offered to account for the prevalence of deception in social affiliations.[6] Social learning theorists (Bandura, 1971, 1977, 1986; Bandura & Walters, 1963) and other researchers (Meltzoff & Moore, 1995; Muller, Hunter, & Stollak, 1995; Perry, Perry, & Boldizar, 1990; J. R. Rogers & Carney, 1994) emphasize that children learn through imitation. As a result, even as adults, their interactions that are duplicitous often resemble the parents' style of relating. Psychodynamic–interactive theory posits that many children learn to distrust their perceptions in social interactions because they have been confused and mystified by "double messages" experienced in the family constellation (Bateson, Jackson, Haley, & Weakland, 1956/1972; Bavelas, 1983; Humphrey & Benjamin, 1986; Mozdzierz, Greenblatt, & Thatcher, 1985; Watzlawick, Bavelas, & Jackson, 1967; Zuk & Zuk, 1998a, 1998b).

Many people give off mixed messages in their couple relationships. For example, during the courtship, a woman notices that her lover is spending progressively less time with her, yet he professes that he still loves her. She doesn't know what to believe. It is crucial that she read her boyfriend's actual behavior in judging the relationship, rather than take his words at face value. To detect deception of this sort, it is important for people to learn to read behavioral cues and body language rather than to depend solely on verbal messages.

> Brad: Any kind of deception starts at a very early age because, for example, my mother, in my case, was like that. No matter how she felt, she had to pretend that she liked me. She didn't honestly say, "Look, I want to go do something else besides sit here in the room with a baby." You're not quite sure what's going on. You know that she doesn't really behave like she likes and respects you, but she's saying she loves you. So, to this day, if someone says "I love you" to me, it doesn't mean anything, or I think they're making it up. But if someone acts loving, then I start to feel anxious because I don't know how to respond to a real feeling of love.

Relationships Are Often Based on Emotional Hunger and Desperation

Many individuals experience feelings of longing and desperation that they mistake for love. They fail to make a distinction between emotional hunger, which is a strong need caused by emotional deprivation in childhood (Bornstein, 1993; Firestone, 1985; Parker, 1983), and feelings of genuine love and concern. Feelings of emotional hunger are experienced as deep internal sensations, ranging in intensity from a dull ache, to a sharp painful feeling, to generalized anguish. Close contact with an emotionally hungry person has the opposite effect of nurturance: The more time spent with this type of person, the more debilitating the effect. In contrast, genuine love sustains, nurtures, and enhances the well-being of the other (Firestone, 1985, 1987a, 1990b).[7]

People seek relief from painful primal feelings in the selection of new objects, and when they find temporary respite, imagine that they have found love. Here the participants describe their insights into the origins of these feelings of emotional hunger and desperation. They disclose that in the past they often felt driven to find in a particular partner, the "missing piece" to fill the emptiness or void:[8]

> Donald: I think I must believe that something is basically wrong with me, that I'm not very worthy, that's why I've pursued women who would flatter me . . .

> Natalie: I think that comes from growing up in a certain type of family environment. I think a lot of people who are looking

for relationships are looking for something that they never, ever got. So they've created this fantasy in their heads of what they imagine they are looking for and then they go out and look for this, the thing that they never got growing up.

Like Natalie, a number of the participants recognized that they sought relationships in an attempt to satisfy emotional hunger and strong dependency needs. They discovered that their efforts only left them feeling more empty and dissatisfied.

Raymond: I think that my family was very empty, but I chose not to look at that, and so I didn't consciously think as a child, "Oh, my family's empty." What I did instead from the time I was about five or six, I started to build a fantasy of what it would be like when I finally met a girlfriend and got married, and had a family, and all my emptiness that I felt in my family was lumped into that fantasy.

That's what I've been looking to have fulfilled every time I enter into a relationship. Someone said they brought "old baggage" to each new relationship. Well, I bring in a whole household full of emptiness looking to be satisfied by that and it's inappropriate to the situation and it can't be fulfilled.

Carolyn: The relationship with my father was such that he had a hard time expressing whatever feelings he had toward me, so I always felt unlovable and desperate towards him. I was always trying to get something from him that wasn't available, so I took that into my life in search for someone that I wanted that with.

Desperation and emotional hunger contribute to a basic insecurity and an inner dread that one will never be chosen or loved. To relieve these feelings, many men and women quickly attempt to extract promises of love, devotion, and commitment from a partner. They tend to form an imagined connection, a *fantasy bond*, wherein they use each other to alleviate their feelings of emotional hunger and longing from the past (Firestone, 1985, 1987a). This process has a negative impact on relationships.

Few Long-Term Relationships Are Made Up of High-Level Choices

People actually find few potential partners whom they admire and would choose, who would in turn choose them for a long-term relationship. In mate selection, there are high-level and low-level choices. Most people make their selection from a small pool of available prospects; this is often a low-level choice. In other words, these men and women essentially "take what they can get." A few people are able to select from a pool of many available prospects; their selections can be conceptualized as high-level choices. Most people, however, have a limited number of prospects from which to choose when it comes to finding a marital partner whom they really find attractive and admire, and who would also choose them as a mate.

For example, Mark, a single, attractive, energetic 35-year-old businessman, appraises the choices that have been available to him over the years:

> Mark: There are a number of women who have been interested in being with me, but usually they weren't the women that I would have chosen to be with for an extended period of time. Thinking back, I realize that when I take into consideration the women I would have chosen to be seriously involved with who were also interested in me at the time, the number turns out to be very small.

In an effort to rationalize making a low-level choice, people tend to aggrandize a low-level choice. He or she is soon "one in a million"; the relationship becomes "a match made in heaven." This transformation of a low-level choice into a high-level one implies a certain degree of self-deception as well as deception of the other, as is manifested in a fantasy bond.

> Lewis: Based on what you [Mark] said, then every choice of mine has been a low-level choice.

> Raymond: I think that most of my choices have been medium-level choices. But after I enter into the relationship I prop them up so that in my mind they become a high-level choice.

People recognize, consciously or unconsciously, that they are not a high-level choice of their mates. This fosters a sense of insecurity. Both sexes are fearful that their partners may someday make a better choice, and as a result, they make strenuous demands that their mates prefer them over all rivals, particularly sexual rivals. This poses an essential contradiction, because when questioned individually as to whether they feel that they are better than most, men and women would say, "No, I'm just your ordinary, average person. Sure, I do some things well. I have some good qualities, but basically, I'm just like everyone else." Yet men and women demand from each other that the illusion that they are special be maintained and tend to be punitive when confronted with evidence to the contrary.

The reality that women have left the more insular environment of the home and are now actively participating in the workplace exacerbates men's fear that they will lose the preference of their mates. An interesting trend came to my attention in private practice. Talking with various men in individual psychotherapy, I discovered that most of them became suspicious and wary when their wives left home to return to college or pursue careers. They were apprehensive, obsessively concerned, and paranoid about their wives' independent activities. Indeed, these husbands sensed that once their mates had an opportunity to be associated with other men, they would inevitably become involved sexually. Initially, I treated their fears and foreboding as paranoid presuppositions. In fact, they had no basis in reality in terms of their wives' motivations at the time. Interestingly enough, in nearly every case, as these women became more independent and developed more self-esteem, they actually did make other choices. They felt more self-possessed and attractive and often became involved in sexual liaisons that were painful for their spouses. In retrospect, these men's suspicions had been paranoid only in the sense that they preceded what later became a threatening reality.

This example in no way implies that women are different from men in regard to their infidelity or that women are always unfaithful. In general, when people of both sexes are free to move about, they frequently become involved sexually and often move on to different choices, underlining the fact that preferences are unstable over the course of time.

High-Level Choices Can Be Made for Negative as Well as Positive Reasons

High-level choices, those based on strong attractions in which there were many prospects, do not necessarily imply positive choices. On an unconscious level, the need to relive the experiences of one's childhood in present-day relationships exerts a distinct influence over one's choice of a partner. People have powerful tendencies to select mates who are similar to a parent or other family member as part of a repetition compulsion. Many people go on to a succession of choices in the same (nonproductive) mode that previously caused them trouble. Andrea draws attention to this fact:

Andrea: On the basis of what we were talking about earlier, that people repeat the same patterns they learned in their families, you might go out of your way to pick a really crummy person so you could have another crummy relationship.

Carolyn: That reminds me of my situation in high school because I was fairly popular, and a lot of guys wanted to date me. And there were a lot of nice guys. But instead of choosing to date the nice guys, I was always attracted to one or two guys that were more like my father. They were kind of mean guys. And those were the guys that I dated. So my choices were not in my interest, really.

Andrea: It's a little embarrassing to say, but I never had that problem of not having many choices because there was always a lot available to me. I really did have a lot of choices. For some reason, I was the kind of girl that everybody wanted to take home and introduce to their parents, so I didn't have problems like that. But my problem was that when somebody was interested in me that I really liked, it was very difficult for me to accept that, and I even eliminated choices because they made me feel too anxious.

Evaluating marital satisfaction poses a serious problem. Longevity in a relationship does not imply that it is a productive or satisfying relationship. Relationships based on a strong fantasy bond may endure, but they usually manifest a gradual erosion of the spirit, individuality, and emotional health of the partners. In a relationship it is the individuals who matter, not the couple or family unit. Couples and families are merely abstractions, not real entities. The individuals concerned are very real and do matter. Similarly, one can only analyze the value of a social system or society by analyzing its effect on its members: If the individual members are flourishing, it is constructive; if they are impaired or suffering under the social process, then it is obviously destructive.

My colleagues and I also noted that level of maturity and the capacity for relating to another as a separate person affects one's selection of characteristics in a mate. If one is an emotionally mature and independent person, one is more likely to emphasize adult companionship, friendship, and mutual interests, whereas if one is immature, one seeks dependency ties and personality characteristics in the other to compensate for one's perceived negative traits or deficiencies.

Carl: I'm looking for friendship, a real friendship that is equal. The part that feels best is the friendship with the woman. Also intelligence, a sense of humor, a person who is active, who likes to do a variety of things.

Carolyn: I'm looking for someone who has similar values to mine, someone who has a point of view towards life that's similar to mine, not exactly the same, but their main values are similar—that seems important.

Andrea: I thought of a funny word, appreciation, someone who appreciates me and who I appreciate.

Sheryl: I think appreciation is one step up from love, because it makes you feel seen, yet it's so sad to be appreciated for who you really are.

Andrea: Also appreciation doesn't have anything to do with what you do, it's just what you are. It doesn't have anything to do with what the other person can get from you. There are no strings with appreciation. It's really separate.

Several participants mentioned desirable qualities in a mate that have been identified to be characteristics sought by men and women in many different cultures:

Lewis: Attractiveness, humor, and companionship are the most important qualities I'm looking for in a woman.

Jeff: Someone who's lively and who has some joy in life, who really enjoys things, has her own independent interests.

Natalie: If I saw a man with a child and he had loving feelings toward that child and was very sweet toward the child, that would be a plus. That would be something I would look for in a man.

According to evolutionary psychologists, both male and female mating strategies are determined primarily by patterns that gradually evolved through the process of selective adaptation (Buss, 1992, 1994; Buss & Barnes, 1986; Buss & Schmitt, 1993; Symons, 1979; Trivers, 1985). These theorists postulate that men are looking for women who are youthful and attractive: qualities that signify many years of reproductive possibilities. Men are also attracted to women who are vital, lively, and healthy, who possess qualities that are indicative of the physical stamina required to survive long enough to successfully raise their offspring. Women are seeking two important qualities in a man: (a) "good genes," that is, those traits that are valued as signs of strength and power in a particular culture; and (b) the *ability* to provide care for their children as well as the *desire* to remain in close proximity to them and their offspring (Kenrick, Sadalla, Groth, & Trost, 1990).[9]

People Tend to Confuse Sex With Love

Both men and women tend to confuse sex with love. In particular, during the early phase of a relationship, most people mistake the initial attraction and pleasure in sex for love. When an initial strong sexual attraction is followed by a period of distress or conflict, it is often indicative of a relationship that has been formed based on feelings of inadequacy. When this is the case, the specific qualities that men and women find initially irresistible in their respective partners tend to be complementary to, or the opposite of, their own personality characteristics. For example, a passive, reserved man is likely to be drawn to an extroverted, gregarious female, and vice versa. As the relationship develops, these qualities or behavior patterns become exaggerated, in this example, with one partner becoming increasingly domineering while the other develops deferential, submissive responses. This type of polarization is characteristic of an addictive attachment or fantasy bond. The very qualities that were once so attractive become sources of irritation and resentment. This phenomenon is exemplified in the old adage that "opposites attract"; however, they may eventually repel. On the other hand, people who select a partner based on positive traits they possess in common with the other person are more likely to form enduring and satisfying relationships.

> Mark: I have the same interests that both Carl and Jeff said, but I tend to be drawn to women who have many other qualities that perplex me, qualities like aggressiveness. I wouldn't have said that I was drawn to those women, but I must be, because I end up with women who can be aggressive, ones who are very sexually feverish [laughter] ones who are wildly energetic in that way, frenzied sexuality, passionate. By the way, it's very different from loving sex. I'm attracted to it [frenzied sexuality], but it doesn't make me feel good when I'm involved in it or afterwards.

As Mark indicates, love and sex may be very different, and therefore have differential effects on an individual. Jane, 25, was involved for several years with a man who had a serious problem with alcoholism. She admits that prior to their breakup, she believed that she was deeply in love because of the intense sexual attraction between them.

> Jane: I felt like the last relationship I was in was a good relationship because the sexuality felt right to me, and I felt like I was okay sexually. So then everything that I noticed in my boyfriend that wasn't what I wanted or was below my standards, I just pushed away or made an excuse for it. I just kept thinking, but it's okay, so who cares that he has these problems and these characteristics that are very different than me, or he has ideas about things that are very different. The sex is good, and that's what's important. It's really embarrassing to say this, but I really lived for four years based on that.

In another meeting, Jane discusses her sexuality further:

> Jane: As an adult, I've typically been attracted to men who appreciate me for the way I look, the way I am sexually, how I appear to them, my appearance, my image. I feel totally out of place to be appreciated for other things, like being a nice person or that I'm intelligent or that I'm good company. I feel totally out of place in that situation.

> Carl: I think everything you see in the media shows sex as separate from love. I know that I grew up thinking that they were totally separate things.

> Raymond: In the later stages of a relationship when everything has turned to absolute shit and there's nothing good going on

between me and the woman I'm with, if it's still sexual, I'll use that as verification that I'm still loved.

As Carl noted, the media inadvertently contributes to the views held by many people in our society that love and sex belong to two separate and distinct categories. It is significant that so many people find it difficult to combine these qualities in a long-term relationship. People who have suffered painful childhoods are often deeply saddened by love and tenderness in their sexual lives. There is a tendency to avoid this sadness. Positive responses threaten to alter the sense of identity formed in the family, which leads to tension and anxiety. Consequently, the combination of love and sexuality can precipitate separation anxiety. In fact, the sex act itself is a real, but temporary, physical connection followed by a sharp separation. Physical intimacy manifested by close, affectionate contact is followed by a distinct awareness of boundaries. These separations often foster resentment, although the anger and hostility can be unconscious (Firestone, 1984).

> Marilyn: It's very hard for me to combine sex and love in a relationship. In my mind, I have them as two separate things. I'm very easy being loving and enjoying a loving relationship outside of the sexual situation. But I have a hard time feeling the love when I'm in a sexual situation with my boyfriend. I'm afraid of the intimacy, of the loving feelings for some reason.

> Carl: All my life, I've felt that there's no way a woman's really going to like me. That's why right now I have a lot of trouble with a woman who loves me, who has feelings for me. I can't handle it. I don't want to feel that pain, it's very early pain.

Although the closeness that is brought about by the combination of love and sexuality can arouse painful feelings from the past as well as concerns about potential loss of one's mate and other existential issues, it has the potential for providing the most satisfaction and happiness.

People Feel They Are Failures Unless They Succeed in Finding Mates

People generally do not perceive themselves as a whole unit; they act as though they are incomplete in and of themselves. They operate under a basic assumption of personal deficiency or core inadequacy, akin to "original sin." Many of our participants revealed feelings that they were unlovable, based on the introjection of a negative identity in their childhood years:

> Carolyn: I realized that I've always tried to fix something in myself through a relationship. But now I know that I can't really

look towards another person to fix that. I know it's in me to realize that I'm not going to get that from anybody really. I have to feel whole and okay on my own.

Mark: I have a lot of insecurity about my sexuality, my masculinity, almost all aspects of my life. Insecurities, weaknesses, and desperation for someone to kind of fill these voids that I have. When I think about it that way, it's very difficult for me to pursue the kind of person I'm looking for because I'm really looking to quell these pains that I have. I'm not really looking for someone who is independent and attractive, I'm looking for someone who doesn't make me feel weak, who covers that up.

Because people have many insecurities and perceive themselves as deficient, finding a mate and getting married takes on a surplus meaning. Societal expectations about what men and women are supposed to do arouse considerable tension. The state of being married is not simply perceived as customary, but also as an indication of normalcy in our culture. If one is not married or cohabitating by age 30, one runs the risk of being categorized as peculiar or deviant.

The ability to find and keep a partner gives those with a sense of inferiority and low self-esteem a sense of security, status, and a feeling of belonging. On the other hand, the state of being single, separated, or divorced signifies failure. People's basic feelings of personal inadequacy and unlovability are confirmed when they experience difficulties in finding a partner, when their mates are unfaithful, or when their relationships are disrupted through separation or divorce.

During the seminars, an important truth emerged about intimacy: that many people are intolerant of love and intimacy, the very thing they say they find the most desirable. People usually fail to sustain meaningful relationships because love makes them feel vulnerable once again to the threat of rejection and loss.

Marilyn: If I show a man that he's really important to me and that I really do love him, as soon as I even have that thought, I don't even have to say it, I think to myself, "Don't say it, just don't show it, don't let him see how you really feel."

Jane: People hang onto that feeling of being unlovable because it's almost lifesaving. It feels like you can't let go of it in some way. First of all, there's sadness, like deep pain in changing that view, you know. It stirs up so much—it's agonizing and painful.

Raymond: I think people end up carving out a niche in their family where they don't feel what's really happening to them, and they're content to go through their lives in that niche. They don't want to have that niche disturbed and if somebody really loves you, that takes you into the full impact of what happened to you. You have to feel what happened to you as a child. So you're willing to even hold onto negative thoughts about yourself. It's a security. It's how you survived and how you learned to live your life.

CONCLUSION

In this chapter, we depicted a complex and perplexing overview of relationships. In this service, we recounted the attitudes expressed by individuals who participated in a series of seminars about personal affiliations.[10] As a result of our explorations into the problems of people in various relationship constellations, we have been compelled to take a fresh, more exacting look at the subject. Despite some of the "hard truths" about relationships, there is no need for pessimism. In facing the truth, people can challenge their defenses and develop more tolerance for love and sexual gratification.

In the chapters that follow, we explore the core issues noted in this chapter that prevent people from maintaining closeness and intimacy in interpersonal relationships. The analysis is followed by the description of a method to cope with these problems, both from a psychotherapeutic and a social perspective.

ENDNOTES

[1]Recent census reports showed that the "fastest growing marital status was divorced persons. The number [of] currently divorced adults quadrupled from 4.3 million in 1970 to 17.4 million in 1994" (Saluter, 1996, p. vi). Buss and Schmitt (1993) stated that "estimates of adultery among American married couples range from 26% to 70% for women and from 33% to 75% for men" (p. 204).

[2]Family systems theorist Murray Bowen (Kerr & Bowen, 1988) asserted that people select marital partners who are at similar "levels of self-differentiation." He described a common scenario in which, over time, one partner advances to a higher level of self-differentiation, while the other remains at the same level. Conflict or divorce is the typical outcome of this differential rate of growth and individuation.

[3]Ford and Beach (1951) found that "In 84 per cent of the 185 societies [nonindustrial] in our sample men are permitted by custom to have more than one mate at a time" (p. 108). The one industrial society studied by Ford and Beach (American society) was described as a "single mateship" society. Daly and Wilson (1983) noted that "a majority of human societies permit a man

more than one wife if he can afford them" (p. 88). "Polygynous unions remain rarer than monogamous ones, however, even within those societies that permit them" (p. 282). Usually, only members of the elite classes, i.e., wealthy and/or politically powerful men are able to take advantage of legalized polygamy in these societies. "In most Moslem countries, polygamous marriages are restricted to the upper classes and form no more than 4 to 5 per cent of all marriages" (Tucker, 1993, p. 37).

Murdock (1967) found 137 human societies that had monogamous marriage practices and 708 that had usual or occasional polygyny. See also Lockard and Adams' (1981) analysis of over 4,000 dyadic groupings in the United States in terms of preferred mating patterns (serial polygamy or monogamy) of men and women.

[4]"The adaptedness of any particular organism comes to be defined in terms of its ability to contribute more than the average number of genes to future generations" (Bowlby, 1982, p. 56). The particular time period involved is referred to as the "environment of evolutionary adaptedness" (EEA) or ancestral environment. "Only traits that would have propelled the genes responsible for them through the generations in our ancestral social environment should, in theory, be part of human nature today" (Wright, 1994, p. 38).

Slavin and Kriegman (1992), citing Mitchell (1985) and Trivers (1985), noted that:

> Deception is a pervasive, universal intrinsic feature of all animal communication. In the pursuit of their own inclusive fitness, organisms do not simply communicate in order to convey truth to others, but, rather, to convey tailored images of both self and environmental realities: to hide certain features and selectively accentuate those that they want others to perceive. (p. 151)

Slavin and Kriegman also argued that "a child must possess reliable ways of dealing with the inherent parent-offspring conflict and ambiguity of developmental relationships as well as monitoring deceptions—deliberate deceptions in addition to unwitting, well-meaning ones" (p. 150). Gilbert (1989) noted that self-deception and deception have psychological and physiological costs, despite their adaptability. These costs include the "defensive exclusion of negative information that may lead to a poor choice of partner" (p. 232).

[5]"The theory of natural selection says the following: If within a species there is variation among individuals in their hereditary traits, and some traits are more conducive to survival and reproduction than others, then those traits will (obviously) become more widespread within the population. The result (obviously) is that the species' aggregate pool of hereditary traits changes" (Wright, 1994, p. 23). After approximately 14 generations, a specific (new) trait would "constitute more than 99 percent of the population" (Daly & Wilson, 1983, p. 6).

[6]See *Vital Lies: Simple Truths* by Daniel Goleman (1985), an exposition of the

various forms of deception (and self-deception) that are manifested in families, groups, and social organizations.

[7]In his book *Parental Overprotection*, Parker (1983) discussed a number of components of overprotectiveness that are similar in many respects to my description of the manifestations of emotional hunger (Firestone, 1990b), for example, intrusiveness, excessive psychological control, infantilization, encouragement of dependency, excessive contact, prevention of independent behaviors, strictness, and parental obsessiveness. Parker cited a number of research studies that had uncovered these factors, including studies by Perris, Jacobsson, Lindstrom, von Knorring, and Perris (1980) in their development of the EMBU ("own memories of child-rearing experiences"). Parker, Tupling, and Brown (1979) developed the Parental Bonding Instrument (PBI) to measure various components of overprotectiveness. Bornstein (1993) found that "in samples of adolescents and adults . . . high levels of parental intrusiveness and authoritarianism and low levels of parental nurturance and positive involvement were associated with increased risk for psychopathology" (p. 23). The studies reported by Bornstein used the Parental Orientation Scale (POS; Ryan, Deci, & Grolnick, 1986) and the Children's Reports of Parental Behavior Inventory (CRPBI; Schaefer, 1965).

[8]The children's book, *The Missing Piece* by Shel Silverstein (1976), makes the point (humorously) that the need to search for someone to fill the perceived or imagined gap in one's personality is universal and detrimental to the individual.

[9]There are significant gender differences in several specific qualities that are sought in selecting a partner for marriage. For example, Kenrick et al. (1990) found that females were more selective in terms of their mate's "family orientation" than were males, whereas males were more selective in terms of their mate's physical attractiveness. Females sought mates who were ambitious, emotionally stable, powerful, had high social status, were popular, wealthy, had good heredity and good earning capacity. However, at the level of "trait requirements" for a sexual partner, there were larger gender differences than at the level of selecting a partner for marriage. In other words, males were nearly as selective as females when considering requirements for a long-term partner. Kenrick et al. cited a study conducted by Buss and Barnes (1986) showing that "males were generally more selective regarding physical attractiveness, whereas females were more selective regarding traits related to resource allocation" (Kenrick et al., 1990, p. 114).

[10]Excerpts from the videotaped seminars in this chapter are part of a documentary *Exploring Relationships* (Parr, 1997a).

2

WHY RELATIONSHIPS FAIL

The theory suggests that at an unconscious level, the combination of the defensive distortions based on the primary fantasy bond and the consequent distorted threat of death is of such power as to sometimes defeat our chances of success in life, in work, in love—defeat us in the areas of our greatest competence or longing.

Stuart Boyd (1982)

The distinguishing characteristic of selfhood . . . is not rationality, but the critical awareness of man's divided nature.

Christopher Lasch (1984, p. 258)

Throughout history, major breakthroughs in science have repeatedly shattered people's sense of omnipotence. Copernicus' discovery that the earth is not the center of the universe and Darwin's (1859/1958) assertion, several centuries later, that humans are merely evolved animals were enormous blows to people's self-confidence. Subsequently, Freud's (1924/1953) theory of the unconscious mind challenged people's trust in the one quality they believed distinguished them from animals, their rationality.[1]

Freud contended that men and women were directed by unconscious or partly conscious motives they were unaware of, yet which affected every aspect of their lives.[2] Later, he went on to describe people's destructiveness toward themselves and others as indications of a fundamental inborn tendency toward self-destruction (Freud, 1925/1959). The postulation of this death wish further undermined man's confidence because it suggested that there are forces within people that are directed toward their own demise and antagonistic to others. I do not disagree with Freud's description of man's aggressive behavior toward self and others, prevalent throughout history. However, I reject his conceptualization of a death instinct as such, and instead perceive aggression as derived from frustration. Regardless of causal analysis, the observations of man's aggressiveness and self-destructiveness are alarming and generally give rise to a disheartening view of man's future.

In my work, I have gone on to emphasize the split in the self-system between forces that are constructive and goal-directed, and a destructive thought process alien to people's best interests (Firestone, 1984, 1985, 1988, 1997a, 1997b). These negative thought processes can be brought to the surface in voice therapy, and when expressed, reveal a tremendous amount of aggression toward self. The terror of recognizing this intimate enemy constitutes another threat to our sense of security and self-assurance.

Negative attitudes toward self and others based on this split have a profoundly devastating effect on personal relationships. Nowhere is this insight more important than in understanding the psychodynamics underlying the way individuals relate to each other in their most intimate associations, because angry thought processes directed both toward ourselves and those most important to us predispose alienation in relationships (Firestone, 1990e). In becoming aware of these destructive thoughts, my associates and I began to develop a better understanding of the ways people damage themselves and others, and why they do so.

At those times when negative thought processes based on the internalization of parents' destructive attitudes and defenses predominate in one's thinking, serious distortions of oneself and others are introduced into personal interactions; this is particularly true in one's closest associations. Moreover, when an individual is under stress, there is a breakdown in the self-system. When the person is "not himself," the self is fractured into parental and childlike behaviors that fit the model of transactional analysis. To the extent that individuals act childish or parental, they do real damage to their spouses and family members. Parental behaviors, childish reactions, and noncoping responses in particular cause a serious rift between partners and are the basis of marital and family disputes.

In summary, a basic division exists within each person's psyche: One part is harmonious with the individual and his or her goals, while the other part is alien and opposed to his or her best interests. The alien part, made up of a systematized destructive thought process or "voice," predisposes suspicion, defensiveness, distancing behaviors, and compulsive habit patterns that cut off feeling responses. As such, it supports each dimension of an inward lifestyle.

RELATIONSHIPS: A DEVELOPMENTAL PERSPECTIVE

As noted, the major problem in interpersonal relationships is each person's psychological defenses based on destructive voice processes and the distortions each partner introduces into the relationship (Firestone, 1985, 1987a). To fully understand these factors, one must examine how children react to stress and pain in their formative years and how they subsequently resolve to protect themselves against future hurt and vulnerability.

Children are faced with pain and anxiety arising from two major sources: (a) negative experiences within the family such as emotional deprivation; rejection; and overt or covert aggression on the part of parents, family members, and significant others; and (b) fundamental human problems, that is, the dawning awareness of aloneness, aging, and death as inevitable processes in life (Firestone, 1994). They react to psychological pain from all sources by making the best adaptation possible to preserve a form of rationality and sense of unity. Under stressful conditions, rather than suffer ego disintegration or fragmentation, they cut off feeling for themselves and tend to depersonalize. They identify with the aggressor or negative agent and incorporate this alien point of view toward self and others that persists into adult life (see Firestone, 1997a, chap. 5). Once children defend themselves in this manner, they are reluctant to recover their feelings—to reinvest in feeling for themselves and others.

Psychological defenses are subject to malfunction in a manner that is analogous to the body's physical reaction in the case of pneumonia. The presence of organisms in the lungs evokes cellular and humoral responses to meet the invasion, yet the magnitude of the defensive reaction leads to congestion that is potentially dangerous to the person. In this disease, the body's defensive reaction can be more destructive than the original assault. Similarly, defenses erected by vulnerable children to protect themselves against a toxic environment eventually become more detrimental than the original trauma. In this sense, people's defenses, formed under painful circumstances, become the core of their neurosis or psychosis (Firestone, 1997a).

The Fantasy Bond

Early in the developmental sequence, the infant or child compensates for emotional deprivation by forming the primary defense, which I refer to as the *fantasy bond* (Firestone, 1984, 1985). The *fantasy bond*, originally an imagined fusion with the mother or primary parenting figure, is highly effective as a defense because a human being's capacity for imagination provides partial gratification of needs and reduces tension.[3] This leads to a pseudoindependent posture, and the more an individual comes to rely on fantasy, the less he or she will seek or be able to accept gratification from other people in real relationships.

The Primary Defense

The fantasy bond is the *primary defense* against separation anxiety, interpersonal pain, and existential dread. Once a fantasy bond is formed, it predisposes inward behavior patterns, including a preference for fantasy gratification over real satisfaction, a reliance on substances as painkillers, patterns of withholding behavior, tendencies toward isolation and passivity, self-critical attitudes, and cynical, hostile views of others. When pseudoindependent attitudes prevail, they give rise to a self-protective lifestyle manifested by distortion and distrust of others, particularly in close relationships.

Several years ago I delivered a lecture outlining the development of a comprehensive theory of psychological defenses.* The material it contains elaborates the theory underlying relationship problems. Quoted extracts appear on the following pages:

> The primary defense occurs at a time when the child would be in great danger if he were abandoned by the parent. That's why a person is afraid to take a chance again. If he takes a chance on another person, he fears that he will be exposed to the anxiety and the fear and the pain that he went through at the time when he was helpless and dependent. That is why in adult life, people generally tend to relive rather than live, that is, to repeat the patterns of the past and to defend the primary fantasy in their defiance, and avoid the real gamble or real adventure of taking a chance on other people. They would rather repeat the same pattern than take a chance on something new. They are afraid that if they react with emotional integrity, if they really cry out, if they really ask, if they really scream for help, that it won't come, and they'll be in the same panicky, frightened state they were in when they were little.
>
> But if people *could* get back to that feeling in adult life, they could see through it and see that, as adults, they don't really need the parent they have internalized, that they really can be free. The trick in therapy is to get them to take that chance again, to get them to really ask, to really take a chance. And once they do, once they really ask and they feel the pain, they also feel free because it isn't like they imagined. They're not helpless and dependent. These defenses set in, however, when the child *was* really helpless and dependent.

Self-Parenting Process

The self-parenting process is a manifestation of the fantasy bond wherein the child (and later the adult) both nurtures and punishes him- or herself internally. The process involves self-nourishing thoughts and habits as well as self-punishing ideation and behavior.

Self-nourishing propensities persist into adult life in the form of praising and comforting oneself, vanity, eating disorders, addiction to cigarette smoking, alcohol, and other drugs, compulsive masturbation, and an

---

*In this lecture format, I used the generic "he" to indicate both genders.

impersonal, self-feeding, repetitive style of sexual relating. Self-critical thoughts, guilt reactions, attacks on self, and self-destructive actions are examples of the punitive component (Firestone, 1990c, 1993).

Both self-nurturing and self-punishing behaviors are regulated by an internal thought process that is detrimental to self, which I refer to as the "voice." The voice ranges from minor self-criticisms to major self-attacks and fosters self-nourishing habit patterns, isolation, and self-destructive lifestyles. The voice may also be conceptualized as a secondary defense consisting of negative hypotheses about the interpersonal environment that justify and support the primary defense. The person imagines: "I can take care of myself. I don't need anyone else. I am my own parent." The voice process functions to support and confirm a person's retreat into an inward fantasy state. In effect, the voice represents the language of the overall defensive process.

> When children are rejected or hurt, they tend to imagine themselves as one with the destructive parent to somehow protect against the hurt and pain and rejection by that parent. Children defend this primary fantasy of fusion but, in so doing, must also incorporate the parental rejecting attitudes; that is, they have to maintain the self-concept that fits in with the early situations. Later on, they often resist information about themselves and their worth that contrasts with the way they tended to see themselves, based on the parental rejection.

The voice, the system of negative thoughts, feelings, and attitudes about oneself and others, is inextricably tied to the internalized idealized image of one's parents (Firestone, 1985).

> The child cannot afford to find fault with the parent and see the parent as bad, because then his situation is truly hopeless. To defend against that pain and that despair, the child sees himself as bad and idealizes the parent. He wonders if by performing, if by trying to please, or by doing the right thing, he can get the parents to love him. If he took the other position and saw the parents as at fault, his situation would appear more precarious. That is why this defense works.
>
> The fallacy is that the parents, to varying degrees, are unable to love because of their own problems, because of their own inadequacies, so the child can't get what he needs from them—it's impossible. He goes through life trying, in symbolic form, to get that love and goes through those maneuvers that he thinks will please, or will get the parents to love him. Actually, the specific behaviors that may have worked in the family situation usually have adverse effects on personal relationships later on. The child becomes somewhat paranoid in relation to other people and avoids closeness. His actions don't make sense and he appears self-destructive because he avoids good relationships and clings to bad ones. He develops patterns with the people he selects in life which are repetitive of the past and frankly damaging, and he seems trapped in those patterns.

Pseudoindependence

The self-parenting process represents a desperate attempt on the child's part to deny his or her true state of aloneness, helplessness, and vulnerability. It is manifested internally in fantasy as well as externally through the use of objects and people in one's environment. The result is a pseudoindependent posture of self-sufficiency—an illusion that one has the ability to sustain oneself without the need for others (Firestone, 1984).

> I've talked a lot about the primary fantasy and it is important to define it. To compensate for rejection and emotional deprivation, the child becomes joined in his fantasy with the all-powerful parent, and in this, he develops a sort of pseudoindependence. In other words, he is both the bad, weak, needful child and the all-powerful, all-giving, all-controlling God-like parent, all at once. He resists anything which threatens that pseudoindependence. He establishes, in fantasy, a kind of independent "I don't need you" attitude. In denying his needs and his wants in relation to other people, he becomes a system unto himself.
>
> The more seriously disturbed a person is, the more seriously damaged he is, the more he creates this fantasy, and resists real relationships and real closeness and real feeling toward real people. The more he is caught up in this division, this dualistic notion of himself as the bad, needful child and the strong, omnipotent parent, the more dysfunctional his real relations are with people. In other words, that whole system of the incorporation of the parent into himself and the incorporation of the rejecting attitudes is a system which he then tries to protect against any other kind of experience. This is the basis of resistance in therapy—the fear of changing the image of himself and forming relationships that are different. So the person appears to act in a way that is destructive to himself.
>
> The connection between the primary fantasy and the pseudoindependence, and the passivity that goes with that, and the internalization of the real parent and that parent's evaluation of the child, that is, the self-concept which is based on interacting with that parent, represents the fundamental resistance to a better, more constructive life. People are resistant to changing their image of themselves, and they're resistant to forming associations with people who would behave toward them in a different way.

The Fantasy Bond in Couple Relationships

The term *fantasy bond* is used to describe both the original imaginary connection formed during childhood and the repetitive efforts of the adult to make fantasized connections in intimate associations. This defensive process leads to a subsequent deterioration in later personal relationships (Firestone, 1987a).

In the course of the developmental sequence, psychological equilibrium is achieved when an individual arrives at a particular solution to the basic conflict between relying on internal fantasy processes for gratification and seeking real satisfaction in the external world. This equilibrium is generally attained at the expense of satisfying object relations and may be actually threatened by warm or constructive events that contradict early childhood experiences. To protect the fantasy process from these "positive" intrusions, most people tend to recreate the original conditions within their family.

> First of all, people tend to select partners who are like people in their early lives because those are the people that their defenses are appropriate to. It's like a mirror image of the primary fantasy. It's an externalization of the primary fantasy, and it leaves a person's defense system intact. At a party or social gathering, they'll be drawn to people who manifest familiar characteristics. They feel a sense of comfort and ease in those situations. They recreate the past by finding people who are like the ones in their past environment, and on top of that, they distort the people around them and see them as more like the people in their past, and if all else fails, they'll try to provoke responses in people which will duplicate the past.

Psychotherapy

Regardless of the specific techniques, interventions, or therapeutic approach, patients must become aware of their ongoing needs and desires and use the therapeutic situation to break into their pseudoindependent posture, ask directly for what they want, and learn to come to terms with their anger at being frustrated (Firestone, 1985, 1990c, 1993). A significant part of the therapeutic process is that therapists need to react to patients authentically, with discipline and boundaries, in helping them to make the transition from relying on illusions of connection, pseudoindependence, and self-parenting behavior to seeking and finding satisfaction in personal relationships and career.

> The overall aim of therapy is to help the patient to take a chance again, that is, to really ask for what he wants, to find out and to establish his needs in an honest way, to admit them honestly, to become vulnerable, to be frustrated, and to learn that frustration doesn't kill him. He has to then face his anger toward the frustration in an honest way, become an independent adult, not hang on to the past, and attempt to form new types of relationships that are satisfying. It takes a good deal of courage to reach out to other people once one has been hurt. A person must learn to avoid maneuvers that are pro-

voking and discourage closeness and to break down the defense process, which inevitably leads to anxiety. Unlike psychoanalytic theorists and others who believe that defenses are necessary, my associates and I conceptualize that defenses *are* the illness and that people can exist without deception of self and others. They can be truthful and straightforward, and not defended and dishonest in their associations.

Psychotherapy has to help the person to recognize his pseudoindependence and his defiance and not act it out. If he acts it out, he cannot get better. If he manipulates and provokes other people and controls their behavior, he ends up merely reliving the past and he doesn't change and he doesn't give up his defenses. He has to learn to give up his defenses and honestly ask for what he wants and honestly take a chance. He has to sweat it out when things get close with other people, and he has to learn to suffer the pain of being loved and not provoke rejection—not get people to attack him and thus get him off the hook. When the relationship is good, when he thinks well of himself, he has got to sweat that out, like an addict who goes cold turkey. He has to take a chance and not damage the relationship. He can feel like damaging it and he can share that he feels like damaging it, but he must not do it. If he does, he ends up back where he started—there's no growth. If he sweats it out, then he does grow.

The core of resistance is the fear of giving up the primary fantasy and being left feeling alone. Even though negative thoughts or voices are destructive, they are a form of companionship, and resistance represents a fear of losing that companionship. But when a person really does take a chance, it isn't as painful as anticipated, and he feels better. When he does sweat it out, he expands his world. When he does get at the real feeling, he develops his capacity to love. He is more direct, sincere, and happy. He really feels good.

But there is tremendous resistance to really honestly asking, especially in the form of dialogue. There is tremendous resistance to calling out to the parent or substitute object and asking for love again when it wasn't there originally, and facing the fact that it isn't there and that it is impossible to get from the parent. The person must really give up and recognize that he is never going to get the love he wanted from his parents. When he does that, he also recognizes that he doesn't need love in that form anymore, and he can accept real love and closeness for the first time.*

---

*One problem in many group therapies is that some psychologists have a feeling that honest confrontation is necessarily helpful. It is not always so. For example, confrontation is often valuable with people experiencing borderline personality disorders and very destructive when working with patients with narcissistic personality disorders. The neurotic patient who is attacked for repetitive acting-out behavior just becomes more stubborn and confused. It is not therapeutic to merely attack negative behaviors. A therapist has to help clients face their pain and express their irrational, infantile feelings and primitive longings and desperation. This process of identifying early wants and experiencing the emotions involved enables people to emerge as independent individuals who are more honest and less defended.

DIMENSIONS OF THE DEFENSIVE PROCESS

Addictions and Self-Gratifying Modes of Sexuality

Addictions are an integral part of the fantasy bond or self-parenting process. They represent the self-nourishing component in the fantasy of self-mothering and also reflect a fundamental choice away from relationships (Firestone, 1993).

The self-parenting process can be understood as an addictive psychonutritional system wherein because of early deprivation, the person imagines that there are limited quantities of nourishment available in the interpersonal environment and chooses to nourish him- or herself. The child (and adult) unconsciously rejects real gratification and gives up goal-directed activities to hold on to the safety of a fantasy world over which he or she has complete control.

The use of substances to satisfy oneself is closely correlated with oral deprivation and maladaptive parenting. When children suffer unusual frustration, they resort to compensatory self-nourishing habit patterns. Later, there is an attempt on the part of these individuals to comfort themselves and relieve their own tension. In every case, the addiction supports a pseudoindependent posture and an illusion of self-sufficiency. Sexual relationships can also be used as painkillers. They can function as a means of partially gratifying primitive longings and deeply repressed oral needs.

> I would like to describe the relationship between food and sex and the primary defense and how that works in terms of nonrelating. In order to understand that, you have to remember that the primary defense supports the idea that "I don't need anyone. I can take care of myself." This can result in a denial of needs, whether these needs be oral or sexual or for love.
>
> To understand where a person is in this defensive process, it is valuable to examine his or her sexual life and sexual fantasies because these reveal the person's exact attitude toward the giving and taking of love in relation to other persons. (In this system of ideas, the sexual attitudes relate to the underlying oral symbolism, in that the penis symbolizes the breast, the vagina symbolizes the mouth, the semen symbolizes the milk, and the full belly the pregnancy.) The compulsive eater, the compulsive masturbator, the compulsive drinker, all in one way or another are saying the same thing. They are saying, "I don't need you, I can feed myself, I can take care of myself." Also in avoiding sex or turning away from genital sexuality, the person is saying, "I don't need sex, I don't need you, I don't need another person," which represents this pseudoindependent, defiant state of turning away from one's needs in relation to others.
>
> It is almost as though some people have a fantasy that they can meet their own sexual needs, that in a sense, they can "feed" themselves.

One schizophrenic man felt that milk came out of his penis, symbolizing the breast, and that he was on his own system, that he didn't need nourishment from outside of himself. And the irony was that while he was imagining his independence and his self-sustenance, he was totally helpless and would indeed have starved to death if he were not taken care of by other people. Yet in this fantasy, the primary fantasy, he was his own mother, he was feeding himself, he could take care of himself.

Interestingly enough, the only two direct exchanges of bodily fluids between people in life are breast-feeding the baby and depositing semen from the penis into the vagina. Basic attitudes toward the giving and receiving inherent in sexual intercourse are related to the old feelings of breast-feeding, early training, and early oral experiences. This is particularly true in schizophrenic patients. A good deal of their symbolism can be directly analyzed on an oral level, but this is also true, although more subtly, on many levels for other people.

People who are much less disturbed, but avoid relationships and closeness by turning away from their needs instead of asking for what they want from other people, may become hard or tough. In our groups, we talk about hardness and toughness, and we see this as part of a defensive style of relating that is hurtful and destructive. For example, a man may act macho and maintain a dishonest posture of invulnerability that masks his real needs for love and care. He may have difficulty in giving or offering love because of a fear of being depleted. A woman who is acting tough, controlling, or castrating may not desire to hurt the man so much as to protect herself or to avoid the recognition that she wants anything from the man. She is trying to drive him away so that she won't get hooked or become dependent upon him for gratification and run the risk of being hurt again. Her toughness or lack of vulnerability is based on turning away from real wanting.

Similarly, the compulsive eater, the user of drugs, the alcoholic is denying his dependence on other persons and has this pseudoindependent attitude—"I can feed myself, I have my own bottle." A well-respected professor at a university was married to a paranoid and controlling woman who dominated every aspect of his life. After years of marriage, these manifestations reached the delusional level and she was eventually hospitalized. Free from the daily interrogation, harassment, and attack, the man began to feel excited about the possibility of a positive future. Women responded to him favorably and his sex life not only improved but was very gratifying. Perversely, he was unable to tolerate this gratification and turned away from it. He was so frightened by his newfound independence, sexuality, and popularity with women that he went from social drinking to more serious drinking, killing off his feelings through alcohol. Interestingly enough, although he was extremely mild-mannered and meek, when the subject of his drinking came up in therapy, he became very angry and abusive and acted out in the negative transference. It was the only place he manifested direct anger.

Sexual problems are often manifestations of a turning away from seeking gratification from or offering to other persons, whether expressed through sexual symptoms in the male of premature ejaculation or retarded ejaculation, or through impotence; or in the woman through being frigid or unresponsive. In all of these examples, there is a turning away from closeness and the exchange of real feelings between people and a movement toward relying on sex more as a method of self-gratification.

In most cases, the woman who experiences difficulty in having an orgasm during intercourse is attempting to avoid dependence, avoid the feeling of gratification from outside herself. If she were free, she would be allowing the other to satisfy her. She would be actively receptive. But in her defended state, in her distrust, in her fear of taking a chance, she will not allow sexual gratification. She will not become dependent on an organ that she does not have, the penis, to gratify her. At the point of intercourse, she may draw the line, that is, not allow herself to respond. Often when she can work out this distrust, she will be able to have an orgasm during intercourse. However, this usually happens as a result of changing her basic attitude, her basic defensiveness, a basic breakdown of the primary fantasy, rather than attacking the sexual problem directly through specialized techniques often used by sex therapists.

A woman who may be avoiding sex, or avoiding men, or avoiding closeness with her mate, may also be saying in effect, "I don't need to be fed." She doesn't want to be thrown back to feelings of infantile dependence on the breast which led to so much pain earlier in life. So she won't allow the man to give her that gratification. It is a denial of the wish to be fed, just as the compulsive eating is a denial of the wish to be gratified from the outside and the statement: "I can feed myself." On a sexual level, anger may come about when she feels that she wants something from a man. Many women avoid being attractive and alluring by putting on weight, thereby discouraging men from approaching them, because they resent dependence on someone outside themselves to gratify them. In this case, they are directly feeding themselves and acting out the primary self-parenting process. In indulging in this process, it is not the actual weight as such (except in extreme cases of obesity) that puts the man off, but rather the woman's negative attitude and feeling about her body which discourage her from wanting sex and inevitably affect her partner's attraction to her.

The same is true with men in relation to sex. A man may feel resentful of needing a woman sexually and at the same time, often through masturbation, sustain the infantile fantasy that he can take care of himself, that he doesn't need her. Also he may have a fear that a woman, the mouth, the vagina, will drain him, will take everything from him, will eat him up alive. So when a man feels unloved or inadequate or empty emotionally, he feels uncomfortable about giving, about feeding, about making love to a woman, and he may back off from all of those. He may feel that he is unable to care for or satisfy a woman. He may avoid her sexually, become uncommunicative or distant, and in many other ways restrict his interactions. When he feels her sexual demands or her wanting something from him as hunger, he may be particularly withholding and unresponsive. He may want to be the baby; he may want to be fed.

On a sexual level, the primary defense, the pseudoindependent fantasy, may be expressed as a feeling of sexual independence. Some men support this fantasy through compulsive masturbation, and some women actually fantasize about having a penis, almost pretend, almost believe that they have their own penis, almost feel vulnerable to castration as though they possessed a penis.

To summarize, the way people relate to the opposite sex tells a great deal about where they are in their development psychologically, and in their growth, their independence, their attitudes about life. The majority of problems in relationships clearly indicates the neurotic defense or primary fantasy and the secondary fantasies that sustain it. That's why when we talk about sex in our groups, it often ends up that we get back to very basic issues related to giving and receiving, accepting or rejecting love.

Aggression and Pseudoaggression

Genuine Aggression

For didactic purposes, we can distinguish between genuine aggression and pseudoaggression. Human beings are not inherently aggressive, destructive, or self-destructive; they become angry, hostile, violent, or suicidal because of the pain or frustration they experience in relation to deprivation of basic needs and later in relation to death anxiety.[4]

I would like to distinguish between genuine anger, hostility, aggression—and pseudoaggression. Genuine anger and aggression occur as simple, irrational, feelingful reactions to frustration. When we don't get what we want, we get angry. If we deny our wants and we don't get what we want, we still get angry, but we don't know what we are angry at. We are confused, and we tend to get into difficulty and into cloudy issues. But anger is a simple reaction to frustration. The fact that we are taught to be reasonable only means that we tend to deny our anger when it doesn't appear to make sense, and that is how we get into trouble. The point is that we are angry, irrationally, whenever we are frustrated in what we want. When we don't get what we want, we feel angry, and we feel angry in proportion to the frustration, not in proportion to the reasonableness of whether we should have got what we want or not, or any of those other considerations, or whether it was adult to want it in the first place.

On a feeling level, that's all there is to it. It just requires simple acceptance. But often, proponents of religious dogma preach that even thoughts are evil and punish people for feeling anger. In contrast, if people feel their anger, they're more likely to have the power and the strength to resist it, to control it. So in regard to anger or any other emotions, we must feel them fully. On the other hand, we must *choose* how to act; how we act comes under moral code, whereas how we feel should come under no restrictions. People who have learned this principle are able to live their lives more fully and more honestly. They're more in control of their emotions as far as their actions are concerned. They tend to act more in their own interests and manifest less destructive behavior toward others.

Righteous indignation—feelings that dwell on being victimized or abused—are one of the strongest issues in marital discord. This type of anger, justifying one's anger, leads to an internal process of "stewing in your own juices" to the point where there are overdramatic reactions of rage that powerfully destroy romantic feelings and love for one another. This process of righteous indignation and feeling victimized actually tears relationships apart.

Withholding and Pseudoaggression

Both anger and anxiety are aroused by anything that threatens the self-parenting process. This type of anger, or pseudoaggression, functions to push away positive experiences that don't correspond to the person's image of him- or herself formed in the family. Happiness in a love relationship often triggers anxiety states, which in turn lead to aggressive or withholding responses.

By inhibiting or reducing the responses of both giving to and taking from objects in the external world, one limits and controls emotional transactions with others (Firestone, 1985). In couple relationships, people often hold back the traits that are the most desired or prized by the partner, usually with little or no conscious awareness.[5] For example, a woman who had shared her boyfriend's sense of adventure and interest in outdoor sports during the courtship phase was disappointed when during the first year of marriage, he gave up skiing and other physical activities they had shared. A man who complimented his bride on being a "good sport" on her first camping trip was gradually disillusioned as she began to complain about the weather and the accommodations on subsequent vacations.

> Pseudoaggression is not a genuine anger; that is, it is not a response to frustration. It is an attempt to manipulate, to push away, to control, and to avoid other people who threaten the primary fantasy of "I don't need anyone." When people tempt us by being exceptionally loving or close, we tend to push them away and establish distance. We accomplish this by being defiant, by attacking, by acting out withholding behavior patterns, by provoking, and then the person *does* pull away. These maneuvers actually affect the relationship and maintain the neurotic equilibrium—they make it safe again. In other words, pseudoag-

gression is anger that is used to provoke rejection. To maintain distance from other persons, we use anger to ward off closeness. When somebody is nice to us and warm to us, we may attack them to get them angry at us so that we don't have to face that closeness. Becoming distant from one's partner or not being sexually responsive are also ways of cutting off genuine relating. Withholding is a self-defeating, suicidal process, an inward process that insulates us and helps maintain a posture of pseudoindependence.

In addition, self-nurturing lifestyles in which we cater to ourselves, for example, where we're overly concerned or worried about our space, are socially acceptable versions of an inward process that is really harmful. On the other hand, a healthy person will have boundaries, but would not exclude transactions. Withholding is a holding back of emotional transactions, of in and out, of giving and taking.

It is frightening to be close, to want, to really feel love, to feel worthwhile. All of those things are frightening, but we have to take that chance. We have to sweat through that rather than act out, in order to get better. But often instead, we become pseudoaggressive and withholding, that is, we provoke rejection and distance in other people by acting in a way which will make the other person move away from us.

GUILT AND SHAME

Because people's internal conflicts are primarily unconscious, they are generally unaware of the circle of guilt and shame that limits them. An important distinction has been made in the literature between guilt feelings and shame. Shame is associated with the pre-oedipal level, and guilt is more associated with the oedipal level of development. Shame is a primary affect related to my concept of negative parental introjects* internalized during the pre-oedipal stage, whereas guilt has been identified as self-critical feelings experienced in relation to one's actions (C. Goldberg, 1991, 1996; Kaufman, 1980; Lewis, 1971; Morrison, 1989). Voices represent both types of attacks: a sense of deep humiliation for perceived inadequacies as well as self-recriminations for behavior. Both shame and guilt play a significant role in breaking down relationships.

The Two Modes of Guilt

Neurotic Guilt

Neurotic guilt can be defined as feelings of remorse, criticism, or self-attack for seeking gratification, for moving toward one's goals, and for

---

*Negative parental introjects refer to negative parental attitudes and feelings of hostility that are incorporated by the child during the formative years.

pursuing one's wants. Becker (1964) has described neurotic guilt as "the action-bind that reaches out of the past to limit new experiences, to block the possibility of broader choices" (p. 186). When children are taught that personal wants and desires are selfish, there is a resultant guilt reaction and movement toward a state of selflessness. However, our wants and desires make up a major part of our identity. When they are suppressed, we don't know who we are, and without a sense of self, we lose compassion for others (Firestone, 1987b, 1997a).

> I would like to say something about guilt and shame. They represent the internalization of the parental rejecting attitudes in relation to the simple body needs and feelings of the child. When parents reject the child's need for love or closeness, they imply that the child is "selfish" or bad for wanting these things. The child internalizes this image that he is bad and that his needs are wrong.
>
> The immature or helpless parent who is unable to really give and provide love for his child tries to get love from his child, tries to get his child to be very adult behaving and tries to get the child to deny his simple needs. This type of parent cannot distinguish emotional hunger, an anxious attachment, from real love or a positive attachment.
>
> A healthy person has to learn again to be "selfish." We have to learn to be honestly selfish, that is, we have to honestly face our needs and our feelings and face what we really want from others in our relationships. The more we face our simple wants, the more we can be straightforward in our expression to the people closest to us and to ourselves. We have to give up parental, rejecting, critical, evaluative attitudes toward our simple wishes and feelings. We have to feel what we want and stop accusing ourselves of being babyish when we want things.
>
> When we pursue our goals in an honest and direct manner, without deception, we actually are more moral and tend to have respect and empathy for other people. There is a sense of value for both ourselves and others. Following one's own motives and inclinations, within acceptable limits (with the exception of violations of the other's boundaries), does *not* lead to chaos or immoral behavior. On the other hand, the hypocritical attitudes and dishonesty inherent in turning away from our needs often leads us to be more destructive or hostile to friends and loved ones.

Existential Guilt

Existential guilt is triggered by holding back or withholding one's natural inclinations. It is generally experienced by individuals when they turn their backs on their goals, retreat from life, or seek gratification in fantasy (Firestone, 1987b, 1994; Maslow, 1968; May, 1958; Yalom, 1980).

> There is a kind of guilt that is appropriate, an existential guilt for retreating from life, going against our own being, against our own na-

ture. We are pained by a sense of alienation from ourselves and others. That type of guilt, that type of pain, is like a warning signal that we're off the track. We're cut off from ourselves; we're cut off from our feelings when we go against the nature of our body, when we go against our "selfish" impulses and feelings. That kind of guilt I would call an existential guilt. It is a guilt about running away from our experience, our honest experience, which is all that we have. That is our life, our vitality.

Existential guilt is inevitable when we turn away from ourselves, and it's not "a bad kind of guilt." It also follows that if we respect our own individuality, our own feelings, and our own wishes, this respect would extend to other people through the process of identification—in other words, people will behave in a moral way. They don't have to be coerced into it—they don't have to be tricked into it. You can't impose this type of behavior from the outside. But a person who is acknowledging of his own wants and needs will tend to behave morally and in a way that is respectful in relation to other people. There is a natural guilt, in other words, related to going against yourself and an extension of that natural guilt to being disrespectful to others and to violating the rights of other individuals. It simply follows.

But the haranguing guilt feelings of neurotic individuals, the torturous pain that they put themselves through, the self-critical thoughts, all of that is an internalization of the parental rejecting attitude—punishing themselves for feeling, for wanting, just as they were punished early in their lives. In that sense, neurotic guilt is always a negative thing. All people have to cope with neurotic guilt, and we can do that by struggling to maintain our integrity in relation to our needs and desires. In the course of therapy, if you stay honest, you'll gradually get over the guilt and fear and you'll hold the territory, but if you capitulate, you'll lose the ground. So if you hang in there and act on what you know to be right, even though you have an emotional attitude that it's wrong, you'll develop in time to where you *can* expand your life and have more fulfillment.

People acting out patterns of guilt and self-destructive machinations powerfully affect their mates and loved ones. Many marital quarrels are about the destructive patterns we see in our mates that take them away from their lives and away from their relationship with us. In fact, there is an enormous amount of animosity and quarreling regarding the self-destructive habit patterns that partners see in each other.

To summarize, fantasy, self-nurturance, and inwardness play major roles in an individual's retreat from close relationships. In the early years of life, children retreat to an inward, self-protective posture characterized by the progressive use of fantasy and self-nurturing behaviors to alleviate psychological pain (Firestone, 1990b). As adults, they may come to prefer these forms of internal gratification over seeking satisfaction in real relationships.

The fear of intimacy is closely related to a generalized fear of individuation and death anxiety. The child who forms an imagined connection with the parent or primary caretaker cannot easily differentiate him or herself at later stages of development. This lack of individuation, in turn, seriously interferes with his or her developing and maintaining close relationships.

A CONCEPTUAL MODEL OF RELATIONSHIPS

In understanding and treating the problems that individuals encounter in their intimate relationships, it is necessary to develop a model of healthy relationships and, in a similar manner, to characterize disturbed modes of relating. My in-depth study of the psychodynamics involved in couple and family relationships led me to conclude that all people exist in conflict between tendencies to pursue real gratification in their interpersonal relationships, and propensities to rely on internal sources of gratification, that is, fantasy, the use of substances, and inward habit patterns (Firestone, 1997a).

It is our contention that the fantasy bond or illusion of connectedness and the inward lifestyle it predisposes that defends the primary fantasy are the key elements responsible for distress and disharmony in relationships. As described previously, the degree of fantasy involvement characterized by withholding, inward behavior patterns, and alienation can be represented on a continuum, with healthy functioning at one end and schizophrenia at the other extreme. People's relationships range from mature reciprocity and loving relationships to a partial breakdown in relationships expressed in the addictive attachments of neurotic or "normal" individuals, to a total breakdown in relating manifested by schizophrenic patients.

The degree of inwardness as well as the frequency and intensity of the voices that control self-protective behavior patterns could potentially be assessed using a self-report questionnaire. This instrument could then be tested to determine its ability to predict the degree of emotional health manifested by individuals in their relationships, as well as the quality of their relationships and style of relating. I have already developed a scale, the *Firestone Assessment of Self-Destructive Thoughts (FAST)*; Firestone & Firestone, 1996, to predict self-destructive behavior that overlaps, to some extent, behaviors of men and women in relationships.* Preliminary studies are currently being planned to develop another scale, made up of items representing negative thoughts and attitudes, specifically designed to mea-

---

*The FAST is an 86-item self-report questionnaire used by clinicians as a risk assessment instrument with which to evaluate patients' suicide potential, to identify clusters of other self-destructive thoughts as part of formulating a treatment plan, and to use as an outcome measure.

sure inward behavior patterns and the inability to relate. This instrument may prove valuable in the future for use as part of a psychotherapeutic treatment program.

In couple relationships, each partner is strongly influenced by his or her voice process. Negative thoughts and attitudes generate pseudoaggressive behaviors, withholding habit patterns, emotional distance, and in some couples, interpersonal violence. In clinical studies, the origins of the voice have been traced to early family interactions (Firestone, 1988, 1990b). Because human beings are able to conceptualize themselves as objects, they are also capable of incorporating critical and aggressive attitudes toward self from others in the environment when they are under conditions of stress. As children, they develop a mode of intrapsychic communication, made up of negative thoughts toward self and others, that seriously compromises their ability to accept love, closeness, and intimacy as adults.

Note that mate selection based on deficits in each partner leads to a continuation of negative voices regarding the topic of those deficits. The projection or externalization of each partner's hostile attitudes or "voices" onto the other predisposes dissension within the couple, and they become intimate enemies. This type of projection is a major destructive factor in relationships.

In conclusion, the major threats to intimacy within couple relationships can be traced to the developmental history of each partner. Psychological defenses operating within the parents of the respective partners are transmitted to them as children on an unconscious level. They develop attitudes similar to those of their parents, both toward themselves and toward the opposite sex (sexual stereotypes), and imitate their parents' inward behavior patterns and lifestyle (Firestone, 1990b). Our therapeutic goal is to help people move toward more constructive and healthy forms of interaction in their intimate associations. By helping individuals develop better mental health and relinquish powerful defenses that interfere with intimacy, we help them to move on to a better life with mates and family members.

ENDNOTES

[1]Thomas Kuhn (1970) conceptualized these and other upheavals in the way people thought about themselves and the world as "scientific revolutions." He wrote that each discovery of Copernicus, Newton, Lavoisier, and Einstein "necessitated the community's rejection of one time-honored scientific theory in favor of another incompatible with it . . . and each transformed the scientific imagination in ways that we . . . need to describe as a transformation of the world within which scientific work was done. Such changes, together with the controversies that almost always accompany them, are the defining characteristics of scientific revolutions" (p. 6).

[2]Freud (1924/1953) wrote that "The first of these displeasing propositions of psychoanalysis is this: that mental processes are essentially unconscious. . . . Yet . . . the acceptance of unconscious mental processes represents a decisive step towards a new orientation in the world and in science" (pp. 25–26).

[3]Research has shown that fantasy can be rewarding under conditions of physical deprivation. In one study (Keys, Brozek, Henschel, Mickelsen, & Taylor, 1950), volunteer subjects deprived of food and kept on a minimum sustenance diet reported that they spent hours daydreaming about food, which partly alleviated their tension and hunger drive. Empirical studies conducted by Silverman, Lachmann, and Milich (1982) showed that the message "MOMMY AND I ARE ONE" presented subliminally (on the tachistoscope) ameliorated symptoms in schizophrenic patients and in some groups of nonpsychotic individuals.

[4]There is a tendency on the part of some theorists (Freud, 1920/1955, 1925/1959, 1923/1961; Klein, 1932; Menninger, 1938) to confuse man's potential for aggression with innate drives. The capacity for aggressive emotional reactions should not be mistaken for an instinct for aggressive behavior. This differentiation has serious theoretical consequences. Freud (1920/1955) contended that the aggressive drives (id) based on a death instinct, are so powerful that they must inevitably prevail over reason (ego) or conscience (superego). I subscribe to the view (N. E. Miller & Dollard, 1941) that aggression is primarily frustration-derived and that human beings are not inherently destructive, aggressive, or self-destructive. My understanding of human aggression also takes into account social learning theory (Bandura, 1973; Bandura & Walters, 1963; Berkowitz, 1989). See Okey's (1992) review of theoretical approaches to aggressive behavior and Lore and Schultz' (1993) and Eron's (1987) summaries.

[5]Examples of withholding behavior patterns in relationships can be found in George Bach and Ronald Deutsch's (1979) book, *Stop! You're Driving Me Crazy*. See also *Fear of Intimacy: An Examination of Withholding Behavior Patterns* (Parr, 1997b) for further examples from videotaped seminars.

3

AN ETHICAL PERSPECTIVE: HUMAN RIGHTS ISSUES IN PERSONAL RELATIONSHIPS

If it is not only power and coercion that enslave man, then there must be something in his nature that contributes to his downfall; since this is so, the state is not man's first and only enemy, but he himself harbors an "enemy within."

Ernest Becker (1975, pp. 39–40)

To develop a better understanding of relationships, we find it worthwhile to examine the parallels between the psychodynamics in couples and families and those operating in larger groups. An important analogy can be drawn between political systems, family systems, and interpersonal relationships. Human rights issues apply to all of these social phenomena.

In attempting to understand fundamental group dynamics, it is useful to study the patterns of psychological defense manifested by individual members. People form defenses to cope with excessive conditions of stress experienced in growing up. Once formed, these defenses lead to a wide range of behaviors that limit, restrict, and damage self and others. In the process of forming groups or societies, individual patterns of defense are pooled and combine to form cultural attitudes and social mores. Once established, cultural prerogatives based on defense formation then reflect back on people, cutting deeply into their autonomy and depriving them of vital experiences necessary for reaching their true potential (Firestone, 1985, 1996).[1]

THE ETHICS OF SOCIAL STRUCTURES AND INTERPERSONAL RELATIONSHIPS

Issues of power, control, and human rights enter into interpersonal relationships. From an ethical standpoint, one can compare the functions of a state or political system with those served by the couple and the family in terms of the extent to which they either support or violate the rights of the individual.

Social Systems

The principles of the good society call for a concern with an order of being . . . where it matters supremely that the human person is inviolable.

Walter Lippman (1955, p. 165)

A key consideration in analyzing the functions of a social system is what the state is offering its citizens, that is, to what extent does it provide for the welfare of its constituents? The ideal state would be concerned with economic security for its members as well as with the protection of their personal freedom and basic human rights. Philosophically, this type of government would place value on the life of each person over the survival of the system itself. Individuals would be considered as an "end in themselves" and never as the means to an end providing benefit to the system (Kant, 1781/1965). Granting preeminence to the individual rather than to the state or any of its institutions is logical as well as ethical; as noted previously, systems are merely abstractions, whereas people are real, living entities.

In contrast, when protection of the state or a political system takes precedence over the individual, the needs of most citizens are not served; instead, they generally suffer economically, politically, and personally. Governments operating on this premise perceive issues of human rights as a low priority, thereby setting the stage for oppression and tyranny. The concept of the ideal system as described in Plato's *Republic* (trans. 1955), and Sir Thomas More's (1551/1949) *Utopia* can be contrasted with the nightmarish illustrations of Huxley's (1932) *Brave New World*, and Orwell's (1949/1954) *Nineteen Eighty-Four*.

All social systems involve a certain amount of compromise in relation to the rights of the individual (Rawls, 1971). Obviously some sacrifice of individual freedom is necessary to live in a social order; however, it is a matter of degree. Totalitarian or authoritarian states impose a myriad of rules and restrictions on their citizens, while on the other hand, the democratic state permits more personal freedom, mobility, and possibility for members to improve their economic status.

The totalitarian state best represents a viewpoint that values the system over the individual. Totalitarian governments are tyrannical in nature in that they demand conformity and submission. The efforts of their political leaders are often directed toward categorizing and grouping persons as a means of control and manipulation (Marcuse, 1955/1966; Turner, 1978). Havel (1990) described the "self-momentum" of impersonal power manifested in authoritarian systems as "the blind, unconscious, irresponsible, uncontrollable, and unchecked momentum that is no longer the work of people, but which drags people along with it and therefore manipulates them" (p. 166). Unfortunately, most citizens living under this type of regimen are willing to submit because they can escape the terrifying responsibility of freedom. In a sense they are in collusion with the social system. In writing about the conditions that existed in 19th century imperialist Russia, Dostoyevsky (1880/1958) described the individual's propensity to renounce freedom and to submit to the manipulations of the power structure: "Man has no more agonizing anxiety than to find someone to whom he can hand over with all speed the gift of freedom with which the unhappy creature is born" (p. 298).[2]

Corruption, manipulation, and other iniquities exist even in a democratic society. All societies establish conventional means and mores that are effective in controlling the membership, and, in most instances, these conventional attitudes and stereotypic views restrict people's thinking, increase their hostility, and negatively influence their behavior toward one another. Social conventions become ritualized activities that reinforce a collective conscience and form the foundation of social relationships in society. These rituals permeate every nuance of our daily life (Durkheim, 1912/1965; Goffman, 1967) and are frequently inhibiting and repressive.

In addition to the threat to individual freedom, social institutions and conventions often have other negative influences on social behavior. For example, the rights of individuals are largely dictated by the legal system. The court, as a social institution, presumably maintains the safety of children by establishing and enforcing definitions of maltreatment, neglect, and abuse. Child welfare agencies are bureaucratic extensions of the social system supporting children, yet these institutions have sometimes overlooked the welfare of children in support of the primacy of the biological family in the child-care role. The idealization of the family, regardless of the degree of its dysfunctionality, often helps its members avoid critical issues that are vital to mental health.[3] Instead of challenging destructive family practices, our society reinforces and supports the formation of fantasy bonds within the couple and family. The emphasis is on preserving the *form* of the relationship or family constellation, while disguising the fact that the *substance* or quality is lacking. We have in a sense normalized the discourse so that the once perceived dysfunction becomes the accepted norm, becomes produced *truth* (Foucault, 1975, 1980). It is the production of these truths that shapes human experience rather than human experience that shapes the production of truth. Restrictive and irresponsible practices of the social system, as well as their idealization, have significant detrimental effects on each person.

The resultant loss of meaning can be seen in the high rates of homicide and suicide, drug addiction, depression, and random acts of violence among adolescents.[4] Many young people, once the most serious critics of the status quo, currently manifest attitudes of apathy and hopelessness. Most members of society remain prisoners of their own internal programming while continually reinforcing the socialization processes that damaged them. Contemporary social practices generally have a powerful delimiting effect on people's personal freedom, healthy sexuality, personal integrity, and natural drive for affiliation with others.

These practices become the expected norm rather than the exception. They become institutionalized routines that are unchallenged by the individuals they affect. In effect, they become self-fulfilling prophecies. The self-fulfilling prophecy advanced by Merton (1957) is based on a statement by W. I. Thomas (cited in Merton, 1957), "If men define situations as real, they are real in their consequences." The self-fulfilling prophecy occurs when inaccurate definitions of situations or circumstances elicit behaviors that make the inaccurate definitions true.

Couple and Family Systems

The ideal couple or family would attempt to gratify the physical, economic, and emotional needs of each individual and enhance the personal development of children. There would be a minimum number of rules and restrictions, allowing for optimal freedom and autonomy.

In contrast, the less-than-ideal couple or family tends to function in a manner that exerts excessive control over each person through rules and rituals that favor obligation over choice and image over self. Unnecessary restrictions, manipulations, and power plays, as well as the mystification needed to deny the fact that such controls exist, cause considerable harm. It is absurd to serve an abstraction, that is, to place primary value on any social institution, whether it be the couple or family, without considering the well-being of the individual men, women, and children.

In recent years, attention has been focused on specific forms of interpersonal relationships in which survival of the dyad or system appeared to be valued over the well-being of the individual. Clinicians and theorists have written about family systems that are similar in many respects to the totalitarian state and have described a number of these systems' suppressive and cultlike practices. For example, in reporting findings from a sampling of dysfunctional, "normal," and optimal families, Beavers (1977) wrote the following: "Severely dysfunctional families invade and attempt to distort individual reality. Midrange families believe in external absolutes and attempt to control by intimidation and coercion. Only the optimal families showed many areas free from efforts at thought control" (p. 147).[5] Tedeschi and Felson (1994) asserted that "people who rarely if ever use coercion with others make an exception in the case of their children" (p. 287). They called attention to the "high levels of coercive behavior, including bodily force, verbal and physical punishment, physical isolation, and deprivation of resources" (pp. 290–291) in American families. Their social interactional model postulates that parents' coercive behaviors are "designed to influence children, promote retributive justice, and assert and defend [their parents'] favorable identities" (p. 290).

Other theorists have described couple and family systems that demand loyalty, whether it is deserved or not. In these relationships, control through guilt and a sense of obligation characterizes the interactions between members and supports the perpetuation of destructive family ties. In their book *Invisible Loyalties*, Boszormenyi-Nagy and Spark (1984) emphasized that "in families, as well as in other groups, the most fundamental loyalty commitment pertains to maintenance of the group itself" (p. 40). These theorists noted that the meaning of words such as *loyalty* and *justice* eventually becomes corrupted within the context of most traditional families.[6] They went on to describe the types of manipulations typically used by family members that arouse guilt in others by calling into question their loyalty to the family:

> The real forces of bondage or freedom are beyond observable power games or manipulative tactics. Invisible loyalty commitments to one's family follow paradoxical laws. The martyr who doesn't let other family members "work off" their guilt is a far more powerfully controlling force than the loud, demanding "bully." (p. xiii)

Family systems theorist Murray Bowen (Kerr & Bowen, 1988) argued that in most relationships and families whenever there is an increase in anxiety, "each person feels pressured to act in ways to preserve the attachment" (p. 84). In describing the functions served by the traditional or "normal" nuclear family, R. D. Laing (1967) wrote as follows: "The family's function is to repress Eros; to induce a false consciousness of security; to deny death by avoiding life; to cut off transcendence; to believe in God, not to experience the Void; to create, in short, one-dimensional man; to promote respect, conformity, obedience" (p. 65).

To identify those aspects of society and family life that have a destructive effect on human experience, we must first conceptualize those attributes that are essentially human, such as the capacity for deep feeling, rationality, and the ability to use abstract symbols. In addition, compassion for self and others and the search for meaning are of special significance. We must be sensitive to both cultural and family influences that in any way limit or pervert these qualities. Regardless of other considerations, if any aspect of these fundamental human attributes is damaged by society or family life we must consider that socialization process to be oppressive and abusive.

In summary, to a certain extent, social systems and institutions ignore important issues of human rights. Similarly, many families intrude on and violate the human rights of their members, that is, their right to live and develop as individuals. Many parents, for example, fail to "let their child be" in the sense of allowing his or her real personality and unique qualities to emerge. The spirit and personality of the child are damaged by such intrusions. This abuse of personal freedom can eventually evolve into an issue of human rights within the person: The child who is mistreated goes on to mistreat him- or herself in much the same manner. The damage is then perpetuated in new relationships and, perhaps most painfully, in relation to one's children, thereby completing the cycle (Firestone, 1990b).

We must conclude that human rights issues, values, and ethics are unavoidable in an analysis of couples, family relationships, and social structures. However, the conventional approach to these subjects often ignores these issues and indeed, they are deemphasized or completely overlooked by many practitioners in the mental health profession.*

The question arises as to why most individuals are susceptible to machinations of oppression and tyranny whether practiced by one's mate, family, or political system. A number of social and psychological factors are known to contribute to people's tendencies to submit their will to another person or a group. The answer is complex and multidetermined, and one must consider the basic philosophical assumptions of members of a social system in approaching this issue.

PHILOSOPHICAL ASSUMPTIONS THAT HAVE A DAMAGING IMPACT ON RELATIONSHIPS

One major problem insufficiently stressed by social critics involves certain core assumptions about human beings that are inherently false and that negatively impact relationships. These presumptions are implicitly believed, to varying degrees, by most people, and are more or less "common knowledge." One reason analyses of these assumptions become important is the fact that speculations about human nature function to a considerable degree as self-fulfilling prophecies. For example, the assumption that human

---

*With respect to taking the conventional approach, many marital and family therapists *implicitly* endorse the perspective "Can this marriage or family be saved?" rather than "Can these human beings be helped (or saved)?" as being the most important question to address in their work.

nature is basically destructive supports the belief that without the absolute sovereignty exercised by the state, war would be inevitable (Hobbes, 1651/ 1909). When people act on this belief, they shy away from seeking alternative solutions, arm themselves, and assume an aggressively defensive posture. The paranoia and counterparanoia eventually set off the violence.

Some basic assumptions that have implications for how we consider human nature include the following italicized statements:

Human beings are basically inadequate or deficient in and of themselves. Most people grow up feeling that something is inherently missing in them. They imagine that to be a whole person, they need to find someone to fill the space or void. As individuals operating on their own, they feel flawed in some basic sense and believe that one must find one's "soulmate," that is, some special person out in the world that will make them complete. This belief is reinforced in popular culture and in contemporary music and literature. The main character in the popular movie *Jerry McGuire* states, "you complete me." This presumption increases men and women's desperation to find partners, leads to premature choices, and later leads couples to elevate and reify the relationship out of proportion. Subsequently, too much is expected from couple relationships and marriage as people attempt to satisfy all their needs in one relationship. This expectation causes a good deal of human misery.

A person must subordinate him- or herself to the preservation of the couple, family, or society's norms or else he or she is abnormal. If a person fails to fit into these systems, for example, does not live up to society's expectations to get conventionally married and have children, he or she is considered odd, immature, or psychologically disturbed. Within this framework, all deviations from conventional modes of living are suspect. Conformity and adjustment to society are considered moral and healthy; nonconformity to societal expectations is perceived as abnormal and a threat to society.

Peter Shaffer's (1974) play, *Equus*, illustrates this basic assumption. In the play, the psychiatrist, Dysart, is torn between his pledge to take away the pain and torment of his young patient, thus allowing him to return to society as a "safe" adjusted member, and his instinct to allow the boy to retain his individuality and live with his pain. He chooses to blot out the pain and incidentally some of the most vital parts of the youngster's personality, rather than run a minor risk of harming society. Dysart is tormented with guilt about the threats to the boy's spirit posed by the therapy. In one scene, he cries out in anguish: "Look at him! . . . My desire might be to make this boy an ardent husband—a caring citizen—a worshiper of abstract and unifying God. My achievement, however, is more likely to make a ghost!" (pp. 123–124).

Although the play depicts an extreme situation, it exemplifies the dilemma all psychotherapists face. Dysart's choice reflects the goal of most contemporary treatment programs, that is, to cure patients of their manifest symptoms and quickly readjust them to society.*

People are born bad; they require rehabilitation, cleansing, and purification. When people conceptualize the origin of life as dirty or sinful and believe that they must cleanse themselves to be pure, they set up conditions that define and limit the course of their lives, particularly their sexuality. The concept of original sin is a presumption that the human body and its sexual functions are bad or dirty.[7] Negative attitudes about one's person, formed in early childhood, are later extended into the adult's sexual sphere. Shame, guilt, and restrictive views about sex make it an area that is fraught with anxiety, pain, and guilt for many people.

Some children come to confuse sexual functions with anal functions during toilet training. On some level, they assimilate the verbal and non-verbal cues that communicate the disgust and displeasure that some parents feel to an inordinate degree while changing diapers. Most people maintain the belief that they are somehow basically bad or unclean throughout their lives. Social systems that overemphasize personal cleanliness and order are particularly dangerous. Attitudes of ethnic superiority incite people and foster hatred. "Ethnic cleansing" represents this perverted point of view carried to its logical extreme, whereby members of the "ingroup" act out violence against the "outgroup." In a social structure based on such prejudice and racist attitudes, individuals within the disenfranchised and oppressed group tend to act out the negative stereotypes assigned to them (Firestone, 1996). When people are perceived as being basically bad, flawed, or evil, they tend to behave accordingly. For example, the "bad" child usually goes on to live out the self-fulfilling prophecy imposed by parents whose child-rearing practices are based on negative assumptions about the nature of the child.

Another important supposition, akin to the concept of original sin, states that the infant possesses innate aggression—a perspective reflecting Freud's (1925/1959) concept of the "death instinct." Klein (1948/1964) deemphasized parents' role in the psychological disturbances of their children by stressing that the child projects his or her own rage onto the parents and then feels persecuted and paranoid. Our perception of the real issue is that the child's aggression is derived primarily from the frustration of his or her wants and needs; it does *not* stem from an inborn instinct for aggression.

Freedom necessarily leads to anarchy and chaos; therefore, restriction is essential. Many people believe that without the imposition of strict rules,

---

*Therapists who place social conformity above the personal interests of their patients perform a great disservice. Just as the physician upholds the oath of Hippocrates, the therapist should be devoted to the cure of his patient above all other considerations, both personal and social. One notable exception is where the patient could be considered to be physically harmful to him- or herself or to other members of the community. In that case, the therapist's primary obligation is to protect the rights of others.

regulations, and sexual prohibitions, human beings would neglect their basic responsibilities to family and community, parents would abandon their children, and the family, the most important agent of socialization for future generations, would be threatened with extinction.

One notable example of this myth is the expectation that without restrictions or laws against nudity, sexual promiscuity would run rampant, dangerous sex drives would be unleashed, and the incidence of rape and sexually transmitted disease would rise at an uncontrollable rate. In actuality, in a number of European countries where there are fewer restrictions in relation to nudity, for example, where women are allowed to be topless on the beaches, there are few if any disturbances based on these relaxed standards. On the other hand, unnecessarily harsh restrictions on people's sexuality, imposed by moral code, custom, or distorted views, interfere with personal fulfillment and sexual maturity. Frustration due to suppressive moral codes contributes to a generalized increase in hostility and a proliferation of perverse sexual practices.[8]

The nature of love is generally considered to be constant and invariant. For many individuals, the "happily ever after" characterization of love engenders promise that things will always be the same, if not better. Love, like any other natural feeling, arises spontaneously, is inconsistent, and can be affected by a wide range of external conditions and internal states. Even in a good relationship, there are always emotional highs and lows in the ebb and flow of loving feelings.

Furthermore, when love is conceptualized as an unchanging process, feelings of love and hate toward the same person appear to be irreconcilable. Because conflicting attitudes coexist in all relationships, it is advantageous to recognize mixed feelings without becoming alarmed. Because ambivalence is often perceived as illogical, people strive for a singular view at the expense of reality. In the process of banishing negative feelings from consciousness, men and women frequently act out hostility indirectly in a destructive manner. Recognition of these feelings enables one to avoid projecting them on to the other and serves to better regulate aggressive responses.

People who have difficulty accepting ambivalent feelings in their realm of experience tend to categorize self and others as being either all good or all bad. They think in black and white terms, ignoring the reality that human beings have two sides and possess both positive and negative characteristics.

Parents have unconditional love for their children. Most people believe that parents instinctively and unconditionally love their children, and therefore, deserve respect and affection. Mothers, in particular, are idealized (Badinter, 1980/1981), and all of their responses are perceived to be pure and selfless; yet this presumption is simply not accurate. When observing the behavioral manifestations of so-called loving parents in everyday situations, it becomes apparent that this idealistic image is false. Many parents complain that their children are rejecting or disrespectful; however, it is reasonable to assume that children *would* love and respect parents who treated them properly. Why would they respond lovingly and respectfully to parents who are destructive in their actions and cause them a great deal of psychological pain?

The precept of unconditional parental love is a fundamental tenet of society. Actually this myth causes considerable guilt in parents who have difficulty accepting whatever negative feelings they have toward their children, and parental guilt reactions only compound problems of child-rearing.

In conclusion, people who accept the premises noted above, whether consciously or unconsciously, tend to become increasingly cynical, indifferent, and duplicitous in their overall world view and personal interactions. The short-sighted view of oneself and others generated by these assumptions leads to a sense of malaise and increased aggression and self-destructiveness in the larger society. Lastly, social pressure to conform to societal mores and expectations based on these fallacies helps maintain a negative status quo that militates against the initiation of preventive measures based on sound principles of mental health. Insight into these faulty attitudes could help to challenge the abuses of power that exist in contemporary society and in so many interpersonal relationships.

THE PSYCHODYNAMICS OF POWER AND CONTROL IN RELATIONSHIPS

How do manipulations of power and control work in interpersonal relationships? Why are they generally so effective? How do the defenses and personal qualities manifested by each partner intermesh to create relationships characterized by power struggles and conflict? The answers are extremely complex. However, the underlying dynamics can best be understood through a careful, objective analysis of early environmental conditions that lead to the formation of psychological defenses and can indicate how these defense mechanisms are replicated in adult relationships.

Manipulations are generally effective within the couple and family because most adults have not succeeded in outgrowing or transcending the fears and pain of their childhood experiences. Residuals of the hurt child exist to a certain extent in every person; no one has completely left behind the primitive fear, longing for love, feelings of helplessness, and guilt experienced during the formative years (Firestone, 1990b). Ironically, the defenses that many people originally formed in an attempt to protect themselves against painful feelings later cause them a great deal of trouble and render them more susceptible to abuses by others. Distortions of self, others, and the world that are inherent in being defended are introduced into new relationships, coloring all important interactions. Most people end up fighting ghosts rather than struggling with fundamental issues of personal gratification and self-actualization (Bloch, 1978, 1985; Caspi, 1993; Crittenden, 1985; Fraiberg, 1982; Fraiberg, Adelson, & Shapiro, 1980; Moeller, Bachmann, & Moeller, 1993; Neumann, Houskamp, Pollock, & Briere, 1996).

For example, manipulations that precipitate guilt reactions exert a powerful influence over people's lives.[9] These maneuvers "work" because most people were taught to be selfless as children, that is, to accommodate to unnecessary prohibitions at the expense of self. They were conditioned to believe that they were "selfish" for expressing their wants and needs and learned to be indirect and fundamentally dishonest about their desires. As adults, they continue to act on these distortions of self and are often manipulative themselves as well as vulnerable to manipulation by others.

Methods of Control

Manipulations and power plays are manifested in three important ways in personal relationships: (a) bullying, domination, and the use of force, (b) threats that arouse fear reactions, and (c) maneuvers that trigger guilt feelings in others.

1. Domineering or authoritarian individuals control other people overtly through aggressive parental behaviors that reward and punish, indicate approval and disapproval, and sometimes actually impose physical punishment.

2. Threats of reprisal or loss of economic security by members of a couple or family are clearly intimidating. Abandonment threats are a particularly effective means of control. These maneuvers work because abandonment fears are experienced with dread by so many people. Even when they would like to escape from a bad relationship, if there are threats of being left by an undesirable partner, or if their partner actually leaves them, they usually suffer emotional trauma. The reason behind this paradoxical phenomenon is that being left supports internal thoughts and feelings adverse to the self, feelings that one is unlovable, bad, inadequate, or worthless. Many parents use threats of abandonment or sending the child away to promote obedience (Bowlby, 1973). Needless to say, this is destructive because it arouses extreme fear and insecurity as young children are completely dependent on parents for survival.

3. Close scrutiny reveals that many marriages and family constellations are characterized by controlling behaviors that are less obvious but nonetheless intimidating. Guilt-provoking responses on the part of one member or another cause considerable harm. There is a kind of terrorism practiced in personal relationships that makes one individual accountable for the unhappiness of the other. The tyranny of weakness and illness exerted by masochistic, self-denying, or self-destructive individuals clearly has a powerful manipulative effect. For example, a woman's tears will frequently establish submission to her will. Irrational or microsuicidal behavior is also intimidating. A father's habitual drinking often controls the behavior of his wife and the entire family. Threats of self-harm or actual suicide are particularly effective. Many people unconsciously use self-destructive machinations to gain leverage over mates and family members. Although these manipulations are often effective, they are not worth the price to the perpetrators.

Within a couple or family, the more insecure the partners or family members, the more they need to control and manipulate others. Similarly, the extent to which people submit to controls is proportional to the degree to which they feel insecure, fearful, and guilty. Partners in a couple tend to establish a balance or equilibrium in that one or the other will act dominant or parental and the other submissive or childlike (Willi, 1975/1982). This pattern may vary in that partners exchange roles from time to time, depending on the specific issues confronting them. Members of a couple are in collusion to maintain their style of relating and react adversely to any changes. When the balance is upset, one or the other will attempt to manipulate the situation back to the status quo (Kerr & Bowen, 1988).[10]

Early Environmental Conditions That Predispose Insecurity

There is a direct relationship between the ethical concern about destructive manifestations of control or manipulation in relationships and the patterns of anxious attachment developed early in life.[11] The conceptual model of relationships introduced in the previous chapter may be further elucidated by examining the negative environmental conditions that impinge on children and their style of coping with these toxic elements. One early manifestation of the defensive process can be observed in the quality of the attachment the infant or child forms with the parenting figure. Studies have shown that many infants develop attachments to parents or caretakers based on feelings of anxiety and insecurity rather than on feelings of basic trust and a sense of security (Ainsworth, Blehar, Waters, & Wall, 1978; Bowlby, 1973, 1982; Main, 1996; Main et al., 1985; Rutter, 1997; Steele, Steele, & Fonagy, 1996). When this is the case, these patterns of anxious attachment can later contribute to the deterioration of adult relationships (Bartholomew, 1990; Brennan & Shaver, 1995; Feeney & Noller, 1990; Kirkpatrick & Davis, 1994; Latty-Mann & Davis, 1996; Shaver & Clark, 1994; Simpson, Rholes, & Phillips, 1996).

The conditions that foster the formation of secure and anxious attachment patterns can be delineated (Belsky & Isabella, 1988; Cicchetti & Toth, 1998; Firestone, 1990b; Spieker & Booth, 1988; Steele et al., 1996). Ideally, the mother or principal caretaker would offer sensitive care and relieve the infant's anxiety without being overprotective. As the child grew older, she would provide appropriately varied responses, alternating spontaneous contact with letting go of her offspring. In terms of attachment theory, this child would be likely to form a *secure attachment* with his or her parent or caretaker (Chisholm, 1996).

The ideal conditions favoring a secure attachment rarely exist. All children, to varying degrees, suffer emotional pain and anxiety that necessitate the building of defenses. In the early stages of an infant's development, intolerable feelings of anxiety and isolation are often conveyed through the physical interaction between the mother and child. It is impossible for an anxious mother (or caretaker) to hide her fears and anxieties from her infant (Jacobson, 1964; Mahler & McDevitt, 1968; Mahler, Pine, & Bergman, 1975; Stern, 1985). The authors and other observers have noted a form of withdrawal in mothers who appear to be unaffected or unmoved by the emotional experience of feeding or caring for the child, and who avoid eye contact with their infants (Bolton, 1983; Welldon, 1988). The symptoms that develop in the infant as a result of inadequate or insensitive caretaking are a general dissatisfaction indicated by excessive whining and screaming, an inability to relax against the mother's body, and a desperate clinging to the mother or a pushing away from her (Cassidy & Kobak, 1988; Main, 1990; Main & Hesse, 1990). Toddlers and young children categorized with *anxious–ambivalent* or *anxious–avoidant* patterns of attachment exhibit many of the same signs as well as other symptomatology (George & Main, 1979; S. Goldberg, 1997; Greenspan & Lieberman, 1988; Lieberman & Pawl, 1990; Main, 1990).

It is important to make the distinction between parents' feelings of love and those of emotional hunger to understand one of the major factors that contribute to the formation of a secure attachment versus an anxious or avoidant attachment between parent and child.[12] With some exceptions (Parker, 1983; Tronick, Cohn, & Shea, 1986; West & Keller, 1991), these two emotional states and the associated behaviors in parents have not been sufficiently differentiated from each other by developmental theorists. Immature, emotionally hungry, or overprotective parents exert a strong pull on their infants that drains them of the emotional resources necessary for healthy personality development.[13] Symptoms may take the form of either clinging to (anxious–ambivalent attachment) or avoiding the parenting figure (anxious–avoidant attachment pattern), depending on the specific type of parenting experienced by the child.[14]

Role of the Voice in Maintaining Psychological Equilibrium in Adult Relationships

Research Background

A considerable body of research on attachment theory has accumulated that investigates the quality of early attachments and the effects of an anxious attachment on children and adolescents in terms of depression, learning disabilities, and other emotional disturbances.[15] Other studies have demonstrated that differential patterns of attachment are generally repeated and expressed through different styles of relating in adult romantic attachments.[16] Over the past decade, researchers have consistently emphasized the need for further investigations into the underlying mechanisms, that is, the "internal working models" or thought processes responsible for the repetition of abnormal or maladaptive attachment patterns over the life span (Benoit, Parker, & Zeanah, 1997; George, 1996; George & Solomon, 1996; Main & Goldwyn, 1984; Owens et al., 1995; Pianta, Egeland, & Adam, 1996; Shaver, Collins, & Clark, 1996; Sperling & Berman, 1994; M. J. Ward & Carlson, 1995).[17] According to attachment theorists (Bakermans-Kranenburg & van IJzendoorn, 1993), internal working models or "current 'state of mind' with respect to attachment relationships determines parents' sensitivity to their infants' attachment behavior, and, in turn, shapes the infants' own internal working models of attachment" (p. 870).

We conceptualize the "voice" as a fundamental part of the "internal working models" that explains the dynamics involved in interpersonal relationships. Clinical studies investigating the structure, functions, and origins of the negative thought process, or voice, have clarified its role in the intergenerational transmission of negative parental attitudes, behaviors, and defenses (see Firestone, 1990b, pp. 88–89). The voice, an intrapsychic mechanism that is primarily responsible for the perpetuation of parental defenses in succeeding generations, also influences the type and quality of attachments formed by adult individuals in their couple relationships (Firestone, 1997a). The psychodynamics described here (and in chapter 2, this volume) elucidate the important link between early defense formation, specific defensive processes regulated by the voice, and interactions between the couple that function to preserve the self-parenting process and maintain psychological equilibrium.

Once people have achieved a stable balance between reliance on the self-parenting process and pursuit of gratification in the real world, *anxiety will be aroused by anything that threatens either the self-parenting process or object dependence, that is, anxiety is aroused whenever an individual's state of psychological equilibrium is disturbed.* Anxiety states may be described as having a bipolar causality. Anxiety can result from especially rewarding experiences, personal growth, and involvement in more gratifying relationships, which threaten an individual's defensive identity and disturb the core defense or fantasy bond.[18] On the other hand, anxiety can result from personal failure, frustration in interpersonal relationships, physical illness, separation or loss, and death anxiety. The rise in anxiety results in both aggressive and regressive reactions (Firestone, 1997a).[19]

The psychodynamics underlying Freud's (1920/1955) concept of "repetition compulsion," and its primary function of maintaining psychological equilibrium are discussed below in terms of (a) the concept of a provisional identity; (b) externalization of the voice in adult relationships; and (c) defensive maneuvers that repeat the past in new associations.

The "Provisional Identity": Identity Formed in the Family

In most families, each child is assigned a provisional identity that is integrated into the family system. Children are defined and categorized by parents and carry these labels with them into adulthood. The accuracy or reality of these assigned characteristics is rarely challenged or subjected to objective scrutiny, yet they play a significant part in life. Children are defined as "the quiet one," "the pretty one," "the wild one," "the smart one," "the selfish one," "the bad seed," and so forth. This programming is well established, and later these introjects determine each person's style of relating to other objects.[20]

The process of assigning a provisional identity is a result of the parents' tendency to project their own self-hatred and negative voices onto their children. Later, parents criticize and punish their children for these projected qualities. In the process of projection, the child is basically used as a waste receptacle or dumping ground; the parents disown weaknesses and unpleasant characteristics in themselves and perceive them instead in the child (Bowen, 1978). In most cases, children accept parental attributions and take on the assigned negative identity while maintaining an idealized image of their parents. As adults, they feel anxious and guilty to move away from these definitions, even though they may be negative or degrading.

The provisional identity described here refers to an identity assigned to, or induced in, the child by parents and other family members. It is important to note that these labels do not make up an individual's "real" self or identity. However, many people mistake the imposed identity for their real selves, and act accordingly.

Destructive attitudes toward the self are assimilated by the child through the defense of identification with the aggressor. Under stressful conditions, the child identifies with the powerful aggressive parent rather than experience the painful feelings of being a weak and vulnerable child. Because each person's self-concept is regulated by these hostile thoughts and attitudes, a self-attacking posture is aroused whenever the individual steps out of the defensive mode or modifies his or her negative self-image in a positive direction.[21] A person's provisional identity, in conjunction with the habit patterns and lifestyle that support it, may evolve along a developmental pathway very different from one the individual might have followed had he or she been allowed to develop freely.

Externalization of the Voice in Interpersonal Relationships

The voice functions to perpetuate the provisional identity in adult relationships. Rather than cope with the positive anxiety inherent in achieving a warmer, more satisfying relationship, people usually attempt to preserve psychological equilibrium and maintain their provisional identity by externalizing their voice in the new relationship. This helps to explain why so many people remain in bad relationships.

Externalization of the voice represents an end in itself because each partner is able to avert or reduce anxiety by perceiving the other person as his or her critical parent to affirm his or her negative identity. Both individuals use the other to represent the negative view they have of themselves, thereby preserving their negative self-image. For example, a woman whose internal feeling of being unlovable centered on self-critical voices about her physical appearance gained considerable weight in the months following her wedding. Her husband's anger and sarcasm about her weight gain and his gradual withdrawal from their sexual relationship reaffirmed her image of unlovability. In another case, a man identified negative voices that women did not see him as a real man and revealed disparaging thoughts concerning his body, general appearance, and sexuality. It turned out that his current girlfriend had become increasingly irritated by his desperation, passive-aggression, and compensatory catering behavior and eventually had come to see him as he saw himself.

The process of using one's partner as the agent of attack rather than being at the mercy of one's own self-accusations diminishes internal feelings of anxiety and self-hatred. Often, it is less painful to defend oneself against outside attack than to experience the torment and sense of division in recognizing the enemy within. Finally, by externalizing the voice, both partners are also able to deny negative experiences they encountered in their families, to displace or project them onto the current relationship, and to relive painful aspects of their past in interactions with their partners.

Defensive Maneuvers That Repeat the Past in New Relationships

To preserve their provisional identities, people must modify the responses of their loved ones, in a sense "working them over," in a manner that maintains equilibrium and reduces tension and anxiety. The intolerance of accepting a new, more positive orientation leads to behaviors that significantly alter the feelings of their mates. As noted in chapter 2, individuals attempt to recreate the original conditions within the family in their present-day relationships through three major modes of defense: (a) selection, (b) distortion, and (c) provocation.

Selection. People tend to select mates who are similar to one or another parent or family member because they feel familiar and comfortable with them. They feel relaxed when their defenses are appropriate. The defended individual externalizes the introjected parental image by using the new partner to maintain the good parent–bad child system. Thus, people are often attracted to someone who physically resembles their father or mother, aunt or uncle, and so forth, and often choose mates whose behavior patterns and style of relating are similar to key family members.

Distortion. Perceptions of new objects are altered or distorted in a direction that corresponds more closely to members of the original family. Not all distortions are negative. Both positive and negative qualities from the past are attributed to significant people in the individual's current life. Any misperception, whether exaggeration of admirable characteristics or of undesirable traits, generally creates friction in new relationships. People want to be understood and seen for themselves, and distortion triggers hurtful, angry responses.

Another important issue relevant to distortion is the need to maintain an idealized image of the parents. To serve this end, people project parents' undesirable qualities onto others. They focus a kind of selective attention on their mates, attempting to prove that the new objects have negative traits similar to one or both parents. Fantasized images superimposed on one's mate based on past relationships are generally maladaptive and lead to dysfunctional modes of relating.

Provocation. If these first two maneuvers fail to recreate the past and maintain the defense system, men and women will manipulate their loved ones to elicit familiar parental responses. To a large extent, they behave in ways that provoke angry, punishing reactions. For example, husbands and wives withhold the affectionate, loving responses that were originally desirable. They provoke anger and rage in each other with forgetfulness, thoughtlessness, and other manifestations of direct or indirect hostility. Ultimately, partners are provoked to the point where they actually find themselves speaking out the other's "voices" in an angry reaction to the provocation. Most people are largely unaware that their behavior may have the specific purpose of inducing aggression or withdrawal in others. In general, the most tender moments in relationships are followed by these provocations, which create distance between the partners. Each pulls back to a less vulnerable, more defended place and reestablishes his or her psychological equilibrium. Many marriages fail because each partner incites angry responses in the other to maintain a "safe" distance.

All three maneuvers—selection, distortion, and provocation—operate to preserve the introjected parent by externalizing the parents' point of view in new associations. The fear of losing the fantasy bond or self-parenting process compels people to retreat to a more familiar, less personal style of relating, one that may recapitulate the type of attachment they originally formed with the parent. In this manner, the partners transform the new situation into one that more closely corresponds to the environment in which their defenses were established.

CONCLUSION

It is we who introduce purpose and meaning into nature and into history. Men are not equal; but we can decide to fight for equal rights. Human institutions such as the state are not rational, but we can decide to fight to make them more rational. (Popper, 1966, p. 278)

The tyranny and manipulations that exist within social systems parallel interpersonal phenomena that seriously impair individuals. Immaturity, hostility, duplicity, role-playing in the family system, the illusion of connection between family members, and withholding behaviors can have devastating effects on the minds and feelings of young people. Each of these behaviors can be viewed ethically and morally as representing infringements on the child's basic human rights.

A certain amount of frustration is inevitable in life; therefore, psychological defenses are inevitable: The question is one of degree rather than absence or presence. Even in the best families, there is frustration, not only from interpersonal interactions within the family itself, but from painful existential issues of separation, aloneness, aging, and death. It is important to recognize that when family interactions that arouse frustration and anxiety reach proportions that seriously interfere with the psychological development of children, we must consider them abusive. It is incumbent upon us to recognize those elements of couple and family interaction that have the most destructive effects on the individual. Only by becoming aware of these issues can people begin to change these patterns.

Most people have strong resistance to perceiving destructive elements that operate to varying degrees within so many families. The nuclear family is regarded as the bulwark of society by most people. Its image must be protected at all costs. This resistance and the failure to recognize the child's inherent rights go hand in hand with the myth that parents have unconditional love for their children and therefore know best how to raise them. In supporting the family system and protecting parents' rights over their children, we often unwittingly condone the harm done to children "for their own good."

We must try to overcome our prejudices and narrow views of couples and family life and objectively examine dehumanizing practices. In this endeavor, we need to seriously reconsider our priorities in terms of social and family values. We need to learn to treat children respectfully as individuals and not intrude on their unique qualities. We need to develop couple relationships where we allow the other person to live and flourish. Education and understanding of the dynamics underlying harmful couple and family interactions could help people progress in this direction. The goal is not to reject marriage as an institution or to dismantle the family, but to build more constructive associations that, like a true or "ideal" democratic system, would meet the needs of the individual and support his or her personal development and movement toward self-actualization.

ENDNOTES

[1]Marcuse (1955/1966) made a similar statement regarding the collusive relationship between individuals who fear freedom and the society that oppresses them: "The struggle against freedom reproduces itself in the psyche of man, as the self-repression of the repressed individual, and his self-repression in turn sustains his masters and their institutions" (p. 16).

[2]Olson (1962) explained the meaning of the phrase "the anguish of freedom" from an existential perspective: "What is called the anguish of freedom would more accurately be called 'anguish before the necessity of choosing.' The anguish of freedom is really anguish over the fact that one *must* choose" (p. 51).

[3]Another consequence of idealizing the family can be seen in certain legal sanctions that protect the rights of parents (and the family unit) over the rights of individual children and condone child abuse in the name of discipline. For example, Garbarino and Gilliam (1980) note that in 1974, the Texas legislature enacted legislation containing the following statement: "The use of force, but not deadly force, against a child younger than 18 years is justified: (1) if the actor is the child's parent or stepparent . . . (2) when and to the degree the actor believes the force is necessary to discipline the child" (p. 32). McFarlane and van der Kolk (1996b) also noted in "Trauma and Its Challenge to Society" that the larger society has "a stake in believing that the trauma is not really the cause of the victims' suffering" (p. 27). McFarlane and van der Kolk (1996a) concluded as follows:

> In recent years . . . the prevailing social attitude to victims has been that they are mendacious, greedy and vengeful. . . . This in-

tolerance of victims of trauma, rather than of the circumstances that lead to those traumas, is a function of a willingness to accept the seemingly inevitable conditions that lead to traumatization: crime, wars, poverty, and family violence. (p. 573)

[4]For example, suicide is the third leading cause of death for young people between 15 and 24 years of age, with 100 suicide attempts for every completed suicide occurring among this age group (McIntosh, 1998).

[5]Beavers (1977) noted that the "midrange group [of families] is probably larger than any other group, including healthy families, no matter how generously defined" (p. 83). "The average . . . midrange families would probably be closer to the normal than [healthy families]" (p. 124).

[6]Boszormenyi-Nagy and Spark (1984) cited the original ethical basis of family loyalty and then stated:

> The ethical obligation component in loyalty is first tied to the arousal in the loyalty-bound members of the sense of duty, fairness, and justice. Failure to comply with obligations leads to guilt feelings which then constitute secondary regulatory system forces. The homeostasis of the obligation or loyalty system depends thus on a regulatory input of guilt. (pp. 37–38)

Incidentally, there has always been a good deal of public condemnation and fear of cults. And for good reason—cults exemplify extremes of conformity and submission. Their practices of thought control and other forms of intimidation are potentially dangerous and have even ended in mass suicide or violence. However, cultlike practices exist, to varying degrees, in many interpersonal relationships and family constellations. In a similar manner, these patterns lead to dangerous consequences in relation to mental health.

[7]See Elaine Pagels' (1988) *Adam, Eve, and the Serpent.* Pagels' scholarly recounting of early Christianity shows that the basis of the belief that people are born bad probably originated in the 4th century in the teachings of Augustine, who reinterpreted the creation myth. Augustine believed that because Adam and Eve disobeyed God, the human race inherited a nature irreversibly damaged by that sin. Spontaneous sexual arousal is punishment for the sin of disobedience as well as being proof that the "flesh" or body invariably disobeys the will. Pagels noted that Augustine identified sexual desire as evidence of, and penalty for, original sin, thereby implicating the whole human race.

[8]In *The History of Sexuality*, Michel Foucault (1990) explained "the negative relation" of sexuality and power in our culture:

> Where sex and pleasure are concerned, power can "do" nothing but say no to them; what it produces, if anything, is absences and gaps; it overlooks elements, introduces discontinuities, separates what is joined, and marks off boundaries. Its effects take the form of limit and lack. (p. 83)

Later in the same volume, Foucault described more subtle forms of sexual "repression":

> We are often reminded of the countless procedures which Christianity once employed to make us detest the body; but let us ponder all the ruses that were employed for centuries to make us love sex, to make the knowledge of it desirable and everything said about it precious. Let us consider the stratagems by which we were induced to apply all our skills to discovering its secrets, by which we were attached to the obligation to draw out its truth, and made guilty for having failed to recognize it for so long. (p. 159)

[9]Patricia Crittenden (1995) discussed how young children learn coercive, manipulative behavior to elicit parental attention and guilt in "Attachment & Psychopathology" (pp. 375–376).

[10]See chapter 3, "Individuality and Togetherness" in Kerr and Bowen (1988) for clarification of Bowen's concept of balance in a relationship and description of various unconscious maneuvers that poorly to moderately differentiated partners manifest when this balance is threatened.

[11]See Jeremy Holmes' (1995) history of attachment theory "Somebody There Is That Doesn't Love a Wall." Batgos and Leadbeater (1994) cited John Bowlby's (1980) definition of attachment as "an enduring affectional relationship between child and caregiver, the purpose of which is to provide protection and nurturance for the child" (p. 161).

[12]Attachment theorists (see Ainsworth et al., 1978) initially identified two patterns of anxious attachment: anxious–ambivalent and anxious–avoidant. Subsequently, researchers (see Main & Solomon, 1986) identified a third, a disorganized attachment pattern, in extremely disturbed children. See also Lamb's (1987) critique of attachment research, summarized by Field (1987) in "Interaction and Attachment in Normal and Atypical Infants."

[13]The videotape documentary *Hunger Versus Love* (Parr, 1987) illustrates this concept. The video portrays emotional states manifested by a parent that would tend to predispose the formation of anxious attachment patterns between the parent and child. See Main and Hesse (1990), in which the parent *"may even subtly indicate a propensity to flee to the infant as a haven of safety"* (p. 177) under fear conditions.

[14]Bowlby's (1973) formulations about specific defenses formed by anxiously attached infants provide support for this thesis. Shaver and Clark (1994), in their interpretation of Bowlby's conceptualization, noted that "if the . . . set of attachment behaviors repeatedly fails to reduce anxiety, the human mind seems capable of deactivating or 'suppressing' the attachment behavioral system, at least to some extent, and defensively attempting to become more self-reliant" (p. 112).

[15]See Bowlby (1979); Brazelton and Cramer (1990); Brazelton and Yogman (1986); Brody (1956); Cole-Detke and Kobak (1996); Crittenden (1995); de Jong,

(1992); Fonagy et al. (1995); Grossmann, Fremmer-Bombik, Rudolph, and Grossmann (1988); Kestenbaum, Farber, and Sroufe (1989); Main (1990); Ricks (1985); Rosenstein and Horowitz (1996); Sroufe (1985); Stern (1985).

[16]See Bartholomew (1993); Bartholomew and Horowitz (1991); Bretherton, Ridgeway, and Cassidy (1990); Feeney, Noller, and Hanrahan (1994); Hindy and Schwarz (1994); Scharfe and Bartholomew (1994); Shaver and Hazan (1993).

[17]Attachment researchers (Batgos and Leadbeater, 1994; Bowlby, 1973, 1980, 1982; Bretherton, Ridgeway, and Cassidy, 1990) have proposed that "internal working models" represent children's beliefs about self and relationships and mediate their attachment behavior. These formulations agree in substance with our own findings, both those regarding the voice process that influences different styles of relating in adult relationships and those related to children's reactions to the intrusiveness manifested by many emotionally hungry parents.

Bretherton (1996) has discussed the concept of a working model as it relates to narratives or "scripts" of significant events in childhood. See also Haft and Slade's (1989) paper, "Affect Attunement and Maternal Attachment: A Pilot Study."

[18]It is important to differentiate the specific use of the word *bond* from its other uses in the literature. It is not a bond as in *bonding* (a secure maternal–infant attachment) in a positive sense, nor does it refer to a relationship characterized by real loyalty, devotion, and genuine love. Our concept of the fantasy bond uses *bond* rather in the sense of bondage or limitation of freedom. It describes an *imaginary connection* to a parent rather than a real attachment (Firestone, 1985).

[19]In another work (Firestone, 1997a), I noted that "resistant behavior in or out of therapy represents an attempt to maintain psychological equilibrium by minimizing or avoiding both *negative and positive* anxiety states" (p. 76).

In his chapter, "Why Maladaptive Behaviors Persist," Caspi (1993) argued that "internal working models" are highly resistant to change. If these internal working models

> screen and select from experience to maintain structural equilibrium ... [then] once a schema becomes well organized, it filters experience and makes individuals selectively responsive to information that matches their expectations and views of themselves. ... The course of personality development is thus likely to be conservative because features of the cognitive system may impair people's ability to change in response to new events that challenge their beliefs and self-conceptions. (pp. 349–350)

In discussing the role of internal working models, Sroufe (1988) asserted that "anxious attachment does not cause later peer incompetence, anxiety, antisocial behavior, or depression, but it may likely represent a developmental context that makes the emergence of such problems more likely" (p. 30).

[20]An area having considerable research potential is indicated by the findings of M. Main and associates. In studies using the Adult Attachment Interview (AAI), these researchers (George, Kaplan, & Main, 1985) demonstrated that the

intergenerational transmission of attachment patterns was significantly correlated with the coherence, consistency, and openness of the individual's narratives about attachment experiences. Incoherent and inconsistent narratives were found in adult subjects whose children manifested patterns of anxious attachment. The narratives were hypothesized to be influenced by the subject's state of mind, particularly his or her "internal working model" (thoughts, feelings, beliefs and expectations regarding attachment). See van IJzendoorn (1995) for validity and reliability studies of the AAI. Fonagy, Steele, and Steele's (1991) correlational study assigned Probable Experience and State of Mind scale ratings to AAI transcripts, which reflected parents' capacity for understanding mental states:

> Based on prenatal administration of the Adult Attachment Interview to 96 primiparous mothers, we were able, in 75% of the cases, to successfully predict whether an infant would be coded securely or insecurely attached (B/non-B) to mother at 1 year in the Strange Situation. (pp. 900–901)

[21]Research conducted by Ainsworth et al. (1978) with respect to patterns of anxious attachment tends to support our findings regarding internalized parental attitudes that make up the insecurely attached child's negative identity. Batgos and Leadbeater (1994) reported that Ainsworth et al. (1978) "describe a sense of being unlovable and unworthy of comfort and help as a defining feature of anxious/ambivalent attachment. Thus, a punitive and critical stance toward the self is present, along with anxiety about relationships" (p. 172).

4

THE IDEAL COUPLE RELATIONSHIP

> It is also good to love: because love is difficult. For one human being
> to love another human being: that is perhaps the most difficult task
> that has been entrusted to us, the ultimate task, the final test and
> proof, the work for which all other work is merely preparation.
>
> Rainer Maria Rilke (1908/1984, pp. 68–69)

The professed goal of most men and women is to find love, companionship, and fulfillment in an enduring romantic relationship.* Learning to give and receive love is central to an individual's sense of well-being; it is a fundamental aspect of being human. Although in general, love is a natural response to being treated with love (just as anger and hostility are natural responses to cruel treatment), extending one's capacity to love is a skill that one needs to learn, just as one develops any other expertise. The process of learning to love is frustrating and complicated for those who experienced rejection or subtle (and not-so-subtle) forms of hostility as children. This is especially true in learning how to accept love because the beloved suffers a recurrence of painful feelings from the past when he or she attempts to let love into his or her life. Both giving and receiving love, exchanging psychonutritional products, are inhibited by primal pain. Inwardness and defensiveness restrict the flow of feelings in either direction.

Young people falling in love for the first time usually have little perspective about the possible future of their relationship. For many of these young lovers, desperation and anxious attachment patterns lead to pre-

---

*When discussing couples, I am referring to all relationships, including those between women and men; men and men; women and women; men and women and children; and friendships between all types of individuals. I use the term *men and women* as a way of referring to the modal type of interaction rather than indicating an exclusive category. Again, it is important to acknowledge that my insights and attitudes about relationships apply to all the forms of relationships noted above.

mature commitment to relationships that later become unsatisfactory. Rubin (1983) has described the sentiments of young people in love:

> "I love you"—words that hold out the promise that loneliness will be stilled, that life will at last be complete. Once, not so long ago, we heard those words and thought about forever. Once, they signaled the end of the search, meant that we would marry and live happily ever after. Now, we're not so sure. (p. 1)

Moreover, traits experienced as appealing at the beginning of a relationship can later become undesirable. A man originally attracted to a woman's naivete, childlike dependence, and distractibility may find these same qualities to be a detriment in his marriage when his wife fails to manage her share of their affairs. Or a woman who finds her lover's assertiveness and outspoken opinions charming may subsequently come to resent his domineering nature and insistence on always being right.[1]

Because of the complexity of the problems involved, genuinely successful, loving relationships are difficult to achieve in our society, yet they represent our highest ideal. The success or failure of an intimate relationship is strongly influenced by one's choice of a mate. Selecting a person with the right characteristics is perhaps the most important prerequisite for attaining the ideal of a close personal relationship.

On a more personal note, it caused me pain to be prescriptive in delineating these positive or ideal qualities. The task of summarizing the vast amount of information gathered through years of observation and discussion with couples in my practice and in the reference population tends to oversimplify complex issues of relating. Part of my distaste is that this manner of presentation can sound somewhat banal, reminiscent of a style prevalent in the popular literature and advice columns. Nevertheless, it serves an important purpose to outline and elucidate the factors that have been found to be the most significant in contributing to positive relating.

QUALITIES TO CONSIDER IN SELECTING A MATE

According to Schnarch (1991),

> another of the wondrous and terrible facets of love is that loving increases the capacity of the lover to love, making the loved one all the more dear and irreplaceable. And that makes the inevitable loss of the partner all the greater. . . . So one is well advised: Loving is not for the weak. (p. 594)

Choosing a partner for marriage or a long-term relationship is clearly a critical issue in each individual's life. Obviously, there is no perfect mate who would manifest all the positive attributes necessary to ensure one's happiness in a relationship or marriage. Nevertheless, it is worthwhile to describe the traits that this ideal person would most likely possess. The most powerful deterrent to a negative outcome in a couple relationship can be found in the positive personal characteristics and propensities of the individual partners: qualities such as optimal mental health, a willingness to be vulnerable to another person, and an ability to maintain distinct personal boundaries at close quarters.

The choice of a mate has important consequences because the personal qualities of one's partner determine the course of one's life in many unforeseen ways. There are a number of fundamental tenets on which the ethics of interpersonal relationships are based, and these principles should be seriously considered when appraising the personal qualifications of a potential partner. One difficulty arises when we attempt to define the positive attributes useful in mate selection because the verbal descriptions we choose have lost much of their original meaning. Many have become clichés; the words that depict the subtleties of love have been exploited and have become banal through manipulation and overuse. Advertising campaigns, the media, television in particular, and so forth have cheapened the meaning of these words.

Everyone would agree, for example, that honesty is an important character trait to look for and identify in a potential partner. But what do we really mean by *honesty*? What observable behaviors reflect the qualities of honesty and integrity? Is the honest person always candid, direct, and self-disclosing in his or her communication? Does a person with integrity never lie, cheat, deceive, or mislead others? To clarify the meaning of these words, it is necessary to operationally define them in terms of observable criteria. In this instance, the term *honesty* is defined by *Webster's Third New International Dictionary* (Gove, 1976) as "fairness and straightforwardness of conduct" (p. 1086). It may refer to a number of observable behavioral operations: (a) an absence of deception or fraud, (b) an absence of duplicity—one's actions correspond with one's words, (c) directness and frankness in communication, (d) integrity—loyalty to one's values and principles, (e) truthfulness—adherence to the facts, and (f) sincerity or authenticity—being oneself in the situation.

As noted earlier, selection is perhaps the most vital factor in a relationship's success or failure. Although it is difficult to identify and assess positive personality traits that will endure, certain qualifications can be evaluated during the courtship phase. In general, an ideal partner is (a) open and nondefensive, (b) honest and nonduplicitous, (c) affectionate and easy-going; (d) mentally and physically healthy, (e) independent and successful in his or her chosen career or lifestyle, and (f) aware of a meaningful existence that includes humanitarian values.

Emotionally healthy individuals manifest a comfortable, relaxed style of interacting and are basically at ease with themselves and the interpersonal world. A strong sense of identity and strength of character are positive attributes to look for in a mate. Flexibility and adaptability to change are desirable qualities as contrasted with rigidity and intolerance. Ideally, a potential love object would be comfortable with physical affection and would not avoid eye contact in his or her personal communications. An individual's physical health is an important issue as well, as both emotional and physical illness in one's partner can eventually take a toll on one's marriage and family life.

Generally, it is advantageous for people to select mates who indicate capability and competency in both career and interpersonal arenas, because these achievements serve to enhance their feelings of self-worth and positive outlook on life.

Maturity and integrity together with a genuine respect for the rights of self and others are positive traits to be sought after. People who possess these qualities attribute a moral or philosophical meaning to life and are invested in goals that transcend the narrow sphere of their existence.

On the other hand, critical or hostile behaviors, a harsh, judgmental style, addictions, or a failure syndrome are negative patterns that eventually lead to painful personal relationships. It is obvious that people who are phony or outwardly dishonest will have a negative effect. Individuals whose actions are not consistent with their words are essentially unreliable and untrustworthy. Attitudes of smugness, superiority, hostility, or any form of cruelty are destructive. People who manifest bizarre behaviors, melodramatic reactions, and histrionics may present serious problems of adjustment.

Individuals who have addictive personality traits, in particular people who are excessively dependent on food, drugs, alcohol, or other substances have a destructive effect in that these addictions represent a defended approach to life that blocks out feeling in intimate relationships. If one is aware of the destructiveness of these addictive patterns, one can detect them in the early stages. Addictive habit patterns as well as self-nurturing fantasies generally interfere with successful need gratification in the real world. It is clear that people who consistently fail in their attempts to accomplish their career goals or plans for the future can have difficulty in long-term relationships.

Lastly, for an indication of what lies ahead in a relationship, one may be well advised to examine the characteristics of the partner's parent of the same sex (the woman's mother and the man's father), particularly the parent's style of interaction with his or her mate. There is a connection between the parent's approach to life and his or her offspring's, caused by strong patterns of identification in growing up. Incidentally, many psychotherapists, sensing this issue, advise clients "off the record" to take a good look at the same sex parent of a potential mate.

Even when people dislike and reject their parent's characteristics, they tend to unconsciously imitate and replicate them. There is usually a strong fantasy bond between mother and daughter, and father and son, a bond that leads to this repetitious lifestyle. Although these characteristics may not manifest themselves initially, they tend to become progressively more dominant in an individual's personality as he or she goes through the life process, that is, becoming engaged, sharing a home, getting married, and having children.

CHOICES BASED ON EVOLUTIONARY THEORY

Unfortunately, most people don't choose their mates on the basis of distinguishing between the positive and negative characteristics described above. Observations and research by evolutionary psychologists indicate that selections are more often based on preferences and mating strategies which evolved from a natural selection process that developed over millions of years. These psychologists (Buss & Schmitt, 1993) have defined specific preferences or strategies for mate selection "as evolved solutions to adaptive problems, with no consciousness or awareness on the part of the strategist implied" (p. 206).

In human evolutionary history, both men and women have pursued short- and long-term mating strategies necessary for solving problems of adaptation. Men and women's preferences for desirable qualities in a potential mate evolved from those strategies that best solved problems related to each sex's reproductive constraints, strategies that basically favor gene survival.[2]

For example, in trying to identify which women were fertile, primitive man had to rely on cues indicating youth and physical health: "full lips, clear skin, smooth skin, clear eyes, lustrous hair, symmetry, good muscle tone, and absence of lesions . . . [as well as] sprightly, youthful gait, and high activity level" (Buss & Schmitt, 1993, p. 208). Today, men still prefer as long-term mates "women who are young and physically attractive as indicators of reproductive value . . . and who are sexually loyal and likely to be faithful as indicators of paternity certainty" (p. 226).

Another premise consistent with evolutionary logic states that "women in long-term mating contexts, more than men, will desire cues to a potential mate's ability to acquire resources, including ambition, good earning capacity, professional degrees, and wealth. This prediction has been confirmed extensively across cultures" (p. 223).

Buss and Schmitt (1993) caution that preferences based on evolutionary predictions tend to be misinterpreted as being "highly intractable, impervious to environmental context" (p. 230). Although their research shows that these preferences persist in modern man, they point out that these trends are not necessarily immutable. Furthermore, basing mate selection on the instinctual response to certain traits rather than considering other equally desirable qualities is not necessarily adaptive in today's world. For example, many men still place too much importance on physical attractiveness in a potential mate, while ignoring women with other traits that might be more predictive of marital satisfaction. Many women still put too much stake in a man's wealth, career success, and social status, while sometimes overlooking prospective partners who exhibit warmth, tenderness, and an interest in children.

Gaining insight into a possible source of one's preferences allows one to make informed decisions in relation to selecting one's mate. In recognizing genetically and evolutionarily determined tendencies operating in mate selection, people can correct for some trends and apply more rationality in making their choices.

IDEAL COUPLE RELATIONSHIPS

Having highlighted some of the issues in mate selection, let us consider the psychodynamics that characterize a healthy couple relationship and contrast them with negative or destructive machinations. Our primary concern is the positive and negative impact these patterns have on the lives of the individuals involved in the couple as well as the degree of self-actualization and fulfillment the individuals experience. The longevity of a relationship is not necessarily a good measure of an ideal couple; people may choose to maintain destructive relationships over an extended period of time. In many cases, the relationship has endured, but the individuals are suffering. Wallerstein and Blakeslee (1995), in reporting their findings from a study of couple relationships, stressed this point:

> People can be held together for decades by lethargy, fear, mutual helplessness, or economic dependency. (p. 14)
>
> The relationship can become a lifeless shell or a collusive arrangement in which the neurotic symptoms of the partners mesh so well that the marriage endures indefinitely. (p. 23)

We are considering the kinds of psychonutritional exchanges that best support the individual lives of the people involved. In our analysis, specific positive and negative modes of interaction that are conducive to success or failure can be delineated or operationally defined in couple relationships (see Exhibit 4.1).

Nondefensiveness and Openness

Two qualities essential in achieving a satisfying and fulfilling relationship are openness and a lack of defensiveness. Nondefensiveness indicates an objective, balanced attitude toward self and others and a recep-

EXHIBIT 4.1
Couple Interactions Chart

Interactions in an Ideal Relationship	Interactions in a Relationship Characterized by a Fantasy Bond
Nondefensiveness and openness	Angry reactions to feedback. Closed to new experiences.
Honesty and integrity	Deception and duplicity
Respect for the other's boundaries, priorities, and goals, separate from self	Overstepping boundaries. Other seen only in relation to self.
Physical affection and personal sexuality	Lack of affection. Inadequate or impersonal, routine sexuality.
Understanding—lack of distortion of the other	Misunderstanding—distortion of the other
Noncontrolling, nonmanipulative, and nonthreatening	Manipulations of dominance and submission

©The Glendon Association, 1999.

tivity to feedback. In contrast, defensiveness refers to behavior patterns that indicate closed-mindedness and nonreceptivity to feedback. In many cases, defensive individuals react with hostility to open confrontation, however mild. Often, they will counterattack rather than examine information about themselves and explore the truth or falsity in a rational manner.

Defensiveness takes the form of intimidating modes of expression that effectively silence the other person, such as changing the subject, "stonewalling," counterattacking, falling apart, and dramatic reactions of rage or tears. People who are self-protective and defensive tend to dramatize criticism and exaggerate it to the point of absurdity. Later, in retaliation, they communicate feelings of defeat and hopelessness to the partner through statements such as "Well, if that's how it is . . . If that's what you really think about me . . . If I'm as terrible as you say I am," or other statements that make the partner regret ever bringing up the subject.

People can be touchy or overly sensitive about certain issues, while remaining open to feedback in other areas. Partners learn quickly which subjects to exclude from their ongoing communications. However, this censorship in the partners' dialogue leads to increased tension within the couple. The negative effect of taboo subjects and hidden agendas becomes progressively more toxic and eventually spreads to other areas of the relationship.

Research studies investigating the psychodynamics in marital conflict have found that defensiveness contaminates a relationship in countless ways. In some cases, defensive attitudes in one partner predispose the withdrawal of the other, whereas in other cases, they lead to rapid escalation of conflict. In both instances, defensiveness as a character trait or typical behavioral response in one or both partners has been found to be significantly correlated with low marital adjustment (Canary, Cupach, & Messman, 1995). In analyzing the quality of verbal communications, Gottman and Krokoff (1989) found that "three interaction patterns were identified as dysfunctional in terms of longitudinal deterioration: defensiveness (which includes whining), stubbornness and withdrawal from interaction" (p. 47).

People who are open and forthright in expressing their feelings, thoughts, dreams, and aspirations have a good effect on relationships. They are honest and direct and are not secretive or self-protective in their communications. Openness also includes a genuine interest in learning and growing beyond one's defense system and self-protective routines. Men and women who are open view life as an adventure and a unique opportunity to find personal meaning, instead of following prescriptions and belief systems imposed from external sources. There is a willingness to take more risks in life and a desire to expand one's boundaries and broaden one's range of experiences.

Conversely, people who are not open to new experiences tend to be inhibited or rigid. They place a high value on certainty and the predictability of habit and routine and respond in role-determined ways. Bill described an incident that occurred in the early days of a significant relationship, which he later identified as indicative of his close-mindedness and rigidity, personal characteristics that he feels contributed to the eventual breakup of the relationship.

> Bill: I feel that when any anxiety comes up in a relationship, the way that I respond is to avoid it, instead of trying to expand myself to the situation to figure it out and to go with it. That's exactly what happened with Carol. It was a new relationship and I felt like I was really in love for the first time in my life. We had just started living together, when one night she said that she wanted to go swimming. It was a moonlit night and the pool was very private. It could have been very romantic, but I just put her down and teased her about how silly she was being. I told her: "It's night. It's so late. The water will probably be cold. Why would you want to go swimming *now?*" I have to admit that at the time I really thought it was a ridiculous idea. She looked disappointed but decided to go swimming without me.
>
> And so I missed out. I didn't expand myself. I didn't take a chance and try something new with her. I didn't get to see her enjoying something. I didn't get to feel her appreciation in doing something with me. I basically shut her out. I know now that my tenseness in that situation and at other times was a major cause of the deterioration that took place in our relationship.
>
> Looking back, I realize that I was avoiding the anxiety of doing something a little bit different. Actually, I was putting my

own routines and comfort ahead of really learning how to love another person.

Honesty and Integrity

Because it is extremely damaging to fracture another person's sense of reality, the personal qualities of honesty and integrity are vital to the well-being of both partners as well as to the health of their relationship. When people are dishonest and lack integrity, adult modes of communication break down. Behaviors characterized as phony, deceptive, role-playing, or coercive generally end in unhappiness. Lies and deception shatter the reality of others, eroding their belief in the veracity of their perceptions and subjective experience. Mixed messages create an atmosphere of confusion and alienation within the couple.

An important characteristic of an honest person's value system is an intolerance of a discrepancy between his or her actions and words. People who are honest and trustworthy represent themselves accurately to others as well as to themselves. To achieve this level of integrity, one must take the trouble to know oneself. This pursuit of self-knowledge presupposes a willingness to face aspects of one's personality that may be unpleasant. In overcoming defenses and personal limitations, people with integrity gradually modify themselves instead of merely hating themselves for their weaknesses or shortcomings. They develop an acute awareness of any remnants of falseness or insincerity in themselves.

Although the majority of people are capable of objectivity in most areas of their lives, their sense of reality in relation to personal, intimate matters is often limited. The greater the discrepancy between the manifest content of a communication and its underlying or latent meaning, the greater the potential for disturbance. Furthermore, within the couple, there are usually implicit prohibitions against making any commentary about these discrepancies, which worsens the situation and leads to increased feelings of alienation.

Studies have shown that in relationships where the verbal communications contradicted nonverbal cues, the partners reported a high degree of marital dissatisfaction. These relationships were significantly more distressed than those where double messages did not characterize the communication pattern (Canary et al., 1995, p. 46).[3] In these studies, the nonverbal negative messages were conveyed through "frowns, sneers, vocal properties (e.g., tense, impatient, scared), and distant or withdrawn body orientation (e.g., hands thrown up in disgust, inattention)" (Canary et al., 1995, p. 46). Duck (1994a) cited findings by Gottman (1979) and Gottman and Krokoff (1989) showing that in these "double-bind" interactions, it was the negative affect communicated nonverbally that predicted the dissolution of the relationship.

Respect for the Other's Boundaries

> Individuals at this level of development [level 1: integration] no longer conceive of the needs for independence and togetherness as conflicting forces, either intrapsychically or interpersonally. Intimacy at this level involves an intense appreciation for togetherness and existential separateness, rather than fusion and merger. This represents the highest levels of individuation and separation of human development, which few individuals attain.
>
> Johnson (1987; personal communication,
cited in Schnarch, 1991, p. 222)

In the truly loving couple, each partner recognizes that the motives, desires, and aspirations of the other are as important as his or her own. Indeed, the ideal partner would conceptualize his or her own freedom and the freedom of the other as congruent, not a contradictory value. Loving implies an enjoyment of the other person's emergence as an individual and a sensitivity to his or her wants and motives. Each partner feels congenial toward the other's aspirations and tries not to interfere, intrude, or manipulate in order to dominate or control the relationship.

Self-reliant, independent individuals demonstrate, by words and behavior, a genuine respect for the boundaries, wants, and priorities of their mates. There is an awareness that to be close to another person, one has to be separate and autonomous. In fact, the closest one can feel to another person is to feel one's separateness, which is an integral part of sensitive, tender feeling toward the other. Only when people are possessed of self, that is, centered in themselves and truly individualistic, are they predisposed to sustain healthy relationships in which the personal freedom of both partners is accorded the highest priority.

People who have developed a sense of their own identity have a greater potential for intimacy than those who rely on others for affirmation of self. In terms of family systems theory, a person who is more independent can be conceptualized as having achieved a high level of self-differentiation (Bowen, 1978; Kerr & Bowen, 1988).[4] These individuals have succeeded, to a large extent, in gradually emancipating themselves from their parents.[5] As a result, they tend to have their own value systems and to set their own courses in life.

Often people fail to make this break. Partners then project one or the other parent into their personal relationships so that often there are, in a sense, four additional people in the room with the couple, probing, directing, and in general interfering with the harmony of the relationship.

A lack of independence in one or both partners predisposes the formation of an addictive attachment rather than a genuinely loving relationship. Tendencies in individual partners to form these dependency ties are fostered by conventional attitudes and assumptions. For example, in our society, most people expect far more security from couple relationships and marriage than it is possible to extract: They have unrealistic hopes that all their needs will be met in a marital relationship. The burden that these expectations put on the relationship is tremendous; obviously, no one person can fulfill such unrealistic expectations or live up to this idealized image.

Many people's actions indicate that they believe, on some level, that by submitting their individuality to a more dominant person, by giving up their independence and unique point of view, they can somehow achieve safety and immortality. On the other hand, this imbalance provides the dominant individual with a false sense of control and invulnerability in relation to life. When this type of demand is put on a relationship, the equality, genuine companionship, and spontaneous affection are effectively destroyed, and the independent strivings and vitality of both partners are diminished to a significant degree.

Physical Affection and Sexuality

Outward expressions of both verbal and physical affection are positive characteristics in couple relationships. Demonstrations of tender feelings between partners are good prognostic indicators for a long-standing relationship. Affectionate exchanges are vital especially in situations where sexuality becomes less passionate and central in the lives of couples: Tenderness and affectionate contact help maintain the original closeness over time.

In a healthy relationship, the sexual relating is spontaneous and close emotionally, rather than addictive, impersonal, or mechanical. Both partners have mature attitudes toward sexuality and do not perceive it as an activity isolated from other aspects of their relationship. They are aware that sex plays an important part in their lives, not in an exaggerated sense, but as a simple human experience. They view sexual relating as a fulfilling part of life, a gift, a positive offering of pleasure to their mate and to themselves. The effect of a natural expression of sexuality on one's sense of well-being and overall enjoyment of life is considerable. The way people feel about themselves as men and women, the feelings they have about their bodies, and their attitudes toward sex can enhance a sense of self and feelings of happiness.

In contrast, within many marriages both partners unconsciously inhibit or hold back natural feelings of sexual desire and its various expressions because of deeply repressed feelings of fear and anger originating in early childhood. They withhold physical affection and appealing personal characteristics as well as other aspects of healthy sexuality. In these cases, sexual withholding is at the core of the couple's problem and causes substantial distress to both individuals. These habitual patterns of withholding are regulated or strongly influenced by the destructive thought processes of the "voice." In some cases, over time, the inhibition of sexual responses can become automatic, and the destructive attitudes may be deeply repressed.

People are the most refractive in their most intimate relations, where there is both an opportunity for an affectionate, feelingful exchange and an animal, physical response. They tend to pull back in one area or the other, avoiding the special combination of love, sexuality, and tenderness that is the most rewarding or ideal (Firestone, 1985).

Affectionate sexuality can gradually evolve into routine, habitualized patterns that act more as a painkiller or drug and progressively diminish the closeness in the relationship. This type of impersonal or mechanical sexuality detracts from the quality of sexual relating and has a negative prognosis for the overall relationship. (See chapter 9, this volume, for further discussion.)

Open Versus Closed Relationships

The issue of open versus closed sexual relationships for couples is quite complicated, no matter which policy is chosen. Generally speaking, it is unwise to be restrictive in a close personal relationship because this tends to foster resentment in one's partner. Yet most people are unable to cope with a partner's sexual freedom without suffering considerable pain. This creates a serious dilemma for most couples. The significant factor is that the partners first agree on a basic policy that is respectful of each other's feelings and desires, and then stand by their principles. The agreed-on principles should not be violated or, at least, the partners should discuss changing the boundaries prior to making any alterations. As one patient put it, "I endorse an open relationship, but hope for the best, that is, that I'll be continually chosen."

Deep and intimate relationships tend to be the most fulfilling when they are not restrictive. Marriages and other close personal associations that are based on respect for each other's independence and freedom are continually evolving rather than static. The "ideal" relationship would be open rather than an exclusive or closed system.

One negative effect of a closed attitude about outside sexual relationships is that in the process of relegating one's own sexuality to another, that is, agreeing to a committed relationship, a person often becomes less sexually appealing. We are referring to limiting the expression of one's sexuality to one other person in a restrictive manner that may go against one's natural feelings. As a result of this type of exclusivity, people often report a decline in their sexual desire and a deterioration in their overall sexuality with one another. In truth, this happens to many couples.

To further complicate matters, many people agree to the principle of fidelity, but later violate the agreement. This deception or violation of trust can have a more damaging effect on the relationship than the sexual infidelity itself. In this sense, affairs cannot be considered to be morally "wrong" if the partners are open and honest and if the affair does not cause either party undue distress. On the other hand, an affair can be considered morally wrong when secrecy and deception are involved, because the personal integrity of the individual partners is more important than the sexual issues.

In our society, monogamous relationships are perceived to offer more security, certainty, and possibility of long-lasting love than nonexclusive relationships or "open marriages." Many men and women are possessive and controlling of their mates in an attempt to compensate for feelings of inadequacy and fears of being in a competitive situation. They tend to act on the assumption that people "belong" to each other because most have been taught early in life that they belong to their families in the proprietary sense of the word. Thus, they do not have a sense that they belong to themselves or that they have a right to their own lives. They do not see themselves or their mates as autonomous human beings. Consequently, they are subject to manipulations that play on their guilt.

In considering the restrictions imposed by an exclusive relationship, one must ask, "Where do I draw the line? Is it wrong to have a cup of coffee or go to lunch with a member of the opposite sex? To give a co-worker a friendly hug? To engage in sex play but not have intercourse?" Most people in contemporary society are well aware that sexuality is pervasive in a variety of situations and cannot be excluded without blocking other aspects of one's life experience.

To substitute obligation for free choice is to give up a vital function that is uniquely human, and it may indicate a relatively low level of self-differentiation (Kerr & Bowen, 1988). Relinquishing or surrendering one's own wants and desires to another may represent a desperate attempt on the part of an individual to avoid the awareness of existential issues of separation, aloneness, and death. The more one gives up of life by denying one's own priorities and choices, the less one feels alone and separate, yet there is a subsequent loss of vitality.

Although any relinquishing or giving away of freedoms constitutes a restriction, this sacrifice may be worth it in some cases. For example, if one partner perceives that an affair would cause the other excessive pain in an especially vulnerable area, he or she may wish to remain exclusive. In general, the best situation for individuals in a couple relationship is to sustain their freedom of choice and not limit or place demands on each other through rules and restrictions. Although restrictive attitudes in marriage violate the policy of supporting the freedom and independence of one's partner, and, in that sense, tend to have a damaging effect on the relationship, this departure from the principle may still be workable. This concession or compromise is more likely to work out when other strong positives are operant in the relationship and all other freedoms are respected.

Empathy and Understanding

Empathy and understanding are fundamental to achieving true intimacy in a relationship. Empathy has been defined as an intersubjective experience that depends on

> seeing the other person in his or her own terms; that is . . . [it] consists not in seeing how I would feel if your experience, X, were to happen to me but in seeing how you feel when X happens to you. (Duck, 1994b, p. 90)

According to Ickes, Tooke, Stinson, Baker, and Bissonnette (1988), understanding is related to the phenomenon of intersubjectivity wherein:

> The two interactants share the ability to determine actively, in varying degrees, certain of the physical events (in particular, the words and actions) that will constitute elements of their common experience. . . . They share the responsibility for determining the degree to which intersubjectivity can and will develop through their efforts to communicate effectively. (p. 81)

These authors suggested that more attention be focused on "intersubjective phenomena that involve the 'meeting' and interaction of two (or more) minds" (p. 82).

Understanding is partly a function of the commonalities that exist between two people, but it can also be a function of their differences. For example, Colman (1995) noted that when partners

> choose each other on the basis of a shared understanding of some mutual deprivation or difficulty [they] soon find that the other's very capacity to "know what it is like" renders them incapable of providing the different experience that is longed for. (p. 61)

When partners talk with feeling and respect for the other about attitudes or values they have in common, each partner feels understood or validated. In good relationships, members of a couple honestly reveal their differences or dissimilarities as well, and this disclosure has the positive effect of making each feel seen and unique. To facilitate understanding within a couple relationship, partners would maintain an ongoing dialogue about their differences as well as about their similarities. By so doing, they lay the foundation for developing greater intimacy.

In contrast, a lack of empathy or understanding between partners has a corresponding negative effect on their interactions and the overall relationship. When people don't feel listened to, taken seriously, or understood by their mates, they suffer from hurt feelings and increased hostility. Feelings of being misunderstood originate in childhood when parents have a distorted view of their children. Many parents find it difficult to feel for their offspring or empathize with them because of their own defenses. Neglect and indifference contribute to painful feelings in children of not being seen, and these feelings carry over into adulthood. Many parents misconstrue their child's motives and attribute an intentionality to his or her behavior that is completely unfounded. For example, parents often misinterpret adolescents' movement toward independence as defiance or rejection (Richman, 1986). The cumulative effect of countless "failures in empathy" (Kohut, 1977) in early interactions with parents sensitizes the child to misunderstandings that occur later in adult relationships.

On a broader level, a basic misconception of the nature of the child exists in our culture. This misconception has a destructive impact on children (Firestone, 1990b). For example, most adults see children in the diminutive, as being less competent and capable than they actually are. Children experience an overall feeling of being unacknowledged for their real capabilities and potentialities. Later, as adults, they experience pain when they feel unacknowledged or misperceived by their mates.

A pattern of chronic misunderstanding in couple relationships can be traced to distorted thinking about oneself or one's partner. This *distorted thinking* or "voice" manifests itself in two principal ways: (a) In negative assumptions or attitudes about the self that lead to feelings of being misjudged. In these cases, the person may think in terms of an internal dialogue, almost as though someone else were saying to him or her: "If he (she) really knew you, he (she) would leave." "No one would love you." (b) In negative perceptions and distortions of the partner which are used in the service of feeling misunderstood or victimized: "He (she) doesn't treat you right." "He (she) just doesn't understand you." "Nobody understands what you feel." Both types of voices, negative attacks on self or others, predispose alienation.

Individuals who grew up feeling misperceived disown and project their angry responses and overreact to their partners. When they project their anger onto their mates, they distort and exaggerate any real irritation or anger they see in the other. They misinterpret mild anger exhibited by the other as deep expressions of hostility and overreact to variations in their partner's moods by taking them too personally. When this occurs, angry situations escalate into open warfare.

The tendency to feel irrationally misunderstood is often related to each partner's failure to develop a realistic, objective view of his or her parents. In general, negative anticipations about others fostered by the voice help maintain the idealized picture of the original family. Children tend to block from awareness those parental characteristics that especially threaten them and project them onto persons outside the family (Firestone,

1985). By judging their parents as right or superior and others as wrong or inferior, children (and later, adults) preserve their illusions about their family of origin. It is clear that if they protect their families at their own expense, there is a tendency to distort their partners' reactions.

Nonthreatening and Nonmanipulative Behavior

Often, members of a couple use a variety of games or ploys to manipulate and control one another. There are many different types of maneuvers employed, which include the following: overly dependent behavior, breaking down emotionally, punishing the other with the "silent treatment," or overpowering their mates with verbal abuse or threats of physical violence. Some people manipulate by the omission of important details in their communications. Since a certain amount of honest sharing of information is necessary in a good relationship, leaving out certain issues can represent a form of lying, deception, or cheating. In some cases, partners actually lie outright and, in the process, distort their mate's perceptions by denying his or her reality. In general, the intentional manipulation or deception of one's partner erodes feelings of basic trust in a close relationship.

The tyranny of the weak through passivity, weakness, passive-aggression, and other forms of negative power is remarkably effective: Using these techniques, people can "keep each other in line." In fact, these maneuvers are commonplace in married life. Individuals can be nagged, badgered, or intimidated into the desired behavior, but the rewards are hollow and short-lived. People can successfully imprison one another, but they damage themselves and each other in the process. The manipulation of another person through provoking guilt reactions arouses anger and tension and subverts any genuine feelings that may exist.

In contrast, partners who are not manipulative or threatening have a positive effect. The absence of control, manipulation, or threat helps maintain the flow of good feelings, which in turn contributes to building trust and feelings of security in the relationship.

Other Characteristics of Healthy Relationships

Successful, healthy relationships are characterized by each partner's placing significant value on building a good relationship. Both would be willing to cope with the stresses that naturally arise in the course of any close association. They would be cognizant that sadness is part of a healthy relationship, that the tender feelings they experience both toward their loved one and from their loved one arouse this poignant sense of sadness.

Free choice rather than obligation characterizes the healthy relationship. Each partner would choose the other primarily on the basis of love, not need. In fact, ongoing choice rather than habit would help to maintain their original excitement. There would be a basic unwillingness on the part of both partners to allow the relationship to become deadened, dull, or routine. Both would be devoted to keeping the romantic spark alive rather than preserving a habitual style of relating in which choices are minimized. They would be concerned with their own personal growth and well-being as well as with their partner's. Neither individual would take the other for granted; instead, each would appreciate and openly acknowledge the other's acts of kindness, generosity, and the giving of sexual pleasure. The couple's interactions would be typified by an ongoing exchange of kindnesses, generosity, and affection.

In successful relationships, the individuals have generally selected their mates on the basis of similar rather than complementary traits. However, when people's choices are made in an effort to fill an emptiness or void within themselves, their relationship is more likely to be unsatisfying or problematic. It is advantageous for partners to have similar goals with respect to their personal relationship as well as to share basic values, beliefs, and philosophies of life.

A fundamental factor contributing to the success of a relationship is that both partners "let each other be" in the best sense of the phrase. These people would basically accept their mates as they are and would not attempt to change them or foist their own interests, beliefs, or values on them. At the same time, they would be open to the new interests, viewpoints, and experiences that their partner has brought to the relationship. In general, people who are tolerant of differences, even in the political or religious sphere, are more likely to have a gratifying relationship than people who are more dogmatic or narrow-minded.

Communication

Genuine friendship between two people is characterized by dynamic, honest communication with feelings of respect and compassion. In a friendship, one gives one's views and opinions, and the other person is encouraged to present his or hers. Good friends don't "dump" their problems or frustrations on each other; rather, both take full responsibility for their own anxieties and difficulties.

In the ideal couple relationship, as in a friendship, communications would be characterized by frankness, directness, and a lack of duplicity, combined with empathy and consideration for the other's feelings. Neither partner would speak for the other, and each would feel free to express his or her thoughts, feelings, aspirations, attitudes, and opinions regarding any topic. There would be a respectful way of asking what the other wants, down to the simplest request regarding plans for the evening, that would acknowledge the will, priorities, and goals of the other person.

Any interaction between two individuals can be analyzed in terms of whether it is conducive to the expression of personal feelings or whether it serves to cut off or obscure them. Communications that are glib, sarcastic, condescending, or a plea for approval ward off closeness and promote a state of inwardness and pseudoindependence in both participants. On the other hand, an open dialogue that is candid, forthright, and characterized by compassion draws both partners closer to themselves and each other. In a relationship typified by real friendship, any hostility or anger existing between partners would not be acted out, but brought out in the couple's ongoing dialogue. Negative perceptions, disappointments, and hurt feelings would be dealt with, then dismissed without holding grudges.

During my years of clinical practice, I noted that men and women who were either newly involved or consulting me independently of their spouses were, for the most part, honest and straightforward in their communication. This was generally not the case with couples who had been in long-term relationships who sought professional help in conjoint therapy.

Typically, newly involved couples were not deceptive or manipulative and did not intimidate each other with words. They didn't feel misunderstood by or blaming of the other, rarely projected their own problems onto the other, and did not feel criticized or defensive in relation to feedback they received. They tried to communicate negative as well as positive emotions more honestly. Furthermore, their conversations were interesting and personal and drew me to them, whereas dialogues between the established couples tended to be dull, repetitive, and blaming, and excluded me as a participant.

In analyzing communications between members of a couple, beyond the more obvious verbal abuse, sarcasm, hostile criticism, and advice-giving, my colleague and I have noted subtle styles that help keep the illusion of connection or fantasy bond intact, for example, partners who talk for each other and use the personal pronoun "we" to describe themselves as a unit. In general, members of a couple gradually lose the ability to directly articulate their wants in relation to each other, and they progressively limit the sharing of important personal feelings. They are especially reluctant to challenge each other in their respective defensive areas and are often retaliated against when they do offer honest feedback.

In their study of "optimal" or unusually healthy couple relationships, Wallerstein and Blakeslee (1995) made the following observations about the relatively few couples whose communications still retained elements of the honest exchanges they had enjoyed at the inception of their relationship:

> Popular notions about marital communication failed to capture the subtlety of the daily interactions between these men and women.

. . . They listened carefully to each other and tried to speak both honestly and tactfully. But they recognized intuitively that true communication in marriage extends far beyond words. It involves paying attention to changing moods, facial expression, body language, and the many other cues that reveal inner states of mind. (p. 335)

CONCLUSION

The most important factor influencing the success of a couple relationship is a selection process wherein the chosen partner exhibits good mental health and is minimally defended. Emotionally healthy individuals have a strong investment in living and respond with appropriate affect to both good and bad experiences. People who are attuned to their emotions tend to retain their vitality and excitement about living. The capacity for feeling contributes to their spontaneity and creativity and adds dimensions to their personality (Firestone, 1988).

By contrast, people who are defended lose access to their innermost feelings and become progressively more superficial, constricted, self-denying, and hostile. People who are involved in close, personal relationships cannot maintain their defenses without having a destructive effect on their loved ones. When people cannot tolerate generosity directed toward them, they will hurt the one who is giving. If they need to think of themselves as inadequate or bad, they will act accordingly, thereby damaging a joint effort to live happily. The woman who cannot tolerate an image of herself as a lovable person will punish the man who offers her love; the man who sees himself as cold and unattractive will be suspicious of a woman who shows an interest in him and will be rejecting toward her. When individuals attempt to protect themselves from feeling existential pain and sadness, emotions inherent in close relationships, they push away the people who care for them the most.

Therefore, to preserve a loving, intimate relationship, each partner would be willing to face the threat to their defense system that positive treatment poses. To be able to accept genuine affection and love, both would be willing to challenge their negative voices, alter any negative images of themselves formed in the family, and give up long-established defenses they usually feel too threatened to relinquish. In addition, they would face the fact that when someone sees them as unique and desirable, an awareness that connects them to positive feelings of personal worth, painful feelings of sadness often arise. Although the processes of loving and accepting being loved, valuing oneself and one's experience, can lead to feelings of joy and happiness, they also increase existential concerns and arouse a poignant, painful feeling about the fragility and preciousness of life itself.

ENDNOTES

[1]Jacob Arlow (1986), in his paper "Object Concept and Object Choice," concluded:

> In practice, we deal with how the individual comes to choose someone to love and how this love is expressed. This is a complex process involving the integration of the individual's total experience. It is usually organized in terms of a few leading, unconscious fantasies which dominate an individual's perception of the world and create the mental set by which she or he perceives and interprets her/his experience. (p. 145)

Murray Bowen (1978) found that individuals with a low level of self-differentiation tended to select mates at a similar low level, resulting in a seriously dysfunctional marriage and new family system. It is likely that their choices were attempts to fill a need or void rather than to advance to a higher level of self-differentiation, a movement that would have aroused anxiety.

[2]According to Buss and Schmitt (1993), men devote a larger proportion of their total mating effort to *short-term* mating than do women. In discussing differential reproductive constraints faced by men and women, they explained that

> Men . . . have been constrained in their reproductive success primarily by the number of fertile women they can inseminate . . . [whereas] women . . . have been constrained in their reproductive success not by the number of men they can gain sexual access to but rather primarily by the quantity and quality of the external resources that they can secure for themselves and their children and perhaps secondarily by the quality of the man's genes. (p. 206)

In *The Coolidge Effect*, Wilson (1981) described the overall difference between men and women's selection processes: "Males have their preferences all right, but they are seldom totally averse to having sex with females low on their preference list [whereas] quite literally many women would not sleep with certain individuals 'if he were the last man on Earth'" (p. 114).

[3]Canary et al. (1995) emphasized that "the nonverbal codes help researchers interpret the meaning of verbal codes; for example . . . agreement accompanied by negative affect indicates sarcasm or disagreement" (p. 46). Gottman (1979) concluded that "the positive-negative dimension of nonverbal behavior thus discriminated distressed from nondistressed couples better than the positive-negative dimension of verbal behavior" (p. 108).

In studies of defensiveness within couple interactions, nonverbal behaviors served as better discriminators of dissatisfied couples. It was conjectured that the negative affect communicated nonverbally during reciprocal chains of confront–confront, confront–defend, complain–defend, and defend–complain sequences in these couples was the most important factor. In general, the implications of a particular message in terms of its meaning to the relationship are largely conveyed nonverbally (Newton & Burgoon, 1990; Watzlawick et al., 1967).

[4]Bowen (1978) described the typical couple in his classic study, *Family Therapy in Clinical Practice*, as follows: "In the average nuclear family living apart from the parental family . . . the spouses are emotionally 'fused' with each other and with the children, and it is difficult to get far beyond the fusion or to do more than react and counterreact emotionally" (p. 545).

[5]Wallerstein and Blakeslee (1995) assert that the first task of partners in the "good marriage" is separating from the family of origin. "Psychological separation means gradually detaching from your family's emotional ties. . . . This emotional shift from being a son or daughter to being a wife or husband is accomplished by *internally* reworking your attachments to and conflicts with your parents" [italics added] (p. 53).

5

CHARACTERISTICS OF THE
IDEAL FAMILY

> In an environment that holds the baby well enough, the baby is able to make *personal development according to the inherited tendencies*. The result is a continuity of existence that becomes a sense of existing, a sense of self, and eventually results in autonomy.
>
> D. W. Winnicott (1986, p. 28)

There is conflict today between idealization and cynicism regarding family life, but in light of statistics related to the quality of family life in our society and its effects, we must concede that what is considered "normal" may have become pathogenic.[1] For example, "in 1997 [in the United States], an estimated 3,195,000 children were reported to CPS agencies as alleged victims of child maltreatment" (Wang & Daro, 1998, p. 3). Nearly 50% of respondents in a national survey reported "at least one lifetime [psychiatric] disorder, and close to 30% reported at least one 12-month disorder" (Kessler et al., 1994, p. 8). It is estimated that a suicide occurs every 17 minutes, and there are 775,000 suicide attempts annually. Homicide is the second leading cause of death among young people between the ages of 15 and 24 years (McIntosh, 1998).

One does not have to rely on statistics to be aware of the widespread damage incurred by children in the process of growing up in an average or "normal" family. It is difficult to ignore the adverse parental behaviors one commonly observes in public settings or the problems of our young people that are continually brought to our attention by the media.

My clinical investigations also tend to support the conclusions stated by others (Briere, 1992; Hassler, 1994; A. Miller, 1980/1984) regarding the prevalence of child maltreatment in the form of physical, sexual, and emotional abuse, and their long-lasting effects. In applying techniques of an

intense feeling release therapy to over 200 patients and research participants, my associates and I found that, without exception, each individual
expressed emotional pain that he or she had previously suppressed. Most
participants made clear connections between painful events in their childhood and problems in their current lives. Prior to reexperiencing these
events in sessions, they had maintained a defensive posture and lifestyle
that had helped them avoid reminders of this psychic pain. I was forced
to conclude that no child enters adulthood without sustaining injuries in
basic areas of personality development that, to varying degrees, disturb
psychological functioning and diminish the quality of interpersonal relationships.

These are some of the reasons we emphasize the pathological aspects
of the norm. As R. D. Laing (1990) said, "Pathology has, or has almost,
taken over, and has become the norm, the standard that sets the tone for
the society . . . [we] live in" (p. xi). In some sense, the norm *has* become
pathogenic; this is a principal reason so many marriages fail, so many families are dysfunctional, and why there is such a high incidence of mental
illness. However, there is no reason to be pessimistic; an awareness of these
destructive patterns and their origins has led to the discovery of methods
to cope with and alter them so that we can move toward the goal of
achieving more healthy families in which to raise our children.

FUNCTIONS OF THE HEALTHY FAMILY

The primary purpose of the family is to nurture the special potentialities of children, facilitate their growth, and enable them to develop, to
the fullest extent possible, their autonomy and sense of self. In considering
the factors conducive to this goal of optimal human growth, readers can
draw an analogy between the developing child and flora and fauna. It is
clear that plants and animals need certain basic elements to survive and
grow; similarly, human beings require specifiable environmental conditions
to develop their full potential. The infant needs food, water, warmth, shel-
ter, and an optimal amount of audiovisual and tactile stimulation to survive. Because human beings are social animals, each person has a basic
need for affiliation with others. The growing child requires contact with
an empathic, affectionate, mature adult or adults who serve as positive role
models. Under ideal conditions, the interpersonal environment would offer
close, genuine experiences that would enhance the developing individual's
search for happiness and meaning in life.

The Concept of Love-Food

To provide infants and children with proper emotional sustenance,
parents must be able to sensitively feed and care for them and be capable

of offering them control and direction (Winnicott (1960/1965b).* I have referred to this function on the part of the primary caretaker as providing *love-food*. Love-food may be defined as a psychonutritional product whereby the parent has both the *intent* and the *capacity* to gratify the needs of the growing child and help him or her adjust to the socialization process necessary to flourish in a particular culture. Emotional sustenance goes beyond the physical body to the spirit of the child (the self system). Psychonutrition embraces two qualities (product and intentionality). In terms of theory, love-food is necessary for survival in both the physical and psychological sense of the word (Firestone, 1957, 1984, 1985, 1997a).†

The provision of love-food requires parents' motivation as well as strength of character. Love alone from a weak parent is not enough, nor is control without love from a strong parent sufficient to provide for the emotional security of the child. For example, when parents are warm, yet immature or ineffectual, they fail to teach the child self-control or self-regulation. If children do not learn to control the acting out of their angry feelings, they become excessively anxious, experience considerable distress, and as a result, repetitiously act out hostility, develop negative attitudes toward themselves, and manifest a high degree of self-hatred. Overpermissiveness on the part of inadequate parents results in children who are not properly socialized, that is, who grow up insensitive to their own boundaries and the boundaries of others.

Conversely, parents who are excessively authoritarian and do not offer kindness and warmth fail to provide the child with the ingredients necessary for a positive life experience. When there is no outward expression of love, children grow up feeling unacceptable and unlovable. Many develop a rigid superego structure that leaves them with little feeling for themselves. As adults, they tend to be suspicious of, and avoid, people who treat them with kindness and tenderness.[2]

Parents who provide love-food have reached a stage of emotional maturity that allows them to be natural, that is, to "be themselves" in interactions with their children. In contrast, parents who are defended, that is, acting out their own provisional identity or a parental role, inadvertently deny their children the experience of knowing them as human and lovable. Children need to feel love for their parents, for the people their parents really are behind the roles. If deprived of this opportunity, children suffer considerable pain. For this reason, books on so-called good parenting that teach techniques can be harmful; specifically learned re-

---

*Winnicott (1960/1965a) used the term *good-enough maternal care* to describe the "holding environment" needed by the infant for ego development.
†I developed this concept while working in a treatment program with schizophrenic patients. The concept of love-food is related to the oral interpretation of the patients' verbalizations and productions and refers to a basic deprivation in the parenting process of these disturbed individuals.

sponses inserted into parents' behavioral repertoire are generally not authentic, and therefore, give rise to mixed signals that damage the child's capacity for reality testing.

Unfortunately, most parents have not developed sufficient emotional maturity to offer their children love-food. Although they provide for the physical survival of their offspring, they tend to have a deleterious effect on their child's special interests and desires, feelings of self-respect, and drive toward individuation. In particular, despite their best intentions, they tend to act out abuses that they themselves experienced in the process of growing up. It is common knowledge in the field of psychology that most parents who physically mistreat their children were abused as children themselves (Briere, 1992; Straus, 1994).[3] However, there is considerably less understanding of the fact that most parents who were emotionally abused as children go on to act out emotional abuse on themselves, others, and eventually their own children (Firestone, 1990b; Garbarino, Guttman, & Seeley, 1986; Shengold, 1989, 1991).[4]

EFFECTS OF THE COUPLE'S RELATIONSHIP ON THE EMERGING FAMILY

The style of relating that evolves between the couple prior to having children tends to determine the quality and type of attachment they form with their offspring.[5] The attitudes and defenses they manifest within the dyad are significant prognosticators of attitudes, practices, and interactions within the emergent family. Imagine a child born to a couple in which each partner has allowed the slow erosion of their love to occur without acknowledging the transformation and, in the process, the child has been diminished in his or her uniqueness, vitality, and sense of self. Then imagine a child growing up in an atmosphere created by two loving, mutually independent individuals who have not subordinated themselves one to the other. It is obvious that the child raised in the latter environment would have a much better chance of developing security, autonomy, and an independent point of view. Ideally, the respectful, affectionate style of co-existence maintained by emotionally healthy parents is at the core of all positive family interactions. A loving, gratifying relationship between two individuals is probably the principal factor that contributes to the healthy development of children born to their union.

In contemporary Western society, the single-parent family is approaching the statistical norm.[6] The number of "blended" families, composed of stepparents and stepsiblings, is also on the increase. In 1990, 11.3% (7.2 million) of children lived in married stepfamilies (Shiono & Quinn, 1994). However, a number of studies have shown that single-parent families often contribute more stability and emotional sustenance to children's lives than conflicted or unhappy couples. "Studies show that children in high-conflict intact families are no better off—and often are worse off—than children in divorced single-parent families" (Amato, 1994, p. 151). Thus, the family (whether traditional, single, or blended) in itself is not the issue; it is the individual defenses and the negative attitudes and propensities of the people involved that are problematic (Johnston, 1994).[7]

BASIC ISSUES AFFECTING THE DEVELOPMENT OF CHILDREN

Bearing in mind that powerful defenses are operating within parents to perpetuate actions within the family that militate against the emotional development of its members, it is still valuable to conceptualize an ideal model of family interactions. In the healthy or optimal family, parents would manifest a number of personal qualities that would contribute to the child's well-being and growth into an autonomous person. We consider two important issues that deserve special mention here: (a) parents' ability to relate to the child as a separate person, not as an object or possession; and (b) parents' capacity to respond personally to the child instead of interacting in a patronizing, strategic, or phony manner (Firestone, 1990b).

In the process of seeing their children as extensions of themselves, most parents tend to intrude on their children's boundaries. These intrusions can range from speaking for the child, using the collective pronoun "we" (indicating an ownership of the child), to going through an adolescent's personal belongings. Parents often extend the criticality and disrespect they feel for themselves to their children. Later, they punish the child on the basis of these projections.

Many children are talked to with baby talk or in syrupy, condescending tones the way some nurses speak to hospital patients. Other parents bombard their children with perfunctory, unfeeling questions. Indifferent questions fail to build a personal relationship with children. Children need to be seen as separate people in their own right and to be related to directly with feeling; they need someone who will listen to them and respond sensitively and realistically to their communications. They need adults who are forthright with them about their own thoughts and feelings. Parents' basic attitudes toward themselves affect the child's development in all cases.

In this chapter, we discuss important dimensions of child rearing that affect positive or negative outcomes: (a) parental ambivalence, (b) emotional hunger versus love, (c) discipline and socialization, (d) open and closed communications, and (e) the advantages of an extended family.

PARENTAL AMBIVALENCE

Parents' feelings and attitudes toward their children are both benevolent and malevolent. These conflicting feelings and attitudes coexist within all people in all societies (Firestone, 1990b; Rohner, 1986, 1991). Rohner conceptualized parents' attitudes as existing on a continuum ranging from parental warmth and acceptance to indifference, rejection, and hostility. On the basis of cross-cultural studies encompassing 35 cultures, he concluded that parental rejection has a universal effect on children and that it can be measured *intergenerationally* (in both parent and child). The patterns of parental rejection assessed by Rohner and his associates included hostility and aggression, dependency, emotional unresponsiveness, negative self-evaluation (negative self-esteem and negative self-adequacy), and emotional instability, a negative world view.*

The fact that parents have strong desires to nurture and care for their children does not negate the hostility they feel at times toward them, and the fact that they have destructive feelings toward their offspring does not nullify their love or concern for them. To the extent, however, that parents fail to recognize their core ambivalence, they may be fixed in their negative influence on their offspring.

Negative, hostile feelings toward children are socially unacceptable; therefore, parents tend to be unaware of or deny aggression toward their children, whether it be overt or covert. It is understandable that parents have powerful resistance to recognizing their core ambivalence. They suffer when they recognize mean, resentful attitudes toward their children. These unacceptable feelings parallel strong conflicting attitudes that parents experience toward themselves. They unconsciously fear that if they recognize negative feelings, they will be more likely to act on them. On the contrary, the recognition of negative feelings allows a person to more effectively cope with aggressive emotions and actually has a positive effect.

The Psychodynamics of Parental Ambivalence: The Core Conflict

All people are divided within themselves in the sense that they have thoughts and feelings of self-worth and warm self-regard as well as those that are self-critical and self-deprecating. When individuals become inward and progressively more involved in self-nurturing habit patterns, they experience considerable guilt and self-recrimination. However, when they honestly pursue their interests and priorities in the real world, they experience a sense of dignity, integrity, and self-respect. Children are exceptionally sensitive to their parents' feelings and attitudes toward themselves

---

*Self-report questionnaires measuring parents' ambivalence toward self and child include the Adult PAQ and the Parent (Mother) PARQ.

and react accordingly. They feel at ease and secure in an atmosphere in which parents have positive regard for themselves. However, if parents have strong feelings of inferiority and are predominantly self-critical or self-hating, the child senses an implicit threat to his or her own security.

The more parents retreat from valuing themselves and avoid closeness with their mates, the more they are limited in their functions as parents, regardless of their stated concern for their children. Self-hating, inward adults cannot offer love or genuine affection to children, nor can they provide the necessary strength and protection to make them feel secure. However, self-reliant, less defended adults are better able to provide a nurturing and loving environment in which to discipline and appropriately socialize the child, while maintaining respect and true regard for his or her individuality.

EMOTIONAL HUNGER

Emotional hunger is a strong need caused by deprivation in childhood. It is a primitive condition of pain and longing that is often mistaken for feelings of love. Parents tend to confuse actions based on these dependency needs carried over from the past with those based on true regard for their children. When acted on, emotional hunger is a powerful feeling that is both exploitive of and destructive to children. As noted previously, sustained contact with an emotionally hungry parent interferes with the development of autonomy in the child.

Emotional hunger is manifested in a wide range of parental behaviors: from an anxious overconcern and overprotection to exploitation or living through a child's accomplishments, to an excessive focus on the child's appearance, or to *parentification*, that is, when children are implicitly asked to take care of their parents. Immature parents often see their child receiving the sympathy and attention that they want for themselves and react with resentment and anger. Some parents respond to their baby as a rival because the baby requires the undivided attention of their partner.

Research studies conducted with clinical populations have documented various aspects of emotional hunger. For example, in her study of the failure of individuation of psychotic children, Mahler (1955/1979) pointed out that

> a complementary pathogenic factor is the well-known parasitic, infantilizing mother who needs to continue her overprotection beyond the stage when it is beneficial. This attitude becomes an engulfing threat, detrimental to the child's normal disengagement and individuation from his second year of life on. Another type of symbiotic parasitic mother cannot endure the loss of her hitherto vegetative appendage, but has to, emotionally at least, slough him off abruptly. (p. 116)

In his book, *Soul Murder*, Shengold (1989) expanded on Mahler's formulations to describe emotionally hungry parents and their effects on their nonpsychotic children:

> Mahler was describing psychotic children whose identity had never been established. My clinical material concerns nonpsychotic children, influenced, seduced, and abused by psychopathic and psychotic parents who induce a regression . . . after the child's individuation has been established. The overwhelmingly stimulating experiences of the child threaten to break through the protective shield against stimuli, and as a defensive measure, a partial reestablishment of the symbiotic relation is needed to deal with the terrible too-muchness. (p. 64)

Bowen (1978) noted that overprotection or oversolicitousness on the part of "undifferentiated" parents are linked to the "family projection process":

> The process begins with anxiety in the mother. The child responds anxiously to mother, which she misperceives as a problem in the child. The anxious parental effort goes into sympathetic, solicitous, overprotective energy, which is directed more by the mother's anxiety than the reality needs of the child. It establishes a pattern of infantilizing the child, who gradually becomes more impaired and more demanding. (p. 381)

Manifestations of Love as Distinguished From Emotional Hunger

Parental love is "behavior that enhances the well-being of children and would exclude those operations that are destructive to the child's sense of self. A loving attitude reflects all that is nurturing and supportive of the unique personality development of the child" (Firestone, 1990b, p. 51).

In contrast to emotional hunger, genuine love nourishes children and supports the unfolding of their personality. Outward manifestations of love can be observed in parents who establish real emotional contact with their children. They make frequent eye contact, display spontaneous, nonclinging physical affection, and take obvious pleasure in the child's company. These parents generally refrain from forming relationships with their children that are exclusive of others. They are aware that love is *not* an emotion that exists in limited quantities and are generous in giving and receiving love in their close relationships.

The difference between loving responses and those governed by emotional hunger can be discerned by objective observers, but it is difficult for parents themselves to make the distinction. The internal feeling state of the parent, the actual behavior of the parent with the child, and the observable effects of the parent on the child's demeanor and behavior are all important factors to consider when attempting to discriminate between manifestations of love and those based on hunger (Greenspan, 1981; Parker, 1983; Stern, 1971).

Parents who are capable of giving love have both a positive self-image and a sense of compassion for the child and, at the same time, maintain an awareness of the boundaries between them. They are respectful of the child and are neither abusive nor overprotective. The tone and style of their communications are natural and easy and indicate an understanding of the individuality of the child.

The effects on the child are probably the most important indicators of genuine love on the part of parents. The loved child actually *looks* loved. He or she is lively, displays independence appropriate to his or her age level, and is genuinely centered in him or herself. In contrast, the child who has sustained contact with an emotionally hungry parent is overly dependent and emotionally volatile.

Effects of Parental Emotional Hunger on the Child

Some children raised by emotionally hungry parents develop a reciprocal hunger toward their parents. They respond to a parent's underlying desperation by developing clinging behavior and fears of exploring the environment on their own. Others become tense when held by their parents or resist physical affection; their bodies tend to become taut and inflexible when they are picked up. Children who avoid or pull away from contact with this type of parent are responding in a manner appropriate to the parent's consuming need to fulfill himself or herself through them.

We have observed a distinguishable characteristic of the "clinging" child's appearance and demeanor when being held by his or her parent. There is an all-too-evident spaced-out look similar to a person on drugs. This is not the expression that is found on the secure child's face. The dazed, forlorn, or pinched expressions on the faces of these children reflect a state of regression. Their obvious discontentment or agitation, manifested when either separate from, or together with, the parent, are signs of emotional deprivation. It is important to stress that sustained contact with an emotionally hungry parent is a significant predisposing condition for psychopathology.

Bowlby (1973), Ainsworth et al. (1978), and Main (1990) described the parents of babies who were anxiously and avoidantly attached as being nervous and hesitant, delaying responses to their infants' crying, and reacting inconsistently to other behavioral cues in their babies. Older children, adolescents, and adults raised by emotionally hungry parents tend to be refractory to physical touch and often feel trapped by close relationships later in life. Adult patients who report having felt drained of their initiative and energy as children, project the same feeling onto their couple relationships, regardless of the reality of the situation. Effects of parental hunger that are frequently expressed in adults are a fear of success, elevated anxiety states, and withholding based on an earlier fear of being depleted.

The concept of emotional hunger has not been sufficiently studied in the psychological literature, yet it is one of the principal factors negatively affecting the child's capacity for individuation.[8] In the course of our longitudinal study of family interactions, we began to question the quality of the maternal–infant bond formed in the early days of an infant's life. As students of human behavior, we need to identify the extent to which this bond or attachment may be based on the emotional hunger and needs of immature parents to form an *imaginary connection* with the child as opposed to real concern and affection for their offspring.

CONSTRUCTIVE DISCIPLINE AND SOCIALIZATION*

Child-rearing is a highly creative task and, like other creative endeavors, requires considerable deliberation. Most parents visualize the kind of person they want their child to become, the positive traits that they would admire in him or her as an adult, and the values they wish to instill in their offspring. Sensitive parents, instead of forming rigid expectations based on an attempt to mold the child in their own image, would try to guide their children in a way that facilitates the gradual unfolding of their (the children's) natural qualities and personal style of being in the world.

The primary purpose of discipline is to help the child develop into a decent, likeable adult, capable of living within a specific cultural milieu without conforming or mindlessly submitting to the socialization process of the culture. In an earlier work, I delineated the guidelines parents could follow in attempting to achieve this goal. Ideally, parents would: (a) avoid unnecessary restrictions, rules, and standards; (b) act as positive role models; (c) reward rather than punish; (d) avoid physical punishment; (e) avoid cynical, judgmental attitudes that reinforce a child's sense of badness; (f) teach their children to control the acting out of hostile, manipulative behavior; (g) discourage prejudicial or stereotypical views in their children; and (h) support their children's independence (Firestone, 1990b).

Avoidance of Unnecessary Restrictions, Rules, and Standards

In a genuinely loving family environment, few rules or restrictions are necessary to accomplish the parents' goal of properly socializing their children. The important rules, those essential for physical safety and health, as well as others that are necessary or useful, are consistently upheld. In

*Portions of the material in this section were taken from *Compassionate Child-Rearing: An In-Depth Approach to Optimal Parenting* by R. W. Firestone, 1990, New York: Plenum Press. Used with permission.

the ideal family, parents would clearly indicate to their child the rules and standards they believe are essential for an optimal upbringing. In situations where definite rules apply, parents would not offer a choice; instead, they would administer their authority and direction in a forthright manner. For example, they would not repeatedly ask the child what he or she would like to do, particularly when it is inappropriate for the child to make the decision. Instead, they would tell the child what is happening, for example: "Now we are going home." Or "It's time to take your bath," rather than asking, "Would you like to go home now?" Later, as the child grows older, parents would explain the reasoning underlying the rules and limits they have established. In the process, they would stress the importance of the child's learning to lead a self-directed life in which he or she maintains his or her standards and achieves his or her goals.

Parents as Role Models for Their Children

In relation to teaching values to their children, parents who act with integrity and responsibility in their own lives are more effective than those who merely apply specific training or disciplinary measures. The processes of identification and imitation surpass by far parents' lectures, rules, rewards, and punishments. For example, there is no better method for teaching a child to be generous than for parents to be generous with their child, with each other, and with other people.

In contrast, when parents act out negative, hurtful behavior, they have an adverse effect on their children. Toxic personality traits in parents not only impact children directly, but are also incorporated into the child's developing personality, influencing the type of adult he or she will become. When parents' own lives are dull and unfeeling, they fail to provide lively examples for their children to emulate. If their lives are shallow, insulated, or self-protective, they fail to inspire their offspring to seek challenges, innovations, or adventure. To encourage children's movement toward self-activation and fulfillment in life, parents would genuinely value themselves, accept their feelings and wants, and actively participate in their own lives.

Rewards Rather Than Punishment in Facilitating Socialization

Effective parents strengthen their child's positive traits by rewarding desirable behaviors and trying to keep punishment or negative reinforcement to a minimum. Positive reinforcement, that is, smiling, taking pleasure in the child's company, verbal praise, and physical affection, has an important impact on learning. On the other hand, withdrawal of these responses and indications of displeasure help modify undesirable behavior in children. Children raised in a loving, accepting environment are anxious to please, and their parents usually have few disciplinary problems with them. However, children who are continually nagged or lectured generally present a problem to their parents. Lecturing, complaining, and scolding on the part of parents are ineffective because they arouse children's resentment and anger yet fail to control their behavior.

Avoidance of Physical Punishment

In the healthy or optimal family, parents would be able to modify their children's negative behaviors as well as control their physically hurtful actions without hitting, spanking, or violently shaking them. When restraint is needed, they would hold the child firmly and would talk to him or her sternly or even move the child physically to get him or her to go where they wish, without striking the child. Because they feel comfortable with their anger, they would be better able to control its expression, and therefore, be more capable of taking a firm, powerful stand in enforcing rules. Their application of disciplinary measures would be consistent with their children's behavior rather than reflective of their own moods.

Harsh, cruel, or sadistic punishment leads to long-standing fears in the child and expectations of punishment from other people. These painful feelings tend to persist into adult life. In general, it has been demonstrated that children who were physically mistreated tend to provoke bad treatment from others to relieve powerful feelings of anticipatory anxiety and eventually mistreat their own children in the same manner (Straus, 1994).

Avoidance of Judgmental Attitudes

Moralistic training procedures, where children are seen as sinful or bad, have profound negative effects on a child. Physical punishment damages the child's psyche, and parents' harsh, judgmental attitudes act to destroy his or her self-esteem. In fact, most children grow up feeling that they are "bad." They have deep-seated feelings of being unworthy, unlovable, unacceptable, or inferior, and search for explanations as to why they feel this way. For example, many children believe they are bad because they cry or feel sad, because they have wants or desires, or because they feel angry or resentful.

As noted earlier, parents tend to label their children's behavior as "good" or "bad," for example, "Were you *good* at school?" or "You're *bad* if you don't listen to me." Continuous bombardment with evaluative statements regarding good and bad behaviors leads to a one-dimensional view of life and the formation of a negative provisional identity that the child carries into adulthood. Judgmental attitudes discourage the child from developing his or her own standards and values.

In contrast, children who are fortunate enough to have parents who act with decency and integrity do not need to be taught moralistic prohibitions or principles; they learn values, ethical principles, and decent behavior through observing and imitating their parents. Sensitive parents would reassure children that they are not bad after they have been punished or reproached. They would stress the fact that although their child's behavior was irritating or offensive, he or she is not a bad person, and unacceptable behavior can be changed. These parents would sometimes use humor to help their child get out of a bad mood or stop misbehaving. They would not only recognize that humor is useful in disciplining a child, but that children also enjoy their parents' being playful and spontaneous.

Parents who actively pursue their own goals in life would teach their children that they are not bad or selfish for having desires and wants. These parents would understand that children's personal motivations are an important part of their identity, and if they turn their backs on these wants, they will be giving up a basic part of themselves. An individual is made up of or defined by his or her feelings, perceptions, thoughts, wants, and idiosyncratic ways of coping with the environment in pursuing his or her priorities. If children are implicitly taught to deny their wants and inhibit their desires, they will be progressively inhibited in pursuing their goals as adults.

Controlling Children's Hostile, Manipulative Behavior

As a general rule, discipline would be practiced with firmness, not cruelty; with understanding, not condemnation; and from an underlying motive of helping the child become not only the kind of person who likes him- or herself, but also the kind of person whom other people would like, respect, and enjoy being with.

Effective parents would deal quickly and firmly with manipulative behavior and manifestations of negative power in their children. *Negative power* is defined here as an attempt to control through weakness, that is, continual crying and whining, temper tantrums, playing the victim, or acting out self-destructive behaviors.

Mature parents would avoid unnecessary power plays—battles of the will—that degrade the child and force conformity and submission. They would refrain from issuing ultimatums and arbitrarily taking a rigid stand, thereby setting up situations that would lead to power struggles. Nor would mature parents be permissive in a way that fosters regressive behavior, destructive acting out, or abusive behavior in their children. In family interactions, rather than acting out hostile recriminations, good parents would attempt to uncover the causes of their child's distress or undesirable behavior. Indeed, the principles of discipline and socialization described here are based on a philosophy that would allow the gradual unfolding of the child's unique personality, vitality, and enthusiasm for life.

Discouraging Prejudicial or Stereotypical Views

Prejudicial attitudes toward people who are different from one's social, ethnic, or religious group confine the child to a narrow view of human nature and the world and lead to distrust and suspicion. They create a fear of "outsiders" that fosters insecurity and interferes with the child's feeling at ease with people of different backgrounds. These negative attitudes, whether racist, ethnic, or sexist, support a self-protective, inward posture that is undesirable for the child's future relationships.

For these reasons, sensitive parents would make every effort to challenge prejudice and stereotypical thinking in their children and adolescents. In relation to sexist attitudes, parents would challenge popular misconceptions and sexual stereotypes, including the view that men are mean, harsh, unfeeling, and not as committed to marriage and family as are women. They would counteract sexist views of women as intellectually inferior, childish, or unreliable, as less interested in sex than men, and as willing to sell themselves out for security. Challenging these prejudices and sexist views has a positive effect on men and women's hostility toward one another and helps ameliorate "the battle of the sexes."

Supporting Independence in Children

One of the most valuable gifts parents can offer their children is support for each step they take toward becoming autonomous, independent adults. In "letting their children go" they encourage their initiative and allow them to progressively take over their own lives according to the level of their ability. Instead of *underestimating* their children's capability for accepting responsibility, they would be aware that they can enter into productive work in the home at an early age. As their youngsters get older, parents would encourage them to expand their participation into progressively more important functions.

In many families, children spend much of their spare time in unproductive activities that neither educate them nor develop their potentialities. Being allowed to vegetate in the home environment creates a sense of worthlessness. Many adolescents if left to their own devices with endless amounts of time on their hands, turn to drugs, gang life, or at the very least, develop negative attitudes about constructive work habits. Often adolescents brought up in this way resent the few domestic tasks assigned to them.

Lastly, good parents would not impose their own interests on their children; instead, they would try to expose them to an abundance of experiences and encourage them to discover their own talents and interests. In family interactions, they would reward their children for speaking up, for verbalizing their perceptions, and for asking questions about "taboo" subjects. In allowing their offspring the maximum independence at each age level, these parents would be tacitly expressing a belief in their potential for making healthy choices.

OPEN AND CLOSED COMMUNICATIONS

> In these [optimal] families . . . intimacy is sought and usually found, a high level of respect for individuality and the individual perspective is the norm, and capable negotiation and communication clarity are the results. There is a strong sense of individuation with clear boundaries; hence, conflict and ambivalence (at the individual level) are handled directly, overtly, and (usually) negotiated efficiently. (Beavers & Hampson, 1990, p. 48)

Although parents have a natural desire to be protective and sparing of their children's feelings, nonetheless, their attempts to protect their children often cause considerably more damage than would confronting the issues. Children who are aware of the realities of life as well as of the shortcomings of the adults they come in contact with have a better basis for coping with the stresses of life. However, there are a number of topics that parents typically have difficulty discussing frankly and truthfully with their offspring. For example, many have trouble honestly admitting their fears and personal inadequacies. They tend to deny negative feelings toward their children and offer them flattery or false praise to cover up their disappointment in them. In general, parents attempt to keep "family secrets" well hidden. They often avoid the subject of sexuality and are reluctant to discuss the issue of death with their children.

Breaking the Idealization of Parents Through Open Discussion

It is important that children not be deceived about significant family matters or the personal lives of their parents. Secrecy and "white lies" about a family member's undesirable personal traits, physical or mental illness, financial loss, business failure, addiction, suicide, criminal activity, or death can have a lasting detrimental impact on a child. It is not necessary for parents to disguise their limitations. It complicates matters for a child who has grown up in a less-than-ideal emotional climate to be told by relatives or family friends how wonderful his or her family is. On the other hand, helping a child to develop an objective, realistic picture of his or her parents will contribute to the child's developing a realistic, nondefensive view of him- or herself as well. These children will not be as threatened in later years when they discover flaws in the personality makeup of both themselves and their loved ones.

Openness About Sexuality and Death

In helping children develop a healthy orientation toward their bodies and sexuality, parents face complex issues because of society's restrictive, exploitive, or distorted views. However, if parents themselves view sex as a natural and simple activity, they would be better equipped to communicate to their children that sexual feelings are acceptable. It is important to not teach children to conform to societal rules in a way that will turn them against themselves. For example, in talking with their children about nudity, mature parents would assure them that there is nothing shameful, ugly, or inherently bad about the naked body, even though there are certain restrictions against nudity in public.

Children who grow up in an emotional climate in which they feel loved and accepted, especially with respect to their physical nature and bodily functions, will not develop sexual dysfunctions as adults or feel confused about their sexual identity. Parents who are emotionally mature in relation to sex implicitly impart healthy attitudes through a wide range of communications and behaviors not directly associated with sexuality. These attitudes relate to a fundamental respect for the individual's mind and body.

Ideally, parents would communicate with their children about death at a level appropriate to their age and ability to understand the concept. However, most parents avoid these subjects instead of being open with their children about death and dying. Many mothers and fathers try to reassure their children with platitudes in an attempt to dispel the painful feelings that accompany the child's growing awareness of death's inevitability. A number of studies have shown that children go through a stage in their development (ages 3–7) where they become progressively more knowledgeable about death (S. Anthony, 1971/1973; Hoffman & Strauss, 1985; Jackson, 1965; Speece & Brent, 1984). Dugan (1977) found that allowing children to go through this stage arouses anxiety states and feelings of anticipatory grief in *parents*.

Parents who do not defensively deny death would tend to share this sadness with their children. They would be able to communicate the fact that death is a mystery for which they don't have all the answers, without making the child feel unnecessarily insecure or fearful. If parents would be willing to endure the sadness and pain of acknowledging their child's mortality as well as their own limitation in time, they would develop a true sense of empathy with their children. In confronting the existential issues of life and death, and telling their children the truth, parents would be offering greater security than when they attempt to offer false reassurance or discourage further dialogue. Rationalizations and reassurances about death tend to suppress the child's feeling reactions of pain and sadness associated with the topic which, in turn predisposes negative consequences.

SUMMARY OF IDEAL FAMILY CHARACTERISTICS

An understanding of the environmental conditions that cause children unnecessary pain can be used to conceptualize the ideal family, an atmosphere that would bring out the full potential of each of the individual members. Within this family, members would be acknowledged, heard, felt, and experienced by each other in such a way as to give them a sense of their own unique identity. There also would be a recognition of each person's sexual identity. An awareness and acknowledgment of each individual's nature is primary and is more important than recognition for his or her performance.

Family interactions would be characterized by a lack of role-playing, surplus power, and manipulation. There would be a respect for real authority, not rule by power. Each individual would be appreciated for his or her individual contributions of ideas, knowledge in specialized areas, or acts of kindness and generosity. There would be a strong belief in each member pursuing his or her wants and priorities and achieving personal goals. Honest selfishness would be preferred over dishonest selflessness. In giving themselves value and importance, family members would naturally demonstrate respect and consideration for others and their goals.

In the healthy family, members would not be seen as having fixed identities; rather, they would be perceived as being in a state of change and as capable of taking an active part in their own growth and development. For this reason, an optimistic, hopeful flavor would pervade the atmosphere. In addition, there would be a spirit of casual sharing, a lack of possessiveness, and an open, easy exchange of products, both tangible and intangible, including feelings, thoughts, ideas, good times, and humor. Every effort would be made to preserve a lifestyle and atmosphere where the feeling and expression of human emotions were not only acceptable but strongly valued and supported. Instead of acting out their anger and hostility, family members would communicate straightforwardly with each other. They would feel free to express any opinion and experience any emotion without self-consciousness. Their humor would reflect the good feelings they have toward each other rather than be sarcastic or cynical.

Overall, the ideal family would offer its members many unusual advantages: a rich, warm, and fulfilling lifestyle, financial security, companionship, the acknowledgment of individual accomplishments, recognition of each member's sexual identity, encouragement of independence, support for each person developing his or her unique abilities, talents, and careers, and opportunity for free and open communication; in summary, all of the desirable qualities of the "good life."

ADVANTAGES OF AN EXTENDED FAMILY

The advantages of the ideal family would be enhanced by extending them to include other individuals. In attempting to provide a nurturing environment for their children, parents would include other people who might be of potential value to the child. An extended family can be defined as consisting of one or more adults in addition to the child's biological parents who have an interest in the child and maintain consistent contact over a period of time. A close friend, relative, godparent, teacher, or counselor can be considered as part of an extended family network. Close association with adolescents or adults in addition to the child's parents or siblings helps to compensate for parents' fears and inadequacies and offers points of view different from the parents' views that expand the child's world and give him or her a more realistic picture of life. This broader view helps break the idealization of parents and provides the child with a more secure base from which to operate.

An extended family relationship offers the child a true friend or ally, a person in whom he or she can confide, an adult who is relatively unbiased and objective concerning the child's relationship with his or her parents. Children in an extended family setting are also provided with relationships that are generally free of the proprietary interest many parents have in their children. They develop more independence in their interactions with adults, rather than remaining overly dependent on one or both of their parents.

An extended family structure can serve all the functions of the traditional nuclear family: long-standing affection, socialization of children, financial resources available in a crisis, and emotional support and guidance. The pooling of wisdom and understanding in a larger group of people is far richer than what would be available in an individual nuclear family. A nonexclusive and open family structure that includes others benefits all members. For example, studies have shown that certain "resilient" children who experienced severe abuse and neglect, yet who developed into well-functioning adults, usually had a relative, family friend, older sibling, or teacher, who took an interest in them and provided them with support (E. J. Anthony & Cohler, 1987; Masten & Coatsworth, 1998; McLoyd, 1998; Werner, 1990).

DISCUSSION

One of the problems facing people who expose the dynamics involved in dysfunctional family practices is that they are thought of as opposing "family values," when in truth, they have tried to simply do justice to the phenomena that they observe. Many people have mistaken my critique of the widespread destructive practices in the nuclear family for an attack on family life in general. The opposite is true; my life with my wife and children represents my highest value. However, I am opposed to families where the behaviors of family members are detrimental and disturbing enough to cause serious damage. Over the years, the accumulating evidence of the prevalence of emotional disturbance and mistreatment of children in "normal" family constellations has caused me to question aspects of the structure and function of the nuclear family. Despite my own personal biases and protective attitudes toward parents, I have been unable to resist the compelling nature of the clinical material that links psychopathology and personal limitation to destructive machinations within the family.

Energy is best directed toward *improving* those interactions within the family that hurt children or interfere with their ongoing development (Minuchin, Lee, & Simon, 1996; Minuchin & Nichols, 1994), while remaining open to extended family relationships and other means for improving the members' lives. Finally, *it is imperative to state that there is no organization or institution of any kind that can substitute for personal, feelingful, and consistent, close relating to children.*

An interesting analogy can be made between the characteristics that are ideal or conducive for good mental health in the family and the dimensions of an effective psychotherapy. In a good psychotherapy, the patient is offered a unique opportunity to be listened to and understood on a deep level. In a certain sense, therapy represents an unusual opportunity for "reparenting." The therapist listens with empathy and compassion, attempting to understand both the "manifest and latent" content of the patient's verbal productions. The therapeutic process is one of inquiry; the therapist suspends judgment while searching and questioning him- or herself regarding the patient and the sources of his or her disturbance. In the same sense, parents who develop a spirit of investigation in relation to their child would be curious about and sensitive to the emergence of his or her unique qualities and behaviors. When their children misbehave, they would speculate about what is troubling them rather than mechanically punishing their behavior.

In general, the good therapist refuses to be alienated from the patient and attempts to maintain a neutral or empathic posture. Mature clinicians refrain from punishing or rejecting the patient for his or her communications, no matter how distorted or negative they are. Obviously, this task is even more formidable in the parenting situation, as compared with the therapy session. Mature parents would maintain consistent contact and resist regressive trends in their own personalities that promote feelings of insecurity.

In effective psychotherapy, there is a strong emphasis on freedom of speech and the expression of feeling. For example, the method of free association used in psychoanalysis permits the patient to let his or her thoughts flow in a stream of consciousness unhampered by the rules of logic or censorship. The patient not only learns to think creatively, but also comes to understand, on an emotional level, that any thought or feeling is acceptable. At the same time, the experienced clinician teaches the patient to confront and examine the consequences of his or her behavior. Similarly, good parents would permit and accept all of their children's feelings, thoughts, and opinions uncritically, while teaching them to control undesirable, aggressive, or provoking behavior.

The good therapist does not assume a posture of superiority or use his or her technical expertise to impress the patient with ingenious interpretations. The same conditions for a good therapeutic relationship can be applied to parent–child relationships. Although children are clearly not the equal of their parents in terms of physical size, power, knowledge, or competence, parents would not use this differential to exploit or overpower them in a way that would make them feel inferior or weak.

Another important dimension of psychotherapy lies in its nonintrusiveness as exemplified by the therapist's acknowledgment of the basic worth of his or her patient and his or her right to an individual existence. Similarly, preserving the child's sense of self through "leaving him or her alone" in the best sense is crucial to good parenting.

An effective therapist does not try to fit his or her patients into a particular theoretical model; rather, he or she is open to learning from them and experiencing the painful personal truths they reveal. By the same token, adults who are not cut off from their child selves would relate to their children with true empathy and understanding as opposed to approaching them with a preconceived concept of what a child is. This would enable them to avoid judgmental evaluations of their offspring's behaviors and personalities. The child who is accepted on this level would be spared the painful feeling of being misunderstood that so many children experience in growing up.

The ultimate goal of therapy is to persuade the patient to challenge his or her inner world of fantasy and risk seeking satisfaction through goal-directed behavior. In the same sense, the ultimate goal of child-rearing is to socialize children in a way that allows them to strive for their goals, shift to a more independent life, and separate from symbiotic ties. Good parents, like good clinicians, would take pleasure in observing the unfolding personality of their children as they emerge from dependency and move toward autonomy.

ENDNOTES

[1]Over the last decade, in the field of psychology, there has been movement toward rationalizing away potentially damaging parental behaviors by denouncing the

idea that these behaviors have important effects on the child's emotional development. In our opinion, this trend represents an effort to protect parents and idealize the family, to keep family life off-limits to objective scrutiny. This trend may be an overreaction to the practice of "blaming parents" prevalent in the 1950s—an unprofessional attitude unnecessarily hurtful to parents (Firestone, 1990b).

[2]Seligman (1975) noted that children deprived of parental love and direction develop an "expectation that events are uncontrollable" (p. 60). They tend to believe that their actions are also uncontrollable, as do their parents. Seligman, who developed the concept of "learned helplessness," also asserted that the lack of provision of "resolvable frustration and conflict" by parents leads to the child's lack of self-control and feelings of hopelessness.

[3]In reporting findings from his research on the effects of childhood trauma, John Briere (1992) stated: "The majority of adults raised in North America, regardless of gender, age, race, or social class, probably experienced some level of maltreatment as children" (p. xvii). Parents feel almost compelled to reenact in interactions with their children, the mistreatment they experienced as children. When parents are prevented from acting out these abuses (for example, in family therapy), they experience considerable distress and anxiety and often develop symptoms themselves. This parental distress in changing attitudes and behaviors reflects the strength of the neurotic reciprocity involved. When their children improve, it appears to make the parents sick (anxious) not to make the child sick, a phenomenon reported by many family therapists (Kerr & Bowen, 1988; Minuchin, 1974; Palazzoli, Boscolo, Cecchin, & Prata, 1975/1978).

[4]In another work, I (Firestone, 1997a) defined emotional child abuse as "*damage to the child's psychological development and emerging personal identity, primarily caused by parents' or primary caretakers' immaturity, defended lifestyle, and conscious or unconscious aggression toward the child.* We must consider it an abuse when imprinting from early interactions with family members has long-term debilitating effects on a person's conception of self and personal relationships, leads to a condition of general unhappiness, causes pain and anxiety in one's sexual life, and interferes with and stifles development of career and vocational pursuits" (pp. 19–20).

[5]In general, most individuals, in their coupling, continually react to present-day events and to each other with dramatic, primal feelings from the past (Firestone, 1985, 1987a, 1990b). Bowen (1976) suggested that when the partners fail to win the love they missed in their respective childhoods, "much [of their] energy goes into seeking love and approval and keeping the relationship in some kind of harmony; there is no energy for life-directed goals" (p. 70). Bowen (1978) also contended that

> the two person relationship is unstable in that it has a low tolerance for anxiety. . . . When anxiety increases, the emotional flow in a twosome intensifies and the relationship becomes uncomfortable. When the intensity reaches a certain level the twosome predictably and automatically involves a vulnerable third person in the emotional issue. (p. 400)

Most often, that third person is the couple's child.

[6]It is estimated that "nearly half of all the babies born today will spend some time in a one-parent family which occurred as a result of single parenthood or divorce" (Shiono & Quinn, 1994, p. 15). In 1992, 25% of "the nation's children under 18 lived in single-parent households" (Women's International Network News, 1993, p. 75).

[7]See Wallerstein and Blakeslee (1989) and Wallerstein and Kelly (1980) for findings regarding the effects of divorce on children in a 10-year longitudinal study. Also see Hetherington, Bridges, and Insabella (1998) for a discussion of factors that contribute to the adjustment of children in divorced families or stepfamilies.

[8]K. S. Rosen and Rothbaum (1993), Belsky, Taylor, and Rovine (1984), Levy (1943), Parker (1983), and Tronick et al. (1986) discussed manifestations of emotional hunger, including parental overprotection and the notion of "affect hunger." Stern (1985) described "overattunement" on the part of some mothers, a "counterpart of physical intrusiveness. . . . Maternal psyche hovering, when complied with on the infant's part, may slow down the infant's moves toward independence" (p. 219). Nervous overconcern, another manifestation of emotional hunger, has been identified by other clinicians as common in "psychosomatic" families. Minuchin, Rosman, and Baker (1978) found that parents in these families exhibited an exaggerated degree of fear and concern for each other's health and welfare. "The children, in turn, particularly the psychosomatically ill child, feel great responsibility for protecting the family" (p. 31).

II

PSYCHODYNAMICS OF RELATIONSHIPS

6

INWARDNESS: SELF-PROTECTIVE PATTERNS THAT RESTRICT EMOTIONAL TRANSACTIONS BETWEEN PARTNERS

Life has taught us that love does not consist in gazing at each other but in looking outward together in the same direction.
Antoine de Saint Exupéry (1939, p. 288)

The term *inwardness* can be defined as a retreat into oneself, resulting in various degrees of a depersonalized mind state and a lifestyle characterized by diminution of feeling for oneself and others, reliance on painkilling habits and substances, and a defensive, self-nurturing posture toward life. When this syndrome of specific traits and behavior patterns dominates the personality, it plays a central role in all forms of psychopathology and is generally detrimental to relationships. The inward posture represents a serious impairment of the ability to engage in emotional transactions and is especially damaging to the capacity for giving and receiving love.

Inwardness represents a retreat into oneself based on early attempts to avoid frustration and emotional pain. What once functioned as a survival mechanism remains in the personality as a dysfunctional, addictive habit pattern. This is to be distinguished from self-reflection, introspection, time spent alone for reading, thinking or creative work, contemplation of nature, meditation, and other spiritual pursuits.

When in this state of mind, one's gaze is focused inward, on oneself, rather than outward toward others. Personal interactions are filtered

123

through this distorted lens of self-absorption, given a negative connotation by the voice, and responded to inappropriately, thereby causing friction and conflict in one's relationships. The more inward the individual, the less capable that person is of relating to another person in an intimate relationship.

MANIFESTATIONS OF INWARDNESS AND THEIR EFFECTS ON RELATIONSHIPS

The major characteristics of the inward person are (a) a tendency toward isolation, (b) self-denial and seeking gratification in fantasy, (c) hypercritical views toward self and others, (d) withholding patterns, (e) use of substances and routines as painkillers, (f) impersonal relating, (g) masturbatory or addictive sexuality, and (h) merged identity and fusion (see Table 6.1). When these traits reach severe proportions, they coincide

TABLE 6.1
Open or Outward Lifestyle Versus Inward or Self-Parenting Lifestyle

Dimension	Outward	Inward
Sociability	Companionable; seeking closeness; positive view of others	Maintaining distance; seeking time alone; cynical view of others
Mode of gratification	Goal-directed behavior; self-fulfillment; self-affirmation	Seeking gratification in fantasy; self-denial; self-destructiveness
Self-concept	Realistic self-appraisal; self-assertion	Hypercritical attitudes toward self; passivity and victimized stance
Withholding	High level of emotional transactions; free flow of giving and accepting love	Limited emotional transactions; refractory to giving and receiving love; holding back of positive responses and desirable characteristics
Addictions	Facing up to pain and anxiety with appropriate affect and response	Using substances and routinized habits as painkillers
Feeling relatedness	Feeling responses; personal states of relating	Cutting off or withdrawal of affect; impersonal relating
Sexuality	Genitality; personal state of relating	Masturbatory or addictive sexuality; "mechanical" sexual relating
Personal identity	Maintaining a separate identity	Merged identity and fusion

© The Glendon Association, 1999.

with indicators of imminent suicide, as noted by many suicidologists, including Edwin Shneidman and David Shaffer (MacNeil-Lehrer Productions, 1987).

Inwardness is an addictive process because it involves tendencies toward isolation and fantasy gratification that have tension-reducing properties. Defended individuals have at their disposal a readily available, effective means for numbing emotional pain. One woman who tended to isolate herself from family and friends described this process as comfortable and familiar. She described her state of mind as so compelling that once she got into that state, she didn't want to come out. She felt that it was worth everything to her, more than her children, more than the people she loved.

Challenging inwardness is a significant step in fostering amicability and growth in a relationship, whereas acting out inward patterns inevitably leads to antagonism and acrimony. For example, one woman was constantly infuriated by her husband's habit of chronic television watching. He spent every night until midnight in front of the TV instead of talking with her, which negatively affected her desire to make love. His technique of retreating into himself was the primary source of conflict in this couple. In another case, a man was provoked for years by his wife's compulsive shopping, which she refused to moderate or change although he repeatedly pleaded with her to do so. The resultant financial problems and continual dissension over this issue destroyed the marriage. Cases in which one partner's alcoholism or drug addiction shatters the other's trust and love are commonplace. All of these defensive behaviors, along with other more subtle inward patterns, inflict serious damage on relationships.

AN OPEN, OUTWARD LIFESTYLE VERSUS AN INWARD STATE

The dimensions of outward versus inward living delineated in Table 6.1 range along a continuum from healthy functioning to serious maladjustment. As described in chapter 2, these patterns can be observed throughout clinical and nonclinical populations, ranging from schizophrenic patients who represent the ultimate in nonrelating or pathological relating, to those individuals who seek to fulfill themselves in a close relationship with another person. Schizophrenic patients retreat into an isolated lifestyle devoid of meaningful relationships, whereas neurotic or "normal" individuals are less refractory to closeness and love. The degree of neurotic or psychotic regression is a function of the degree to which the person depends upon fantasy for nourishment and psychological survival, which, in turn, relates to the degree of early deprivation and parental rejection (Firestone, 1957).*

Aspects of an outward lifestyle of pursuing goals in the real world can be distinguished from those of an inward lifestyle. Signs of inwardness are not separate and discrete: They tend to overlap to varying degrees. However, for purposes of clarity, they are assigned to distinct categories and illustrated by a case study.

CASE STUDY OF INWARDNESS: OVERVIEW

Frank and Janet are intelligent people, attractive and congenial, with similar interests, values, and goals in life. For the past 18 years, these two people and their three children (now adults) have participated in the longitudinal study described in the Preface.† Prior to the study, Frank and Janet, both individually involved in psychotherapy, expressed strong interest in discussing psychological and philosophical ideas and were unusually articulate in talking objectively about aspects of their family life.

At the beginning of their relationship, Frank and Janet appeared to have everything going for them. Yet their defenses and inward behaviors had a progressively negative effect on their relationship, kept them apart, and had a destructive effect on their children's lives. In this analysis, let us consider how maladaptive habit patterns manifested by both partners damaged their interactions on a daily basis and ultimately, after 23 years, led to the dissolution of the relationship.‡ As we observed and interacted with this couple, it became increasingly clear how the characteristics and defenses that each partner brought to the relationship created conflict and dissension. Later, as we came to know the children, we could understand how the dynamics operating in the family had affected their lives. We were able to observe the parents' self-protective, inward patterns duplicated in their offspring as they matured. In other words, the intergenerational transmission of specific negative traits and behaviors manifested by Frank and Janet could be clearly discerned over the course of the longitudinal study.

Incidentally, although this family had many dysfunctional aspects, it

---

*For the prepsychotic individual who is living in a precarious state of inwardness, a single traumatic event or a stressful interpersonal situation can create a panic or confused state that catapults him or her into a psychotic episode. In regressing to a previous level of ego development, the patient's attempts to stabilize and integrate the personality at intermediate stages fail, until finally a very primitive level of equilibrium is reached.

†Within the context of this study, we were able to observe the interactions of the couple and family in their everyday lives and also had access to the personal insights and revelations they expressed in discussion groups and in journals. The material included in this case study was excerpted from interviews with Janet, videotaped descriptions contributed by Frank, and from written memoirs provided by their children.

‡When Frank and Janet first became participants in the longitudinal study, they had been married for approximately 19 years, and their children were in their late teens.

appeared normal, and none of the negative behavior patterns were apparent or showed up in ways that deviated from other families in the communities in which Frank and Janet lived during their children's formative years. On the surface, the family was congenial, the home atmosphere was appealing, and many of the children's friends chose to spend considerable time there.

Frank and Janet met in college and soon became friends. Eventually, they began dating, and within months of becoming sexually involved, Janet became pregnant. The couple eloped, and their son, Don, was born several months later. Janet's motives for getting pregnant were partly conscious, as she revealed some years later in an interview:

> At the time, I was really aware of why I wanted to get married. I was desperate to escape my family after my grandfather died. His death left a household dominated by women: my mother, grandmother, and sister. From the time I was 5, when my father left, until my grandparents moved in with us when I was 16, my mother constantly criticized me and was often physically abusive. My grandfather had served as sort of a buffer between my mother and me, and now I felt I *had* to get away.
>
> Basically, I "used" Frank as a means for making my escape. I had been friends with him for 2 years before we started dating, and I believed that I was really in love. He was attractive, hard-working, intelligent, a very warm, sweet person with a good sense of humor. He was interested in the same things I was and had a quick analytical mind. We were good friends until we started being sexual. But, even before I discovered I was pregnant, I was plagued by guilt about being sexual outside of marriage, and this began to affect our friendship. I sensed Frank was also guilty about sex, because when I told him that I was pregnant, he seemed to take responsibility for the whole thing and insisted we get married immediately.

The psychodynamics in Frank's family were similar in many respects to those operating in Janet's. Frank's mother, depressed throughout his childhood, tended to restrict and infantilize him by focusing on the youngster's illnesses. His father assumed control of Frank's life when he was an adolescent in an attempt to counteract his wife's coddling. In the process of trying to "toughen him up" and "make a man out of him," Frank's father humiliated and degraded him. His father projected fears regarding his own masculinity onto the boy and punished him for any weaknesses he thought he saw in his son. His distorted views of sexuality were also transmitted to the youngster, both on an unconscious level and through overt actions.

On one occasion, Frank's father came to watch a high school basketball game where Frank was playing. During the game, the youngster was changing into a fresh shirt when his father walked onto the court and, in front of the boy's teammates and onlookers, yelled at his son for exposing his "skinny" body in public. Frank was deeply humiliated by his father's bizarre attack. The incident had a powerful effect on him and reinforced generalized feelings of shame and disgust about his physical appearance and sexuality, as well as doubts about his manhood.

To assuage his insecurity about his masculinity, Frank jumped at the opportunity to get married; having a wife and child helped ease his self-doubts, and in his mind proved his manhood. Frank and Janet's attempts to use the marriage to compensate for deficiencies in each of their childhoods, along with their habitual ways of defending themselves, began to take a toll early on.

Consider this case in terms of analyzing the dimensions of inwardness delineated in Table 6.1 and their effects on the relationship as it matured. Although the couple often argued about money, differences in their child-rearing approaches, and political views, the critical concern was that they defended themselves from closeness by acting out inward habit patterns. Considerable discomfort and anxiety would have been aroused in both partners had they attempted to challenge or alter these specific behaviors. However, if they had met the challenge, they would have been more likely to maintain a better, more salutary relationship.

Isolation and Distancing Behaviors

Isolation is a central dimension of an inward, self-protective lifestyle. An individual who feels compelled to isolate him- or herself rationalizes this retreat from a partner with statements such as, "I need some time for myself so I can think things through." "I need my own space." "I'm too busy (too tired; too hassled) to talk things over now, I just need to get away for a while so I can clear my head." Voices encourage the inward person to retreat from social contact and intimacy and spend time alone. This time alone may be contrasted with time spent in relaxing, self-contemplation, constructive planning, or creative endeavors. Instead, it is characterized by an ascendance of critical negative thoughts toward self and others and self-destructive habit patterns.

Soon after the birth of their baby, both Frank and Janet began a gradual retreat from the closeness they had originally felt; their conversations became infrequent, and each became more involved in solitary pursuits. As their family grew, they spent more time alone and away from each other. Each sought solace in passive, solitary activities that were reminiscent of the methods they had used to avoid painful situations in their childhoods. As children, they had chosen solitude and isolated activities over the company of other family members or their peers. As the only boy in the family, Frank was lonely and filled his time by reading voraciously. He felt more comfortable holed up in his room away from his sisters' intrusiveness and the tension and conflict between his parents. Janet had also sought refuge from her mother's endless lectures and deprecating comments in compulsive reading, studying, and sleep. When her mother became physically abusive, she learned to "click off," to mentally remove herself from the situation.

In her marriage, Janet turned to similar methods and routines to remove herself from interactions with her husband and children. She spent an inordinate amount of time reading and taking long walks alone. When depressed, she often slept 12 to 15 hours a day. At night, she typically fell asleep while reading, before her husband came to bed. Even when she was available to her family, she appeared somewhat indifferent and aloof, and her responses were more practical than personal or feelingful. She tended to rationalize her isolation. For example, she defended challenges to her excessive reading by telling herself: "What's wrong with reading? It stimulates your mind, makes you an interesting person. Besides, he reads almost as much as you do." Or, in relation to avoiding sex: "He isn't attracted to you anymore. Why would he want to make love to you, anyway? He's ignored you all day, that shows he really doesn't care."

In Frank's case, his studies necessitated long hours of isolation, which left little time for interactions with Janet and their baby. Later, in his career as an engineer, he again isolated himself behind the locked door of his office, working evenings and weekends. His social times consisted of occasional drinking bouts with his coworkers. Thus, because both partners possessed strong propensities to seek isolation over social interaction, their marriage became less vital and increasingly sterile, and the home they created provided their children with little real warmth or sustenance. In addition, these propensities for isolating themselves had strong modeling effects on their offspring, who developed similar patterns of escape. In a personal journal, their son, Don, described the compelling allure that solitude held for him:

> By the time we left the valley, I was convinced I was evolving into a vampire. I felt threatened being in the open. Daylight made me exposed, vulnerable. I found solace in my dreams where I would discover secret dark rooms behind walls in our house to hide in. After school, I would barricade myself in our shadowy family room. On weekends I never went outside.
>
> Moving to Malibu put a monkey wrench in my carefully refined safe lifestyle. I would sit in our new family room for hours, curtains tightly drawn, attempting to duplicate the numbness which had worked so well for me, for so many years, in the valley. But it no longer worked. I knew, from the moment we first came to Point Dume looking for

homes, that I was seduced by the place. Every moment locked behind closed curtains began to have the feel of waste. Time was beginning to mean something more than just something to be waited out.

Although Don came out of his isolated shell for a time during his adolescence and began to participate in sports (skiing and surfing with friends), nonetheless, his pattern of seeking solitude eventually had tragic consequences. Rejected by his girlfriend when he was 18, he again retreated into the inward, isolated state of which he wrote: "I was living alone, at the mercy of intense self-attacks, which ultimately led to a serious suicide attempt. At this point I entered therapy and began to move toward a more outward, active life." Had Don's parents recognized the dangers of these inward patterns, and had they been more aware of the ways they impact children, they might have been able to challenge these behaviors more effectively.

Preference for Gratification in Fantasy

The inward, self-protective individual spends a large part of his or her waking life dominated by conscious or unconscious fantasies that lead to distortion of everyday experiences. This state is far more extensive than simple daydreams. In the inward state, ideation takes precedence over feeling, and fantasy gratification precludes genuine involvement with other people. The preference for gratification through fantasy has its sources in childhood. Children who are deprived of emotional sustenance gradually compensate with fantasy gratification. This fantasy world is completely under the child's control, where escape from a painful or frustrating environment is available by going into fantasy whenever the need is felt.

Many people come to prefer fantasy, a self-soothing mechanism that is close at hand and immediately rewarding, over an active search for satisfying relationships in the world of reality. Their tendency is to retreat from people, relationships, or circumstances that would fulfill their dreams and meet their needs, while maintaining an illusion that they are acting in their best interests. They imagine that they are still pursuing realistic goals while maintaining a passive stance and sabotaging their lives.

Both Frank and Janet were more cerebral than action-oriented. They tended to live in their heads and imaginations. Both fantasized about happiness in the future, while ignoring actual events in their family that were problematic and needed attention. Again, their reliance on fantasy evolved during their formative years. For example, after Janet's parents divorced, she became increasingly depressed. To compensate for the loss of her father, she immersed herself in fantasies of being an assistant to General MacArthur during World War II. These imaginings would transport her away from a reality that had become intolerable to her.

In much the same manner, Frank had sought relief from his lonely existence by fantasizing about the perfect home and family he would create as an adult. Paradoxically, his fantasy of achieving for his family the happiness and security he had missed as a child prevented him from attaining his goal. Don describes in a journal entry his father's futile efforts to fulfill this dream:

My father bought a new house in the San Fernando valley and set to work on elaborate patios, small gardens, attractive fences, and a neatly tailored lawn. He had an obsession with details. I think that he pictured a family living there in harmony. That dream fueled his enthusiasm. As if all problems would be resolved by the completion of that house. It would close the remaining windows to his past and open the door to his new life. A million hopes attached to finishing the house.

When it was done, its beauty brought the misery in our family to the foreground. He had a wife who had carved out a private world in the back of her mind and had become so withdrawn that we rarely saw her rise from bed before noon, only to return there after she had taken care of the most necessary of chores. A son he was at war with. Daughters he could not relate to. He had tailored the house for a family that did not exist. I think it was a bad awakening which he never recovered from as if he had hoped that it would free him from his own hell. Instead it became it.

When we moved to Malibu, he bought a larger house. It had large overgrown yards. Remnants of a weathered gray fence which bordered, rather than enclosed, a corral which ran to the bottom of a ravine. Once again he saw potential for a beautiful home. He began to live in a picture of how it could look with hundreds of changes. Some large. Some subtle and small. Invariably he would set out on a new project with enthusiasm only to abandon it when it was partially completed. Sometimes so quickly, tools would be dropped and left where they lay. It was not uncommon for someone to be walking through our lawn and stumble over wrenches and pliers, rusted beyond use, lying in the high grass. The projects would then be ignored, as if they had become invisible, and disintegrate over time while he lost himself in the beginnings of another project. Our yard was littered with the small ghost towns of a hundred false starts.

In this manner, he could believe forever that once the home was complete, then everything would be fine. Incompleteness became his sanctuary. Whatever painful truth had surfaced in the completion of the valley house never seemed to fade. I think the failure of achieving a family different from his own slowly ate away at him. Demoralizing him from the inside out more each day. Over time he began to solicit other means to numb his pain. I think that is when his drinking quietly slipped into becoming more than a social activity.

Negative Self-Concept

As previously described, many people cling to negative attitudes toward themselves, hold on to the provisional identity, that is, the way they were seen in their families, and find it difficult to adapt to a more positive or realistic view. In a close relationship, they are tempted to venture out and for a time accept a different, more positive view of themselves from their partner, but soon retreat inward to their habitual way of looking at and treating themselves. They begin to distort their partner and respond to them with negative or fearful expectations. These dynamics were clearly operating in Frank and Janet's marriage.

◆ ◆ ◆

Both partners had critical views of themselves that they projected into the relationship. Frank experienced considerable guilt regarding his perceived failure to bring Janet out of her depressed state. His guilt reactions took the form of self-recriminations and voice attacks such as: "It's your fault she's unhappy. You knew she didn't want to move to California. Why did you take her away from a place that she loved, where she was starting to make some friends? You're an insensitive, selfish bastard!" Although he catered to her moods, for example, preparing meals for the family and serving her breakfast in bed when she was "down," he continued to blame himself for his wife's misery, just as he had assumed the blame for his mother's depression as a child.

Janet's selection of Frank as a marriage partner perpetuated the critical atmosphere in which she was raised. When he was under tension, Frank did tend to become judgmental and parental; however, Janet elicited this type of harsh, critical response by acting incompetent and deferring to Frank.

Essentially, Janet had projected the image of her critical mother onto Frank and played out the role of the less intelligent, inferior child. Toward the end of the marriage, she adopted a more pseudoindependent, antagonistic role, and the couple would argue for hours, sometimes for an entire night. Janet would righteously defend herself and her views against Frank's attacks and his perceptions of reality. Following the divorce, she was shocked at the intensity of her own self-attacks and the self-hatred she experienced when Frank was no longer available to fill the role of critical parent. She realized that defending herself against attacks coming from her husband had given her a kind of strength, whereas now she was left alone with the full intensity of her own destructive thinking and voice attacks that represented her mother's degrading views of her.

Withholding

Withholding is a holding back of positive responses, talents, and capabilities in a retreat from a feelingful life. Withholding refers to distancing oneself by progressively holding back or inhibiting traits that are desired or prized by the other. In personal relationships, the withholding person tends to resist involvement in emotional transactions and refuses to accept love from, or offer love and affection to, his or her partner or children. Withholding is governed by internal voices that direct one's behavior. Free-flowing feeling responses are inhibited by destructive thought patterns such as, "Why should you always be the one to be generous or considerate? What has he or she done for you lately?" "He or she doesn't really love you." "Who needs him or her anyway!"

Passive-aggression, as a form of withholding, represents disguised hostility toward others and may be expressed through fatigue, incompetence, forgetfulness, procrastination, insolence, or sarcasm. These behaviors are directed by voices such as, "You can always run that errand tomorrow. It's not that important. Who does he think he is, anyway? He just takes it for granted that you're here to serve him." Or "You're such a sucker! You always give in to what a woman wants. Don't let her push you around."

Janet's patterns of withholding included refusing to maintain a clean, well-managed household and a disinterest in providing meals for her family. In the area of child care, she failed to discipline the children and instead threatened to "tell your father when he gets home." By making Frank the agent of punishment, she avoided, for the most part, repeating with her own children her mother's physical maltreatment, yet she created a punishing environment for them similar to the one in which she had been raised.

Withholding and self-denial were also manifested by Janet in the couple's sexual relationship. Her diminished sexual interest was fostered in part by her prejudicial attitudes toward men. Her views of men as inferior, sexually driven creatures could be traced directly to her mother's distorted, stereotypic way of thinking:

> My mother would say: "Men, I hate them," in a sarcastic biting tone, maybe as often as 10 times a day, if anything in relation to a man came up. But it was a superior view. She was superior and men were like dirt, little, weak, and dirt. That's how she felt and I projected that feeling onto Frank and then onto Don.

Frank's doubts about his manhood and his adequacy as a provider were reinforced by Janet's views of men. For example, once when he received a substantial raise at work, Frank rushed home and, with pride and excitement, told Janet the good news. He was stunned and deeply hurt by her sarcastic comment that the amount of increase in his paycheck was still inadequate, because it failed to keep up with inflation and the rising cost of living.

It is important to note here that the patterns of withholding and other inward behaviors manifested by both partners reflected a direct imitation of, and identification with, their parents of the same sex. The defenses that Janet resorted to were those used by her mother, and Frank's defenses replicated those of his father. Moreover, each partner's defense mechanisms appeared to complement those of the other. For example, Frank's protective stance and efforts to make Janet happy while disregarding himself corresponded to Janet's unrealistic expectation that her husband "should" take care of her because he was responsible for getting her pregnant. This reciprocal pattern is common in many interpersonal relationships and marriages. These defenses work together to create a new parenting situation similar to the environment each partner experienced as a child.

Use of Substances and Routinized Habits as Painkillers

Self-nourishing propensities arise early in life in the form of self-gratifying behavior patterns that become addictive for the rejected or deprived child. Reliance on this self-support system is proportional to the degree of deprivation. These patterns manifest themselves in eating disorders, substance abuse, routines, habitual responses, and compulsive behaviors. Repetitive behaviors and rituals come to have addictive properties because they function to dull one's sensitivity to painful feelings and lend an air of certainty and seeming permanence to life. Obsessive or compulsive patterns that temporarily reduce anxiety become habitual and later foster more anxiety. In the "normal" range of functioning, many individuals become addicted to routines and personal habits such as excessive television watching, video games, computer use, reading, shopping, and compulsive patterns of overworking.

Although he used rationalizations that justified his hard work, Frank's compulsive pattern of overworking ruled his life and resulted in his sacrificing the closeness he might have had with his family. In a documentary film, he describes how he developed this inward pattern:

There's a recurring dream of when I was a little toddler of running and exploring and sensing life and touching and smelling and sensing things, and then this vise, of being picked up by my mother who was very depressed, who stayed in bed and she wanted me to stay out of trouble, so she put me in the crib in the dark room with her while she took her nap, while she slept, while she whiled away the daytime with the shades drawn. And you could see the light outside, but I had to stay in this crib in this room to stay out of trouble.

My father took over then, as I got older, but it was the same thing. I had to report for work after school. I had jobs to do. "There's work to be done." One day I went to the soda shop where all the rest of the kids went after school, for just a few minutes, and my father came in raging like a bull and he grabbed me by the collar and dragged me out literally by the scruff of the neck. "Don't you *dare* not report to work like you're supposed to. What are you doing here?"

So there was always this creation of demands on me, that a life is not for me. I was thinking of the recurrence of this, that I did it to myself after that. I got my girlfriend pregnant and had three children before I was 23. I was working and carrying 25 hours of engineering because I had this demand to support my family and to finish school.

Then my career in engineering was a succession of going into a job, creating a grandiose scheme—and I would wallow in it. I would wallow in it to the point of where it was consuming, always consuming. I started a career in real estate and development and I enjoyed it. I loved it. But once again it's become a consuming nightmare for me, the financial pressure, pressures of the times. It's devoured me for the past couple of years. The creation of these consuming problems in my life has kept me from having a life over and over again.*

Suppression of Feeling and Impersonal Relating

As noted, the inward, defended state and its opposite, a feelingful state, represent end points on a continuum. Between these two extremes lies the gray area in which most people live. "Normal" individuals are continually contending with the voice; they are not completely possessed by critical voices, and they are not completely removed from feeling. However, their spirit and sensitivity are dulled considerably. Their diminished feelings for self and others makes it possible for them to unconsciously act out destructive behavior toward themselves and their loved ones.

The suppression of feelings begins in childhood. Unable to escape a punishing or toxic home situation, children gradually disengage from themselves as scared, hurting people and become, in a sense, someone other than themselves. In doing so they cut off feelings of compassion toward themselves and sensitivity toward others. In ceasing to identify with themselves, they build a kind of facade or social image. Thereafter, role-determined emotions, conventional perceptions, and secretiveness increas-

---

*This excerpt was reprinted from *Combating Destructive Thought Processes* (Firestone, 1997a) and from the video documentary *Invisible Child Abuse* (Parr, 1995).

ingly replace real feelings, rational thinking, and open expressions of emotion. Self-attacks of the voice and obsessive ruminations that dominate the thinking of the inward person are antithetical to maintaining an ongoing state of feeling.

People who are inward and suppress their feeling responses also tend to view themselves and their partner more as objects than as persons. In relating to themselves in this manner, they give little or no value to their experiences and are often indifferent to their physical health and emotional well-being.

◆ ◆ ◆

Frank and Janet tended to be removed to a certain extent from their feelings, and in their everyday interactions, they related on an impersonal level. (Their personalities could be categorized as more obsessive than hysterical.) Although at times Frank showed real warmth toward Janet and his children, his usual approach consisted of a kind of detached curiosity about people and a preoccupation with trying to find out what made them tick. He attempted to apply his own style of critical analysis in unearthing the reasons for Janet's problems and her depression, which only created distance and animosity between them.

Both partners valued images, appearances, and performance more than feeling responses or simple personal interactions. As children, they had been exploited by parents who fed off their accomplishments and offered them false praise and flattery rather than real acknowledgment or appreciation. As adults, they continued to try to offer and extract this type of buildup in relation to each other and their children in an attempt to compensate for the lack of love in their early environment.

Because his mother had lived through him and praised his intellectual abilities, Frank continually sought praise from Janet for his accomplishments at work. His demand for a buildup diminished the feelings of attraction she originally felt toward him, and eventually caused her to hate him. To disguise her real feelings, she flattered him to his face, but tore him down behind his back in conversations with her women friends.

As a mother, Janet only felt worthwhile and needed when one of her children would become ill. When Don developed a serious illness shortly after his birth, she formed an exclusive attachment with the infant, based on her need to feel special. To her way of thinking, she was the only person who could offer him the kind of care he needed to recover. She repeated this pattern with her younger daughter, Beverly, who contracted whooping cough when she was 3 months old and required constant care for several months. The type of care she offered each child, because it fed her own need for specialness and self-importance, detracted from the real feelings of love and tenderness she might have experienced in relating to them.

The three children learned, through imitation, their parents' methods for cutting off feelings. Each had difficulties relating on a personal basis to the people they chose as partners in their adult associations. In his journal, Don describes how he has struggled to overcome tendencies to suppress his feelings and dull the pain and despair inherent in experiencing one's life:

> Over the years, I have learned about the extreme and unconscious maneuvering I put myself through in order to avoid sadness. (Without obvious reason, I think people build their own machines to defend themselves.) There are times I think that sadness threatens to boil right through my skin. The anxiety I have at those times is my own machinery putting on a second shift to keep it down. Bury it deep. Then there are times that it just pops out, as if it found a small crack in the machine's shell.
>
> Regardless of what may make me sad, I find peace in its aftermath. It clears my mind and turns off a certain mental noise. I realize that in warding off sadness, all my feelings are tampered with and lost. What brings sadness rolling along in me, every time, is letting anything or anyone matter. This ranges from feeling good about having a clean closet to loving someone and everything in between. My life has been a war with my own machinery on everything I wanted. But the most threatening thing, the thing that is the most certain to bring sadness pounding to the surface, is the completion of dreams.

Impersonal Sexual Relating

Many people encounter difficulties in trying to achieve and sustain sexual satisfaction in ongoing relationships because early in life they turned away from external sources of gratification and now seek to gratify themselves internally. They choose fantasy and control while avoiding close, personal interactions. After the excitement and romance that characterize the beginning phases of a relationship fade, partners may become somewhat distant and less sexually attracted to each other. In many cases, they distance themselves emotionally from their sexual partner before their fears of intimacy, rejection, or potential loss reach the level of conscious awareness. They begin to hold back genuine affectionate and sexual responses and unconsciously substitute a more self-feeding or inward style of sexual relating before becoming anxious or fearful. Thereafter, their lovemaking tends to become more mechanical and focused on performance, which often leaves them feeling empty and unsatisfied.

Some men and women use masturbation to avoid being sexual with their partner and may choose this method of self-gratification over having a close, intimate sexual experience. Strong guilt reactions are often attached to masturbation and the excessive use of fantasy during lovemaking, because these behaviors represent a retreat from genuine personal contact with one's partner. The crucial distinction between personal sexual relating and an addictive or impersonal style of lovemaking lies in the awareness of one's partner as a separate person as opposed to the use of the other as an instrument to assuage primitive needs and longings and relieve fears of aloneness, separateness, and death.

◆ ◆ ◆

The sexual relating between Frank and Janet was significantly affected by their fears of being close emotionally and by Janet's sexual withholding which, in turn, precipitated feelings of emotional hunger in Frank. Both retreated from mature, genital sexuality to an immature, more addictive or masturbatory form of sexuality. Janet describes how she felt about being sexual with Frank early in the relationship:

> When we first started being sexual, I really thought that I was giving something to Frank and expected him to feel more interested in me than before. I felt very guilty about sex, and so I felt he should be sympathetic and considerate of my feelings. I remember that I didn't really like having intercourse, but I did like kissing and touching. Looking back, I think that I wanted to be a little girl with Frank. I only wanted him to hold me and tell me reassuring words of love. I must have wanted Frank to make up to me for what I felt I had missed with my father.

While growing up, both Frank and Janet used masturbation as a method of self-gratification to relieve anxiety and compensate for the lack of warmth and nurturance in their home environment. Frank engaged in compulsive masturbation as a young teenager, and once contemplated suicide because he felt so humiliated and incapable of control in this area. As an adult, Janet used fantasy to increase her level of excitement during sex and preferred masturbation over making love to Frank. For her, masturbation became her dominant form of sexual gratification. To a large degree, the lack of sexuality in their marriage was directly related to Janet's addiction to masturbation.

Merged Identity and Fusion

The anxiety inherent in being vulnerable in a new love relationship causes many people to unconsciously attempt to merge and form a unit with their loved ones. In the strictest sense, this merger or fantasy bond exists only in one's imagination, that is, obviously there is no real fusion; however, it manifests itself outwardly in a variety of behaviors that support one's fantasy of being connected or belonging to another person. Men and women who form an imagined connection with each other are avoiding real closeness and affection. Unable to accept the reality of their lack of feeling, they attempt to maintain a fantasy of enduring love. Indications of this merged identity between partners include—among others—a diminished sense of identity in each person, a reliance on the repetition of routines, customs, role-determined behaviors, and special treatment that each partner has come to expect of the other, an idealization or depreciation of each other, the holding back of desirable or lovable traits, and intense feelings of jealousy and possessiveness.

Within a year of getting married, Frank and Janet fell into routine ways of being together that masked the fact that the feelings of excitement they once experienced in each other's company had declined significantly. Gradually the activities that had been spontaneous took on a certain predictability. The Saturday mornings spent in bed, the Sunday afternoon car trips spent house-hunting, the anniversary celebrated with dinner at a lavish nightclub, the annual trip to the grandparents' home, all functioned to preserve the form of love, a shared fantasy of still being in love, long after the substance, the real love had disappeared. These comforting routines occurred in the midst of the couple's acting out destructive machinations with each other, as Frank recounted in an interview:

> It got to be a pattern with Janet and me during the years we lived in the valley and Malibu. She rarely wanted to make love more than once a week, so I would go out with other women from time to time. After a while I started to stay out drinking very late Friday nights, getting totally drunk, and staggering home around 2 a.m. Then came the incoherent, horrible arguments. On Saturday morning, I would feel terrible, contrite, and ask for forgiveness. I would bring Janet breakfast in bed and we would spend the mornings making up and making love. We would reassure each other that things were okay again, when really they weren't. The kids would be in the family room watching cartoons, till past noon. I know they felt confused and completely left out of our lives.

Children born to a couple whose relationship has developed symptoms of a fantasy bond feel excluded and suffer greatly from the lack of emotional sustenance. In addition, they are drawn into their parents' world of illusion and pretense. Most parents still have great difficulty giving up these destructive patterns even after perceiving that their withholding, inwardness, and conflicts are damaging to each other as well as to their offspring. Moreover, in many families, one or both parents select a particular child with whom to form an exclusive attachment that contains some of the same elements as those existing in the couple bond.

◆　◆　◆

During Beverly's childhood illness, Janet formed a strong attachment with her based on Janet's desire to have someone all her own, a daughter similar to her in appearance, interests, and political views. The young girl became her constant companion; Janet took her everywhere she went—shopping, to her painting and exercise classes, and to her college extension classes. Later, as an adult, Beverly wrote some of her impressions of growing up in her family:

> I've always felt alone in my family. Janet was my "protector," and yet I never really knew her fully as a person. I remember being by her side as a "silent shadow," doing everything with her. It was a very symbiotic relationship; an invisible bond, almost like an umbilical cord, kept us together. I partook in her depressing existence. I was perpetually ill in order to be at home and have her care for me. The house was usually so lifeless and dark at these times. It felt dead and gloomy.
>
> My brother and older sister, Don and Sarah, formed an alliance which was exclusive of me. There was a lot of resentment on their part for my being "close" to Janet, and they would physically attack me. Don would chase me around the house, yelling "You're ugly, ugly, ugly!" and call me by a strange nickname, not my own name. I always felt like some strange, weird child around them.
>
> In Malibu, when Don and Sarah had their parties, I went to my room and locked the door. The only interactions Sarah and I had were bitter arguments over possessions. Frank was unaware of my existence completely. I was most struck by his unawareness when some of my parents' friends were being shown around the house by Frank. We had a sewing machine at the time with which I made many of my clothes. When he came to it on his "tour," he said with pride, "Oh, there's the sewing machine—Sarah really does a lot of sewing." I was deeply hurt—it was so obvious that I did most of the sewing. Frank's image of Sarah's accomplishments was so out of proportion to what she actually did and was. But what hurt me even more was that if he didn't see something so obvious as this, it meant I did not exist for him at all.
>
> I used to escape from my family by going to my friend Julie's house almost every weekend. There I was not only accepted, but loved a great deal. The one man who was nice to me was Julie's father. He was openly warm and physical and he showed interest in my life. He was very aware of the damaging side of family life, at one time having been married to a cruel, schizophrenic woman. We would always do enjoyable, lively things together—camping trips, picnics, etc. I was always sad when the weekend ended and I would have to return to my family.

CONCLUSION

Inward and defended habit patterns represent an addictive mode of defense wherein an individual retreats to an emotionally deadened existence. A defensive posture of inwardness and self-nurturance is expressed in a distrust of others and a retreat from exchanging products outwardly, whereas enlightened self-interest and the capability to give and receive products (love) reflects the opposite (outward) posture. When people defend themselves, retreat from life, and seek gratification in fantasy and self-nourishing behavior and routines, there are a number of consequences to their relationships, as we have seen. Indeed, these inward patterns represent the most serious threat to successful relating.

There is a significant loss of freedom and meaningful experience to the individual, a shrinking of life space. The process of disengaging from oneself leads to a fundamental existential guilt in denying life and retreating from loved ones. The process of self-denial activates self-critical voices, is acutely demoralizing, and widens the split in the self-system. Anger, the normal response to frustration, is obscured and may be internalized or projected into one's closest relationships. The former leads to self-denigration; the latter to a sense of victimization and often a counteraggressive stance in relation to one's partner. Thus, human beings cannot be "innocently" defended because the choice to live an inward, self-protective life has a crippling effect on people's interactions within their relationships, their families, and on succeeding generations. In the next chapter, we discuss the remedial procedures both in and out of the circle of friends that had a positive effect on these family members and challenged and altered their inward habit patterns.

7

REMEDIAL PROCEDURES: EXPERIENCES THAT AFFECT INWARD PATTERNS IN THE COUPLE AND FAMILY

To see the depth at which the old ways live inside us, to grasp the power with which they influence adult life and behavior long after we have learned about new ways of being, and to understand fully the source of it all, we must go back to childhood.

Lillian Rubin (1983, p. 37)

In the previous chapter, we illustrated how inward personality traits and defenses seriously damaged the family life of a couple and their children. In this chapter, we describe an unusual set of circumstances and procedures that helped challenge and correct the dysfunctional aspects of each family member's relationships. Our methodology involved identifying negative thoughts and behavior patterns, counteracting them, and developing alternative modes of living. These goals were achieved by the evolution of the members of this family as they were exposed to a variety of therapeutic techniques in the unusual circle of friends cited in the Preface.

The techniques used were not part of an organized or prescribed treatment program, but instead represented an individual search for self-understanding and self-fulfillment on the part of the people involved. There was a general movement in the group of friends toward experiencing feelings and an implicit morality that avoided behaviors that were hurtful and detrimental to each other's sense of well-being. The tendency toward kindness, generosity, and respect for individual rights proved to be a fundamental principle of mental hygiene: These attitudes and pursuits were conducive to good mental health and increased self-esteem.

The remedial procedures started out as general trends but were later developed into refined and responsible therapeutic techniques. They mitigated against social isolation and the use of addictive substances and routine habit patterns that cut off feelings. They supported honesty, integrity, increased sociability, and movement toward better object relations and goal-directed vocational pursuits. People were encouraged to take the emotional risks necessary for self-actualization.

As members of this friendship circle, the authors were able to observe the effects that explorative procedures and corrective suggestions had on members of this family. In considering the progress achieved by each member as well as the limitations that still exist, readers may find it valuable to understand the primary experiential elements involved. These included: (a) personal talks, seminars, and marathons; (b) exploration of feeling release therapy; (c) dissolution of a fantasy bond; (d) development and exploration of preliminary voice therapy techniques; and later (e) the use of voice therapy theory and methodology in a group format with couples and parents.*

The conditions under which these procedures were developed were part of an unusual and comprehensive approach to problems in relationships. Many of the procedures described below have been developed into specialized techniques that are available in psychotherapeutic treatment programs.

EXTENDED TALKS AND MARATHONS

Background

Prior to the group developments described in the Preface, our families, professional associates, and friends socialized extensively and discussed ideas in the fields of philosophy and psychology. In October 1972, the same people became interested in meeting for an extended period of time away from the city. During these weekend gatherings, they were able to break through many defenses and reach their deepest feelings. Encouraging each other to role-play parents and other family members, they released powerful feelings that at times approached a primal level of expression. They gained

---

*The techniques that evolved functioned as a pilot study to determine hypotheses that could later be tested in more formal therapeutic settings. See Part III, this volume, Countering the Inner Voice: Methods and Theory for a description of these therapeutic techniques. The techniques and fundamental ideology have been described in professional journals and books (e.g., The Fantasy Bond, Voice Therapy, Psychological Defenses in Everyday Life, Compassionate Child-Rearing, Combating Destructive Thought Processes, and Suicide and the Inner Voice), and 38 videos used in training mental health professionals.

considerable insight about how painful experiences from childhood influenced their present-day actions and relationships.

Frank and Janet were among the participants in the extended discussions. Janet, who attended one of the first weekend marathons, reported feeling separate and distinct as a person. She was gratified by the fact that others acknowledged her as a woman and found her intelligence and vitality appealing. She was more aware of her own sexual identity than she had been for a long time. As the weekend went on, Janet became closer to her feelings and developed compassion for herself as a child growing up. She also understood and empathized with painful experiences that other people disclosed.

> Late Friday evening, after we had been talking for several hours, one of the participants, who was somewhat withdrawn, revealed that he was deeply embarrassed by his apparent lack of feeling. He asked a friend, who was bothered by his lack of response, to play the role of his stepmother, who had accused him of being cold and unfeeling. During the confrontation, other people expressed similar emotions toward him, and soon this man, who couldn't remember ever crying before, broke down and sobbed deeply.
>
> Afterward he said that at first he had thought the sounds of sobbing were coming from someone else. I was deeply touched to see this man, who said he had always been removed from his emotions, feel so much for himself and other people. I had a lot of feelings for myself, too. I realized that, like this man, I had cut off my feelings as a child. I was painfully aware of how much I had lived on an intellectual level since then, trying to protect myself.

In a meeting that Frank attended, he participated in an exercise where each person revealed the one thing that they felt most ashamed of. As Frank listened to other men speak openly about their sexual fantasies, their fears of sexual inadequacy, and their guilt about sex, he began to feel a sense of relief from the guilt he had experienced about masturbation and the hatred he felt toward himself for being a sexual person:

> Before the meeting that night, I had often thought that life would be so much simpler without sex. Like if I had no urgent sex drive, things with Janet would have been all right, life would be easy, there would be no guilt, no remorse about infidelity, no arguments, no need to get drunk to get rid of the guilt.
>
> But in listening to the other men talk, I slowly began to realize that sex was natural. I know that sounds obvious and I would have said that I believed intellectually that sex was natural, but on a deep level, I felt tremendous guilt and shame about being a sexual person, having sexual drives. There were a couple of men there who I admired for their strength, their warmth, and their acceptance of themselves and their sexual feelings. I noticed they weren't at all secretive about feelings I had always kept hidden. These men talked about sexuality and

women in a way that was very different from the way the guys in the Air Force had talked, in that macho style, bragging, making sex seem dirty and secret. A distinction was formed in my mind between clean, natural sexual feelings and guilty, dirty, nasty views of sexuality.

This weekend was the beginning for me of having a whole new perspective on sexuality and relationships with women. I no longer felt inward and secretive about my sexuality. The way both men and women spoke about sex challenged my old conception of sex as being something sinful, which had made me feel isolated and removed from other people. I no longer needed to drink and go to bars to try to relieve my guilty feelings. As time went by, I developed an entirely different view of myself as a man, which really has changed my life for the better.

Both Frank and Janet reported that the meetings were meaningful to them in that they felt closer to themselves and other people and were able to see their lives with unusual clarity. They said they were inspired by people expressing themselves personally and honestly and being so accepting toward one another. They noticed positive changes in the facial expressions of their fellow participants and felt more relaxed and alive themselves. Each person came to participate in the meetings independently and separately, not as one half of a couple. Frank and Janet flourished in the new surroundings because, as Janet noted above, each was treated as an individual. It became obvious to them that, in contrast to these weekends, they generally lived their day-to-day lives in a more emotionally deadened state, cut off to a considerable extent from their feelings. It was apparent that the new situation seriously challenged Frank and Janet's inward behavior patterns and improved their relationships.

The experiences of these weekends gave Frank, Janet, and the other participants a sample of the kind of life they wanted to live. They had heard reports of other encounter groups (then in vogue), where people had achieved a heightened sense of self-awareness and feelings of compassion that had eventually dissipated. In contrast, our friends and colleagues valued the closeness and camaraderie of the shared weekends and wondered how these elements could be incorporated into their everyday lives so that they would have a lasting effect. In an effort to maintain this enriched way of being, they began to change their habitual modes of living. Motivated by their experiences in the extended talks, they gradually succeeded in creating a lifestyle that brought the warmth and aliveness of those weekends into their everyday lives.

The clinical psychologists who were involved in these weekend encounters were personally gratified and intellectually stimulated because the meetings expanded their insights into their therapeutic practices. They were enlightened and fascinated by the theoretical discussions. My quest was directed toward understanding resistance in psychotherapy. The encounter groups and seminars provided ideal conditions to investigate the major factors underlying people's fundamental resistance to change.

EXPLORATION IN FEELING RELEASE THERAPY

As noted, in the marathons, participants began to have emotional reactions that were primal in nature, that is, deep expressions of intense childhood trauma. In 1973, we investigated methodologies that might help people who had reached points of resistance. One approach involved feeling release therapy. While lying face up on a mat, participants learned to breathe deeply and to allow sounds to escape as they exhaled. They were also encouraged to say or blurt out any thoughts that came to mind while using this breathing technique. As a result, they were able to revive deeply repressed feelings.[1] Following the release of intense feelings, they interpreted their primal experiences, analyzed the content of their thoughts, feelings, and memories, and gained insight into the dynamics underlying the pain, rage, and sadness they were expressing.

During the 3 years that we studied this procedure, Janet and Frank underwent a number of basic changes in their attitudes and feelings toward self and others. They became softer and more emotionally responsive; both were closer to their feelings, especially feelings of sadness, than they had ever been. Experiencing their sadness also allowed them to feel more joy in their lives. Through the release of feeling, they were able to more clearly understand their childhood situations and observe how they were repeating them in their present-day lives.

In one of his first primal sessions, Frank became aware that his sense of freedom and movement had been severely restricted by his mother. He relived a scene from his early childhood (a scene that occurred repeatedly in his dreams), in which in the midst of exploring his world, he was suddenly snatched up by his mother, thrown in his crib, and imprisoned there for what seemed to him to be an eternity. He realized that he had essentially repeated this pattern, that of constricting his own freedom, throughout his life.

Janet discovered that her deep feelings of shame originated in her mother's severe toilet training regimen. She understood that this had become a deep part of her self-concept and played a negative role in her sexual life. In addition, during a series of sessions, she recalled inappropriate sexual behavior on her father's part that had started when she was a toddler and had developed into more serious acts of molestation following her parents' divorce. Although she had previously been involved in psychoanalytically oriented therapy and had recognized ambivalent feelings toward her father, she had not remembered the sexual involvement with him before the feeling release therapy.

As a result of these sessions, Janet understood why she had always blamed herself for her father's leaving. At the same time, she uncovered an important source of her fear of her mother and subsequently other women: The secret activities with her father led her to fear her mother's competitive feelings and possible retaliation. Janet's guilty feelings about sex were also related to these incidents. She experienced particular guilt in remembering the pleasure she felt from her father's sexualized attention.

The couple's son, Don, also participated in the feeling release therapy. In a journal entry, he described a childhood experience he relived during a session, and discussed his insights:

> In the session, I was aware first of the slamming of a screen door. The sound sent a chill down my back. I was in my room, and my father had just come home from work. Then I heard a sort of low level buzzing as my mother quickly told my father about her day. This was followed by a moment of silence, then my father's voice: "Goddamn that kid!" followed by "That simple little shit, where is that son of a bitch?"
>
> Then my door slammed open. My father was standing in the doorway, biting down hard on his lower lip, clenching and unclenching his hands until they froze into the fist position and then he moved toward me. He swung and then caught himself in the middle, like a runner who just realized he had started a race seconds before the gun had gone off. He stopped his swing in mid-flight, for just a second, as if he were wrestling with himself to gain control over a rage on the loose. He soon lost this internal battle and the beating began.
>
> In the session, I had an image of my mother standing quietly in the hall looking into the room. At first with a kind of "I warned you what was going to happen, you should have listened." But as the beating continued, that look soon faded and she began pleading with him to not hit me anymore. "He's only a child, don't hit him anymore, leave him alone—damn it!" In the middle of the yelling, crying, pleading, I was looking at her, wondering why the hell she wanted this to stop when she was the one who had pushed the button in this bizarre chain of events. I felt a huge amount of anger and also a feeling of complete helplessness during this part of the session.
>
> After the session where I reexperienced the pain of that beating and felt how much I had wanted to escape, I thought again about my father—and my grandfather. My father had wanted to escape, to get far away from everything that resembled small towns, their churches, their talk, their limited opportunities, their prejudices, but most of all, away from my grandfather.

Frank, Janet, and their children, like the other members of the group, became far less defensive after they experienced the deep feeling sessions. Previously, Frank had reacted with belligerence to negative feedback. From these sessions, he learned to listen and consider the reality and unreality of what was said, which had a profoundly positive effect on his personal relationships. All the participants became aware of the pain and sadness they had been suppressing in their everyday lives. Don became more invested in his life and began to take steps to overcome his passivity and procrastination at work; he felt more at ease in social situations, trusted people more, and began to develop close friendships. The most significant changes in Frank and Janet were the openness they developed in revealing thoughts and feelings they had always kept hidden and the compassion they began to feel and express. Feeling release therapy, like the personal discussions and marathons, expanded each person's ability to relate to and trust other people.

During this study, much time was spent evaluating the results, recording and transcribing the material from individual and group sessions, and appraising people's progress. We concluded that feeling release therapy represented a significant advance over free association as a technique for recovering memories and experiences from one's childhood. The participants interpreted their own material and integrated it without assistance or intervention from the facilitator. An extra bonus for me was the fact that the uncovered material validated many of my theoretical formulations regarding the neurotic process.

DISSOLUTION OF A FANTASY BOND

Relationships that are based on a fantasy bond wherein people choose to remain together because of feelings of desperation and fusion become extremely debilitating to the individuals involved. Although Frank and Janet grew and developed personally and in their relationships with others, that is, with friends and children, they maintained destructive styles of relating with each other. Eventually, after 23 years of marriage, they separated and divorced. Although painful, the divorce had an overall positive effect on both individuals. It allowed them to achieve perspective on the inward, self-protective behaviors and attitudes each had brought to the relationship, behavior patterns that gradually eroded the original feelings of love between them. Exposing destructive elements of the fantasy bond and feelings of merged identity that had existed in the family opened up the possibility for individuation and genuine relating on a more personal basis for all the family members.

After the divorce, Frank and Janet and their children continued to participate in the friendship circle and in the seminars on couples and family relationships that followed. They revealed details of their defensive styles of relating and the specific means by which they had reinforced each other's inward and isolated way of life. Janet recalls her initial reaction to the separation and the insights she subsequently gained as a result of her participation in the group discussions:

> Immediately after the divorce, I felt free for the first time being separated from Frank's critical attitudes that reminded me so much of my childhood. My good feelings were short-lived. Later, I became very anxious. I noticed that I was constantly questioning and criticizing myself in ways more vicious than Frank or my mother had ever done. I had intermittent thoughts that I was ugly, unlovable, and dirty, and that I didn't belong anywhere. It was difficult to stop these attacks on myself. I couldn't even identify what was making me feel so bad. Since Frank no longer criticized me, I became aware of my own critical attitudes toward myself that I had internalized since childhood.
>
> I realized that in some way Frank had been essential to me, in a destructive way, but still necessary. I had used him as an externalized critical parent. Until we separated, I never had to face how much I hated myself, how worthless and unlovable I felt, or how fearful I was of really living on my own without a "concerned" protector.

After several months, as Janet developed more understanding of the sources of her fear and self-hatred, she began to enjoy her freedom. Summing up her feelings at that time, she said:

> To be tied by a fantasy to Frank was a terrible thing for me as well as for him. I realized how many years of my marriage I had spent being depressed. After separating from Frank, I felt more alive and spontaneous than I had in years. I also recognized that I had loving feelings toward Frank and began to understand my ambivalence. I realized that idealizing him and disapproving of him were both inappropriate responses.

As their fantasy bond broke down, Janet, who had idealized Frank and seen him as more intelligent and competent than she was, began to perceive herself as an equal. Frank, who had lived for years with Janet's depression, felt free of this constraint and looked forward to living a life unencumbered.

> At first right after we separated, I had a stark feeling of fear, "Who the hell am I?" I felt disoriented, strange. On the other hand, it was such a relief to be away from the constant arguments that had developed as our relationship unraveled. The worst time before the final separation was when we sold the house in Malibu and moved into the marina. The fights were terrible and humiliating. One night, it got so bad that Janet ran crying from the apartment. Later, a guy knocked on our door asking if she was all right. You can imagine how relieved I was to have a reprieve from this sort of situation. I had time to think about myself, to find out who I really was.

Frank and Janet also learned, by listening to the stories of other couples, how compulsive routines (that had given them comfort, but that were based on their fears of being separate and individuated) had detracted from the happiness they could have achieved together. They developed an understanding of how to avoid acting out destructive forms of relating that inevitably create distance and alienation in relationships.

The intellectual discussions among the couples and families in the group enabled Don, Sarah, and Beverly to develop a more realistic view of their parents—their strengths and their weaknesses. All opinions were encouraged and respected, including those of children. No one interfered when the young people described their perceptions of their parents and other adults, whether positive or negative. There were also opportunities for them to observe their parents interacting with other people in a variety of situations. The formal ties and roles of "mom" and "dad" were gradually discarded, and they related to their parents more as friends, with mutual respect for one another's individuality. The formalities or form of the family declined, while the substance of the friendships and each person's feelings for the other increased. In one meeting, Don was aware that he was viewing his father with more objectivity and with real feeling:

> My father talked tonight. I was one of many, in a room of friends, as he told the story of his business failure. He spoke in a monotone, like the sound of a distant helicopter, numbed from the reality of the story he told. As if it wasn't him it had happened to. Like he was reiterating a story he had read in the paper. I noted the pain in his friends, in my friends' faces, as his story unfolded. People who cared more about the content of what he was saying than he was feeling that evening.
>
> As he spoke, I leafed through my emerging memories. I understood the waves of angry procrastination I have always had to endure whenever I reach the point, in everything I do, where the end of a project is within a simple, uncomplicated, and nondramatic grasp. I had an image of myself as a child, with a strange compassion I don't remember having for myself before. Not like I suddenly was "getting in touch with the lost child within me" or any bullshit like that. Just that I was aware, tonight, of the pure power and energy fueling a young boy's desire to love his father. How much I wanted to admire him, how much I wanted to have him be someone I would like to grow up to be. At that moment, I had a feeling of painful empathy and love for him.
>
> I was aware of the reasons. I knew, from both my observations and stories my father told, that his father viewed him, used him, in the capacity of free slave labor. For the most part, that was the extent of their relationship.
>
> This night, hard realities settled in around me. I looked at him across the room. Disheveled and tired. Like a machine because he had no sense or feeling that he was broken. Like a machine because that is how he treated his body and mind, as if it were a detached and poorly maintained vehicle that could always be replaced.

DEVELOPMENT AND EXPLORATION OF PRELIMINARY VOICE THERAPY TECHNIQUES

The social milieu provided the setting for early investigations into voice therapy (VT) procedures. Beginning in 1977, my associates and I focused on the exploration of self-destructive thought processes. We identified negative attitudes and behaviors that limited people and sabotaged their successes. As these investigations proceeded, the participants came to recognize that they had internalized their parents' negative as well as positive attitudes toward them. They learned that these angry, hostile attitudes lived on within them in the form of a systematized point of view, punitive toward self and distrustful of others. Our studies showed that people also identified with and imitated their parents' defended ways of living, addictive tendencies, and limitations. Destructive thought processes or internalized "voices" generally influenced behavior patterns that represented their parents' explicit and implicit prescriptions for living.

In group meetings, individuals learned how to identify the contents of this hostile point of view by saying their self-critical thoughts in the second person: "You are worthless; you are unlovable," as though someone else were talking to them. They were shocked at first at the intensity of the anger and sadness they experienced when verbalizing these thoughts.[2] Most identified these destructive cognitions as originating from interactions within the family that had been particularly painful or anxiety-provoking. Their understanding of the voice process motivated them to alter behaviors influenced by this inimical way of thinking.

Voice therapy gave Frank and Janet insight into forces within themselves that had handicapped their development in the past and that now prevented them from fully embracing the kind of life they had always wanted. It also gave them a perspective on their parents' point of view toward them, toward their relationships, and toward life in general. Janet uncovered voices representing her mother's view of men; essentially, that men were mean, harsh, driven by sexual desires, yet stupid and inferior to women. She traced the source of her own distrust of men to her mother's views and was aware that they were reinforced by her father's early abandonment. In voice therapy sessions, she revealed her distrust and paranoia regarding Frank and other men:

> Don't be such a fool! Don't trust him. He's eventually going to leave you anyway. He's just like all other men; they're such idiots. They don't give a damn about feelings, all they're interested in is working all the time, making money.

After identifying the content of these voices, Janet was able to relate in a more friendly manner to men and develop closer relationships.

Frank became aware of voices that accused him of not being a real man, and at the same time that urged him to work hard to prove his manhood:

> You're such a wimp, such a sissy, a real mama's boy. You're never going to amount to anything; you're a lazy good-for-nothing. The least you can do is learn how to work. That's the least you can do, you stupid shit! You've got to work hard. You'd better get to work. Look, you've got to provide for your family. If you don't work hard, earn a good living, you're nothing, a nobody, not a real man.

Both Frank and Janet gradually modified these types of negative thoughts and attitudes toward themselves and each other that were part of the provisional identity that was formed in their families of origin. They recognized that prior to their involvement in voice therapy, they had accepted, without question, these core beliefs. It was interesting that they experienced corresponding voices. For example, Janet realized she had been stubbornly invested in thinking that she was unlovable, unfeminine, basically different from other women, while Frank held on to views of himself as not being masculine, different from other men.

The couple's adult children took part in the voice therapy exercises as well and uncovered thoughts influencing specific inward habit patterns that were limiting factors in their lives. Fears of competitive feelings and retaliation from rivals, based on the emotionally incestuous entanglements in the family, had a debilitating effect on each person's adjustment. For example, as a child Don had been close to his mother. His father had seen him as a rival and on an unconscious level, wished to dispose of him. This unconscious wish was manifested in an incident when Don was 8 years old.

One evening at the dinner table, Don was telling jokes and receiving positive attention from his sisters and mother. As the joking and laughter continued, his father grew more and more quiet. Suddenly, he flew into a rage, accused Don of being a troublemaker, and threw the boy out of the house. As a result of these types of traumatic incidents, Don identified with his father's rage and developed hostile angry voices, the most extreme of which told him to do away with himself. At the same time, a fear of men was formed, accompanied by voices that warned him that men were dangerous and threatening. Don experienced anxiety whenever he began to compete for women or achieve success in business. At these times, he tended to retreat to a more inward, passive posture, which, in turn interfered with the pursuit of his personal and vocational goals.

As his business became more successful and expanded, Don became aware that he had surpassed his father, who had recently suffered financial setbacks because of poor business decisions. This awareness precipitated a severe state of anxiety in Don that took the form of paranoid thoughts toward other men. At one point, he began to experience occasional suicidal thoughts reminiscent of those that had tormented him prior to his suicide attempt when he was in his late teens.* In a voice therapy session, Don explored his current situation, examined the source of his fear of men, and went on to verbalize the malicious thoughts he directed against himself:

> I'm afraid of standing out. I actually feel paranoid toward other men in my life like I'm going to get in trouble by continuing to be successful, which is insane, if I really just say it out loud. But it's a gut level fear. For years after that incident where my father made me leave the house, there was all this talk of military school. "Let's try to find a military school. I can't do anything with this kid."
>
> In terms of the voices that I have today, they are the feelings a rival would have toward someone else, like:
>
> What are you doing here? You're not supposed to be here (loud voice). Get out of here. Go find a gun. Pull the trigger. Blow your head off! Just blow your head off! [intense rage, yelling loudly] Smash your head. Smash it! Blast your brains! I don't want a piece left of you. I want you to die horribly. I want you to die in pain, pain, pain! Blow your head off! [cries deeply]

Later in the session, Don connected the contents of the sadistic voice he incorporated from his father with painful incidents in his childhood.

> It's really the way that I felt my father was. I feel like the only way I could have survived there was just to stay out of his way. I had to blend into the carpet. I couldn't stand out. I had to be invisible in the family. I know that the intensity of this voice has to do with my trying to be different in my life in a way that I've never been before in terms of being successful.
>
> I realize that there are reasons why I haven't competed in my everyday life. These fears were projected onto every other man in my adult life and onto every situation, so I'd have a gut level feeling of not being able to compete. I'd feel like men were going to kill me. Right now I don't have that feeling. Instead I feel like it has to do with the past. It has nothing to do with my real life now.

Following this session, Don experienced a substantial improvement in his friendships with both men and women and in his business, based on a diminution in his fears of being competitive. In his own sessions, Don's father, Frank, became aware that he had been subjected to the same kinds of threats by his father, and that he had tried, but usually failed, to suppress his rage and control the impulse to act out the same pattern in relation to Don.

In analyzing findings from applying the procedures of voice therapy, we found that no other techniques bear more directly on understanding

---

*Portions of this session are taken from an article titled "A New Perspective on the Oedipal Complex: A Voice Therapy Session," by R. W. Firestone, 1994, *Psychotherapy, 31*, pp. 346–349. Used with permission.

the inward process. From this point on, insights gained from the application of this method served as a guideline to combat inwardness and the limitations people experience in developing intimate relationships.

USE OF VOICE THERAPY THEORY AND METHODOLOGY IN A GROUP FORMAT

Couples Groups*

In seminars about couple relationships, participants progressively disrupted inward defensive patterns that were interfering with closeness and feelings of intimacy.† In one group, Don examined the reasons he had difficulty maintaining a long-lasting relationship with a woman:

> If I meet a woman for the first time and she's attractive, I'll project my voice onto her. I believe that she's thinking that I'm a little boy, that I'm very nonsexual, that I'm definitely not a man, that women think it's fun to joke around with me, but I'm not to be taken seriously.
>
> I know it's very painful for me to shake this unreal view of myself and understand that it's what I'm really thinking about myself, not what the woman is thinking. Often I think that women don't like me and I'll even act in a way to draw out that kind of response.

Don realized that this tendency to put himself down in relation to women was directly linked to his inclination to idealize them. In exploring this subject further, he became aware that his need to seek women's approval was based on feelings of emptiness and desperation that persisted from childhood.‡

> I feel like I turn a relationship into something to satisfy an emptiness in me and in that the person that I'm involved with is no longer even the person. It's just like they're someone else that I've been able to plug into that slot from relationship to relationship my entire life. And that's very distressing to me because it's highly impersonal.
>
> So I feel wary of getting into a relationship again because right now I'm at the place where I'm beginning to let myself have my life and I'm enjoying myself and I relish my times in all my interactions with everybody and that feels really good to me. That is what I give up when I get into a relationship. Those things no longer have any value at all to me. I just care about having this attachment to this person and that's the only thing that means anything to me.

---

*Statements in this section were excerpted from the video documentary *Voices in Sex* (Parr, 1990b).
†See the Methodology section in chapters 12, 13, and 14, this volume for a description of procedures and group processes in couples' seminars using voice therapy techniques.
‡Don's statements are excerpted from the video documentary *Fear of Intimacy: An Examination of Withholding Behavior Patterns* by G. Parr (1997b).

Basically I withhold my life from myself and in reality I think that's what the person really was drawn to originally, my being an outgoing person, being a free person, doing whatever I do naturally, and those are the things I shut down on. I take those back; I hold them inside myself and I just attach myself to this woman and it's totally meaningless. It doesn't mean anything anymore.

By recognizing the destructive attitudes he held toward himself and the desperation he felt toward women, Don had insight into his intolerance of giving and accepting love (a fundamental aspect of inwardness). He gradually learned to free himself of the self-defeating, restrictive way of thinking that had always caused him distress in the early phases of a relationship. After his experience in these talks, he felt he had the courage to risk being vulnerable in a new relationship.

In the couples' groups, participants could see that the projections they imposed on their mates caused them considerable distress. They realized that they tended to provoke responses in the other that justified these false perceptions. Individuals learned to give away their negative thought processes to each other and understood that a good deal of their pain was based not on actual events, but on how they perceived these events.

Parenting Groups

Since 1978, 24 children were born into this friendship circle. Because their parents had learned much about the kinds of interactions that had hurt them in their formative years, they wanted to avoid treating their children in a similar manner. They began to meet on a regular basis to apply their new understanding to the problems they encountered in child-rearing.

The primary goals of the parenting groups were (a) to increase parents' awareness of the damage they had sustained in their upbringing and its effects on present-day relationships with their offspring, and (b) to help parents develop a sense of compassion toward themselves and their children. The participants used insight to modify attitudes and behaviors as in traditional psychotherapy. In addition, they continually shifted from a retrospective exploration of themselves as children and the sources of their limitations and negative attitudes toward self, to an investigation of themselves as parents and ways in which they extended these hostile views of themselves to their offspring. In other words, two processes were occurring concomitantly as parents examined the links between their past and present on a deep feeling level. This dual focus helped the participants have more compassion for themselves by developing feeling for what had happened to them as children. We found that regaining feeling for themselves was perhaps the key element that enabled parents to alter their child-rearing practices in a positive direction.

In the parenting groups, the participants (26 men and 23 women, including Sarah, who had married and had two sons) became increasingly willing to admit their underlying attitudes toward themselves and the ambivalent feelings they experienced in relation to their children. Many parents who identified negative thoughts about themselves became cognizant of how they projected these negative attitudes onto their children and went on to reveal the origins of their own self-deprecating attitudes.

In some cases, participants at first failed to recognize the significance of painful childhood experiences and even looked back on them matter-of-factly or with humor. On further examination, however, they found that the incidents had left deep psychological scars. These parents were gradually able to reexperience the depth of feeling associated with the original trauma and to gain perspective. They became more sensitive to the painful emotions expressed by others in the group and developed greater empathy for their children.

The procedures of identifying negative thoughts toward oneself and toward one's children were found to be effective when applied in the parents' group setting. The methods that were used in the specialized parenting groups have been incorporated into a systematic program for other parents as a form of preventative mental health.[3]

GENERAL EFFECTS OF THE SOCIAL MILIEU

The family's involvement in the circle of friends allowed Frank and Janet and their children to intermingle with a wide variety of interesting people, to increase their knowledge of self, and to develop a new, more constructive point of view not only about themselves but also about their children. As Don commented,

> I think the biggest thing that was different from living in my family was that my friends here saw me as different from how I was seen there. My family existed in a careful vacuum where everyone had a specific role. Any action you might do which did not match the checklist of what your role in the family was, simply was not seen. It was not even there. My role was the troublesome son who should not be there, the son who was the root of all the family's problems, the son who would amount to no good.
>
> When I left home at 19, I first surrounded myself with friends who, in some form or another, provided me with the same boundaries and roles I had in my family. There were subtle digging jokes among these friends that were pretty nasty, now that I think about it.
>
> Then I met my friends here, many people, from all walks of life. It is important to mention that these were people that I would not have picked to be close to. Not because they were unlikable, just that they were all from extremely different walks of life and varied greatly from

the type of friends I was used to making. We were all different, but we had one strong common trait: We were dissatisfied with our lives and wanted to improve them.

Living and working with people I would not have necessarily picked is one of the most important aspects of my adult life. I think it shattered the vacuum of my family and in many ways ensured that I would not be able to surround myself with friends who duplicated my family. In this, I learned that people should be somewhat suspect of their motivation for seeking the kind of friends and mates that they want around them in their life. I was suddenly with people who I had a clean slate with, people who liked me for things that I didn't even know I had in me, and this was a rich feeling.

Living in an open atmosphere and extended family orientation in which people were supportive and friendly helped family members develop beyond certain rigid boundaries they had imposed on themselves and each other. In the group discussions, the shared wisdom and knowledge about couple and family relationships helped Frank and Janet challenge inward patterns, modify their addictive attachments and habit patterns, and become more outward and congenial. In recognizing the voices that were limiting them and by counteracting these destructive thoughts, they moved closer to their personal and vocational goals and improved the quality of their relationships.

The high level of social interaction between people militated against isolation, a key element in an inward, self-destructive lifestyle. In Frank and Janet's case, isolation was a particularly stubborn habit pattern. The couple as well as their children participated in the seminars and discussion groups where people openly shared their knowledge and insights, revealed important aspects of their personal lives, and most important, where expression of feelings was encouraged. This process broke into this couple's tendency to be impersonal in their communications and style of relating.

The adventurous lifestyle and shared projects provided opportunities for family members to be generous and allowed them to contribute their skills to various projects, which had the effect of counteracting their tendencies to be withholding. For example, Frank taught the teenage crew the sailing, navigational, and engineering skills he had acquired over the years. Don comments on the contrast between his present-day situation and the self-centered existence and withholding patterns that he once considered normal:

In our family, nobody ever did anything nice for anyone else. All the kids had separate rooms, with our own TV. Our parents had their separate room and everybody was impersonal. There was no courtesy, no consideration, no involvement, there was no real friendship. But then when I started being friends with people here, things were very different. Like someone might say to me, for example, "I'd like to help you with that." Or "I thought about you today, I bought you this because I remembered you said you liked it." There was this kind of knowing who you were—things that seem very simple here, and such a part of my life now, had been totally missing in my family.

CONCLUSION

In chapter 6, we explained how personal defenses formed early in life interfered with Frank and Janet's capacity to relate closely and were the primary factors in the dissolution of their marriage. In this chapter, we demonstrated how they were able to change many of their inward patterns, such that each family member is respectful of the other and sensitive to their feelings. In reviewing their progress, we noted that the majority of their inward characteristics were altered in a favorable direction. A lingering problem for the members of this family is their habit of working compulsively in a manner that detracts from their happiness and fulfillment in life. Despite this ongoing problem, their overall adjustment has improved in most areas, and they have found much more satisfaction in their personal relationships with each other and other friends.

We derived much wisdom from the longitudinal study that led to an understanding of the primary difficulties in relationships, and we developed specialized techniques to cope with problems of intimacy. In particular, the dynamics of the sensitive social environment challenged tendencies toward distancing behaviors and isolation. In addition, feeling release therapy helped people get closer to their feelings and become less defensive. Understanding the fantasy bond helped them relate more honestly, maintain a sense of self, increase their independence, and positively affect their sexual lives. Voice therapy helped them understand the core issues in relationship problems and was particularly effective in understanding self-attacks and the ideation behind addictive and withholding behavior. The couples groups helped them recognize and retract the projections of their self-attacks onto their partners and led to more compassion and empathy. The longitudinal study yielded many hypotheses that appear to apply well beyond this limited reference population; however, these must be tested through empirical research. We hope that other researchers will investigate the concepts and hypotheses developed here.

In our own research efforts, we have been able to establish a significant correlation between destructive thought processes and suicide attempts with over 1,300 subjects (inpatients and outpatients). We are also involved in a study to investigate the hypothesis that voices toward others are correlated with violent behavior. Using the same methodology employed in the suicide research in a new study of prison inmates, we found that subjects with a potential for violent behavior could be distinguished from nonviolent subjects. Currently we are studying the efficacy of voice therapy in treating depressed patients and developing procedures to better understand and predict trends and outcomes in personal relationships.

In concluding this section, it is important to reiterate that defenses formed in childhood are temporarily adaptive in that they cut off anxiety, pain, and the fear of disintegration, yet they create subsequent problems. The defense system eventually becomes the enemy and is particularly destructive in personal relationships. These patterns can be altered using techniques that mitigate against isolated inward behaviors, bring people closer to their feelings, and increase their awareness of the destructive forces within them. By modifying these destructive patterns and taking the necessary risks involved in maturation, people can move toward increased closeness and caring in personal relationships.

Follow-up note: In the past year, Janet and Frank have become involved again. Their interactions are very different than they were during their marriage. Recently Frank described how he felt with Janet: "The kind of relationship we have now is what I always wished for during our marriage. There is none of the drama or conflict that we used to get embroiled in. Things are really simple between us; we don't have a stake in holding onto old ways of thinking or reacting to each other. We have conversations now that are interesting, the way they were when we were first friends. I think that what we've learned over the years has had a huge effect on the way we get along today."

ENDNOTES

[1]The primary goal of feeling release therapy is to put individuals in touch with painful feelings from the past that they found too threatening to allow themselves to experience fully as children. The sessions consisted of daily, five-times-a-week, 1 1/2-hour sessions that took place over a period of 5 weeks, followed by several months of once- or twice-a-week sessions. The large majority of people who went through this therapy were able to learn the technique of breathing deeply and letting out sounds within a few sessions. Some began sobbing almost immediately, while others moaned loudly or shouted angrily, for example: "Leave me alone," "Get away," "I don't need you." Some cried loudly for help: "Please hold me," "Don't go away," "Look at me." People's physical movements and verbal expressions generally became much freer as therapy progressed. Almost every person seemed to be genuinely reliving, with intense emotional reactions, events and feelings from the past. They connected present-day limitations and emotional distress to painful incidents in childhood.

[2]The therapeutic techniques to which the concept of the voice has been applied is a cognitive–affective–behavioral therapy, known as voice therapy (VT). Its purpose is to separate and bring into the open elements of the personality that are antithetical to the self as a result of the internalization of negative parental attitudes and damaging childhood experiences (Firestone, 1997a).

[3]The *Compassionate Child-Rearing Parent Education Program* incorporates videotapes of the parenting groups into a comprehensive 6-week course for parents. Preliminary evaluations using Rohner's (1991) Mother PARQ and Adult PAQ instruments show improvement in parents' self-esteem and positive attitudes toward their offspring following the classes.

8

THE FANTASY BOND IN COUPLE RELATIONSHIPS

The universal psychopathology is defined as the attempt to create in real life by behavior or communication the illusion of fusion.

Hellmuth Kaiser (cited in Fierman, 1965, pp. 208–209)

In the snug little world where both Johan and I have lived so unconsciously, taking everything for granted, there is a cruelty and brutality implied which frightens me more and more when I think back on it. Outward security demands a high price: the acceptance of a continuous destruction of the personality.

Ingmar Bergman (1973/1983, p. 123)

Most people have a fear of intimacy and at the same time are terrified of being alone. Their solution is to form a fantasy bond—an illusion of connection and closeness—that allows them to maintain emotional distance while assuaging loneliness and, in the process, meeting society's expectations regarding marriage and family. Destructive fantasy bonds exist in a large majority of couple relationships and are apparent in most families. The process of forming a fantasy bond greatly reduces the possibility of achieving a successful personal relationship.

As noted in chapter 2, the self-parenting process or fantasy bond is manifested internally in fantasy and externally through the use of others in the interpersonal environment.[1] In general, people tend to nurture and punish themselves in much the same manner as they were nurtured and punished as children. They use new relationships and their partners to externalize their particular mode of self-parenting. The formation of a fantasy bond leads to a sense of pseudoindependence and restricts the flow of both giving and receiving love. By introjecting the negative, hostile, or defensive parental attitudes and at the same time retaining painful "primal" feelings formed during the early developmental phases, an individual develops the fantasy of being at once the good, strong parent and the weak, bad child. When a fantasy bond develops in an adult relationship, aspects of self-parenting are externalized, and individuals may alternately act out either the grandiose, critical, punitive parent or the helpless, worthless child with their mates.

Over the past decades, my concept of the fantasy bond has become integrated to some extent into the mainstream of psychological thought.[2] A popular version of the concept has become familiar to the general public as the term *codependency*. In earlier writings (Firestone, 1985, 1987a, 1990b, 1997a), I cited the work of other theorists, beginning with Hellmuth Kaiser (Fierman, 1965) and including Karpel (1976) and Wexler and Steidl (1978). Kaiser's germinal idea that a delusion of fusion represents the "universal psychopathology" is analogous to my conceptualization of the fantasy bond as the primary defense mechanism in neurosis.

DEVELOPMENT OF THE FANTASY BOND IN A COUPLE RELATIONSHIP*

Men and women are most likely to become romantically involved at a stage in their lives in which they are breaking dependent emotional ties with their families and experiencing a sense of separateness and independence. As they reach out and risk more of themselves emotionally, they tend to attract others with their vitality and enthusiasm. In the first stages of the relationship, they tend to let down their defenses and to be open and vulnerable. Their positive emotions are intensified; the sun looks brighter and the grass greener; and they feel a heightened sense of joy and closeness.

Although this state of being in love is volatile and exciting, at the same time, it can be frightening. The fear of loss or abandonment as well as the poignant sadness often evoked by positive emotions may become difficult to tolerate, especially for those who have suffered from a lack of love in their early lives. At the point these individuals begin to feel anxious or frightened, they retreat from feeling close, gradually giving up the most valued aspects of their relationships, forming a fantasy bond just as they did in childhood.

This retreat from closeness and intimacy is an outgrowth of the adjustment the individual made in responding to the early environment. By the time they reach adulthood, most people have solidified their defenses and exist in a psychological equilibrium that they do not wish to disturb. Although they may be relatively congenial with more casual acquaintances, there is a deterioration in friendly and respectful feelings as a relationship becomes more meaningful and intimate, because the new love object now threatens to disrupt this psychological balance by penetrating their basic

---

*Portions of the material in this section are taken from *Combating Destructive Thought Processes: Voice Therapy and Separation Theory* by R. W. Firestone, 1997, Thousand Oaks, CA: Sage. Used with permission.

defenses. Conflict develops as the partners strive to maintain their defenses, while at the same time, they attempt to hold on to their initial feelings of closeness and affection. The two conditions tend to be mutually exclusive. Eventually, one or both partners usually choose to sacrifice friendship and love in order to preserve their respective defended states.

Early Symptoms

When two people first become romantically involved, there are generally feelings of genuine companionship as well as a strong sexual attraction between them. However, when the affection and friendship in the new relationship contrast sharply with the unhappiness and rejection of the past, the participants unwittingly attempt to eradicate the difference. One early symptom of deterioration is diminished frequency of eye contact between the partners. This is a sign of curtailed relating and indicates an increasingly impersonal mode of interaction. As the relationship deteriorates, a fantasy bond replaces the original loving feelings and behaviors. The couple's style of communication tends to become less honest, more duplicitous, and characterized by small talk, bickering, speaking for the other, interrupting, and talking as a unit. Both partners may begin to manipulate by playing on the other's guilt or provoking angry or parental responses. Self-doubts and self-critical thoughts are often projected onto the mate, leading each person to complain about the other.

As these methods of relating take a toll on the relationship, other symptoms of the fantasy bond become more apparent. Individuals who in the early phases of their relationship spent hours in conversation begin to lose interest in both talking and listening, and spontaneity and playfulness gradually disappear. Often the partners develop a routinized, mechanical style of lovemaking and experience a reduction in the level of sexual attraction. This decline is not the inevitable result of familiarity, as many people assume. It is due to deadening habit patterns, exaggerated dependency, negative projections, loss of independence, and a sense of obligation. As one or both partners in a bond begin to sacrifice their individuality to become one half of a couple, basic attraction to each other is jeopardized. In fact, people in a fantasy bond often experience themselves as an appendage of the other person, and the other as an appendage of them, a condition that causes their feelings of sexual attraction to wane. All of these have a distancing effect on the couple, and the partners come to rely on a fantasy of closeness and love that is no longer evident in their behavior toward each other.

As the fantasy bond develops and partners begin to withhold the desirable qualities in themselves that attracted the other, they tend to experience feelings of guilt and remorse. Consequently, both begin to act out of a sense of obligation and responsibility instead of a genuine desire to be together. In spite of the fact that there is less real affect or personal feeling in a fantasy bond, potential losses or threats to the imagined connection often evoke dramatic emotional reactions. This emotionality, which contains distortions based on the frustrations and pains of early childhood, is often mistaken for real caring about the relationship. As the process of deterioration continues, the couple's emotional responses become progressively less appropriate.

Symptoms of a fantasy bond often appear following a commitment that originates as an expression of the partners' genuine feelings toward each other. Partners may be refractory to the level of love being expressed at these times and react by creating a fantasy bond. The commitment may be to living together, to marriage, or to starting a family. Partners use these commitments as *guarantees* of continued love and security—external indications of a fantasy of connectedness. For those with a poor self-image and strong dependency needs, this sense of belonging to another person, of being loved "forever after," offers a reassurance that is difficult to resist. On the other hand, for mature individuals, a mutual commitment that expresses the desire to be associated with another person throughout life can remain an expression of deep feeling rather than become an attempt to find ultimate security (Firestone, 1985).

Form Versus Substance

Individuals who form destructive ties usually resist accepting the fact that they have lost much of their feeling for each other and have become alienated. They attempt to cover up this reality with a fantasy of enduring love, substituting form for the substance of the relationship. The conventional form of relating consists of the convenient habits and superficial conversation that many partners come to depend upon to maintain their fantasy of being in love. Everyday routines, customs, and role-determined behaviors provide the structure and form of the relationship. People's capacity for self-deception enables them to maintain an internal image of closeness and intimacy, while they act in ways that contrast with any recognizable definition of love. R. D. Laing (1961) described this phenomenon in the following: "Desire for confirmation from each is present in both, but each is caught between trust and mistrust, confidence and despair, and both settle for counterfeit acts of confirmation on the basis of pretence" (pp. 108–109).

A COUPLE

Ralph and Karen became involved at a juncture in their lives when both were open to the possibility of a new relationship. Ralph, 56, was divorced and seeking a partner, and Karen, 40, had recently separated from her husband. Initially, there was a strong sexual attraction between them, and as the months went by, their relationship became closer and more meaningful. In an interview, Ralph described the first year of the relationship:

> Ralph: When Karen first arrived here from Canada, we got involved. I knew she was interested in me, and I liked the fact that she was attracted to me. I liked her energy and enthusiasm and the fact that we enjoyed the same activities: boating, flying. But I realized that sometimes the way she talked bothered me. It didn't seem real.

Karen was born in Italy, immigrated to Canada, then to the United States, where she met Ralph. She was drawn to his honesty, strength, and forthright manner of communicating his thoughts and feelings. However, because of her own insecurity and low self-esteem, she found it difficult to believe that Ralph could be attracted to her.

> Karen: The most interesting part of my relationship with Ralph was the immediate attraction I felt toward him, a deep and immediate attraction. But then, when he asked me out, I didn't want to believe him. Right from the beginning, I didn't really believe that he wanted to be with me. I knew I was attracted to him, but I didn't trust that he wanted to be with me. I would tell myself, He doesn't really like you. You like him, but he doesn't like you as much. He's not the kind of person who would like you. He's from a different background to begin with.

The patterns of defense that each partner brought to their relationship had their sources in their early childhood experiences. Ralph grew up in a household dominated by a strict, perfectionistic father, a loner who was frugal and extremely distrustful of his wife and women in general. His mother was emotionally hungry and intrusive. He recalls: "The first thing I can remember is the focus of my mother—her constant criticism and disapproving eyes. I remember just being ignored by my sisters. So I was amazed to discover that the first woman I went out with was genuinely interested in me. It was really something!"

Karen learned to subvert her own desires in favor of a man's wishes through observing her mother's childlike dependency and servile style of interacting with her father. The only affection she received as a child was the seductive attention from her father, which exacerbated her hunger and longing for real love and acknowledgment. In recalling her childhood, Karen said: "I was very desperate toward my father. But I never got anything real from him, and I thought Ralph was going to be able to give me that. If he liked me and I really believed him, then I felt that I would be okay, somehow acceptable."

Manifestations of the Fantasy Bond

In this case analysis, we will consider a number of manifestations of the fantasy bond in couple relationships in general and specifically examine the psychodynamics involved in the formation of an addictive attachment between Ralph and Karen. It is important to note the destructive thoughts and attitudes each partner brought to the relationship that contributed to a collusive pattern of defensive relating.

Progressive Withholding of Qualities Valued by One's Partner

Men and women who have been damaged in early family relationships attempt to control the amount of love and satisfaction they receive from their mate by withholding personal qualities originally valued by the partner. In holding back traits and actions that are lovable and would elicit tender responses, they are, in effect, manipulating each other to a familiar level of relating, rather than remaining close and learning to tolerate feeling particularly loved and chosen.

As Ralph and Karen's involvement became more serious, their relationship was significantly affected by Ralph's withholding. His style of holding back was not new; as a child, he protected himself from his mother's intense focus by becoming suspicious and self-contained. In other relationships, he had often inhibited affectionate and sexual responses especially when he felt a woman's wanting. At times, he misinterpreted his partner's natural sexual desire as desperation or excessive dependency. His tendency to hold back affection and sex was regulated by a wide range of negative thoughts or voices, which he reveals in the following interview:

> Ralph: I do have feelings for Karen, but in bed, it's different. I want to satisfy her, but I have voices about that. I tell myself: You'd better satisfy her, goddammit, because if you don't, she's going to be pissed off the next day and you haven't done your job. It doesn't take that much effort. So why don't you just do it? Stop being such a withholding son of a bitch. I know I have a lot of voices about being old, too—You're too old for sex—that preoccupy me these days.
>
> So when I get into bed, I have all these voices, and a lot of times I just want to avoid them and go to sleep. It's not quite a disinterest in sex, it's more that I don't want to deal with the thoughts that are going to come up when I do start being sexual. It just makes me tired and I want

to go to sleep and it bothers Karen. She can't sleep; sometimes she leaves the bedroom and sleeps on the couch.

Karen describes the negative thoughts she experienced in reaction to Ralph's withholding:

> Karen: When we were together, just sitting close, I'd be thinking to myself: Well, maybe you could hold his hand now. No, don't hold his hand now. He wouldn't like that. Or if I was lying in bed next to him, I'd think: Do you think it's okay to put your arm around him now? You'd better wait for him to make the first move. Then I'd wait awhile and think: It's taking too long, better do something. You'd better make it happen. It would be a total world within myself, thinking about when he would give me something or be affectionate or touch me.

Karen's desperation and attempt to find the kind of love that would make up for the lack of warmth and affection in her childhood tended to push Ralph away, whereas Ralph's pattern of sexual withholding served to increase her feelings of emotional hunger. In terms of attachment theory (applied to adult relationships), Karen could be categorized as "preoccupied" (preoccupied with attachment), which is hypothesized to be an outgrowth of an earlier anxious–ambivalent attachment, while Ralph could be categorized as "dismissing" or "fearful," an outgrowth of an avoidant attachment pattern (Shaver & Clark, 1994).[3]

Idealization of the Partner

A couple's disappointment in and critical views of each other stem partly from their tendency to idealize their spouse as they idealized their family in the past. Often when a partner is made aware of the weaknesses and foibles of the other, he or she becomes angry and resentful because this idealization is shattered. In the case under consideration, Karen's tendencies to aggrandize men led to many problems in her relationship with Ralph:

> Karen: I always saw myself as coming from a different class and background, being an immigrant, from a poor background in Italy. Ralph went to a really good Eastern school, had a profession, and seemed to be a person who was very straightforward and honest. I was attracted to those qualities, but I thought that people who had those qualities wouldn't be interested in me.
>
> I didn't think very highly of myself, so it was exciting at first that he liked me, that he continued to ask me out. From the beginning, though, I didn't quite trust him, but I covered it up. A lot of the time I was really trying to be

okay. I can see now that in my trying so hard, I got into trouble because I was never quite myself when I was trying to be okay, trying to be the kind of person he would like. I was always looking for signs, thinking Maybe he'd like this kind of a girl. Then I would try to make myself more what I thought he would like.

I didn't have a sense that he liked me for me, for what I was, so it was very tense between us. He would say, "Just relax." So in a way, I felt like a child, like I was trying to be a good girl. If he was critical or disapproving, then I felt devastated. I would tell myself, Look, you'll never get him to like you now.

Ralph had ambivalent feelings in relation to Karen's idealization of him. On the one hand, he enjoyed the attention, exaggerated focus, and flattery. He liked that she sought his advice and opinions and deferred to his wishes. On the other hand, when her expressions of adulation became too blatant, he would experience feelings of embarrassment and anger. One summer while on vacation Ralph received a lengthy "love" letter from Karen that offended him because it stood in contrast to his more realistic views of himself:

Ralph: Last year, I was vacationing in Europe and Karen was unable to join me for two weeks because of her job. So I guess she must have missed me a lot because I got this romantic letter from her. At first I felt good just to hear from her. But after a few sentences, the letter became so flowery and sticky that I had to put it down.

It's funny, there I was, sitting alone reading this letter, but I could feel my face getting red—like I was embarrassed in front of myself reading the words. It's humiliating right now just talking about it, but she wrote things like "My dearest" (she never called me dearest!) and "I miss your handsome face; I especially miss your body, the muscles in your shoulders and arms, your strong legs, your feet—you have beautiful feet. And I miss your penis." *That* was embarrassing. But it went on and on. "I miss seeing you stride across the deck. I love the way your body moves. I love your stroke, your powerful stroke slicing through the water when you swim" and so on and on. It actually made me sick. I had to stop reading after a certain point, the words she used were ludicrous.

Jesus Christ, no one can be that wonderful! So I was forced to acknowledge to myself that Karen really didn't see me clearly most of the time. It was painful to realize that on some level, I wanted that kind of adoration from her, and probably from every woman I've been involved with. But it had put a kind of pressure on me to live up to their expectations.

Karen's idealization of Ralph and the expectation that all her needs would be met in their relationship placed a tremendous burden on him. Essentially Karen made Ralph feel that he was the source of all her happiness. Obviously, no one person can fulfill such unrealistic expectations or live up to such an idealized image. Otto Rank (1941), in commenting on people's tendencies to try to achieve safety and immortality from an "ultimate rescuer," wrote as follows:

> As a rule, we find . . . in modern relationships . . . one person is made the god-like judge over good and bad in the other person. In the long run, such symbiotic relationship becomes demoralizing to both parties, for it is just as unbearable to be a God as it is to remain an utter slave. (p. 196)

Loss of Independence and a Sense of Separate Identity

Perhaps the most significant sign that a fantasy bond has been formed is when one or both partners give up vital areas of personal interest, their unique points of view and opinions, their individuality, to become a unit, a whole. The attempt to find security in an illusion of merging with another leads to an insidious and progressive loss of identity in each person. The individuals involved learn to rely more heavily on habitual contact, with less personal feeling. They find life increasingly hollow and empty as they give up more aspects of their personalities.

In addition, the propensity to surrender one's independence and individuality is encouraged by the conventional belief in the myth of everlasting love. This false assumption supports people's resistance to understanding the source of deterioration in their relationships by supporting their imaginary view of connection and oneness, while real closeness is deteriorating.

Karen realized that she had become progressively less independent the more focused she became on the relationship with Ralph:

Karen: Looking back, I know I had some kind of fantasy going in terms of keeping Ralph connected to me. The connection consisted of trying to get certain signs from him that he loved me. But what kept it going was the fact that each thing I got was only momentary. So even if I got that special something, it was great for the moment, but then it was gone, and I would feel alone. In that state of mind, I couldn't be alone. I needed to be always thinking of him, how was I going to get it again from him. That was my total focus. I became much less interested in many of the activities I usually enjoy, teaching drama to children, yoga classes, etc., and concentrated my attention more and more on Ralph.

Polarization of Parental and Childish Ego States

In a fantasy bond, people often polarize into a parental posture or exhibit childlike behaviors. In this case, Karen tended to act out the childish role in the relationship, while Ralph responded in an authoritarian, parental manner.

Karen: I don't know why, but every time Ralph and I work on anything together, I end up getting so nervous and tense. The other day, we were going to wash the boat and he asked me to find a hose so we could scrub the hull. I was really anxious and began searching all around for a hose. I must have looked at him with this scared expression on my face because he said, "Look, if you don't want to do it, if you're going to be like that, I'd rather do the whole job alone."

I know I was anticipating that he was going to eventually get angry and criticize the way I worked. So I was thinking on some level, I guess, that he was some kind of an ogre. What's so puzzling though is that I never act that way with anybody else. I'm a pretty competent person in practically everything I do, so it has something to do specifically with this relationship.

Ralph: I'll admit I can be a pretty critical person sometimes, and I really can't stand people who are incompetent. But with Karen, it's totally ridiculous. She's smart, well-coordinated, and has many responsibilities in her job, but with me, she acts like a little girl almost every time we try to do something together. And I end up feeling like I'm the meanest guy in the world. It really ruins the good time we've been having if one of those situations develops. So I try not to ask her for help on the boat or on any other project that requires two people to cooperate.

In general, by regressing to childish modes of relating, people are able to manipulate others into taking care of them and thereby preserve the imagined security of the original fantasy bond with the parents. Behaviors that elicit or provoke parental reactions—worry, fear, anger, and even punishment—act to cement the fantasy of being connected to another person. The partner acting out the parental role disowns his or her child self, denies feelings of fear and helplessness, and acts out an authoritarian manner. This type of interaction tends to prevail with occasional role reversals. As a result, it is rare that both partners are relating from an adult ego-state.

Jurg Willi (1975/1982) described this polarity in his book *Couples in Collusion*:

> *In the disturbed partner relationship we often observe that one partner has a need for over-compensatory progression while the other seeks satisfaction in regression. They reinforce this one-sided behavior in each other because they need each other as complements* (p. 24). *This progressive and regressive behavior is a major reason for the mutual attraction and the resulting bond* [italics in original]. (p. 56)

As long as these manipulations and the corresponding reactions are in operation, both partners feel inextricably bound to each other.

By acting out these complementary parent–child roles, people often elicit the exact voice attacks that they are experiencing internally. Tansey and Burke (1985) defined this unconscious process of projective identification as follows: "Projective identification, although having intrapsychic characteristics, represents an interactional phenomenon in which the projector unconsciously attempts to elicit thoughts, feelings, and experiences within another individual which in some way resemble his own" (p. 46).

In analyzing Ralph and Karen's relationship, one can observe how Karen adopted the role of the more regressive partner, while Ralph assumed the more progressive (over-compensatory) role. This polarization fostered increasingly defensive behavior on each person's part, especially in the area of sexuality. Karen became more desperate and demanding in her advances, while Ralph became more rejecting and withholding in his responses.

Karen: It was such an odd feeling to be secretly trying to please Ralph and then his not taking any notice at all. I had a voice like, You're trying so hard, and look at him, you still can't satisfy him. You still can't make him happy. You still can't be right, can you? No matter how hard you try.

And I'd be angry too. I would think to myself: He's such an asshole. Can't he see that you're trying. He's lucky that you're nice to him. He just doesn't know or appreciate what you're doing for him, what you're giving him.

It was such a familiar feeling because it was how I felt all my life in my family. I could never get it right. I could never get them to like me, or be the right kind of girl, a good Italian girl. I wasn't quite good enough or proper enough. And of course, I couldn't say anything about what I wanted from my parents; after a while it got so I didn't even know anymore what I wanted.

For many years, Karen used Ralph and the relationship to validate negative views of herself while continuing to complain that Ralph withheld affection and sex from her. For his part, Ralph persisted in criticizing Karen for what he called her "cloying" affection, phoniness, and lack of independence. This style of complaining is common in couples who have formed a fantasy bond. The partners complain ineffectively and avoid directly challenging their mate's defensive behaviors. They ward off each other's feelings so that neither has to experience the vulnerability and sadness that genuine love, sensitive treatment, and tenderness might arouse.

Ralph and Karen were locked in this type of collusive defensive pact with each other until Karen began to alter her influence on the destructive cycle.

Current Status of the Relationship

Ralph and Karen's relationship matured as the communication between them became more equal. Karen began to emerge from the childlike, dependent role she had assumed during the earlier phases of the relationship. However, in the area of sexuality, Karen and Ralph remained locked in an escalating, reciprocal cycle of emotional hunger and withholding and the relationship was at a stalemate. Here Karen recounts an incident that made her aware of the role she played in this destructive pattern.

Karen: Ralph and I had gone away for a weekend. We flew to Las Vegas, picked up a friend's boat and went boating on Lake Mead. It was the closest time we've had in a long time, very affectionate and a lot of fun. There was a very relaxed feeling between us. We had personal conversations which were meaningful to us. I felt like an equal friend and partner in all the activities of the weekend.

After boating, we found a very nice hotel and decided to go to dinner. I showered and got ready to go out. Ralph was relaxing on the bed when I got out of the shower. I felt like I wanted to make love, but was afraid he wouldn't want to (which has been a pattern). I tensed up and got focused on how he didn't really want me. Then when he dozed off, I got really angry and started thinking to myself, Here you are, all vulnerable and wanting and all he wants is sleep. Just leave him alone. I was furious and thought, "You asshole! I'm going for a drink, you jerk. Just see what happens when you wake up and I'm not here. See how it feels to squirm like I'm squirming." I told myself, Look, he doesn't really want you. Face it! Get dressed and leave.

So I left the room, went to the bar for a drink and collected myself. After about 45 minutes, I went back. Ralph woke up and immediately noticed I was different. He asked me what was wrong, but I wouldn't tell him. He guessed I was angry and upset that we hadn't made love. He said he would have later, but he wanted to rest and eat dinner first. But I wouldn't drop it. I was quiet and cold through the whole dinner. Finally, much later that night, I decided to drop my grudge and we talked about it. Afterward I realized some important things about my-self.

I recognized that I had turned him into a bastard that I had to get away from, a person who doesn't give me what I want. In my mind, I had become a victim of a man who is mean and not understanding of my needs. I really believe it would have been an almost perfect weekend and it would have shattered the belief I have that he doesn't care, if I hadn't acted the way I did. Because as I've become more open and more myself and "adult," he has responded lovingly. I can't take it. It's hard to admit this truth, but I know it in my bones. If I hadn't tampered with the feelings that were happening between us, we would have had a close night—sexual or not is not the point— it would have been a close, sharing night together. And I stopped it. I pulled away. I walked out.

Karen's insight into her part in perpetuating Ralph's tendencies to withhold his affection and sexual responses helped disrupt the couple's habitual style of relating (or nonrelating). She began to alter behaviors that had reflected her constant focus on Ralph's responses to her, especially in the area of sexual relating. This development enabled both parties to explore other ways they had been using each other in an attempt to find security in reliving patterns of the past. This exploration, in turn, led to a significant improvement in the overall relationship.

RESISTANCE AND THE FANTASY BOND

The child, and later the adult, uses the fantasy bond as a defense against the awareness of aloneness, separation anxiety, and eventually death anxiety (the ultimate separation experience). Once a fantasy bond is formed, people often choose to protect it at all costs. Their principal goal then is to maintain the safety and security of this imagined connection, and they come to prefer fantasy gratification to real satisfaction and love from others. Thereafter, the arousal of an awareness of separateness or individuation is anxiety-provoking and often leads to hostility toward the people and circumstances that could offer the individual the greatest satisfaction. There is resentment inherent in separation experiences that inevitably follow real closeness, although the anger and hostility are often unconscious.

For this reason, a satisfying sexual experience can be a major disruption to the fantasy of being connected. The sex act is a real physical connection followed by an immediate separation. Close affectionate contact is inevitably followed by separation; real communication involves sharing of thoughts and feelings followed by a distinct awareness of boundaries. In a fantasy bond, the above situations are avoided; natural movement in and out of closeness is intolerable to those people who have become dependent upon repetitive, habitual contact with little feeling. Genuine love and intimacy challenge the fantasy of connection and arouse an acute awareness of mortality. Viewed in terms of defending the fantasy bond, many irrational, self-limiting, neurotic responses begin to make sense.

Threats to the fantasy bond also create anxiety because they reawaken painful feelings that were operating at the time the original defense was formed. Therefore, people often avoid positive experiences, distort and misperceive loving situations, and may even provoke negative outcomes. To the degree that they are defended, people no longer want or pursue what they say they want. Once a fantasy bond has been formed, experiences of genuine love and intimacy interfere with its defensive function, whereas *symbols* of togetherness and images of love strengthen the illusion.

In general, people have the most difficulty in their intimate relationships because the closeness, sexuality, and companionship threaten their internal methods of gratifying themselves. Instead of altering their defensive posture and inward habit patterns and allowing positive intrusion of friendship and love into their inner world, most people choose to distort their perceptions of their loved ones. Tender moments in their relationships are followed by pulling back to a less vulnerable, more defended place.

THERAPEUTIC APPROACH TO DISRUPTING FANTASY BONDS

A major problem with many psychotherapies is that both the therapist and the patient refuse to challenge the core defense—the fantasy bond. Intense reactions and strong resistance are inevitable when separating from illusory connections with one's mate or family. For this reason, the therapist is often afraid of retaliation from one or the other partner or family members. Furthermore, therapists may conform to standard beliefs about the sanctity of the couple and family to avoid seeing the destructive processes within their own marriages and families.

Many patients incorrectly equate breaking the fantasy bond with terminating the relationship itself. In actuality, exposing destructive ties opens up the possibility of a renewed and better relationship. It is important for patients to recognize that, for the most part, divorce or rejection of the other may represent a step backward into an inward, unfeeling, or self-denying life. Despite the many rationalizations offered for breaking up or leaving a long-standing relationship, in the majority of situations, patients are preserving their defensive structure rather than challenging themselves and moving toward a positive life choice.

Unless manifestations of the fantasy bond are identified and consistently challenged, there will be no sustained therapeutic progress. Therefore, in an effective psychotherapy, destructive bonds are exposed and understood in the context of each individual's fears and anxieties. This approach assists the couple in relating to each other on a more positive basis and frees them to experience genuine loving feelings. A completely effective therapy must challenge all aspects of each partner's inward lifestyle and behavior patterns. Partners are encouraged to acknowledge the projections they have made by identifying and counteracting their negative voices toward themselves and their partners. In addition, defensive elements brought to the relationship from each partner's original family constellation must be exposed and altered. Each person must challenge the idealization of his or her parents and the corresponding negative self-concept.

Defensive patterns are interrelated, and efforts directed toward changing any one aspect interfere with other defenses and cause anxiety. Furthermore, the disruption of any specific defense is an indirect threat to the core defense: the self-parenting process, the illusion of pseudoindependence, and the fantasy of fusion. The ultimate goal of therapy is to persuade each partner to express and cope with his or her inner world of fantasy and to risk seeking satisfaction through goal-directed behavior and real relationships.

Steps for Disrupting the Fantasy Bond in Couple Relations

There are a number of steps that individual partners can initiate to break into the fantasy bond they have formed with each other and recapture some of the original vitality of the relationship. Partners can (a) admit the existence of a fantasy bond and stop denying that they have become distant and their actions are no longer loving; (b) reveal feelings of anger, hostility, and withholding patterns and admit critical, hostile voices toward themselves and their partner; (c) face the psychological pain and sadness involved in attempting to resume intimacy; (d) expose their fears of individuation and separation, including the fear of loss or death of their partner as well as their own death; (e) move toward independence and respect for each other and establish true equality. Disrupt reciprocal patterns of dominance, submission, and defiance; (f) develop a nondefensive posture toward feedback and an open and honest style of communication; (g) move toward increased interaction with others—extend circle of family and friends to provide better reality testing; and (h) if necessary, plan temporary or long-term separations.

In conflicted couples, partners tend to selectively focus on events and interactions with each other that provide confirmation for their negative voices. In addressing this dynamic in couples he was treating, psychologist

Dan Staso (personal communication, 1998) composed the following guidelines that explain how individuals typically distort information and feedback, based on their negative beliefs about self and others. His goal was to assist his clients in identifying false beliefs promulgated by the voice so that each partner would become less defensive in his or her communications with the other.

> Negative beliefs cause us to filter out information long before it reaches our conscious mind. This system of false beliefs filters in information that is consistent with our long-held assumptions and filters out information that contradicts it. The results include: failure to see opportunities as they arise or to create opportunities; reluctance to utilize resources that are easily available or to assert oneself for simple things that could potentially lead to new possibilities and opportunities; failure to believe others when they offer support; refusal to accept help from those who could make a difference; reluctance about asking for assistance/help; using poor judgment to alienate those who are helping or have helped and could do more.
>
> What you believe is true about you at the deepest level eventually manifests itself in an "illusory reality." If you believe you aren't lovable or acceptable, you will be compulsively driven to act out in a way that (1) pushes people away; (2) provokes them to make comments about your actions that you grossly magnify out of proportion as to their significance (the perception is that the world stands still and time freezes as the noted infraction implies a permanent change in your social acceptance, only adding to the acting out); and (3) causes you to falsely interpret people's actions as a reaction to you. You read people's minds and convince yourself you've been right all along despite the fact there is minimal and often contradictory evidence for such interpretations.
>
> This "illusory reality" explains your behavior but often confuses others involved in your social interactions. It is rare for other people to accurately guess your true motivation. Just as you do with others, other people personalize interactions they have with you and mistakenly assume you are behaving rationally in relation to them. Since you are acting inappropriately to the situation, they can intuit something is amiss, but unless they know you extremely well, they will guess wrong. The more emotionally significant the event and the more ambiguous your behavior, the more they will project their own worst fears into the meaning behind your behavior, thereby triggering painful feelings. Your actions then appear abusive or punitive, when in fact it is only your defense protecting you against changing your self concept. (personal communication, 1998)

Through the process of identifying negative thoughts and beliefs about self and others, men and women are able to take back their projections and assume responsibility for their own behavior, which reduces the tension in the couple's interactions.

CONCLUSION

The nature of a fantasy bond is the central concept of my theory and explains people's compulsion to relive the past with new objects, that is, to form illusory connections that invariably lead to a reenactment of defensive styles of interacting developed in childhood. Once a fantasy bond is formed, individuals are reluctant to take a chance again on gratification from others. This process of reverting to outmoded defense patterns interferes with the establishment of secure and satisfying adult relationships characterized by feelings of humanity, compassion, and equality.

A fantasy bond is the antithesis of a healthy personal relationship where individuals are free to express their real feelings and desires. This destructive tie functions to perpetuate feelings of distrust, self-hating thought processes, and the inward behavior patterns that each person brings to the relationship. In their destructive coupling, men and women surrender their unique points of view for an illusion of safety and a fantasy of eternal love.

Positive change takes place only when the fantasy bond in the original family is investigated and its reestablishment is challenged in the current relationship. It has been our experience that, as fantasy bonds were understood and relinquished, many of the men and women in the reference population manifested new energy, self-possession, and vitality and were able to become loving companions and allies (see chapter 14, this volume).

ENDNOTES

[1]Beebe (1986) and Zelnick and Buchholz (1990) emphasized that a number of theoretical perspectives now recognize the early, active self-protecting abilities of infants and their later elaboration into maladaptive, addictive habit patterns.

Bollas' (1987) description of the "self as object" is similar in some respects to the conceptualization of the self-parenting process. Bollas stated:

> It is my view that each person transfers elements of the parents' child care to his own handling of himself as an object. (p. 59) If we look closely at our patients we would probably all agree that each has his or her own sense of existence but that, by virtue of the persistent pathology of their defences, they live by disowning the self. (p. 63)

[2]A rapidly expanding body of research on adult romantic attachments tends to

support the formulations regarding the manifestations of the fantasy bond in couples and families. These studies show the continuity of defensive patterns of anxious–ambivalent and avoidant attachment through the life span and explain how these patterns are maintained by "internal working models" of self and attachment figures. Studies conducted by Shaver and Hazan (1993), Shaver and Brennan (1992), Kunce and Shaver (1994), Owens et al. (1995), Holmes (1995), and others demonstrate the persistence of these patterns. See also a report from a large National Comorbidity Study (N = 8,098) with respect to attachment style and psychopathology in "Adult Attachment in a Nationally Representative Sample" (Mickelson, Kessler, & Shaver, 1997).

[3]Shaver and Clark (1994) described disturbed attachment patterns that appear to fit closely the case of Ralph and Karen:

> The avoidant type seems to cope with attachment needs and a variety of threats and stresses by using emotion-avoidant strategies, denial of vulnerability, and repression. . . . They have had to deny vulnerability and disengage their attachment behavioral system to live amicably with an attachment figure who disliked close bodily contact or rejected the then-infant or child for other reasons. The anxious-ambivalent, or preoccupied, type is . . . perpetually vigilant, somewhat histrionic and anxiety-amplifying rather than anxiety-denying. This pattern emerges, according to theory, when an attachment figure seems unreliable and unlikely to respond unless anxiety and anger are dramatically and insistently experienced and displayed. (p. 123)

Shaver et al. (1996) emphasized the role played by "internal working models" in transmitting attachment patterns from one generation to the next, that is, from a particular pattern between a caregiver and an infant to a specific style of relating between partners:

> In the study of attachment, the role of appraisals can most easily be seen in relation to anxious-ambivalent, or preoccupied, individuals. Their vigilance is an indication that they lean toward a particular interpretation: "He or she is leaving me, cares more for someone else, will lose interest if I don't make a scene". . . . Lying behind dismissing avoidance there is probably a complex network of beliefs: "If I get too close, I am bound to be hurt; life is better when one doesn't risk deep involvement; life is safest when one relies on oneself" (p. 48).

The beliefs cited by these authors tend to coincide with the negative thought patterns or voices reported by Karen (preoccupied) and Ralph (dismissing-avoidant).

9

WITHHOLDING IN COUPLE AND FAMILY RELATIONSHIPS

Of all animals . . . [man] is the best equipped for action in the external world. But his supreme uniqueness lies not only in this. Of all animals, paradoxically, he is at the same time alone in *being able to stop external action completely, and to keep activity going in controlled inner thought processes alone.* Thus the same mechanism that enables him to find an external world more rich than any other animal permits him to lose the capacity to act in it.

Ernest Becker (1964, p. 73)

In this chapter, we describe patterns of withholding, including sexual withholding, that significantly interfere with people's ability to sustain closeness and intimacy in their relationships. Withholding is a major dimension of inwardness that profoundly affects personal associations and family life. This defense refers to a withdrawal of positive emotional and behavioral responses from others and includes a holding back of pleasure or fulfillment from oneself (self-denial) as well. In close relationships, withholding individuals resist involvement in emotional transactions, refusing to take love in from the outside or to offer love and affection outwardly. The degree of withholding depends on the extent of damage incurred during the formative years. The generalized reduction of emotional commerce with one's partner is characterized by the reluctance or outright refusal to exchange psychonutritional products.* As such, the process of withholding serves the purpose of protecting and maintaining the fantasy bond.

Withholding in the broader sense not only refers to the holding back of affection and sexuality but also relates to limiting one's capabilities and a tendency to retreat from leading a productive, fulfilling life. Whenever individuals hold back or restrict behaviors or qualities that were once an

---

*Psychonutritional products include expressions of affection and sexuality; acts of kindness, generosity, and empathy; communication, eye contact, humor; and other positive behaviors.

important expression of their personal motivation or identity, they are no longer goal-directed and are, therefore, prone to failure in their personal or vocational pursuits.

THE PSYCHODYNAMICS OF WITHHOLDING

Withholding behavior patterns develop early in childhood as a defense against interpersonal trauma and are later crystallized when the child becomes aware of death as a reality. Environmental conditions that are especially conducive to generating and maintaining patterns of withholding or self-denial include: intrusive parents who disregard the personal boundaries of the child; immature parents who attempt to feed off their children's accomplishments; sadistic parents who delight in denying the child gratification; withholding parents who are unable to accept or offer love and affection in relation to their children; or a family atmosphere characterized by neglect or hostility. To be refractory to a child's loving responses is particularly damaging in that it denies the child a sense of him- or herself as a feeling, loving person.

When children are hurt or frustrated, they depersonalize to varying degrees and tend to withdraw their emotional investment in self and objects; a process of decathexis occurs. This process leads to a reduction of pain and anxiety at the expense of emotional vitality. Hurt children stop wanting real affection (become self-denying) and at the same time abrogate natural feelings of love and affection toward their parents. They learn to arrest the flow of natural feelings, rely on fantasy processes, and develop a defensive attitude or posture toward life to keep real experiences predictable and manageable and to maintain equilibrium. The withholding person perceives spontaneous responses and free-flowing interactions with others as risky and potentially painful, and fears a loss of control.

The individual who is being withheld from is often left feeling emotionally hungry. The awareness that feelings and responses are being withheld by the other provokes longing and desperation. Withholding behaviors reflect an exaggerated fear of being emotionally drained by parents and family members who are intrusive and tend to take credit for the child's accomplishments. In these cases, children inhibit the expression of those qualities and talents in which their parent or parents take a proprietary interest. For example, Bill, 32, has never married and has difficulty in his personal relationships. As a child, his mother lived vicariously through the youngster's accomplishments, using them to enhance her own self-esteem.[1]

> When I was about 6 or 7 years old, I was happy at school and I brought home a picture one day that I'd drawn that I really enjoyed—it was a rocket ship or something like that. I was really proud of it and I gave it to my mother. She said, "Oh, this is great!" and I was really happy

to get her praise. Then she put it up on the wall and in subsequent weeks, she told all her friends about it and told me how great I was for drawing it. After a while I hated it and I never drew again because I lost any feeling that it was mine. It became her picture in essence, and it's a process that I take forward today because I don't allow myself to want things because I think there's a feeling that I'll lose them. I'll lose my own being as a person. It will be snatched away from me and I try to fight against it, but I do it unconsciously.

I've often wondered, "Why can't I have close friendships with both men and women?" and the thoughts I had about that were directly related to the fact that there were no boundaries between myself and my mother. She always treated me like we were the same person. So today if someone wants to touch me or if I feel someone really wanting to care about me or if I want to reach out to someone, the feeling is that I can't stand the pain—it's too painful, I curl my shoulders up. It's almost like an anxiety attack, and I think to myself, "Whoa, this is too far! What's going to happen?" It's not a rational feeling like "Oh, I'm going to die," but it's like an emotional pain in my chest and I'm just terrified.

In general, emotionally hungry or immature parents exert a pull that leaves their children feeling empty. The same person these children turn to for love and nurturance is seeking nurturance from them, so they self-protectively turn away from potential sources of gratification. Individuals raised in this type of emotional climate are often suspicious of the motives behind expressions of generosity from others, and they feel a need to limit their own acts of giving due to fears of being depleted.

PASSIVE-AGGRESSION

Passive-aggression due to suppressed anger is one form of withholding. It is characterized by the presence of oppositional, negativistic traits and behaviors and expressions of indirect hostility (Firestone, 1985). A certain degree of frustration is inevitable in the developmental process, but it is often compounded by inadequate or rejecting parenting. Such frustration leads to a combination of intense rage and emotional hunger, for which the child usually has no acceptable outlet. Children often manifest these negative feelings indirectly by withholding desired responses from parents.

Because of the power differential within the family, children tend to develop a passive–aggressive orientation and express aggression and hostility through assertions of negative power: whining, sulking, falling apart, or refusing to respond. They learn to control parents through regressive behaviors, noncompliance, incompetence, dawdling, and procrastination. When aggressive feelings are unacceptable or suppressed, the child finds a way of "getting under the parents' skin," while concealing more direct feelings. The use of negative power is more effective than a direct power play against a stronger or more powerful opponent. Children discover that by *not* performing, by not doing what the parents want, they are able to exert a considerable influence. When they indirectly act out anger toward the parent, there is some measure of release.

Defiance manifests itself in early childhood, partly as a desire to express independence and separation from parenting figures; nevertheless, continued defiance beyond a certain age is symptomatic of a more general withholding. In some cases, withholding takes the form of a more active rebelliousness or stubbornness. These children actually develop a sense of self from being defiant, from going against parental wishes and directives.

For example, one man had been openly defiant as a child and had stubbornly refused to concede to his parents' demands. In his job as a salesman, he knew that he should spend 3 hours a day making cold calls to develop new contacts, but he found it almost impossible to make the calls. Even after his sales manager reprimanded him for his lack of cold-calling, he tended to put them off until the end of the day, promising himself to make up for it the next day.

Children who hold back talents and abilities, for example, who refuse to function or perform at their level of capability in school, later have difficulty living up to their potential in their chosen careers. Eventually they adopt an overall style of holding back that operates even in areas where they themselves want to excel. These individuals have learned to say "no" to everything, including their own wants and aspirations.

The child's early strategies of holding back from the people who are the most significant, at a period in life when the child is the most vulnerable, eventually evolve into major character defenses in the adult. Because the specific traits of withholding are unconsciously determined and closely tied to the self-parenting process, they are usually resistant to change.

THE EFFECTS ON RELATIONSHIPS OF WITHHOLDING

There are countless examples where people withdraw or begin to hold back their most desirable or lovable traits to modify their partner's loving feelings toward them. Once, during a particularly romantic evening, a newly married couple experienced a level of closeness that touched both of them deeply. In the course of the evening, the man told his wife that she looked beautiful with long hair and that he loved the way it fell to her shoulders. The next afternoon, on an impulse, she went to the hairdresser and had her hair cut extremely short. When she met her husband for dinner that evening, she was mystified by his look of shock and the anger and disappointment he expressed.

In another case, a man refused to complete his doctoral dissertation.

It was not only important to him but to his wife, who had supported him through graduate school. This man, who was characteristically passive in his interactions with his wife, expressed his anger and aggression indirectly by withholding the final step in the process of becoming self-supporting. In so doing, he alienated his wife and created considerable distance in the relationship.

Men and women withhold their responses in many situations of everyday life: Wives fail to share financial responsibility and refuse to stay within an agreed-upon budget, husbands promise to spend a weekend with their wife and family and then insist they can't get away because of work, and children procrastinate in doing their homework or cleaning their rooms. These manifestations of withholding in personal relationships are so commonplace that they tend to be accepted by many people as "normal"; nevertheless, they have a powerful undermining effect on the family.

Many people who are married or in long-term relationships tend to engage in behaviors that detract from their attractiveness: They may gain excessive weight, relax their standards of personal hygiene, or become careless about the way they dress. Withholding behaviors often take the form of one partner first offering, then withdrawing, help or support from the other. For example, an accountant offered to take care of the monthly bills for her family. Although the family was on a tight budget, she invariably paid them late, incurring excessive late charges.

Generally speaking, most people say that they want love, admiration, closeness, loving relationships and long-lasting ties. However, they are often refractory to these gratifying experiences, that is, they tend to recoil from rather than move toward them. In the process, they act out withholding behaviors to distance themselves from their loved ones and from potentially gratifying experiences.

WITHHOLDING AS A DEFENSE AGAINST DEATH ANXIETY

The seemingly perverse, hostile, or provoking behavior often directed toward those who love, befriend, or choose us is understandable in relation to the issue of death anxiety. As we are chosen or valued, we are drawn into a greater emotional investment in a life that we must certainly lose. We fear this increased sense of vulnerability and will often act out destructive responses that interfere with closeness and intimacy (Firestone, 1994). In general, positive experiences that lead to individuation and self-expression and the sense of being valued and specially chosen have a powerful impact in terms of the anxiety and stress they arouse. For this reason, individuals attempt to modify these experiences rather than go through painful feelings of existential awareness. The following case study illustrates how people often react negatively or even with hostility to loving feelings being directed toward them.

Case Study

Natalie was raised in South Africa by parents who, according to Natalie, were somewhat neglectful and alienated from their children. As an adolescent, she developed self-destructive patterns of drinking and promiscuity that eventually began to concern her father. She was persuaded to travel to the United States for an extended visit with family friends. Natalie's father hoped this new situation would provide the teenager with a different, more constructive environment. In an interview that took place some 4 years after she left her home, Natalie talked about how her life changed for the better.[2] She also reveals her adverse reactions to finding love and happiness:

> Both my parents were very self-centered in that they didn't have that much to give. They didn't have loving feelings to give and I think that no loving feelings were drawn out of me, and I was kind of left to be by myself. I felt rejected. I felt hurt, but I knew that loving feelings existed somewhere in life. I knew that there was some hope somewhere. I would go looking for it but then I would be rejected again. I withdrew everything that I wanted to get or wanted to feel and I took those feelings back into myself.
>
> This happened all the way until I was 18, and then I met Jeff and his family who were very different towards me. They took me in immediately with loving feelings and caring feelings, feelings that I'd never ever experienced. So here I am now in a situation where suddenly I'm having loving feelings directed towards me and being seen for a person I've never been seen as before. I can accept it for a while, but then I turn around, and I think that life is so short. Immediately those loving feelings go away because I think it would be so painful to lose what has been directed towards me.

Natalie goes on to describe how adopting a withholding posture protects her from painful feelings of vulnerability, yet creates distance and alienation in her relationship:

> When Jeff and I are sharing the same feelings about life in general, for example, one moment we're sitting together and we're talking, and we're expressing really thrilling feelings but also painful feelings, and it's very equal, just two people looking outward at life together, and he expresses a loving feeling towards me and it is really thrilling. I feel so seen and so loved and so much like I have worth. But after that I turn around and have a thought like, "life is so short," and in response to that I act nasty or I say something that is critical or I am just

withholding. An hour later he'll come and ask me, "Is there something wrong?" and I really think about it. And I'll say, "no," I'll really think that nothing's wrong.

But then I realize what I've done is I've taken away from him the kind of person I was when we were having that moment. Because even though I may not be acting nasty or critical in any way that other people could see, it would be very subtle. I wouldn't be the way I had been, thrilled and excited. I'd be sort of lifeless, cut off to the loving feelings, to feelings about my life. And he notices that because it's an intimate relationship.

Withholding or self-denial is acted out in an ongoing sexual relationship in an effort to negate that which is alive, pleasurable, or spontaneous. People become sexually withholding partly to escape an awareness of being connected to their body which is vulnerable to illness, aging, and death. In addition, the guilt and self-hatred associated with withholding behavior patterns serve the purpose of narrowing down or trivializing life experience so that people can escape the full awareness of their existence and subsequent mortality.

WITHHOLDING AND SEXUAL RELATING

Withholding, a defense based on an intolerance of intimacy, is an important factor in the development of sexual problems. Most people encounter difficulties in trying to achieve and sustain sexual satisfaction in ongoing relationships because early in life they turned away from external sources of gratification to gratify themselves internally.

Two Modes of Sexual Relating

There are two distinct modes of sexual expression: an inward, masturbatory style of sexual relating in which sex is used primarily as a narcotic, and an outward form of genuine contact that is a natural extension of affection, tenderness, and companionship between two people. The use of sex as a narcotic is directly analogous to physical addictions such as alcoholism and other forms of substance abuse in that the sexual experience acts like a painkilling drug to cut off or inhibit feeling reactions. It represents a movement *away* from real intimacy and emotional exchange between two people, and *toward* a reliance on sex as a mechanism for self-gratification that places a limitation on mature genital sexuality.[3]

Sexual experiences can be conceptualized as existing on a continuum between these two modes of sexual expression. Sexual experiences appear to be the most fulfilling when they are the outgrowth of affectionate feelings (Balint, 1952/1985; Kernberg, 1980).[4] During love-making, whenever there is a switch from close, emotional contact to a more self-gratifying style of relating, the transformation is hurtful to the well-being of the individuals involved. For example, many people report feelings of emptiness, a sense of dissatisfaction, boredom, and irritability following sexual experiences in which an inward or a less personal mode of relating predominates.

Self-gratifying modes of sexual expression are symptomatic of a fantasy bond. It is important to reiterate that in most cases, men and women distance themselves emotionally from their sexual partner *before* their fears of intimacy, rejection, or potential loss reach the level of conscious awareness. They begin to hold back genuine affectionate and sexual responses and unconsciously substitute a more "self-feeding" or inward style of sexual relating before they become anxious. The automatic, unconscious nature of defended, self-nourishing modes of sexual relating compounds the problem of treatment for many sexually distressed couples.

Satisfying sexual relations are not restricted to relationships in which the partners are deeply involved or committed. A spontaneous sexual encounter between two people who are more casually involved can be satisfying, both physically and emotionally. The crucial distinction between the two modes of sexuality is not the stability, longevity, or depth of the relationship. Some people are so limited in their sexual functioning that they find it difficult to tolerate any experience that combines sexuality with affection and friendship. The determining factors are related to an awareness of one's partner as a separate person, as opposed to an unfeeling or impersonal use of the other as an instrument for one's own gratification. When sex is used for control, power plays, manipulation, security, or self-soothing, that is, for purposes other than its natural functions of shared pleasure and procreation, there is generally a deterioration in the sexual relationship.

Manifestations of Addictive Modes of Sexuality

Withdrawal and the dissociation of feelings during the sex act can become habitual or can occur intermittently. A self-gratifying mode of sexual relating is characterized by a number of specific behavior patterns and associated feeling states: (a) elements of control and sexual withholding in one or both partners, (b) increased reliance on fantasy with corresponding emotional distancing, (c) guilt reactions associated with reacting impersonally, and (d) the emergence of negative self-attitudes and critical or hostile attitudes toward one's partner.

Control and Sexual Withholding

The basic characteristics of a self-protective, addictive style of sexuality center on issues of control. Sexual withholding refers to holding back or inhibiting natural sexual desire and its expressions: physical affection, touching, physical attractiveness, and all other aspects of one's natural, healthy sexuality. Although this particular form of self-denial and withholding takes place primarily in the privacy of the bedroom, its damaging effects are not contained there. They are widespread and affect every aspect of family life.

Habitual patterns of self-denial or withholding have a progressively deadening effect on the feelings of excitement and attraction usually experienced at the beginning of a relationship. Adults who have become sexually withholding experience spontaneous sexual interactions and sexual intimacy as threatening to their defended state. Consequently, they try to regulate or direct various aspects of the sex act, that is, dictate the frequency of love-making, the time, the place, the conditions, movements, positions, and manner of expressing affection. Passive or covert forms of control, such as seductive behavior followed by rejection, appear to be more common than overt, aggressive maneuvers.

Fantasy and Emotional Distance

Many men and women distance themselves emotionally from their partner by fantasizing during sex. Here Leonard, 45, attributes the loss of excitement and intimacy with his wife to his compulsion to fantasize whenever the relationship became close and deeply personal:

> What bothers me most is the loss of sexual excitement in my marriage. This excitement, the kind that comes before actually having sex, makes me feel so looking forward to making love, but then I somehow deny that excitement to myself. It seems paradoxical—the relationship and the excitement are available to me, yet in place of them, I substitute fantasies about having that same thing with somebody else.
>
> This pattern has been present in all my relationships and both marriages. I have that excitement with a woman until I develop a close relationship; then that dies and I fantasize about somebody else. It makes me sad to know that I'm missing a meaningful part of my life and that I have a kind of negative control over my sexuality, in a sense.

The compulsive use of fantasy to enhance sexual excitement indicates a denial of the need for the other that fosters emotional distance. The secrecy and inwardness involved in protecting these fantasies from exposure tend to intensify the guilt associated with fantasizing during a sexual experience. This is especially true when sexual fantasies contain incestuous, sadistic, masochistic, or other forbidden components. Analyses of sexual fantasies reveal patients' attitudes toward the giving and taking of love in relation to other persons, as well as the extent to which they have retreated to an inward style of self-gratifying sexuality. The symbolic interpretation of these fantasies is valuable in understanding each person's mode of functioning in interpersonal relationships.

Guilt Reactions

Manipulations to control one's partner, the holding back of affection and sexual responses, and other maneuvers to create emotional distance precipitate strong guilt reactions in the withholding person. When individuals defend themselves against painful feelings stirred up by a close, personal relationship, they are aware, on some level, that their retreat is hurtful to their loved ones. This causes them considerable guilt. Mrs. S, recently divorced after 12 years of marriage, addresses this issue:

> Mrs. S: The self-hatred and guilt that I felt in pulling away sexually and knowing on some level that I was doing it was torturous. I felt that my reactions to my husband were often based on guilty feelings. I would try to act enthusiastic about making love so I wouldn't have to feel so guilty. Also, I know I started to use sex in a way to soothe myself, rather than to feel alive and excited.

Negative Thoughts Evoked During Sex

Sexual experiences that are of a more masturbatory, self-nourishing nature are characterized by the intrusion of negative cognitions into one's thoughts prior to, during, or following the sex act. Self-critical attitudes as well as thoughts reflecting animosity toward one's partner ("voices") can erupt into consciousness at any time during a sexual experience, intensifying performance anxiety and feelings of self-consciousness. Even the slightest voice attack can interfere with an individual's ability to perform or take pleasure in making love (Firestone, 1990e).

For example, during intercourse, a man might find himself thinking: "You're not going to be able to keep your erection," and actually begin to lose his sexual feelings and sensations. Similarly, many women report having worries about their performance, such as "You're not moving right." "You're not going to be able to have an orgasm." "You can't make him feel good."

Men and women often have negative voices that criticize their bodies: "Your penis is too small." "Your breasts are not attractive (too large, too small, the wrong shape)." "Your vagina is too large." Voices about one's partner can also interrupt the flow of feelings during love-making: "He's not touching you right. He's so insensitive," or "She's not really excited. She's just pretending to be turned on."

The voice process regulates patterns of sexual withholding. In responding to these subliminal voices and following their prescriptions, individuals inhibit many of their spontaneous, natural responses during sex.

In shifting their focus to concerns about performance, people tend to concentrate on the technical aspects of sex in an effort to complete the act.

Effects of Both Modes of Sexuality on Interpersonal Relationships

The quality of a particular sexual experience is influenced by each partner's sexual orientation, that is, whether it is based on a core defense of fantasized self-sufficiency or on the pursuit of a healthy interdependence with another. Individuals who have a more self-gratifying or defended orientation toward sex often feel dulled and somewhat empty following such an experience. In addition, feelings of self-reproach associated with the use of fantasy, the intrusion of negative cognitions, and the awareness that one is using another person as an object rather than relating personally, can contribute to feelings of emotional hunger, alienation, and depersonalization. These negative feelings contrast with the satisfaction, on a feeling level, that follows fulfilling, intimate love-making.

When either partner is sexually withholding, the sex act becomes progressively more impersonal and tends to lack tenderness and compassion. Sex then becomes an inward experience, wherein one partner utilizes the other in a symbolically self-feeding process rather than relate as an equal adult in the sex act.

CONCLUSION

Withholding is part of a self-destructive or microsuicidal process that represents an attempt to gain control over potential loss or separation. Both men and women tend to hold back positive responses from their loved ones as part of a basic defense to create emotional distance in their relationships. Self-denial and withholding lead to the obliteration of a person's most desirable qualities in an effort to ward off loving responses from his or her partner. Progress in therapy requires that the patient become aware of his or her typical methods of manipulating the environment through withholding responses. One needs to learn both how to be loving and generous to others and how to accept love and friendship.

Sexual withholding affects the core of the couple's emotional life. The dynamics involved are complicated and difficult to work through. In seeking to regulate the amount of gratification they allow themselves from external sources, individuals frequently alter their basic orientation to sex as well as to the sex act itself. Therapeutic interventions directed toward the personal development of each individual can help break patterns of withholding affection, positive qualities, and sexual responses, allowing both people to recapture their original feelings of love and sexual attraction.

ENDNOTES

[1]This material was excerpted from the video documentary *Invisible Child Abuse* (Parr, 1995).

[2]This interview was excerpted from the video documentary *Fear of Intimacy: An Examination of Withholding Behavior Patterns* (Parr, 1997b).

[3]Kernberg (1980), Fromm (1956), and others have stressed that one criterion for "mature" sexuality and love relations is an individual's development of an ability to extend "self-love" (primary narcissism) to the love objects (persons). Mollon and Parry (1984) observed a specific form of narcissistic disturbance in otherwise functional individuals. These patients attempt to protect themselves against potential injury to the self by "turning away from dependence on others" and then cling "to a torturous inner world which, although painful, is at least felt, unconsciously, to be more controllable" (p. 141). Lacan (1982) contended that feminine sexual maturity does not, as many theorists have insisted, imply "the transformation of the clitoral into the vaginal," but rather the *transformation of "auto-erotic libido into object libido"* [italics added] (p. 129). In the authors' terms, this would imply a transformation from self-gratifying forms of sexuality into a reliance on others for satisfaction in interpersonal relations. Kernberg (1980) suggested that mature love relations are dependent on the achievement of *libidinal object constancy*, that is, the investment of libido in another person or persons.

[4]Kernberg (1980) described a continuum of sexual love in terms of "the capacity—or rather, the incapacity—to fall and remain in love" (p. 278). At one extreme on Kernberg's continuum are "narcissistic personalities who are socially isolated and who express their sexual urges only in polymorphous perverse masturbatory fantasies" (Level 1). At the other extreme (Level 5) is "the normal person who has the capacity to integrate genitality with tenderness and a stable, mature object relation" (p. 278). Kernberg asserted that genital sex requires a leaving behind of the parental figure of the same sex.

10

MEN

Despite the fact that predictions based solely on gender are often inaccurate, social institutions in the U.S. continue to expend enormous efforts to support stereotypes and to generalize about gender differences in behavior.

Bernice Lott (1997, p. 22)

SEXUAL STEREOTYPES

Traditional views of men and women create animosity between the sexes and undermine interpersonal relationships. Most people lack trust in the opposite sex. They manifest cynical, suspicious attitudes that interfere with forming and sustaining intimate relationships. They lack empathy, find it difficult to talk honestly, and are often mutually disrespectful.

Sexual stereotypes confuse people's thinking about the differences between men and women by placing them in artificial categories. For example, men are typically seen as focused on sex and as impersonal in their relationships with women. In thinking about this issue, I am reminded of an unsophisticated, rugged teenage boy, who became involved with a highly intelligent, refined woman in her late twenties. This was the young man's first sexual relationship; he was 18, full of life and sexual energy. One would have thought that sex was the only thing on his mind when he was with his girlfriend. The irony was that after the couple had spent several evenings together, he complained to a friend about the lack of emotional closeness and communication in the relationship. It seemed that his girlfriend only wanted to make love, but he yearned for meaningful conversation. "I want to get to know her," he said, "but she doesn't want to talk; she just wants sex."

This young man's story should not be brushed aside or considered merely an exception to the view that is prevalent in current literature. Some sexual stereotypes do correspond to research findings regarding specific differences between men and women. However, when these are incorporated into the destructive thoughts and attitudes of the voice process, they take on a connotation of hostility and denigration that goes beyond the real gender differences authenticated in the psychological literature. Furthermore, social psychologists have stressed that gender stereotypes are consensually validated by most members of society and that many have negative implications. For example, Geis (1993) has asserted that "because consensus defines 'the truth,' it also transforms gender stereotypes from assumed facts into values" (p. 31).[1]

The story of the teenager contradicts society's conception of men and points out that in most aspects of their psychological makeup, men and women cannot be categorized according to their gender identity. Their behavior should not be explained, interpreted, or judged by conventional standards that emphasize gender differences.[2] It is probably of much greater value and importance to explore the similarities.

Consider, for example, the point of view of an intelligent, articulate woman who described her subjective experience of making love. She said that she felt that when she was fully involved emotionally in the sex act, she didn't see herself as a "woman" per se, but felt simply like a person, a human being, very similar in wants and desires to her husband. In a discussion group, she spoke out strongly against society's exaggerated focus on the differences between men and women:*

> I think that conventionally, men and women are seen in such strange ways that are never examined and never even questioned, and I thought that it has to enter into the way that two people are sexually. Men are seen as wanting sex and women as not wanting sex. Also women are seen as being feelingful and sensitive, and men are seen as not having any feelings.
>
> The image you have about the sex act is of this weak little woman and this man with all these powerful sexual feelings and she succumbs to it, but she just wishes he would be a little bit more romantic and feel a little bit more about it. This is all such a lie!
>
> Men are every bit as romantic as women. Women are every bit as sexual as men. Why, for some reason, society makes such a distinction between men and women in this area is a mystery to me. The only way it's nice is if both people are the same—in their feelings of wanting to make love, in their feelings of being romantic and close emotionally, and I think that to the extent to which people believe these stereotypes, it really hurts their sexual relationship.
>
> And I think that men buy it every bit as much as women. They

---

*The following statements are excerpted from the video documentary *Sex and Society: Everyday Abuses to Children's Emerging Sexuality* (Parr, 1990a).

think that they're gruff and aggressive and insensitive, and you see it all over the place in magazine articles: "How to tell a man how to touch you," "How to teach him to be sensitive." It's a bunch of bullshit! As a woman, you know as little about being sensitive as he does, or as much. There's not much difference.

Making love must be a terrible experience for so many people because they go into it with so many crazy ideas about it that ruin the nice time that they could have together. I really think that these conventional stereotypes make men and women different and make them enemies.

This woman's point of view differs from the popular consensus. Despite the advances of the so-called sexual revolution, sexist attitudes still permeate people's thinking and profoundly influence their behavior. Moreover, several researchers in the area of gender studies recently warned their colleagues that the general public tends to misinterpret the findings of published research on this controversial subject. For example, according to Beyer and Finnegan (1997), results from many studies, polls, and surveys have been cited "as evidence for the existence of pervasive gender stereotypes which might ultimately lead to discrimination" (p. 1). On the other hand, according to Halpern (1997), "research is the only way in which psychologists can distinguish between those stereotypes that have a basis in fact (i.e., are statistically associated with one group more than another) and those that do not" (p. 1091). She goes on to comment: "Of course, research always takes place in a sociopolitical context that guides the research questions that are asked, the data that are collected, and most important, *the way the data are interpreted*" [italics added] (p. 1091).

Geis (1993) asserted that general knowledge about the world "shapes and guides our perceptions and actions automatically. . . . [This] includes all the old gender stereotypes as tacit or implicit beliefs" (p. 11). These "implicit beliefs interpret perceptions of males and females from the time they are born" (p. 14). Indeed, most adults grew up in families where they learned inaccurate and misleading information about themselves and their counterparts. These sexual stereotypes reflect underlying attitudes of negativity and hostility that can be as damaging to human relations as racial prejudice.

In considering our views about men and women, readers will find some information that substantively disagrees with certain conventional views and biases. Several differences and similarities are noted, with an emphasis on equality and compassion for both sexes. One difference between the sexes, based on evolutionary theory, is that men and women use different strategies in selecting their mates because they must solve different adaptive problems (Buss, 1994; Buss, Larsen, & Westen, 1996; Buunk, Angleitner, Oubaid, & Buss, 1996).[3] For example, the tendency of men to be more random and to seek variety and for women to be more selective has been observed to be universal across human societies (Wilson, 1981). On the other hand, a number of traits and skills assumed to be more characteristic of males than females (and vice versa) actually show only mild to moderate variation between the genders (Hyde & Plant, 1995).[4]

The information in the sections on men and women was gathered during hundreds of interviews with a wide range of patients as well as from discussions with people in the circle of friends. After many years of honest collaboration, participants in this reference population have arrived at a number of conclusions that may be startling to the average person. It was only because their rapport in the group setting reached a level of openness wherein they felt free enough to confide their innermost thoughts that they achieved this unusual depth of understanding. The stimulation of each other's ideas and personal development over the years led to the unearthing of very basic knowledge about men, women, and sexuality. Our clinical observations of men and women who had the opportunity to be unusually honest and open with one another have led us to believe that many gender stereotypes are exaggerated and destructive.[5]

Although these ideas may deviate from contemporary psychological thought and public opinion, the findings presented are not speculative.[6] They are closely related to data gathered from the men and women in the circle of friends described in the Preface. After years of openness, the conclusions and hypotheses described in the following chapters have become common knowledge for these individuals. What may appear to be radical at first glance is worth considering, evaluating, and reevaluating in relation to one's own personality and relationships.

A DEVELOPMENTAL PERSPECTIVE

Men are much maligned in contemporary society. Prevailing attitudes, many of which are blatantly inaccurate, mitigate against a deeper understanding of their humanness. Most men accept these negative evaluations as factual and are confused about the nature of manhood. They share society's point of view about their inadequacies and failures, causing them to turn against themselves and other men.

Children inevitably suffer varying degrees of damage in their early relationship with their primary caretaker, usually the mother, the most important figure in their lives at the time when they are the most dependent and vulnerable. As boys grow into manhood, their personalities are affected on a deep level by residuals of maternal deprivation and rejection. As a result, the majority spend their lives searching for the gratification of these unfulfilled needs and longings, commonly seeking new objects in a symbolic attempt to reconnect to the mother. The anxiety and insecurity from early childhood are therefore perpetuated in current relationships.

The defenses formed to cope with the pain and hurt of early years interfere with the achievement of real intimacy and adult sexual relating.

Most men grow up feeling alienated from other men and find it difficult to relate to them beyond a superficial level. They do not believe that other men experience the same feelings of inadequacy, desperation, and fear that torment them. They feel isolated and very much alone in their suffering, which they often try to disguise with a defensive, macho exterior. Once this defensive armor is pierced, however, one frequently finds a self-doubting, self-critical human being, driven alternately by the fear of being rejected or of being consumed by a woman. Consequently, some men subordinate their priorities to cater to women's wishes and desires, while others are defiant and hostile or act indifferent to the women in their lives. To compensate for internalized negative attitudes toward themselves, many men continually seek approval and reassurance from women. Only when their partner feels happy and satisfied do these men relinquish their self-attacks.

Boys are in serious conflict in relation to their fathers. They want nurturance and love, while at the same time, they feel competitive, often experiencing hostility, envy, and feelings of rivalry directed toward them from their fathers. Later, friendships and associations with other men are affected by the emotional residuals. Success or an unusual achievement, for example winning over a male rival, takes on the symbolic meaning of surpassing the father, which activates intense fear and guilt reactions. There is also a sense of loss.

The importance of the father as a role model for the male child is another factor that cannot be overemphasized (Neubauer, 1986). Many fathers automatically idealize women as mothers and in the process defer to them in relation to child-rearing practices. As a result of this inequality, children do not benefit from positive influences their father could have on their childhood. Many boys grow up feeling that they have no ally or protector in their father. They tend to closely observe and incorporate their father's style of relating to the mother; they notice when he caters or sells out, is intimidated by her tears, or gives in to her control. They also observe and identify with their father's hostile and defensive attitudes toward women. His weaknesses as a role model pose a serious limitation to the development of a strong sense of identity and maleness in his son.

In addition, many fathers unwittingly support the mother's view of men as being mean and unfeeling. Women reinforce this stereotype when they use their husbands as agents of punishment in child-rearing such as by saying, "Just wait till your father comes home. Then you are really going to get it!" Consequently, children learn to view male strength and power in a negative light. Park (1995) emphasized that

> what the boy needs is a father's help in dealing with the emotional
> pressures that come from his mother. He needs to learn that there are

other views of masculinity than those which she propounds, and that what she says to him has more to do with her own past experiences than with him. (p. 23)

On a social level, economic conditions, changing cultural patterns, and the feminist movement have been responsible for many changes in men and women's relationships. The latter criticized many aspects of men's behavior as being sexist and oppressive. Although modern men are generally more sensitive, softer in a positive sense, and less macho than their predecessors, they often lack a fully developed sense of self and the autonomy necessary to offer companionship and support to women in a relationship. Overall, men are in a state of transition and are dissatisfied with, and confused about, their roles and their relationships.

Attributes of Men That Contradict Contemporary Stereotypes

Men are required culturally to mask their feelings, yet when I have seen them in the therapy setting and in situations where feelings are accepted, I have found that they are as feelingful and emotionally expressive as women. Moreover, they have equally strong desires for a lasting affiliation with another person and are often just as interested in procreation and child-rearing. For the most part, men tend to underestimate their sensitivity and capacity to feel for children; at the same time, they idealize women in this regard.

In our observations of men and women in the reference population, as men overcame biases due to early conditioning as to appropriate sex-role responses, they came to openly express the same depth of feeling as the women. We found that fathers were as concerned, compassionate, and caring for their children as mothers. Although some gender differences continue to exist, men have taken an active interest, not only in their own children, but in the children of others. They have exhibited the same involvement and concern as women.[7]

Men are not innately indifferent to women's feelings and moods, although as a result of early training, they may have become generally desensitized to feeling. Although many men assume protective attitudes that are demeaning to women, as the men in our ongoing discussion groups developed insight and understanding, they became more empathic and related to women with a sense of companionship and equality.[8] Most of these men demonstrated a consistent concern for their partner's well-being. Interestingly, the times they reported feeling their best seemed to coincide with the times when their partners' overall mood was a positive one of strength and self-possession. Overall, their mates' happiness and companionship were a central issue.

Factors That Contribute to Men's Feelings of Sexual Inadequacy and Inferiority

Nowhere is there more shame or humiliation for men, or so much confusion and misunderstanding between men and women, as in the privacy of the bedroom. In his lectures, R. D. Laing often quipped that "the bedroom is the most dangerous room in the house." In our seminars, as men and women revealed honest feelings in relation to their sexuality, these controversial findings came to light:

1.   A man's emotional and sexual responses are strongly related to a woman's genuine sexual desire. A woman may act interested or aggressively pursue sex, but without feeling and genuine desire for the man, her partner will have difficulty responding sexually and find it necessary to resort either to fantasy or masturbatory rubbing for gratification. Moreover, men generally blame themselves for sexual failures and tend to deny their mate's influence, even when they are intellectually aware or critical of the woman's effect.

2.   In general, the way women feel about themselves and their physical appearance has considerable impact on their partner's sexual desire. The times women in the discussion group admitted feeling less interested in sex coincided with those times when their husbands reported experiencing sexual difficulties. Many women revealed that during pregnancy they felt disturbed and embarrassed by the changes in their bodies and pulled away from their husbands. A husband's decline in sexual response is often related more directly to the woman's feelings about her body than to a diminished interest in sex on his part due to her pregnancy.

One young woman, Carol, who doubted her attractiveness and lovability, talked about making love to reassure herself that she was desirable. When she felt particularly self-attacking, her husband was usually unable to have an erection and felt mystified and demoralized by his failure.

Carol: Sometimes I didn't really feel like a sexual woman, but I still sought it out. I wanted some kind of comfort or reassurance, and I wanted to be soothed in some way and babied. I recognize now that there's a big difference between that kind of motivation for making love and really wanting to be close to my husband.

The first way is just like an unfeeling, really unfeeling kind of love-making. It's viewing a man as an instrument. I mean, that's a terrible phrase to use, but I think it's really true.

Jim (husband): Lots of times during that period, Carol would approach me and she would even suggest that we go to bed early. We'd get in bed and I'd feel like,

"God, I'm really falling apart here" because I wasn't interested. I didn't respond. I couldn't make love, and it was driving me crazy.

Many men suffer from feelings of sexual inferiority and inadequacy; however, there is no realistic way for them to evaluate their performance. They have secret doubts and rarely receive objective feedback. Their insecurity about their masculinity is partly based on the fact that they believe that "real men" feel sexual at all times and under all conditions. They have criticisms about their bodies, their physical stature, and the size of their penises. In a seminar on sexuality, several men addressed this subject:

John: I have attacks about every part of my body. I have thoughts toward myself like: Your chest doesn't look like a man's; you look fat. And your penis is small—look how small it is. Your penis doesn't look like a man's penis; everything about you is wrong. How can you possibly expect to attract a woman if you look like this?

Dr. Firestone: It's amazing that most men, for example, during physical education or going to a gym, taking showers, notice other men and so often feel inferior. They feel that their penises are smaller than the majority of other men. It's a statistical impossibility for the majority of men to be inferior to other men. [laughter] Yet if you were to listen to them they all seem to feel that way.

Eugene: In the locker room situation, I always looked at myself, at my penis, and thought I was smaller than any other guy in my P.E. class. Then I came to an interesting conclusion. I looked at myself in the mirror from the side and I thought, "Hmm, penises look smaller from the top than they do from the side, so I was able to rationalize that away to some extent. [laughter]

Because destructive thoughts and self-attacks leave men confused and unsure about their sexuality and masculinity, they have a strong need to have their manhood validated.

Case Example

A 19-year-old adolescent entered therapy suffering from a severe depression of several months' duration. His girlfriend of 2 years had found a new boyfriend and suddenly rejected him, precipitating symptoms of anxiety and self-recrimination. In exploring his reactions to the loss, the young man discovered that it wasn't the rejection itself that had devastated him. It turned out that in the couple's last argument, his girlfriend said she was ending the relationship because she found him unsatisfying as a lover.

The negative evaluation of his sexuality reinforced his inner doubts about his manhood and sexual performance. His real suffering and torture centered on the theme of sexual inadequacy; his girlfriend's criticism served to activate his own destructive thought processes, internal voices that attacked his manhood.

Further investigation revealed that these voices were related to identification and incorporation of his father's negative self-image. In addition, his mother's seductive attitude toward him put pressure on his developing sexuality. (A seductive relationship with the mother often stimulates intense oedipal rivalry and leads to powerful feelings of inadequacy in the growing boy.)

Several months later, the patient entered into a new relationship and his depression seemed to disappear overnight. He felt elated; he told me he felt "great." He said, "My girlfriend told me that I was the nicest man she had ever been with sexually."

It was obvious that the young man took this new evaluation to mean that now he was "okay" sexually. His reactions indicated that he still sought definition and a buildup from a woman to cover up his self-doubts. He was still vulnerable to depression as long as he needed reassurance from his girlfriend about his sexual performance.

In dealing with feelings of inadequacy, suppression and compensation are always ineffectual. They end up preserving, rather than relieving, one's doubts and fears. Only by exposing and working through the underlying dynamics can a person develop strength and security.

Male Vanity

One of the most agonizing issues for men lies in their insistence upon being preferred at all times by the women in their lives. Basically, men tend to demand that they be preferred over all rivals. This poses an essential contradiction, because the same men, when asked if they feel that they're better than most other men, would say "no." Yet they feel as if they are entitled to this unconditional preference from their partner. This unrealistic requirement causes considerable misery and conflict in marriage.

The insistence on a false buildup and dishonest reassurance causes many women to resent and even hate men. Indeed, male vanity leads to considerable aggression from women. Although women resent men's demand for a buildup, they also realize that it gives them leverage and control in their relationships. One woman, recently divorced, was honest and straightforward in admitting that early in her marriage, she had learned how to build up her husband as a way to keep him dependent on her. However, she felt guilty about her behavior and eventually came to hate her husband and herself. Much later, she realized that her fears and insecurities from childhood had compelled her to use this form of control.

> I knew how to listen to him with an enraptured look on my face. I knew how to make him feel that he was the smartest person I knew about practically every subject. He had a huge amount of vanity about being a great writer, and I thought to myself, "I can treat him like a great writer and he'll need me for that."
>
> I saw all the different areas where he was weak and I knew that those were inroads. I knew that I could create dependency in him. Then, as the relationship went on, I hated him when he would say stupid, embarrassing things in public situations. I hated him, but I never once told him. I never once treated him like a person. I never gave him a chance. I was totally involved in this manipulation and hated myself for it.
>
> I knew he would give me anything I wanted as long as I built him up, especially in the areas where he felt weak and that were really important to him. That was the deal, and it's that way in most marriages I see. Men will do anything women want them to do as long as they support the man's vanity. They'll support you, take care of you, and you don't have to do anything.

Manipulations that support men's illusions of superiority are debilitating to the men and damage each party's sense of reality. For example, women who are more successful or intelligent than the men in their lives often relate as though they are inferior. They submit to men's so-called superiority in matters of logic, practicality, and worldliness. When a woman surrenders her individuality and gives up her dignity and self-respect to build up a man's sense of importance, the result is a tragic personal loss for herself and her mate.

Within a monogamous contract, men's illusions about being preferred are protected by social sanctions against infidelity. Traditionally, the role society has assigned to women restricts their freedom of movement and prevents them from coming into contact with other men. In this sense, a man can use social mores to maintain the image of being the most preferred male, the "king of the castle."

Even when these cultural sanctions appear to be working, they often backfire. Women who are restricted, for example, those who remain at home, still come into contact with men. One patient, an insurance inspector, related many stories of housewives who were flirtatious or tried to seduce him. Men recognize that in pursuing certain occupations, for example, divorce lawyer, driving instructor, or personal trainer, careers that bring them into close contact with women, they stand a good chance of becoming sexually involved.

Relationships that are based on free choice rather than obligation can, and often do, endure when the man does not demand a buildup from a woman, but has the self-respect and maturity to face himself realistically.

CONCLUSION

Men face a difficult task in challenging their defenses and transcending traditional masculine role-determined behavior. Their struggle requires courage in facing internal conflict as well as external social pressures that foster conformity to rigidly defined sex-roles. Men need to challenge their idealization of women, especially in their role as mothers, and, in order to mature, abandon the quest for "the perfect love" based on infantile needs. Their unfulfilled primitive needs for safety and security from childhood are rarely gratified in adult relationships. Men must come to terms with the remnants of childhood insecurity that place heavy unrealistic demands on the women in their lives. As men develop real personal power, they become more attractive to women and more capable of sustaining intimate relationships. In relinquishing their illusions, they are drawn to women who are affectionate, independent, and strong, and take pleasure in respectful and equal companionship with them.

ENDNOTES

[1]Geis (1993) described the "fundamental attribution error" wherein one attributes people's behavior to their "internal personality dispositions" (p. 29). She contended that "committing the fundamental attribution error, we assume that high-status behavior is dispositional in men and subordinate behavior in women" (p. 38). "Gender stereotypes operating as implicit expectations bias perception and treatment of women and men, and the results of the discriminatory perceptions and treatment—sex differences in behavior and achievement—then seemingly confirm that the stereotypes were true all along" (p. 37).

[2]The concept of *gender* is generally distinguished from the concept of sex. Walsh (1997) states: "Sex refers to the biological differences between women and men; gender relates to the normative expectations attached to each sex. Gender is viewed, therefore, not as a trait inherent in an individual but as something that is socially constructed" (p. 7). Halpern (1997) uses the term *sex* to refer to "differences between men and women regardless of their origin" because she believes that "biological and social influences are not separable" (p. 1091).

[3]Buss (1994) asserted that "In evolutionary terms, men and women are identical in many or most domains, differing only in the limited areas in which they have faced recurrently different adaptive problems over human evolutionary

history. For example, they diverge primarily in their preference for a particular sexual strategy, not in their innate ability to exercise the full range of human sexual strategies" (p. 18). Buunk et al., 1996, wrote: "Over human evolutionary history, men have faced a profound adaptive problem that has not been faced by women: uncertainty in their parenthood of children" (p. 359). "Women have faced a different set of adaptive challenges . . . if her mate becomes interested in another women [sic] she risks losing his time, energy, resources, parental investment, protection, and commitment" (p. 360). Their studies showed that women exhibit more distress in response to emotional infidelity, whereas men are more disturbed by sexual infidelity.

[4]See Hyde and Plant's (1995) commentary on Eagly's (1995) article, "The Science and Politics of Comparing Women and Men" in which they stress the fact that "meta-analyses indicate great variability in the magnitude of gender differences across different behaviors" (p. 159). "Of the effect sizes for gender differences, 25% are in the close-to-zero category, but 10% are in the large category and an additional 3% exceed one standard deviation in magnitude" (p. 160). They also call attention to the lack of consensus among feminist empiricist psychologists regarding sex differences. They note that those adhering to the *minimalist perspective* perceive sex differences as small or null, whereas feminists from the *maximalist perspective* argue "for large psychological gender differences . . . or for more complex positions that recognize that some gender differences are small and others are large" (p. 159).

[5]In the authors' opinion, two examples of exaggerations of the differences between men and women in terms of their style of communication are those set forth in Tannen's (1990) book, *You Just Don't Understand* and Gray's popular works beginning with *Men Are From Mars: Women Are From Venus* (1992). Contrary to these writers' assumptions regarding large gender differences in modes of communication, several studies have shown that men and women are similar, both in the importance they place on communication and in their communication skills. Findings by Burleson, Kunkel, Samter, & Werking (1996), who studied men and women's communication skills in relationships, suggested that "when both within-sex and between-sex comparisons are made, similarities between the sexes often outweigh the differences" (p. 220). Similarly, Aries (1997) concluded that "men are capable of sharing intimately and can do so when the situation demands it" (p. 95).

[6]The scope of gender studies and empirical findings related to sex differences in current psychological literature is too broad to summarize here; however, it is worthwhile to note that the political and social implications of the debate tend to bias some of the findings and cloud the relevant issues. A synopsis of the controversy regarding sex differences and their generalization to popular gender stereotypes can be found in a series of papers published in the *American Psychologist*, March 1995. In this issue, Eagly (1995) and Hyde and Plant (1995) both emphasized the political context in which empirical research comparing the sexes has been conducted. Eagly reported some areas where studies found substantial sex differences (e.g., facial expressiveness, attitudes toward casual intercourse, and others) but concluded as follows: "Yet, most aggregated sex-difference findings appear to be in the small-to-moderate

range" (p. 151). Marecek (1995) challenged "the view of gender [that] holds that the categories 'man' and 'woman' are natural, self-evident, and unequivocal . . . [and that] regards sex-linked behaviors and traits as fixed and stable properties of separate, autonomous individuals" (p. 162). In the same volume, Buss (1995) summarized numerous studies and concluded that "most tests of general cognitive ability . . . reveal small sex differences. The primary exception . . . occurs with spatial rotation. This ability is essential for successful hunting" (p. 166), an ability that would have attracted women and thus been differentially selected in men during the EEA. Buss concluded that "evolutionary psychology possesses the heuristic power to guide investigators to the particular domains in which the most pronounced sex differences, as well as similarities, will be found" (p. 167).

The reader is also referred to summaries and critiques of gender studies in *The Social Psychology of Gender* (Burn, 1996), *Bridging Separate Gender Worlds* (Philpot, Brooks, Lusterman, & Nutt, 1997), and *Women, Men, and Gender: Ongoing Debates* (Walsh, 1997). Evidence supporting a hormonal basis for sex differences in brain structure and functioning can be found in *Brainsex* (Moir & Jessel, 1989) and *Handbook of Behavioral Neurobiology: Vol. 11, Sexual Differentiation* (Gerall, Moltz, & Ward, 1992). In his article "Sex Differences in Social Behavior," Archer (1996) offered a synopsis of the two major explanations given for observed sex differences in human social behavior: social role theory and the evolutionary principles of Darwinian theory.

[7]It is interesting to note that in the small pilot study reported in chapter 14, this volume, two of the four male partners scored higher than their female counterparts on the role orientation subscale of the *Marriage Satisfaction Inventory-Revised* (MSI-R; Snyder, 1997). Their scores reflected an even greater sense of fully shared responsibilities across all relationship domains than did those of their female partners.

[8]In two large studies that examined the components of empathy, Snodgrass (1992) asserted that status is a "social context that is confounded with gender" (p. 154). Her studies indicated that "women have no advantage in interpersonal sensitivity when they are leaders as often as are men. This suggests that sensitivity is more related to status or role than to gender per se" (p. 158). In a critique of some feminist research, Burn (1996) reported that measures of empathy utilized in these studies found larger sex differences on self-report questionnaires than on physiological measures. This finding suggests that males may "be unwilling to portray themselves as empathic because doing so is inconsistent with the male gender role" (p. 57).

A review of gender research suggests that some feminist studies stress the similarities between men and women in cognitive abilities and instrumentality, yet emphasize the differences in emotional expressiveness and empathy (Chodorow, 1978; Gilligan, 1982; J. B. Miller, 1976). With respect to this type of bias, Walsh (1997) commented: "Some feminists have reservations about a theory that glorifies women's relational skills. One problem, they argue, is that it replaces the old male model with a new model of female chauvinism" (p. 360).

11

WOMEN

A HISTORICAL PERSPECTIVE ON WOMEN

A major influence in the lives of modern women is the fact that, for centuries, they have been subjugated by a patriarchal society (Gilligan, 1996). As a result, most women accepted the socially defined identity of being the "second sex," and consequently, felt incapable of actively determining the course of their lives. This lack of access to real power led them to adopt indirect or passive techniques in trying to fulfill their human potentiality.

Historically speaking, biological factors played their part in the evolution of the inequality between the sexes. In terms of physical strength and overall body size, women were clearly the weaker sex. Originally, biological factors contributed to the formation of an unequal power structure based on the division of labor by sex difference. However, women's tendencies toward passivity and control through weakness appear to result more from suppression and social bias than from biological determinants. Psychoanalyst Jean Baker Miller (1976) pointed out one of the important reasons that women felt compelled to resort to negative power:

> It is not surprising . . . that a subordinate group resorts to disguised and indirect ways of acting and reacting. While these actions are designed to accommodate and please the dominant group, they often, in fact, contain hidden defiance. (p. 10)

Over many generations, the internalization of outwardly compliant, but inwardly defiant, behavior patterns have become as detrimental to women's development as the social forces that made their use necessary. It is important to note that passive–aggressive responses result in manipulative behavior that may be only partially conscious, yet is obstructive to harmonious relations between men and women.

STEREOTYPES OF WOMEN

Both men and women tend to perceive women as basically weaker than men in areas other than size and strength; both genders see women as needing special protection. Social attitudes that emphasize female helplessness, powerlessness, and vulnerability support women's passivity and feelings of victimization. In commenting on their tendency to maintain a victimized position in spite of its maladaptive aspects, J. B. Miller (1976) writes the following:

> It can sometimes seem much easier to be, and remain, the victim than to struggle for oneself. . . . The victim does not have to confront her own desires to change the situation, her own power to do so, nor the anger that has mounted and accumulated over her victimized position. (p. 122)

Maintaining a victimized stance may not only be easier, it can also be a highly successful maneuver. Women's displays of helplessness, childishness, victimized complaints, and unnecessary incompetency not only are effective in manipulating men but these behaviors also tend to agitate and provoke anger. After provocations of this sort, men feel guilty and ashamed of the hostility aroused, a fact that gives even more leverage or power to these machinations. The tyranny of the weak represents an amazingly effective technique in undermining the individual (or group) in power by playing on guilt feelings. In our culture, this "underdog" position is generally supported by social mores and institutions.

The experience of Mr. B, a 31-year-old man, demonstrates how stereotypic views of women as the weaker sex are operant in our society:

Case Example

Mr. B was on a first date with a woman he had recently met. During dinner, she drank several glasses of wine and seemed somewhat disoriented as they left the restaurant. Mr. B drove her to her apartment, but when he said good night, she refused to leave the car and began to cry. Mystified and somewhat frustrated, Mr. B attempted to reassure her and then offered to walk with her to her apartment. When he tried to coax her out of the car, the young woman grabbed on to the steering wheel with both hands and became hysterical, yelling, "Leave me alone!"

At this point, a car pulled up. Drawn by the woman's cries, two men from the other car (who Mr. B later described as "big, tough, and menacing") jumped out and grabbed Mr. B, dragged him from his car, and were about to hit him, when one of their female companions yelled: "Wait! He's not hurting her! *She's* the one who's crazy!"

Fortunately, the woman had seen the situation for what it was and intervened just in time to save Mr. B. Later, Mr. B revealed he had been terrified of being beaten up by the two men. "I knew I was a goner when I saw them running toward me. I realized that nothing I could say would stop them. Their reactions made sense. They naturally assumed that she was the victim, because she was a woman and she was crying, and so I was the attacker. They probably saw it as an attempted date-rape. It's amazing that the men's girlfriends saw what was really happening. I think in the same situation I would have re-acted exactly the way the men did."

In this incident, the men who came to the woman's assistance were acting on the stereotype that men are sexually driven and aggressive and that women must be rescued and protected from men's "animal" nature. In general, both sexes are continually being shaped and directed by stereotypes in destructive ways that don't necessarily lead to distortions of this magnitude, but do cause alienation between men and women. Indeed, women are not inferior, impractical, emotionally immature, dependent, or in need of special protection. They are not inherently less sexual or sexually inhibited. They are equal to men in intelligence and resourcefulness.

Manipulations through weakness, helplessness, and withholding are counterproductive to women's real goals of attaining equality with men. The hostility and resentment underlying subservient, passive behavior patterns in women complicate their relationships and contaminate their natural love and affection for the men in their lives. The tragedy is that men and women have a natural affinity for each other that, in the absence of these learned manipulations, would lead to affection, tenderness, and sexual intimacy. Yet in the complex interaction between women's reactions to cultural prejudices and generations of faulty child-rearing practices, many men and women eventually end up as enemies.

THE MOTHER–DAUGHTER BOND*

Women's strengths and weaknesses are transmitted from one generation to the next within the family context. The imprinting of these traits

---

*Portions of this section were adapted from *Compassionate Child-Rearing: An In-Depth Approach to Optimal Parenting* by R. W. Firestone, 1990, New York: Plenum Press. Used with permission.

and behavior patterns on the daughter's personality through the mother's influence as a role model is a powerful dynamic operating in women's lives. As adults, women pass on these characteristics to their daughters, both through direct instruction and through the process of imitation and identification (Firestone, 1990b).

The Central Role of the Mother

In our culture, the role of the mother as the primary caretaker has important implications because she exerts the most profound influence on the family. Some degree of frustration is inevitable in a child's early interactions because no person can successfully anticipate the needs of another at all times. However, when this frustration is compounded by immature or rejecting mothering, it leads to emotional hunger in the child and fosters hostility. These negative feelings have no acceptable outlet in most cases and therefore manifest themselves in the formation of psychological defenses and withholding behavior patterns.

In the case of female offspring, where the identification with the mother is stronger (Chodorow, 1978; Deutsch, 1944; Hudson & Jacot, 1995), the daughter's hurt or angry response is transformed into a form of withholding that resembles the mother's personality traits and patterns of defense. Although children of both sexes are adversely affected by their mother's rejection and manipulations, it appears that daughters tend to imitate their mother's behavior patterns more than sons.

The mother–daughter bond, so valued in our culture, may be the single most limiting factor in a woman's life. Friday (1977), in *My Mother/My Self*, observed that

> there is a great deal of data that says an unresolved relationship with her mother sets a woman's mind in certain nonautonomous patterns, encloses her in fear of certain experiences, often stops her from going after what she wants in life, or, when she finds what she wants, keeps her from taking from it the gratification she needs. (p. 35)

Despite the many volumes written on this subject since the publication of Friday's book,[1] there is still a dearth of information about critical issues at the core of the identification between mother and daughter. In no other relationship is the identification between individuals as intense, far-reaching, and powerful. This phenomenon not only has the potential for perpetuating mature, *positive* personality characteristics, but also an equally strong potential for projecting negative characteristics into future generations. However, the negative effects of this identification process often outweigh the positive (Fenchel, 1998a; Firestone, 1990b; Welldon, 1988).

Girls who suffer maternal deprivation carry elements of exaggerated need into subsequent relationships with men. The anger, resentment, and search for nurturance continue to complicate friendships and relationships with women as well. Paradoxically, the more painful and frustrating the interactions with a withholding mother, the more the daughter tends to incorporate her mother's noxious attitudes and behaviors (identification with the aggressor). This imitation takes place in spite of the fact that the daughter is often critical of these traits in her mother. To the degree that she maintains these characteristics, she suffers from self-hatred and demoralization that often play a significant part in depression.[2] Left unchallenged over time, the distinction between the daughter's personality and the incorporated negative traits becomes increasingly less obvious until the defended posture of the mother becomes dominant and the pattern is repeated with her own children.

The effects of this imitative process can be observed in couple and family relationships. For example, when a mother represents herself as an asexual woman and allows herself to deteriorate physically, it has a destructive effect on her daughter's sexuality. Ms. V made an important connection between her mother's style of relating to her father and her own issues:

> Ms. V: I rarely saw any sign of sexuality between my parents. My mother was kind of overweight and childish. The only image I have of her showing any sexuality at all was sometimes at night, she would drink some wine and get slightly drunk and giddy and come on to my father in such a strange way that made everybody uncomfortable. Then she would go to bed, and he wouldn't go to bed for hours. When he finally did, there was a lot of arguing. So any idea of her being sexual was horribly embarrassing to me, because she was so unattractive and childish.
>
> But I realize that in being sexual myself, I just can't believe that I can actually excite my husband. I'll be making love and I'll think to myself, There's no way he's going to be excited by you. I sometimes feel as embarrassing and as unappealing as I saw my mother. It's sad to think of that because I never realized before that I thought of myself in the same way I thought of my mother.

In a popular movie depicting the evolution of a couple's relationship, the woman, in the midst of nagging and complaining to her husband, suddenly commented, "Oh my God, it's finally happened! I've turned into my own mother!" Many women can identify with the sentiments this character expressed. Negative identification with the mother often takes the form of self-critical thoughts or "voices" about the body, issues regarding weight, breast size and shape, genitals, and overall sexual performance. It is common for American women to feel critical of their weight in a way that diminishes their sexuality.

Repercussions of the mother–daughter bond have a negative effect on women's relationships with men, and later, with their children. However, it is more important to emphasize the powerful limitation this bond may impose on each woman's sense of self. Its stultifying impact on her feelings of self-worth, achievement, and personal power is far greater than most clinicians realize.

Anxiety and Guilt Aroused by Movement Away From the Mother–Daughter Bond

The process of individuation, whereby children increasingly differentiate themselves from their mothers, occurs naturally throughout children's lives. Each step is generally accompanied by reminders of existential aloneness and separation anxiety. The developmental task of individuation is a difficult transition for children of both sexes. The son, in differentiating himself from the mother, gradually shifts his identification to the father. The daughter remains finely tuned to the mother (Chodorow, 1978; Genevie & Margolies, 1987).[3]

Thus, each step in a woman's development toward sexual maturity is filled with conflict. On the one hand, she is driven to seek independence, express her love and sexual desire in relation to a man, and have her own children; on the other hand, she is compelled to hold back this natural evolution in order to maintain the maternal connection.

There are crucial times in women's lives when they are fearful of moving away, symbolically or literally, from the mother: when they pursue a mature sexual relationship with a man, when they marry, when they establish their own household, and when they become mothers. Each step in the movement toward individuation and separation from the mother creates a sense of fear and guilt.[4] Many times these powerful emotions cause women to retreat during these critical periods and revert to dependency bonds and sameness with the mother, behaviors that offer an illusion of safety and have anxiety-reducing properties.

Marriage

A woman may bring any number of assets to marriage—compassion, wisdom, intelligence, skills, an imaginative spirit, delight-giving femininity, good humor, friendliness, pride in a job well done—but if she does not bring emancipation from her mother, the assets may wither or may be overbalanced by the liability of the fear of being a woman.
Joseph C. Rheingold (1964, p. 451)

Movement toward sexual intimacy with a man symbolizes a step away from the mother, as well as a loss of the hope of ever satisfying one's longing for maternal love. Women are necessarily ambivalent; they are drawn to marriage as an imitation of their mother, yet they fear it as a step toward further individuation.

Marriage and the attainment of sexual maturity often arouse a woman's fear of her mother's jealousy, envy, and vindictiveness, feelings that many women have experienced since early childhood. As she matures, a daughter may actually fear retaliation from the mother for seeking adult sexual fulfillment. Rheingold (1967) drew attention to this aspect of the separation–individuation process as it affects women: "In the psychotherapy of women one regularly discovers an association of the masochistic or hostile dependent kind of relationship with the mother and the fear of mutilation and annihilation as punishment for feminine self-fulfillment— indeed, for just being a female" (p. 96).

According to Rheingold, most young girls are terrified of their mother's feelings of hostility and jealousy, and as a result, they attempt to turn to the father for protection. However, this move toward the father is similarly fraught with danger because of the mother's envy, and the girl retreats once again. Caplan (1981) described how daughters often adjust to their mother's envy:

> It is a heavy burden to feel envied by one's mother. This is especially true because anger so often accompanies envy. . . . How does a daughter deal with her mother's competitiveness with her or jealousy of her accomplishments? Often, she does one of two things (or tries both at different times): She reduces her efforts to achieve . . . and she puts emotional or physical distance between herself and her mother. (p. 120)

In our experience, we have found that both separation anxiety and fear of the mother's envy or vindictiveness are experienced by women at crucial points in their sexual development. In addition, many women who are successful in their personal and vocational pursuits experience intense guilt reactions in having gone beyond the mother—in particular, a self-denying, asexual mother.

Rather than cope with the guilt, separation anxiety, and fear of retaliation inherent in moving away from the mother, some women find themselves experiencing a renewed closeness with their mothers following marriage. Commenting on this "reunion," Friday (1977) wrote the following:

> When we move into an apartment of our own, when we find a job, take a lover, get married and have a child of our own—in all these important rites of passage away from her [mother], as we take one step forward, we take another one back, and find ourselves doing things her way. *Becoming like her overcomes our separation anxieties* [italics added]. (p. 435)

Pregnancy and Childbirth

Having a child is a fulfilling and rewarding experience for most women. However, it symbolizes a final separation from one's mother, which can arouse intense anxiety. As Friday commented: "There are two times in women's lives when the unconscious drive to become the mother we dislike speeds up. The first is when we become mothers ourselves. The second is when our mother dies" (p. 450).

Starting a new family signifies the end of childhood, causing many women to cling to dependent, childlike patterns of behavior during the pregnancy and following the birth of the baby. Conventional views of a pregnant woman's helplessness and need for protection also come into play, and lend support to a woman's return to dependency and self-indulgence during this period.

When this type of regression occurs, it usually continues until delivery, when there is either movement toward recovery or a more pronounced retreat into a depressed state. The dynamics of postpartum depression show that the woman is experiencing intense emotional reactions to the reality and responsibilities of being a mother. Benedek (1970) emphasized that "pregnancy is a critical phase in the life of a woman. . . . [It] requires physiologic adjustments and psychologic adaptations to lead to a new level of integration" (p. 137). Blum (1977) asserted that

> cultural attitudes toward motherhood may be in conflict with powerful unconscious maternal strivings. In addition to the familiar prostitution fantasies, the clash of infanticidal wishes and maternal ideals is among the deepest unconscious conflicts of women. Infanticidal conflicts are core conflicts in women with histories of postpartum depression. (pp. 176–177)[5]

Blum (1978), in discussing a case of postpartum depression, concluded: "This patient's feelings of loss of maternal closeness and support, separation panic, helplessness, and 'negative ambivalence' predisposed her to her adult depression neurosis" (p. 353).

Women's Fear and Guilt in Relation to Symbolic Substitutes

Women often have a catastrophic fear of other women based on their early relationship with their mother (Rheingold, 1964, 1967). The original fear of loss and guilt experienced in relation to surpassing—and separating from—the mother are frequently transferred to women who serve as symbolic substitutes for the maternal figure. For example, women commonly feel guilty about achieving intimacy and happiness with a man in relation to women friends who are self-denying or have given up their own pursuit of sexual fulfillment or other personal goals.

Many women's fear of their own competitive feelings and retaliation from their peers causes them to withdraw from situations that are potentially rivalrous. I observed this phenomenon in a discussion group that was held for my professional colleagues. One evening, the group, composed of four men and one woman, welcomed a new female member. Almost immediately and in the subsequent sessions, the original female participant, who had been very active, became extremely quiet and faded into the background. The new member flourished, was quite outspoken, and attracted considerable attention from the male participants. Later, this pattern was repeated when two more women joined the group (one at a time), and each previous "new" member, in turn, stepped back and withdrew from her active participation in the group. The group analyzed this peculiar turn of events and found that the women had a basic fear of standing out and competing with the newcomers, which they acted on without conscious awareness.

Often, rather than competing actively in their personal lives or for success in the practical world, women move toward the level of the lowest common denominator within their circle of women friends. They are profoundly affected by women who use the passive–aggressive techniques of falling apart, manipulating through weakness, playing the victim, and expressing suicidal ideation. The latter is particularly threatening. Women's personal lives and goal-directed activities can be affected by negative social pressure when the women close to them use these manipulative techniques.

This type of social pressure is a common phenomenon in the lives of women. For example, a woman may feel reluctant to tell a female friend about the new man in her life, when her friend has complained consistently about being unable to find a man. She would tend to instinctively hold back her own pleasure and happiness to some extent, so as not to hurt her friend's feelings. This process might appear innocuous on the surface, but it can become part of a serious self-denial or pattern of withholding (Firestone & Catlett, 1989).

Many women belong to an implicit "women's club" whose members subscribe to a certain stereotyped attitude toward men and follow prescribed ways of relating to the man in their lives. They alternate between building up their mates to attain status in their peer group and tearing down and ridiculing them in front of the others. Members of this informal grouping share the attitude that women need to manipulate men because men are powerful, but foolish. There is a paradoxical combination of inferiority and superiority in these women's attitudes and behaviors.

A cultural pattern of negative power prevails among women. These patterns are part of the social pressure that operates to keep women in a victimized role. In the process of symbolically reuniting with the mother, many women find themselves selling out their point of view to other women. Socially held attitudes, standards, and codes of behavior reflect those they learned as children from their mothers. This way of thinking attributes to men most of women's dissatisfaction in relationships, marriage, and life. This code implicitly states that although men may understand the practical world, they comprehend little about interpersonal relations, emotions, children, and most important, they do not understand women or know how to communicate with them.

Most women are afraid of not conforming to these stereotypic views. If they choose to relate to men with equality, love, and trust, they are often perceived as a threat by those peers who subscribe to this style of relating and are criticized or denounced for being a "sucker." Moreover, there is social pressure from the media and literature supporting sexist, prejudicial views of men that hold them accountable for the majority of women's misery and suppression.[6]

DIMENSIONS OF FEMALE SEXUALITY

The honest disclosures of women in the reference population have contributed a vast amount of information to our knowledge of female psychology. After many years of open discussion, women reached the stage where they would honestly deal with the issues discussed below without becoming defensive or punitive. From the beginning, women in the longitudinal study were exceptionally bold and forthright. In fact, many were pioneers in addressing and bringing out the truth regarding deep-seated problems in couple relationships. They took more risks than men in altering outdated cultural patterns that separate the sexes.

The women in this group tend to place a high value on their independence. At the same time that they were disclosing patterns of withholding and other defensive maneuvers, they were fighting for their rights personally, sexually, and vocationally. In their movement toward independence, they did not see men as holding them back; instead, they perceived their limitations as self-imposed, the result of internalizing their mother's negative attitudes and often the guilt about surpassing her. The information that women revealed in the group discussions was shared in the spirit of equality. In giving up self-protective defenses, they achieved considerable strength and maturity and now have a different perspective on themselves and men. Their self-disclosures led to a number of hypotheses regarding women in general:

1. *Although both men and women hold back sexually from their mates when they revert to a defended posture, the tendency to withhold appears to be greater in a woman.* A woman's bond with her mother often takes precedence over her relationship with a man. When she becomes anxious, guilty, or fearful, a woman will often revert to childish responses and become emotionally distant.

Women's withholding behaviors affect the couple's sexual relationship. At times, women may find it difficult to fully experience feelings of wanting or sexual desire. When they hold back their natural responsiveness or enthusiasm for sex, the effects are detrimental to both partners.

Women generally control the sexual situation in the sense that they are usually the decision makers for the couple in relation to the frequency of love-making, the time, place, and behavior that is acceptable. When a woman allows herself to completely experience feelings of sexual desire, she tends to elicit a strong sexual response from her partner. On the other hand, at times a woman may unconsciously inhibit her genuine feelings of wanting and tend to cut off her feelings at various points during the sexual act. This can occur at different stages: at the stage of undressing, at the point of changing from affectional responses to sexual responses, at the point of intercourse (when she may have a fear reaction immediately before penetration), or at any point during the sexual act. These withholding responses usually have an adverse effect on the man's feelings and level of excitement.

2. *Women are able to control men through building up their vanity and by other manipulations of negative power.* In revealing the basic strategies they used in their relationships with men, women talked about how manipulating men by building them up, supporting their narcissism, and pretending to be enthralled with them gave them leverage. However, in spite of building them up in their presence, there was a tendency to tear down men behind their backs in conversations with other women. Women employed a variety of passive—aggressive techniques in an attempt to gain leverage in their relationships, using tears, sulking, and silence, or by acting weaker, less competent, or more helpless than they were in reality.

3. *Most women have a fantasy of being taken care of by men.* Women are often willing to depreciate themselves, belittle their abilities, and function at a lower level to hold on to a sense of being protected, even when the protection is illusory.[7] Although modern women for the most part lead more independent lives than their predecessors, many still wish to be taken care of by a man. They recognize that it would be politically incorrect to reveal this fantasy, yet many studies show that it still exists as part of the "unconscious contract" many couples form. For example, the behavior of Ms. S., a successful businesswoman, is revealing in this regard: She earns ten times the income of the man she is involved with, yet is desperate for his attention, extremely childish in his company, and seeks his help in every area of her life, including financial planning.

4. *Women are more selective in their choice of sex partners, while men appear to be more random.* This should not be interpreted to imply that men are less feeling in interpersonal relationships. Indeed, many women can be unfeeling and impersonal in a monogamous relationship.[8] As long as a woman remains satisfied with her choice of a mate, she usually does not

seek to form a sexual alliance with another man. However, if she meets a man who she perceives as having more prestige, strength, wealth or power than her mate, someone with "better genes," in evolutionary terms, her preference may very well change. At this point, she may reject her original choice and replace him with the new love object. In other words, women appear to prefer being involved with one man at a time (serial monogamy), and their selection of a mate for an exclusive relationship may be, for the long or short term, based on many variables.

Men appear to seek more variety in choosing a mate. However, if they become attracted to another woman, they generally do not want to replace their original choice with the new love object. It appears that men place a high value on the companionship and emotional satisfaction provided by their relationships with women. They tend to relate on a personal level to the women in their lives, and most would not choose to reject their current partner in pursuing a new love interest. If the option of having more than one relationship were open to men, most would probably prefer to include the new sexual partner in their lives rather than divorce or separate from the "old" partner. In other words, men do not tend to support serial monogamy; however, legal sanctions prevent them from creating a more inclusive or polygamous family constellation.

5. *Women and men can have a conflict of interests in forming a relationship with one another.* A long-term relationship or marriage has different unconscious connotations for men and women. For men, marriage can symbolize the fulfillment of their desire for close, affectionate contact with the mother that they have longed for since early childhood. The illusion that they are achieving a reunion with the mother is often based more on a childlike fixation than on a healthy, adult desire for companionship. For women, as noted earlier, marriage can symbolize separation from the mother and a loss of dependency, an anxiety-provoking situation. In this sense, men and women have a conflict of interest and are unconsciously at odds with each other. This conflict of interest arises because the man is motivated to attach to a "mother substitute," whereas the woman is resistant to the symbolic separation from the mother. In this case, both are resisting forming a mature, individuated relationship.[9]

Developmentally, women also have a more difficult sexual role to fulfill in that they must, in effect, change the gender of their sex object. They must successfully transfer the original affectionate, erotic attraction they felt toward the mother to men in their adult lives; on the other hand, in pursuing a relationship with a woman, a man merely extends his feelings for the mother to new objects.

6. *Most women are attracted, emotionally, aesthetically, and physically to other women.* This attraction is probably based on the strong attraction to the mother and is a natural extension of early physical longings.

As women developed a sense of trust in individual and group discussions, they talked more candidly about their feelings toward each other, which included feelings of attraction. They were drawn to women who were energetic, good-looking, and self-possessed. It appeared that these feelings had sexual components, and were similar to men's feelings toward these women.[10] In fact, the women who were the most attractive to the other women were at the same time the most attractive to the men. However, the attraction between these women is not part of a generalized homosexual pattern in their lives.

Although men felt affectionate and warm toward each other, their feelings did not have the sexual component of the women's feelings toward each other. However, it is difficult to say whether this finding represents an essential biological difference between the sexes or is due to cultural influences with strong prohibitions against physical, affectionate, or sexual contact between men.

7. *Women have become better friends based on acknowledging socially unacceptable truths about themselves and each other.* Interestingly enough, when the women in this group recognized their attraction to other women, they reduced their fear of this attraction and incidentally enhanced their relationships with men. These women have become friendly rivals in the process of supporting each other's freedom and acknowledging competitive feelings. They do not act out nasty, bitchy traits or engage in gossip or back-biting political maneuvering in relation to each other or interact in a phony, superficially sweet style.

8. *Pregnancy is a natural part of life.* Women in the reference population do not seek special consideration or care during pregnancy other than observing the medical necessities. Early on, the first of these women to have children set a standard of independence during pregnancy that has been maintained through the years. They had no desire to be taken care of, catered to, or pampered during their pregnancies or the childbirth experience. They had already developed a style of not complaining about the realities of everyday life and saw no need to behave differently during this phase of their lives. Neither did they want to make their pregnancy a self-aggrandizing focus. They avoided the narcissistic inclination to indulge themselves to the detriment of their husbands, other family members, and friends.

All the women worked full time and wanted to continue pursuing their careers along with sharing the responsibilities of child care with their husbands. They looked forward to even more fulfillment and satisfaction in their lives after their babies were born. They wanted to avoid slipping into the conventional "mother" role that they had found undesirable in their own mothers, a role that had often excluded the husbands from a real participation in the raising of the children. Each woman developed a more adult, confident approach to her life as a result of having her baby in a manner that seemed most natural to her.

9. *Child-rearing: Both men and women show a strong interest in and feeling for children.* In the reference population, we discovered that women have the same anxieties about handling newborns as do men. In general, the myth of women being natural mothers did not hold up under close scrutiny but appeared to be based on an idealization process common in our culture (Badinter, 1980/1981).

There is a wide variation among the women in their capability to be mothers, just as there is a wide range of abilities among the fathers for taking practical care of their infants. At times, many of the fathers have taken over the child care functions, and in this respect there has been an increased sense of sharing the responsibilities and joys of raising children. Thus, it appears that men and women in this population were equal along these dimensions.

CONCLUSION

Stereotyped views of men and women have contributed significantly to the hostility between the sexes. Most women have been damaged during their formative years in two important areas of functioning: in their capacity to love, understand, and have empathy for men as well as in their striving for independence and equality. To achieve full maturity, they need to break the negative identification with their mothers and live their lives as separate individuals. The women in the circle of friends who recognized the effects of these identification and imitative processes have moved in the direction of assuming real power over their lives.

It is possible to alter traditional cultural patterns. On a social level, the feminist movement has contributed valuable impetus to women's struggles to achieve personal freedom and equal status with men; nevertheless, some proponents of this movement express certain radical views that are inherently damaging to women. Women need not adopt a superior, hateful attitude toward men in order to challenge inequalities and prejudices that exist in our society. This stance, to which a few feminists subscribe, leads to hostility and counterhostilities between the sexes. These aggressive feelings toward men alienate women from their basic feelings of love and empathy and weaken their striving for independence by supporting the maintenance of a victimized, paranoid position. Women need not sacrifice their sexuality or their love for men to attain equality; to do so would be self-defeating. Many can and do pursue and maintain their rights without turning against the part of themselves that is basically loving and naturally drawn to men.

Understanding the issues involved in the problems between men and women has led to the formulation of a number of procedures that are being used in our couples therapy. Recognizing the sources of much of the tension and pain that exists in male–female relationships, that is, sexual stereotypes, male vanity, female control, and specific gender-related problems inherent in the individuation process, has been valuable in helping couples deal with each of these issues.

By becoming more aware of sexism and distortions of men and women common in our culture, individuals gradually moved beyond these views and developed closer, more harmonious relationships. Explorations of the manipulations typically engaged in by couples underscored the inherent destructiveness of these machinations, and this knowledge helped partners disrupt these patterns in their relationships. The exposure of the dynamics underlying male vanity and female control, that is, understanding how these defensive postures operate in concert to create a collusive couple or family system, was instrumental in our formulating plans or corrective suggestions for modifying these characteristics and behaviors.

Understanding the specific problems that men and women face in differentiating from early attachment figures added substantially to our knowledge of the important steps in the individuation process. Subsequently, we developed methods that help people deal with the anxiety aroused during these crucial transitions. Our familiarity with the dynamics of compensatory behaviors manifested by many men and women led to suggestions for constructive behavioral change.

The methods described in the following chapters are based on many of the ideas discussed here. In particular, our understanding that the more destructive aspects of sexual stereotyping are based on internalized voices led to the development of techniques to counteract these hostile thought processes within the context of couples therapy.

ENDNOTES

[1] Among these volumes are *The Mother–Daughter Relationship* (Fenchel, 1998b); *Mother Love, Mother Hate* (Grizzle, 1988); *When You and Your Mother Can't Be Friends* (Secunda, 1990).

[2] See *Unfinished Business: Pressure Points in the Lives of Women* (Scarf, 1980); *Women and Depression: Risk Factors and Treatment Issues* (McGrath, Keita, Strickland, & Russo, 1990).

[3] In her discussion of the "Female Oedipal Configuration," Chodorow (1978) argued that "for a girl, however, there is no single oedipal mode or quick oedipal resolution, and there is no absolute 'change of object'. . . . A girl never gives up her mother as an internal or external love object" (p. 127).

[4] Guilt reactions and fear of separation from the mother are frequently manifest in adolescent girls in the form of various emotional disturbances. For example, L. J. Kaplan (1984) discussed anorexia nervosa in terms of a failure to individuate from the mother: "In high school and college-age girls anorexia is a solution to the dilemmas associated with becoming a woman" (p. 259). She

noted also how parental prohibitions and perfectionistic attitudes are manifested in "internal voices":

> When the Oedipal triangle is weakly articulated, a child is deprived of the opportunity to own her own conscience. . . . The parental prohibitions and commandments then will continue to be experienced as coming from outside the self, or as alien inner voices. One of the major complaints of the anoretic is that she cannot rid herself of the sense that she always acts on the commands of others. "There is another self, a dictator who dominates me. . . . A little man screams at me when I think of eating." (p. 269)

[5]See "Regression and Reintegration in Pregnancy" (Kestenberg, 1977) and "Affective Experiences and Levels of Self-Organization in Maternal Postpartum Depression" (Menos & Wilson, 1998). Mild to moderate postpartum depression may affect 400,000 women per year (Dix, 1985). Developmental psychologists Klaus and Kennell (1976) suggested that most pregnant women have fears that form the basis for the wide variation in quality of mother–infant relations: "The production of a normal child is a major goal of most women. Yet most pregnant women have hidden fears that the infant may be abnormal or reveal some of their own secret inner weaknesses" (p. 42). Rheingold (1964, 1967) observed similar fears in over 2,500 pregnant women interviewed during a 12-year experimental study. He found that the mother's ambivalence usually continued unabated long after the child was born, although the more negative aspects were either completely forgotten or partially repressed. Dix (1985) stated that "when we give birth, all our own infantile instincts and reactions are reactivated. For some women that might mean reliving ambivalence about our mothers that we experienced as infants: the desire to be separate and the need to merge with her" (p. 139).

[6]See Gordon's (1998) chapter "The Medea Complex and the Parental Alienation Syndrome: When Mothers Damage Their Daughters' Ability to Love a Man." According to Gordon, the media often merely reinforces negative views held by women who manifest hostility toward their mates and "brainwash" their children to imitate their attitudes and behaviors. Gordon cited Wallerstein and Corbin's (1989) study of girls from divorced families, which found that "daughters who identified with hostile mothers had the poorest adjustment [in their relationships with men]" (Gordon, 1998, p. 209).

[7]Many women see men as the "ultimate rescuer" who will save them from death and seek this imagined security at great personal cost (Fromm, 1941; Rank, 1936/1972).

[8]It has been hypothesized by evolutionary psychologists that women's selectivity is partly a function of a biological imperative to find the best genes for their children (Wilson, 1981). In widely varying cultures, women can be observed clustering around the male whose characteristics are valued in that specific society. For example, in the business world, the successful businessman is the most powerful figure; in a motorcycle gang, the toughest, most aggressive rider is the most sought-after; in the world of art, it is the most sensitive, expressive,

or recognized artist who attracts a following among women. Although different groups value very different characteristics, this pattern holds up across cultures. In the reference population, we observed a similar phenomenon. This tendency for women to gather around and move toward powerful men is not necessarily based on love or sensitivity, but on a more primitive desire to produce the strongest offspring and is also related to women's desire to be taken care of.

[9]Both men and women tend to base object relations on the primary object relationship to the mother, and the efficacy of this attachment will have a fundamental effect on their satisfaction and security in their adult relationships (Shaver & Clark, 1994). See also "A New Female Psychology?" (Barglow & Schaefer, 1977).

Other writers have noted the conflict of interest existing between men and women in forming a relationship. Hudson and Jacot (1995) emphasized that a "less familiar feature of female development . . . [which is] a potent source of mutual incomprehension between the sexes, has its point of origin in the rivalry, fantasied or real, between the small girl and her mother." They concluded:

> The daughter/mother bond is not only symbiotic; it is powerfully ambivalent, incorporating both the comforting and alarming, the good and bad. . . . As she cannot express her anger towards her mother without threatening her own identity, the small girl's anger will also tend to translate itself into depression. . . . For women, in other words: Heterosexual intimacy taps automatically into deep reservoirs of unresolved hostility, blame and depression. (pp. 8–9)

> Less obvious is the implication that women will be more likely than men to become depressed in marriages and intimacies *that are going well*. Again the statistical evidence is confirmatory: among the happily married, women are five times as likely to be depressed as men. . . . [this indicates that] a significant source of a woman's discontent lies within herself. (p. 10)

[10]Nancy Friday's books, *My Secret Garden* (1973) and *Forbidden Flowers* (1975) reported the sexual fantasies of over 400 women. Many of the fantasies revealed by these women depicted affectionate, sexual encounters with other women. Friday commented that "What interests me is that if the emotional openness women show one another in their fantasies could be extended to reality, I am sure the result would be, not a soaring increase in lesbianism, but the contrary: a broader, more meaningful heterosexuality" (1973, p. 181).

III

COUNTERING THE INNER VOICE: METHODS AND THEORY

12

VOICES AFFECTING INTIMACY

Our life is what our thoughts make it.
                    Marcus Aurelius, *Meditations*

While investigating the techniques of voice therapy (VT), we have been able to identify the destructive forces underlying the fantasy bond. The 22-year investigation into the structure and function of the "voice" (described in chap. 7, this volume) has significantly broadened our understanding of healthy versus addictive relationships. This chapter describes material gathered during ongoing seminars in which VT procedures were utilized to elicit and identify participants' hostile thoughts and attitudes regarding their relationships. Also included is a discussion of a number of hypotheses about couple relationships that were derived from this data.

Our objectives in this chapter are to report findings from the group sessions, note the important implications for theory, suggest the efficacy of voice therapy as a useful technique for helping couples in conflict, and encourage research utilizing the voice concept to assess the quality of personal relationships.

PSYCHODYNAMICS: ORIGINS OF DESTRUCTIVE THOUGHT PROCESS OR VOICE

As noted in chapter 2, destructive thoughts and attitudes arise as a part of a defensive process. Negative parental introjects or voices internalized during the formative years lead to an essential dualism within the personality. This "division of the mind" reflects a primary split between forces that represent the self and those that oppose or attempt to destroy the self. These elements can be conceptualized as the "self-system" and the "antiself-system." The two systems develop independently; both are dynamic and continually evolve over time.

People possess conflicting points of view about themselves, others, and events in the world, depending upon which aspect of the personality, self or antiself, is dominant. One point of view is rational, objective, and life-affirming, while the other is made up of the destructive thought process or voice that is opposed to the ongoing development, or even survival, of the self. Destructive cognitive processes that make up the antiself-system have a dual focus: They are antithetical toward the self as well as cynical, distrustful, and hostile toward others. Both lead to alienation.

The *voice* is defined as a well-integrated pattern of negative thoughts that is the basis of an individual's maladaptive behavior (Firestone, 1988). It represents an overlay on the personality that is not natural or harmonious, but learned or imposed from without. The voice process is part of an internal form of self-parenting that extends painful experiences in the original family environment to a generalized attitude toward and treatment of self. My associates and I have found that negative voices correlate significantly with suicidal trends. Voices may be conceptualized on a continuum ranging from self-critical or self-deprecating thoughts and attitudes to extreme self-attacks or actual suicidal ideation.

VOICE THERAPY THEORY

Voice therapy refers to the process of giving language or spoken words to the internalized negative thought process. Its purpose is to separate and bring into the open those elements of the personality that are antithetical to the self and predispose hostility toward others (Firestone, 1990d). Voice therapy theory describes how negative parental attitudes, even those that are unconscious, are incorporated.[1] These introjects or internal representations, similar in some respects to the concept of the antilibidinal ego described by Fairbairn (1952) and Guntrip (1969), seriously restrict people's natural development as unique individuals and have a detrimental effect on personal relationships.

Background

In recent years (1991–1996), we developed an instrument, the *Firestone Assessment of Self-Destructive Thoughts* (FAST; Firestone & Firestone, 1996), based on voice therapy theory, to assess an individual's self-destructive and suicidal potential. Scale items comprise self-critical statements, or "voices," that are stated in the second-person format; for example, "You're incompetent, stupid," or "You're unattractive and uninteresting." "Why would he (she) want to go out with you?" After refining the FAST and testing its reliability and validity, we began to focus on the general mental health of individuals with an emphasis on their capacity for intimacy in interpersonal relationships. Subsequently, we conducted a series of discussions on this subject with men and women in the reference population.

Preliminary data from these discussions is posited to assess the quality of interpersonal relationships and the emotional health of the partners involved. The data will serve as a platform on which to develop a questionnaire similar to the FAST, where individuals would identify the content and frequency of experiencing negative thoughts toward self and others. Comparisons across partners in multiple phases of relationships (initial development, long-term relationships, individuals involved in marital therapy, and those who are separated or divorced) are being planned in developing the new scale.[2]

To obtain items pertaining to relationships, we asked participants to think about their interpersonal and intimate relationships and verbalize their negative thoughts about them. We anticipated that they would identify the content of these attitudes and thoughts in an intellectualized format; however, almost immediately after overcoming initial anxiety and self-consciousness, the participants verbalized powerful self-attacks and released feelings of anger and sadness of surprising intensity. The discussions were audiotaped and transcribed.

CLINICAL MATERIAL

Based on this initial inquiry, we derived the following hypotheses:

1. People have considerable hostility toward self and often feel that they are unlovable, factors that lead to desperation in interpersonal relationships.
2. When partners have a similar level of dysfunction, they tend to have reciprocal voices, and their relationships have a poor prognosis.
3. When people choose partners with complementary or opposite traits, often the same qualities that were the basis of the original attraction later become areas of conflict.
4. People's styles of relating are primarily based on their parents' beliefs and prescriptions about relationships. When they break with their parents' programming, they experience considerable anxiety and intensified voice attacks.

5. Men and women's fear of competition is related to the incorporation of their parents' hostile competitive impulses toward them. As adults, they either project them onto present-day figures or experience them as self-destructive attitudes.

Hostile Attitudes and Negativity Toward Self

In using the methods of voice therapy, participants became aware that varying degrees of aggression toward self, as well as sadness and pain, are associated with their voice attacks. It also became apparent that their destructive voices significantly affected the quality of their relationships. To illustrate, in one of the meetings, Dorothy, 35, and recently divorced, gave words to self-depreciating attitudes she had about herself as a woman. When she verbalized her self-attacks in the second person and permitted her feelings to flow, her voice became louder and noticeably angry:

> A lot of times I have attacks that I'm different from other women. You're not like other women. You're never going to have something with a man.

At this point, Dorothy's voice assumed a derisive, distinctly parental tone:

> You're not nice to men. You're not pretty. You're not feminine. You're not lovable. I hate you. I hate you! [loud, intensely angry, rapid speech] I hate your face. You're not right. You don't look right. You don't act right. I'm embarrassed by you. You're not what I want. You don't have the right color hair. You don't have the right kind of hair. You don't have the right looks. You just don't fit in. You won't do what I tell you to do!

After verbalizing her self-attacks and releasing her angry feelings, Dorothy went on to describe the threatening emotional climate that had characterized her home. She recalled specific abusive statements that her mother had directed toward her during her childhood:

> I feel like this was my mother's view of me. It's hard for me to say these things because I think that I'm still afraid of her anger. This feeling is like: I don't want you here. You don't fit into this family. Everyone else is nice. You don't fit in. Everyone else does what I tell them to do. You don't! You don't fit in! You don't look like the rest of us. You're not at all like us!

Dorothy's mother had been verbally and physically abusive to her during her father's extended absences from home. When Dorothy sought her father's help, he failed to intervene on her behalf. In these extreme circumstances, she lived in constant fear of her mother's aggression and, as a result, incorporated the intense hatred her mother felt toward her. As an adult, Dorothy's low self-esteem created a sense of desperation in relation to men. She was aggressive in her approach, which discouraged many potential partners. In her marriage, she was distrustful and preoccupied with trying to elicit reassurances of love from her husband. Her possessiveness, insecurity, and jealousy caused a rift in the relationship, and the couple eventually separated.

Reciprocal Voices Based on Mutual Insecurity or Similar Levels of Dysfunctionality

Partners with similar levels of dysfunctionality often report the same or equivalent voice attacks. For example, Barbara, 34, and Hal, 49, had been involved for 2 years and had grown close to each other. It was at this point that they began to experience problems. Hal had negative attitudes about his age and appearance and found it difficult to believe that a woman would want to be with him on a consistent basis, whereas Barbara felt that she was undeserving of love. Recently, Hal had expressed the desire to marry Barbara. Sensing her hesitancy, he blamed himself for her lack of enthusiasm. His negative way of thinking about himself (thoughts that contributed to a low-level depression) escalated significantly, and he experienced intense psychological pain.

> Hal: Recently, I've had strong attacking voices. They go like this: [snide tone] You're the one that's really weak and you have to do everything to try to hide it. You have to really work hard to make sure nobody sees that. But everybody does see it anyway. [angry tone] You're ugly. You're really old and you don't deserve anything, let alone a woman in your life. You can pretend as much as you want, but women will find out what you really are, no matter how much you pretend to be affectionate and sweet. Those are just words. They'll find out that you have no substance. You don't deserve anything.
>
> When I think about my relationship with Barbara or about women in general, I have thoughts such as the following: They really see through you. They see right through you, and they try to pretend that you're stronger than you really are so that you won't feel bad.
>
> When I just finished saying that about myself, that my affection is not real, I realized that it's the same attack that I have on Barbara, that her affection is made up, it's pretend. She's trying to be something that she really isn't towards you. Women don't want to be a part of your life. They want to have their own lives. It's harder to say specific negative things about Barbara or about women in general.

Later in the meeting, Barbara disclosed destructive attitudes about herself that corresponded to those Hal had disclosed:

Barbara (to Hal):   A lot of my voices are so similar to yours. I was very sad when you were talking because they're identical voices. Especially in a situation where I can feel you looking at me affectionately or wanting to be tender toward me, I think to myself: Don't fool yourself. He doesn't care about you. Who the hell could care about you? He's tricking himself and he's trying to trick you. Just get over it. Get over it! Don't believe that kind of bullshit. You're damaged goods! Nobody's going to care about you like that. You're not going to have anybody care about you like that.

    You think he cares about you? He's just fooling himself and you. He's in dreamland and you're in dreamland, too. Who do you think you are? You think somebody cares about you? You're not somebody that anybody could care about. You've got no feelings and anybody can see that. If he looked at you, if he really looked at you, then he'd see. Then he'd see what's inside.

    You think you can actually let anybody really look at you. Just stand back a little bit. Just keep things nice. Keep things on an even level. Don't let him sit too close. Don't let him in so that he can really see you. You're going to just ruin everything.

Later, she said: "The thing that struck me in this is that I feel like you're tricking me and you feel like I'm tricking you and that we both feel it's all a pretense."

It is significant that both individuals tended to idealize the other, on the basis of their own feelings of inferiority and negative self-images. Barbara exaggerated Hal's importance in her life and built him up, which he sensed on some level, while he tended to idolize women in general and his partner in particular. New difficulties arose immediately after he expressed the desire to marry her. Both of their voices were intensified and took the form of cynical attitudes and suspicions about being tricked by the other.

In another case, Katherine and David, in their early twenties when they met, quickly became involved in a passionate relationship; however, each was insecure, immature, and undifferentiated emotionally from the family of origin. Because of early trauma, Katherine had developed a serious phobia and suffered from recurrent panic attacks, and David was addicted to drugs and alcohol. For a brief period, however, it appeared that each was flourishing in the relationship: David resolved to give up drugs, and Katherine was temporarily free of anxiety symptoms. Later, there was regression in both partners, and they became increasingly intolerant of each others' problems and weaknesses. The insecurity and lack of individuation in each partner were seriously limiting factors, and the relationship was predisposed to fail.

Although this relationship started out with promise, both partners followed the dictates of their respective voices, acting out their hostility and distrust in their interactions. As each became provoked and demoralized by the other's accusations, the relationship unraveled, and they soon went their separate ways. If either David or Katherine had been able to extend love and understanding to the other, or if either could have withstood the adverse reactions of the other and been strong and helpful, the relationship might have survived.

Relationships Based on Opposite Personality Characteristics

A number of participants revealed voice attacks that illuminated the dynamics operating in their relationships. It appeared that people often select a partner with complementary characteristics to compensate for perceived personality deficiencies in themselves. This dynamic is based on negative core beliefs that are supported by the voice process. Willi (1975/1982) has noted that partner selection often results from the search for repressed or missing elements of the self in the partner, which later leads to marital dissension. For example, an aggressive person will tend to be attracted to a passive, submissive person. An individual who needs to take care of others will be drawn to a person who feels the need to be taken care of. These relationships are often characterized by an initial strong sexual attraction. There is a sense of attaining wholeness from this union, when in reality, it weakens both partners as they come to depend on each other for these complementary traits. They eventually come to resent and even hate these qualities in the other, and there is often a serious decline in their sexual attraction.

Bert and Rachel's marriage exemplifies the polarization that can occur in these cases. Bert, a quiet, retiring, easygoing man was initially attracted to Rachel's liveliness, vitality, and outspoken nature. The sexual attraction between them was intense but declined soon after they married. Rachel became progressively more controlling of the couple's life: planning their activities, their vacations, their evenings, and selecting their friends. Bert gradually subverted his wants and point of view in an attempt to hold onto the relationship. The couple eventually separated. Later they participated in the group discussions in an attempt to understand the elements that contributed to the dissolution of their marriage.

In one seminar, Rachel recalled the destructive voices she "listened to" during the troubled phase of the relationship—injunctions that attacked her for being too sexually excited and her partner for being too passive during love-making:

> Don't get so excited. Let him touch you just enough, just enough to let him feel good, but no more. It doesn't feel good. His touch isn't nice; it's too soft, it's too passive, it's not aggressive enough. He's not strong. He's a weak man, so how can you feel that excited with him? Just get it over with. Just let him feel enough to get it over with. Just let him do everything. He needs this. He needs it in order to feel good. Just give in to him and don't feel anything about it!

Over the past months, I've realized how much I began to see you as a weak person. [sad] It was like you became a pitiful person to me, and I had to face the fact that I had made you feel like that and that you had become unattractive to me. And I felt terribly guilty because I knew on some level that I had turned you into a person I couldn't love.

To compensate for his feelings of inadequacy, Bert had a desperate need to find someone who was active and vital and to defer to her more dominant personality. Rachel's more dynamic style and need to control represented compensatory patterns that covered over and helped alleviate her deep sense of insecurity.

The more rejection or deprivation an individual experiences during the formative years, the more a person seeks security and a sense of wholeness through this process. Eventually, these relationships develop into an addictive attachment in that both individuals are using each other as an instrument to assuage feelings of insecurity. This pattern of coupling can only be altered when each individual focuses on developing personally. By challenging the destructive voices underlying their negative core beliefs, men and women will look for different qualities in a partner and be able to move toward relationships that are mutually enriching.

Prescriptions for Living Based on Negative Parental Attitudes

Another significant finding was that sexual stereotypes are extensions of individuals' voice attacks. As noted in chapters 10 and 11 in this volume, defensive attitudes toward the opposite sex held by parents are passed on to their children. We found that the majority of women adopt their mother's negative point of view about men and that men are generally influenced by their father's attitudes toward women.

A number of women in our discussion groups revealed the following views and identified them as reflecting their mothers' spoken and unspoken attitudes toward men and their prescriptions about how to "handle" a man in a relationship:

All men want is sex. They don't want to commit to marriage.

Men are so insensitive. They're so opinionated. They won't let you have your own views about anything.

Men don't have feelings. They don't care about women and they don't care about children.

Men don't know how to communicate with women.

Men just have the ability to walk away from a relationship, at any moment, any time.

Men are from another planet. They speak another language. They just don't understand women.

You've got to build up a man and make him feel really special. You've got to laugh at his jokes, make him feel important, then you'll have him eating out of your hand.

Men reported the following sexist attitudes about women and stereotypic role expectations that they had incorporated from their fathers:

Women are over-emotional, childish, and jealous.

Women think they have to control everything!

Women always want more. They want more than you can give.

You've got to put up with a lot to stay involved with a woman.

Women don't understand the practical things in life.

Women are fragile and sensitive. You have to be careful of what you say to them.

It's a man's job to make a woman happy, so you'd better make her feel good. If you don't, you're a failure.

Case Studies

Ms. J, an attractive computer programmer, had separated from a strong symbiotic attachment and was pursuing a relationship based on mutual respect and affection. In a discussion group she attended with her boyfriend, she recalled her voices about her new relationship:

Ms. J: I had a voice right now when I was thinking about talking: He doesn't want to hear this. Everybody's laughing at you, you know. They're sick of your stupid struggle. You're such a joke. That's my mother's voice, and that's embarrassing in itself. He just wants you to shut up. Just shut up and let somebody else talk.

Ms. J exposed voices that tormented her when she and her boyfriend made love:

While we're making love, my thoughts are the most malicious. They say things like How can you love this man? You don't feel anything, you know. It shouldn't be this much work. Sex should be easy. It should be easy for you.

By verbalizing her voice attacks, Ms. J was able to identify points of view about men that were in fact her mother's:

Ms. J: They only want women for sex. They don't really care about women. They're always unfaithful. In the end, they will always hurt you!

When Ms. J was a young girl, her mother and father divorced. Her mother became bitter and resentful and extended her recriminations and distrust to men in general. Ms. J's movement toward a stable involvement with a man who treated her with sensitivity and tenderness symbolized a break in the identification with her mother and a rejection of her mother's hostile attitudes. When she chose to ignore the dictates of the voice—for example, when she continued to respond affectionately to her partner despite voice attacks—the anger aroused by the break with her mother's programming became intense:

Ms. J: Who do you think you are? [intense anger, voice shaking] You're from me! You are from me! Are you trying to show me up, you little bitch? You can't have anything nice in your life. You're never going to have a nice man! I'll make you believe that he's wrong for you. I'll find a way! You stupid idiot! What are you doing with this man? Look, how do you feel about him right now? Sure, you still like him but why care about anybody that much? Why care about anybody! [loud, strident voice] [pause]

   [To partner]: I feel like the goal is to convince myself that you are not who I want and that you don't want me. After I talked a couple of weeks ago about how I really felt love for you, the voices were more frequent and more malicious, especially when we were making love.

In a later discussion, Ms. J became aware that in choosing a man she could love and care for and who, in turn, loved and cared for her, she was also going against what her father wanted from her. As a result, she experienced other self-attacks and self-recriminations related to her father.

Ms. J: I also have a lot of guilt about separating from my father. These voice attacks are: You know you're my favorite. How could you go away from me? You know I love you. I love you and I need you and I'm going to die without you. It's not a little choice, you know. It's not a little thing you're doing to me. I need that soothing and comfort from you.

   The voices are that I belong to him and I'm killing him, he's going to die without getting what he wants from me, that I'm for him. That's my purpose in life and so now I'm misbehaving. I'm not giving him what he wants. I see my sister doing that, following that exact path, living her life for him.

So now I'm doubting my decision, like, <u>Is this really the man you want to spend your life with?</u>

After articulating the defensive prescriptions for living she had assimilated from both parents, she went on to express her own point of view to her partner:

Ms. J: I realize that I'm continually attacking myself for being phony when I express my loving feelings toward you. But it's a voice, it's not really *my* belief. It feels so nice to really be close to you and be loving, but it goes against everything I ever saw in my family.

Ms. J's progress in healthy relating depends primarily on whether she has the courage to remain vulnerable and open in this relationship. She needs the ego strength to tolerate the inevitable anxiety and guilt involved in making basic character changes, to continue to challenge and overcome her voice attacks, and gradually to adjust to her new identity as a loving woman.

In another case, Mark, 32, revealed a contemptuous voice that he identified as reflecting his mother's views of men and of himself:

Mark: I was thinking about a voice I've incorporated in myself about not being a real man. That was my mother's voice. If I were to say the voices about myself and about men, they would be: <u>You know, you're a weak piece of shit! Just like your father. You're nothing. You can't compete in a man's world. You're just not a man. You'd better grovel. You'd better take care of women. You'd better just take care of us. You give us what we want. You're not a strong man. You never can be. You can't be a man, you don't have a backbone. You just don't have it in you.</u>
       <u>And you're stupid. You think you're smart? You think you fit into the rest of the world, but women run it all. You men are just some drones that are out there. You're just little pieces of shit out there.</u> [loud voice, enraged] <u>We control it all! So just play the role. Play the role like a big man. But you're not really a big man, we both know it, don't we?</u> [sarcastic] <u>We both know that you're not a big man. But just go ahead and play that role.</u>
       I feel these voices from both sides. I feel them from my mother, and I feel them from my father. He felt that same way about himself and about men.

Mark's mother felt superior to men and belittled her husband as well as her son. Mark was attracted to and formed relationships with women who had characteristics similar to those of his mother and tended to cater and defer to them. His submissive behavior and choice of love objects were counterproductive to his goal of having a relationship with a woman who would respect him and genuinely care about him. In the discussion groups, he developed an understanding of the underlying reasons he was attracted to women who were derisive toward men. As a result of his insights, he was able to move in the direction of his stated goal. He was aware that initially he would probably encounter an increase in anxiety and intensified voice attacks as he modified his choices.

> Mark: Today when I heard people standing up for themselves in re-
> lation to their voice attacks, I felt like standing up for myself,
> saying: "That's *not* me. I'm not really a weak piece of shit and
> I don't have to be that way, playing a role." Saying that made
> me very sad. I really don't have to be that way. My thought
> from saying this answer back to the voice is that not only can
> I be different, I can actually have different actions and sweat
> out the anxiety as it comes up.*

Fear of Competition Masks Deeper Fears of Arousing Self-Destructive or Suicidal Thoughts

As noted earlier, the antiself-system is a generalized suicidal process: Negative voices range along a continuum of intensity from mild self-criticism to angry self-attacks and suicidal ideation. Insecure or immature parents often feel considerable resentment and hatred toward their children but suppress these feelings. Children identify with the punitive parent, taking on as their own the parent's aggression and adopting the parent's hostile point of view toward themselves in the form of a self-hating thought process. As adults, self-hating and self-destructive voices are often reawakened in competitive situations. People tend to project onto their present-day rivals the fears of retaliation they originally experienced in relation to the parent.

Based on in-depth interviews, we conjectured that both men and women retreat from competitive situations because they fear the self-destructive thinking that the anticipation of winning can arouse. They are apprehensive about precipitating their own internal malice. For example, Robert was succeeding in his career at a level he had not dreamed possible. At the same time, he was actively pursuing a woman who had recently rejected a friend of his. He spoke about his reactions to both events:

> Robert: Recently I've been getting everything I want in my life—
> close friendships, success, a woman who likes me—and it
> seems like I'm actually scared more from the positive things
> that are going on than any negative things. My father was
> an extremely isolated person, and I feel scared about sur-

---

*See chapter 14, this volume, for material transcribed from a later discussion group in which Mark describes constructive changes in his self-image and style of relating to women.

passing him. I began to have thoughts attacking my desire to be close to B because I feel guilty about winning over my friend. The voices I've been having are really upsetting, like <u>She's not going to want to get seriously involved with you. It's just a matter of time before she realizes it.</u> [louder voice, yelling] <u>You're so stupid! You're so stupid for even wanting this! Such a fucking idiot! You're a child. How can you be a man? I can't believe you even tried to go out with her. This is so fucking stupid!</u>

I feel like I'm drawing a blank, the voices are so angry. <u>This is what happens. You let yourself want something and this is what you get. Punches you right down where you belong. Just go back in the corner. Just shut up! Just stay in the dark! Forget about this. Forget about her. God, what an idiot you are! She's pretty. She's lively. What would she want to do with you?</u>

I think I'm really afraid of the rage I feel right now. I've wanted to talk about these feelings and push beyond them. [crying] Even though I've started to realize intellectually that they're not right, I have no feeling of them not being right. These voices became much more intense and much more frequent when I felt I was succeeding.

In another case, Linda, 24, was frightened of competing with another woman for a man she really loved and admired. She was terrified of winning and became anxious whenever he expressed a strong preference for her. During her childhood, Linda had directly experienced her mother's jealousy and envy. Here she discusses the insights she has gained during previous group discussions about the origins of her anxiety. She then expresses the rage associated with her self-attacks:

Linda: One thing I thought is that I have to go back to my childhood and understand the fear that I felt. The hatred that was directed towards me and the murderous feelings. I know my mother and I know her insanity. And I know the way my father felt toward me, so I can only imagine that scene was crazy, you know. So when I walk into a room now where there's that competition, I feel the same insanity, and the fear and panic, and I feel like running.

As Linda began to verbalize the thoughts underlying her feelings of panic, she experienced a surge of powerful emotions:

Linda: I was thinking about her hatred toward me. And I think (sobbing, loud sounds) I'm trying to say it and it might get emotional but I—[a lot of emotion]—<u>You fucking little bitch! I want to rip you apart! Get out! You're a little fucking child. I want to rip your arms off! I want to hit you in the face! Fuck you! Look what</u>

you've done to me! You've fucked up my whole life! You fucked up everything! You could be dead! You could be dead! Why'd I have to fucking have you? You fucked it all up. I could kill you! I could kill you! Fuck you! [crying]

You're nothing! Don't you understand? You were lucky to be born! That was my mistake! My mistake was that I had you! [crying loudly] It's just too bad I couldn't take that back! It's too bad I can't take that back. [deep sobbing]

I think sometimes I feel like it would have just been really lucky if I would have died as a child. Like lucky for them. Like it would have solved a lot of problems. But she couldn't quite do it exactly—you know what I mean?

Dr. Firestone: That's part of a voice. Thinking that it would solve their problems. Also it's an idealistic picture of them. Nothing would have solved their problems, their attitudes toward each other, or their attitudes towards themselves, either one. But you see, if you take that position, you lose the vitality of what you just said. You really felt the emotions that were directed toward you.

Linda: I appreciate you saying the thing about it being a voice. My immediate reaction in the present situation is that I suddenly have fear in just acknowledging my rival. What it makes me think is that I was probably iced a lot as a child. There I was, this little girl and my mother comes home and she's jealous of me, so she doesn't even say "Hi" to me basically. I don't think there was any warmth or any affection because I was intruding on her situation. I think I'm afraid of really feeling those attacks I was saying; that hatred, the murderous feelings.

Linda's fear of competition was based on the dread that being preferred by her partner would precipitate a self-destructive thought process. Her tendency to regress to a more passive posture can be understood in light of the aggression that was directed toward her by her mother.

Unusual achievement, both personal and vocational, or attainment of a leadership position often precede periods of self-limiting and self-destructive behavior. This is particularly evident when a person's accomplishments surpass those of his or her parent of the same sex. At this point, there is often a significant increase in self-destructive voices and suicidal ideation. It is also important to note that the fear of winning does not preclude the fear of losing. People fear both potentialities: that of being preferred and of being rejected. Both situations arouse intense voice attacks and suicidal impulses, causing men and women to retreat from actively pursuing relationships and to progressively give up their individuality and sense of identity (Firestone, 1990a).

Competition, Jealousy, and Withholding

Competition and jealousy are both aspects of rivalry in personal relationships. Healthy competition reflects an honest striving for one's goals. Competitive feelings are aroused when rivals seek the same love object. At times competition arouses irrational feelings, such as the desire to win for its own sake, with little concern for the object.

An important distinction can be made between feelings of competitiveness and jealousy.[3] Competitive feelings are generally characterized by the relative absence of voice attacks, whereas jealous reactions are fueled by self-attacks and hostile attitudes toward the love object. Jealousy represents hostile, self-hating brooding over a potential or real loss to a rival. When self-deprecating voices or vindictive thoughts against one's partner are ascendant in people's thinking, their feelings of jealousy increase significantly. Their jealous reactions indicate that their focus is more on the rival than on their own desires, and they tend to blame themselves or others for any losses.

Feelings of jealousy are usually experienced more intensely by individuals who deny or avoid feeling directly competitive for a love object. Jealousy disguises the fact that it is one's own self-denial that often prevents one from winning, not the presence of a rival or competitor. Voice attacks and distrust of one's partner are also exacerbated by one's own withholding. When people hold back from their loved ones, they tend to focus on what others are getting and feel cheated, which intensifies their feelings of jealousy and envy. Withholding patterns are manifested in individuals who have retreated from competitive situations because of either their negative voices or their fear of competing. Last, people's fears of intimacy predispose behaviors that ward off closeness in their relationships, which in turn heightens their jealous reactions.

ANALYSIS OF DATA

A preliminary analysis of the narrative data derived from the videotaped discussions is currently being conducted using a grounded-theory approach (Glaser & Strauss, 1967, 1970; Strauss & Corbin, 1990).[4] Once the constructs and coding structure are defined and operationalized, their adequacy will be tested with narrative data yielded from ongoing discussions with participants from the circle of friends and discussions with additional populations. The reliability of the coding structure will be established during this phase of our analysis. Once the narrative data are coded, the relationships among the codes will be empirically examined.

A preliminary examination of transcribed conversations from the series of seminars indicates that the lifestyle of each partner in the couple was directly related to his or her specific voices or parental prescriptions. This parallel was particularly evident in mate selection. Individuals often select partners with opposite character traits in an attempt to compensate for personality deficits. Progressive compensation often leads to disillusionment. The effort to become a complete person through connecting with another by forming a fantasy bond is ultimately doomed to fail.

DISCUSSION

Voice therapy is both a unique laboratory procedure and psychotherapy technique. In the laboratory setting, it has provided the means for eliciting and identifying partly conscious or unconscious elements of the personality. The new perspective made possible by these studies has contributed to a deeper understanding of the basic division within the mind and its pervasive influence on people's everyday lives. Voices predispose people to relive their earlier lives rather than to be spontaneous and goal directed, and to fulfill themselves. Their fear of others, their distrust and hostility, are directly related to the negative voices that are elicited with voice therapy procedures.

THEORETICAL IMPLICATIONS

Contemporary views of marital relationships have attributed the primary causes of marital disputes to the differences in the economic, religious, or political background between the partners. Other theorists have cited different communication styles, career interests, views about child-rearing practices, and attitudes related to division of household labor as prognosticators of relationship satisfaction (Spitze, 1988; R. A. Ward, 1993). Researchers have developed various questionnaires and measures that are designed to predict marital success.

Psychodynamic theorists, focusing on concepts such as the "marriage contract," have attempted to uncover unconscious elements in each partner that have an adverse impact on marital relationships (Sager et al., 1971). This approach bears a close resemblance to the authors' conception. In recent years, family-of-origin research studies have been instituted to validate hypotheses developed by family systems theorists about the intergenerational transmission of dysfunctional patterns of relating (Hampson, Hyman, & Beavers, 1994; Kline & Newman, 1994). Others have investigated how attachment styles or patterns are correlated with interpersonal problems in general (Horowitz, Rosenberg, & Bartholomew, 1993) and in couple relationships (Shaver & Clark, 1994).

Our conclusion, as contrasted with many others, is that most marital difficulties are primarily affected by *partners' disruptive modes of defense based on their negative voices*. In our opinion, the key issues have little to do with economic hardship, differences in background, sexual incompatibility, or imbalance of power. This internal voice process predisposes a lack of tolerance for feeling close to oneself and the other and interferes with true compassion.

In this reference population, there was nothing essentially wrong with the couples involved, except for the defenses and destructive attitudes and beliefs that existed within each person. A number of cognitive–behavioral therapists (Beck, 1988; Waring, 1988; Wile, 1981) have addressed cognitive patterns in each partner that negatively impact the relationship. Segraves (1982), a cognitive therapist, has suggested that in treating distressed couples, therapists need to focus on "faulty cognitive schemas" in each partner to facilitate positive change. Araoz (1982) has described negative beliefs that are primarily unconscious and that "can truly be said to be hypnotic in their power and, therefore, are dangerous because we cannot challenge them rationally" (p. 75).

CONCLUSION

It is valuable for individuals to challenge their negative voices in a psychotherapy that exposes core issues. They must learn to free themselves of self-defeating, restrictive behavior patterns that cause distress in their relationships. Recognizing the enemy within enables people to broaden their experience in living and to significantly improve their relationships. Indeed, there is no defense or relationship problem that is impervious to change, providing the parties have the courage to risk vulnerability in their close associations rather than remain imprisoned by early programming and illusions of connection.

ENDNOTES

[1]For a more comprehensive discussion of voice therapy theory and methodology, see *Voice Therapy: A Psychotherapeutic Approach to Self-Destructive Behavior* (Firestone, 1988) and *Combating Destructive Thought Processes: Voice Therapy and Separation Theory* (Firestone, 1997a).

[2]To investigate construct validity of the new scale, we are considering a battery of instruments that have been designed to assess the mental health of individ-

uals, including the Beck Depression Inventory (Beck, 1978), the CES–D (Radloff, 1977), the NEO Personality Inventory (Costa & McCrae, 1985), and the Rosenberg Self-Esteem Inventory (Rosenberg, 1979). Also included in the battery will be instruments that have been validated for identifying correlations between adult romantic attachment patterns and interpersonal behavior, as well as questionnaires that assess satisfaction, investment, commitment, and conflict in relationships. Several instruments are under consideration, including the Adult Attachment Questionnaire (Hazan & Shaver, 1987); the Relationship Scales Questionnaire (D. W. Griffin & Bartholomew, 1994a, 1994b); the Relationship Conflict Scale (Bodin, 1996); the Marriage Satisfaction Inventory, Revised (Snyder, 1997); and the PREPARE/ENRICH scale (Lavee & Olson, 1993), among others. It is conjectured that scores on the new scale will correlate with specific adult attachment patterns or styles of relating (Dismissing, Preoccupied, or Fearful) in each partner. Following reliability and validity studies, we are planning a longitudinal study of 3 years' duration with selected populations to investigate incremental validity, that is, to estimate the extent to which the new scale adds to our ability to predict future mental health of individual partners and the quality and type of their relationships.

[3]See Sharpsteen and Kirkpatrick (1997) "Romantic Jealous and Adult Romantic Attachment" for a discussion of the differences between jealousy aroused by sexual infidelity and emotional infidelity. It was noted also that avoidantly attached individuals

> were relatively more likely to turn their anger and blame against the interloper [rather than the partner]. . . . Anxiously attached people fo.cused on the implications of the situation for themselves (as tapped by the Sadness, Inferiority, and Fear scales). Despite this, though, they were relatively unlikely to take steps to maintain their self-esteem. (pp. 636–637)

[4]A grounded-theory approach allows for the discovery and definition of data categories derived from context-specific knowledge that is pertinent to negative thoughts about relationships. Essentially, a grounded-theory approach is a process of identifying underlying uniformities in the data in order to develop a set of concepts. Data are reviewed a number of times to hone more precise definitions of the concept and to delineate its properties, and theories are formed as a result of hypothesizing about relationships among the concept properties. This is similar to the approach taken by Luborsky and Crits-Christoph (1998) in their development of the core conflictual relationship theme (CCRT) method to assess and validate observations about the transference relationship occurring during therapy.

Subsequently, the adequacy of the identified constructs will be considered and reconsidered until theoretical saturation is achieved; in other words, no new information is yielded from the analytic process. A text-based, retrieval, indexing and theorizing software system (QSR NUD*IST, 1997) will be used to further refine initial concepts and constructs and to develop coding categories.

13

THE THERAPEUTIC PROCESS IN COUPLES THERAPY

To love one another truly is to walk in the light, to live in truth, to be truly alive, and perfectly free.

R. D. Laing, 1989 (quoting from *Furchte deinen Nachsten wie dich Selbst* by Paul Parin, 1978)

The nature of the fantasy bond as it manifests itself in couple relationships is that both individuals, more often than not, are listening to the dictates of their respective voices. Their communications are filtered through a biased, alien point of view that distorts their partner's real image. Both parties ward off loving responses from the other, using rationalizations promulgated by the voice to justify their anger and distancing behavior. Men and women project their specific self-attacks onto one another and, as a result, respond inappropriately, that is, as though they were being victimized or depreciated by their mates.

The goal of voice therapy with couples is to help each individual identify the voice attacks that are influencing distancing behaviors and creating conflict in the relationship. Patterns of dishonest communication and duplicity can be interrupted by the process of revealing the contents of voice attacks. In identifying specific self-criticisms as well as judgmental, hostile thoughts about the other, each partner is able to relate more openly.

THREE COMPONENTS OF VOICE THERAPY

The therapeutic methodology of voice therapy has traditionally consisted of three components: (a) the process of eliciting and identifying negative thought patterns and releasing the associated affect, (b) discussing insights and reactions to verbalizing the voice, and (c) counteracting self-destructive behaviors regulated by the voice through the collaborative planning and application of appropriate corrective experiences.[1] In therapy, these three components are not necessarily undertaken in the order delineated here. Voice therapy techniques are similar to certain aspects of cognitive, affective, and behavioral therapies. Voice therapy is not interpretive or analytical, in that clients form their own conclusions as to the sources of their destructive thinking.

Identifying Negative Thought Patterns

Identifying the contents of the client's negative thought process is the first step in a three-step procedure in which client and therapist collaborate in understanding the client's distorted ways of thinking. By articulating self-attacks in the second person, the client facilitates the process of separating his or her point of view from the hostile thought patterns that make up this alien point of view. Prior to actually articulating the voice, most clients generally accept their negative thoughts as true evaluations of themselves and implicitly believe them.

The process of identifying the voice can be approached intellectually as a primarily cognitive technique or more dramatically using cathartic methods. In both procedures, the client learns to restate negative thought patterns in the second person as "voices" experienced from the outside. In the latter technique, there is an emphasis on the release of the affect accompanying the voice attacks. The client is encouraged to "say it louder," "really feel that," or "let go and blurt out anything that comes to mind." We have found that clients frequently adopt this style of expression of their own volition. When asked to formulate their negative thoughts in the second person, they spontaneously begin to speak louder and with more intensity of feeling. With this release of emotions, valuable material is revealed.

Discussing Insights and Reactions

Clients discuss their spontaneous insights and their reactions to verbalizing the voice. They then attempt to understand the relationship between their voice attacks and their self-destructive behavior patterns. They subsequently develop insight into the limitations that they impose on themselves in everyday life functions.

Counteracting Self-Destructive Behaviors

Because the procedures of voice therapy expose core defenses and one's basic self-concept, the process of initiating behavioral changes that expand one's boundaries and challenge misconceptions about oneself is a vital part of the overall treatment. Collaborative interventions that effect changes in an individual's behavior are a necessary part of any effective therapeutic procedure. The potential for therapeutic progress is not merely a function of identifying negative thought patterns and uncovering repressed material; personal growth and improving styles of relating ultimately must involve constructive behavioral changes that oppose self-limiting or self-destructive patterns and lifestyles.

Corrective experiences bear a direct relationship to the maladaptive behavior patterns that are influenced and controlled by the client's negative cognitive processes. The therapist and client identify the specific behaviors regulated by the voice that are self-destructive and constricting, and then work together to formulate ideas about altering routine responses and habitual patterns of behavior. The corrective suggestions are in accord with clients' personal goals and ambitions and are specific to those problem areas they wish to correct or improve. These goals always represent personal risk and increased vulnerability in the sense of breaking with psychological defenses that protect the individual from experiencing painful emotions.

APPLICATION OF VOICE THERAPY TECHNIQUES TO COUPLES

Voice therapy procedures are particularly applicable to couples therapy and problems in sexual relating. They are effective in uncovering core defenses that directly affect the compulsive reliving of the past with new objects.

Introducing Voice Therapy Techniques to Individual Partners

The principal technique of voice therapy involves individual partners verbalizing their self-critical thoughts in the second-person format, that is, in the form of statements *toward* him or herself, for example, "*You're* unattractive; *You're* unlovable," rather than "I feel unattractive; I'm unlovable."

Hostile, cynical attitudes toward the other are verbalized in the third-person format, as though someone else were imparting negative information to the individual about his or her partner, for example: "He's cold and rejecting. He doesn't really care about you." "She's so childish and melodramatic. Why would you want to get involved with her?" rather than "I think he's really cold and rejecting," or "I wouldn't want to get seriously involved with her because she's so childish."

The Therapeutic Process in Couples Therapy

In conjoint sessions or couples' groups, partners generally progress through the following steps in the course of treatment: (a) formulating the problem each individual perceives is limiting his or her satisfaction within the relationship, (b) learning to verbalize self-critical thoughts and negative perceptions of the other in the form of the voice and release the associated affect, (c) developing insight into the origins of the voice and making connections between past experience and present conflicts, and (d) altering behaviors and communications in a direction that counteracts the dictates of the voice. This process helps both individuals take back their projections and thereby stop blaming and denouncing the other.

In the sessions, both partners are present as each reveals negative thoughts and attitudes toward him- or herself and the other. In a real sense, they are sharing each other's individual psychotherapy. In tracing back the source of their self-attacks and cynical views to early family interactions, they gain perspective on each other's problems and feel more compassion for their mates as well as for themselves. Recognizing their voice attacks as the primary source of misery in their lives takes pressure off the relationship and has a powerful effect on altering and improving attitudes toward their mates as well as on enhancing each individual's personal growth. Each partner learns to accommodate to the anxiety associated with breaking inward, self-protective defenses and is gradually able to maintain the behavioral changes (Firestone, 1987a).

It is important to emphasize that partners attempt to be sincere and sensitive when giving away their negative thoughts. They try to relinquish critical views and grudges even when their hostile thoughts have some basis in reality. The case that follows illustrates the application of these procedures in the context of a couples group.

Case Study of a Couple

Jeff and Natalie have been involved for 4 years. The beginning phase of their relationship was characterized by friendship, affection, and a strong sexual attraction. At that time, Jeff, 34, had been divorced for 2 years. In his marriage and in previous relationships, he had sought controlling women and tended to be submissive in relation to them. Since his divorce, he had developed a stronger sense of identity and autonomy. Natalie, 22, an energetic, attractive woman, had been involved in a series of casual relationships prior to meeting Jeff. She had difficulty believing that a man would want to be with her on a sustained basis. Both individuals felt different in this relationship: He felt assured and strong, and she had a sense of self-esteem and confidence.

However, as the relationship evolved, there were incidents in which Natalie tried to manipulate Jeff. She became increasingly jealous and possessive and would explode into fits of rage, making nasty innuendos and bitterly accusing him of not caring for her. At first, Jeff refused to submit to her efforts to control him, and they were able to sustain a relationship that was equal and respectful. But as Natalie became more important to him, Jeff became afraid of losing her and gradually subverted his own priorities and relinquished his point of view. Because both partners were distressed by this destructive pattern and were determined to alter it, they asked to participate in a couples' group. The group was composed of individuals who were using voice therapy techniques to improve the quality of their relationships.

Eliciting and Identifying Negative Thought Patterns and Releasing the Associated Affect

In the first session, Jeff focused on his reactions to Natalie's jealousy. He verbalized the specific self-attacks triggered by her anger that increased his feelings of desperation. In doing so, he was able to develop a better understanding of why he was vulnerable to her manipulations:

Jeff: In the past, I used to feel like a mean bastard when I reacted to your [Natalie's] jealousy. But lately I've felt more insecure and desperate. When you have those types of reactions, I really do lose touch with myself in a way where I really become frightened and I don't feel myself. I just feel desperate. The voices are like I'm going to lose you, and I'd better hang onto you.

Dr. Firestone: Say it as a voice. You'd better hang onto her.

Jeff: It's frantic almost, like Is she looking at you? No, she's not looking at you. You'd better get her to look at you. She's losing interest in you. See, you can tell because of the way she's acting right now. She's not interested in you. Call her, get her to say something, get some confirmation that she still cares about you, that she's still interested. She's losing interest. She doesn't want anything to do with you. She's lost all interest in you. You're going to lose her.

You've got to hang onto her. You're never going to find somebody like this again. You're never going to find somebody you like that much again. You're going to be alone, you're going to be miserable. You're going to spend the rest of your life miserable because you're never going to find anybody again like this.

The feeling is that I'm nothing. I'm absolutely nothing and I'd better get her to like me because if she doesn't like me I'm nothing, I have nothing. You're just nothing. Nobody could really like you because there's nothing to you. There's nothing there. How could she like you? How could anybody like you? There's just nothing there.

Following her jealous rages, Natalie invariably felt remorse and made resolutions to be different, but usually failed in her attempts to control her fury. Indeed, jealousy and possessiveness were recurring themes in her life. In the following, Natalie investigates the issues she believed were contributing to her irrational feelings of jealousy:

Natalie: I think that one thing that I lack in my life, especially in my relationship with Jeff, is self-confidence. I have a lot of thoughts that make me feel like I'm an aggressive person and I have to make something happen. If I don't do that then it's not going to happen. I won't have a relationship or I won't have romantic moments.

Dr. Firestone: No one would choose you—

Natalie: Right.

Dr. Firestone: What do you think those attacks on you are?

Natalie: I have thoughts that other people see me as unattractive. I imagine that they're looking at the faults. I know I'm not really ugly, but I imagine that the person looking at me is picking out specific points in me, seeing the bad points.

Dr. Firestone: What do they see? What are the critical things?

Natalie: Well, if I have acne, they see my acne. My mother used to tell me the whole while I was growing up that if one thing would make me look better it would be if I had plastic surgery on my nose. So now if I'm self-conscious, that's all I think the person's looking at. Or I imagine that people look at me thinking that I'm extremely hairy and that's unattractive.

Dr. Firestone: Try to say these things to yourself as though you were the outside person.

Natalie: You're so ugly. You have such a big nose. You're so dark. Your face is so green looking. You're so hairy.

You look like an ape. That's so funny! [sarcastic, degrading tone] Look at you! You have such a huge bum! You have such a huge butt!

Natalie continued by expressing the deep anger and painful feelings of humiliation she felt as she articulated her self-critical voices.*

Dr. Firestone: Try to say those thoughts loudly.

Natalie: It has a joking tone. That's how I think people look at me. It's funny. I think that strangers look at me that way, but if I imagine how my mother looks at me, then it's angry.

Dr. Firestone: Try and say it with feeling, connecting to the pain that you feel about it. Get into it with energy.

Natalie: You look so weird. You look so ugly. When you're talking to me all I can see is the ugly points on your face. You don't even know it! [derisive, snide] You're more ugly than you even think. You have such ugly features. You're so ugly! You're so hairy! It's embarrassing. How can you even be seen in a bathing suit? You have hair all over your legs. You have such a big nose. You're so embarrassing!

Dr. Firestone: Feel it and really express that.

Natalie: It's so embarrassing to say these things. You're so ugly! You have a huge nose. [angry, loud] That's all I'm looking at when I talk to you. You should hide it. It's so ugly and your acne is so disgusting! It's so gross! Why don't you do something about it? You're so dark. But it's not even a nice dark. You're so green and yellow and your skin is ugly. [deep crying] [pause]

Dr. Firestone: How does this relate to getting a man?

Natalie: You have to make something happen. Because if you don't, it's not going to happen. You're too ugly. You're too unattractive. You don't look sexy. You're too big. You're too heavy. Nothing's going to happen. You have to make it happen. You have to look good. You have to walk in a way where you look good. You have to hold yourself better. You can't just be yourself. You have to put lots of makeup on. You've got to cover up all those bad points.

---

*The impact of the sessions cannot be described adequately in words. In viewing videotaped sessions, one can appreciate the depth of pain and anger expressed both by relatively healthy individuals as well as by men and women who are disturbed or conflicted in their relationships.

Discussion of Insights and Reactions to Verbalizing the Voice

In this step, partners discuss the insights they developed while verbalizing the voice and releasing the accompanying feelings. They attempt to understand the relationship between their voice attacks and behaviors that create conflict within the couple. They come to understand the sources of the limitations that they have been imposing on the relationship. For example, as a result of releasing powerful feelings of anger, Natalie became more aware that she had incorporated her mother's hostility toward her and accepted these distorted views as accurate. She had compassion for herself in relation to the emotional mistreatment she had suffered during her formative years. As she developed more insight into the real sources of her jealous reactions, she realized that they were inappropriate in the present-day circumstances.

Dr. Firestone: How do you feel the effects in your life of the feelings that you just expressed? What was the result? What happened to you?

Natalie: I think they really did leave me feeling self-conscious and awkward, especially in one-on-one contact with a man. It was hard for me to just feel comfortable with myself and comfortable with a person looking at me, especially a man.

Dr. Firestone: You said something earlier about being aggressive in pursuing men. How did it tie in with that?

Natalie: It definitely left me feeling inadequate, like I'm not good enough to just have natural responses directed towards me from a man, sexual responses, flirtatious responses, anything like that would have to come from me, because I'm not somebody who would be looked at twice except to look for the bad points. So I felt like if I was aggressive I would be able to get something, like a relationship or a romantic moment or something like that from a man.

Dr. Firestone: What does this make you think of when you think that way? What does this relate to, these negative thoughts?

Natalie: It definitely makes me think of how I grew up. It's so clear to me because it's so much the way I was treated at home. Today they're just voices. But then it was how I really was treated. I can feel that they're inside me now and that they still do affect me, but I don't have that going on in my life today. When I was young I felt like that all the time.

Dr. Firestone:	How do you mean?
Natalie:	Just that I remember my mother would never ever let me borrow her clothes. I knew that they would look good on me but she would never let me borrow them. She always told me that I should have plastic surgery when I get old enough. And she would jokingly say that I look like my father, but in a way where it was derogatory towards him and me. She was always trying to make me do things to make myself look better, telling me that I should do something about myself.
She had hostility towards me because I think that she didn't want me to be attractive. I was not as unattractive as she thought I was (I wasn't even unattractive at all), but she didn't want me to look better than her. Especially when she wouldn't let me use her clothes, she didn't want me to look good in her clothes. She was competitive with me.
Dr. Firestone:	There seems to be some real pain behind the thought that you're unattractive and unappealing. What does it make you think?
Natalie:	It just makes me think that it was unnecessary. That I have a false image of myself which was unnecessarily put on me and that it's sad. If I think of it as happening to another child, it's a painful situation, because it's so undeserved.

Answering back to voice attacks. Some individuals formulate verbal answers to their self-attacks and distorted views of the partner. Initially, following "answering back," there may be regressive trends, but consistent application of the technique can lead to a strengthening of one's point of view and a solidification of therapeutic gains.[2]

Dr. Firestone:	What would you say back to her about these things?
Natalie:	It feels very angry, what I would say back. I feel a lot of anger towards her in relation to this and I feel like: "You're so wrong. You're so wrong. You have no idea what you're talking about. If anyone is ugly you should look at yourself in the mirror. You're disgusting. I'm not like you! I'm not like you at all! So don't even think I'm like you. Don't try and put me in your category because I'm not. I'm not ugly. *You're* the one who's ugly. So leave me alone! Don't tell me I need to change my nose

because I don't. I don't need to change my face at
all. You change *your* face! Don't tell me what's
wrong with me. I'm fine.

Therapeutic progress is best achieved when the exercise of answering
back to destructive thoughts is combined with a gradual, step-by-step collaborative planning of corrective actions that go against the dictates of the
voice. This method (answering back and altering behavior in a positive
direction) is similar in some respects to the technique of systematic desen-
sitization utilized by behavioral therapists (Wolpe, 1969). As this process
continues, the participants gradually accommodate to the anxiety of
change by refusing to relinquish the new territory or give up their real
points of view despite the temporary intensification of voice attacks.

Discussion of Plans for Behavioral Changes That Counteract the Voice

Until individuals learn to take definitive actions that are in opposi-
tion to the dictates of the voice, they tend to repeat early patterns of
maladaptive behavior and continue to distort themselves and their partners. An overall treatment strategy for couples would include initiating
plans to change provoking or withholding responses, to overcome fears of
being close, or to disrupt destructive fantasy bonds. Once they stop controlling the interpersonal environment by manipulating responses in the
other, they generate a new set of circumstances. This, in turn, creates an
unfamiliar, albeit more positive, emotional climate.

Natalie's tendency to act out anger and jealousy had provoked rage
in Jeff. In suppressing his anger, he was caught between feelings of desperation toward Natalie and strong avoidance tendencies. Natalie was aware
that her possessiveness had effectively altered Jeff's feelings for her and felt
determined to reverse the situation. Later in the session, she discussed her
plans to modify her characteristic way of responding to Jeff, thereby leaving
herself undefended and vulnerable. She sensed that she would be taking a
chance, but felt firm in her resolve to control the acting out behaviors and
manipulations that had changed Jeff's feelings for her.

Dr. Firestone: How do you function in a relationship? How do
the voices work in your relationship?

Natalie: I think my jealousy ties into it because if Jeff even
looks at another woman or if he's pursuing something else, I feel like it's a rejection of me because
if only I was perfect that wouldn't happen.

Dr. Firestone: So jealousy really threatens you?

Natalie: Yes.

Dr. Firestone:	And how do you react when you're jealous? How does it affect the relationship?
Natalie:	I feel furious. I don't even know how to explain it. It's, it's a fury. It's—
Dr. Firestone:	How do you express it?
Natalie:	By getting furious, by telling him what a fool he is. By blowing up, by thinking he's an idiot and expressing it with no holds barred, by tearing him apart, by yelling and screaming at him, making him feel he's the worst person in the world. It's like a huge temper tantrum, and once I almost hit him. But it all feels in order to protect myself. The anger feels like it's a protection of myself.
Dr. Firestone:	What's the result of all that?
Natalie:	Well, I think it definitely pushes Jeff away. It probably scares the living daylights out of him. He's lost feelings for me, and it's not the same as it was. I'm not the same as I was. I'm a totally different person in that state. I'm very unlikable in that state.
Dr. Firestone:	So it really caused you a lot of damage.
Natalie:	Oh, definitely, yes. I feel like over the last 6 months, I've recognized these traits and have found them very unattractive in myself and have started to change them. So now I know that I can resist blowing up at Jeff. But I feel like what I've done has already caused damage. I've distorted the type of person that I was to such an extent that his vision of how I used to be is blocked.

Natalie discovered that listening to her "voice" in situations where she felt insecure had caused her to make nasty, angry accusations that she did not really believe. After identifying the specific injunctions of the voice that urged her to retaliate against Jeff at these times, she felt strengthened in her point of view. She reported being optimistic about her ability to control the negative behaviors that she recognized as similar to those of her mother.

Dr. Firestone:	In a way it leads to rejection. The rejection that you anticipated originally—
Natalie:	Exactly. Definitely. But also it's a cover-up. The explosive feelings and the anger and the jealousy, they're a cover-up for how I really feel because at those times it would be a sad feeling of just being

independent and alone, like I am anyway. I really care about Jeff and it doesn't change my feelings towards him when he's independent. But if I were to say that to him, I immediately have the thought, You're so stupid! You're so foolish! How embarrassing. You are such an idiot! How can you say that to him? He is about to go and do something that's not with you, that excludes you, and here you are telling him that you like him and that you feel sad that you're not going to see him and that you'll miss him. That is so stupid! That is so foolish! Don't say that! Be angry! Be furious! Punish him! You have to hurt him back! He's so horrible! How could you even think of being with him? He's so mean to you. Don't show that you're sad. That's the most foolish thing I've ever heard!

Dr. Firestone: Don't show him that you really care, that you have feelings for him.

Natalie: No matter what.

Dr. Firestone: Or you're a sucker.

Natalie: Exactly.

Dr. Firestone: But if you listen to that voice then you disrupt the way things are. You're not the soft sweet person that you like to be.

Natalie: Right. Again, I remind myself very much of my mother in this situation. I remember specific events, I remember her acting that way. She basically taught me how to act that way. I wasn't around anything else. I thought that was the right way to act. I thought that my father was being mean if he didn't pay attention to her. That's the way I feel at those times in my relationship with Jeff, that if he's paying attention to somebody else that it's a rejection of me, but by now I know in reality that it isn't a rejection.

Natalie recognized that her jealous reactions were an imitation of her mother's victimized posture in relation to her father. It seemed, too, that her hostility toward Jeff had masked a deep-seated sense of insecurity and low self-worth as well as feelings of sadness and vulnerability.

Dr. Firestone: So there are really two parts to this. One, you incorporated her negative attitudes about your appearance and your looks, and the other you incorporated her defensive posture toward men.

Natalie:	Definitely.
Dr. Firestone:	You identified with her negative attitudes toward men and the distrust.
Natalie:	Right.
Dr. Firestone:	And the possessiveness.
Natalie:	It's also like they both tie into each other, the possessiveness and negative feelings about all my faults. It's like there's a voice that says, Here you have a man, but you're not so good-looking, so you've got to hold onto him. You finally found someone who really likes you, who really wants to be with you, who really likes sharing his life with you and you have all these faults, so you better hold on to him and you'd better make him know that he's yours. You'd better not show him that you feel sad when he's doing other things. You better not show him that you really like him, that you're really vulnerable, because you've got to hold onto him.
	These feelings aren't so angry now, they're more agitated and desperate. The anger doesn't feel as current inside me. The other feelings, being sad or scared, are so much more current because they go on all the time.

Later in the session, Natalie said,

I felt that something important happened when I was talking today that made me feel more understanding of myself, putting all the pieces together about what goes on inwardly in my mind, and what goes on in reality. I feel like it was easy for me to separate how I live my life inwardly and outwardly and it felt good to me to realize that. And I feel that it will be a progression after I leave here.

After listening to Natalie's descriptions of her insights, Jeff talked about his reactions to the session:

Jeff:	I felt very optimistic from this talk. It felt good to be here. I felt a lot when you [Natalie] were talking. It just felt good to feel something. It's been a long time since I felt like this. It really did make a big difference.

The process of identifying her self-attacks and angry views of Jeff in the session gave Natalie more control over her jealous outbursts. As a result, the couple's relationship improved significantly. The session also gave her clarity about how early interactions in her family had impacted her and led to the formation of a self-denigrating thought process. She made important connections between her mother's views and style of relating to men and her current reactions to Jeff's independence.

Immediately after the session, Natalie experienced a decrease in self-critical thinking and feelings of agitation. A week later, she reported her progress:

Natalie: This week, I have felt so much more aware of myself than I usually do. On an everyday level if I had a reaction to something I understood more where it came from. In understanding more where it came from, I felt like it was easy to resolve and to just think it out, and to not act on any negative reaction I might have at the moment. I just felt much more aware of myself and more feelingful and slowed down.

In the months that followed, as she learned to accept more affection and love, Natalie recognized, on an emotional level, that Jeff had especially chosen her. She became more aware of the times she began to experience voice attacks and was better able to counter the negative thoughts before they reached the point of undermining her good mood and triggering an angry reaction. Follow-up 6 months later indicated that Natalie's emotional state had remained stable, her relationship was a source of happiness to her (and to Jeff), and the couple was planning to start a family.

APPLICATION OF VOICE THERAPY TO SEXUAL PROBLEMS

Nowhere are destructive thoughts or voices closer to the surface and more directly connected with behavior than in the area of sexuality. The intrusion of negative cognitions and attitudes into sexual relationships can have a debilitating effect on each partner's ability to achieve satisfaction in this most intimate aspect of the relationship (Firestone, 1990e). These self-attacks affect people's sexual identity, their ability to both give and receive sexual gratification and pleasure, and they create tension in the sexual situation. Therefore, becoming aware of the voices, identifying their content, recognizing their irrationality, and understanding their sources, are valuable steps in helping couples achieve a more satisfying sexual relationship.

VOICES THAT AFFECT SEXUAL RELATING

Feelings of affection and attraction that lead to a couple's mutual desire to express their feelings sexually are easily dispelled by negative thoughts about their sexual performance. Often, when the transition has been made from an affectionate embrace to a sexual caress, people's "voices" gain ascendancy and can significantly diminish sexual desire as well as positive personal feelings. As noted in chapter 9, this volume, every aspect of love-making is subject to attack by the voice process: men's and women's level of excitement, their movements, their ability to please their partner, and so forth.

Many men and women have negative views about nudity and critical feelings about their bodies that cause them embarrassment in sexual situations. It is interesting that people's self-deprecating thoughts in relation to specific parts of their bodies more often than not are sensed on a subliminal level by their sexual partners, who become less responsive and even tend to avoid touching these particular areas.

Negative thoughts during sex often have an adverse effect on people's physiological responses and on their ability to complete the sex act. For example, a man revealed that as soon as he begins making love, he finds himself thinking as follows: <u>You're not going to be able to keep your erection</u>, whereupon, he usually *does* have difficulty maintaining his erection, and his nervousness increases with each subsequent failure.

When a sexual experience has been particularly gratifying and emotionally meaningful, self-protective "voices" predicting negative outcomes often come into play. These thoughts are degrading to both partners and tend to devalue the sexual act. Some people even appear to change character immediately afterward, for example, by becoming cool and aloof or argumentative.

From our investigations, we concluded that voice therapy procedures are valuable in overcoming sexual dysfunctions based on unresolved conflicts and negative parental attitudes incorporated during early childhood. The techniques can be used to identify a wide range of voice attacks in patients manifesting various symptoms of sexual dysfunction.

Voice Therapy Techniques for Partners With Problems in Sexual Relating

Men and women can use voice therapy techniques to give away their "voices" and maintain personal communication during the sex act, especially at the point where they begin to lose feeling and become more involved in a cognitive process. They can even stop making love temporarily while carrying out this exercise. We suggest that they maintain physical contact while saying their self-attacks and critical thoughts about each other. By taking time to share their thoughts and express their anxieties, they can sustain a level of feeling and maintain closeness rather than becoming cut off from their feelings. The insights and deep feelings from the past that may be aroused can be worked through in the sessions.

CASE STUDY

Mr. and Mrs. R had been married for 3 years and recently started planning a family. At this point, Mrs. R began having problems responding sexually, particularly during foreplay. The following transcription reveals the negative thoughts that each partner experienced while making love.*

Mrs. R (to husband):	I was aware of a voice last night when I was making love with you. When we first started, it felt so sweet to me, it was especially tender, and I could tell that you felt sweet toward me—that's the word I think of, "sweet." You were holding me and you said "sweetie." As soon as you said that, I started to attack myself. I started to think: Oh, sure, you're sweet!
	It's a mean voice like What's so sweet about you? How long do you think you can keep this up? It's really sarcastic. How long are you going to make him think you're sweet? I could tell that I started to get into a thought process and became cut off from my feelings. Then sex started to feel impersonal and it lost that sweet feeling. As soon you said that word, it triggered that voice.
Dr. Firestone:	Do you remember voices you have had at other times?
Mrs. R:	Yes, like, Can't he tell that you don't feel anything? Can't he tell that you're not nice? He always thinks you're nice. What's the matter with him? It starts to rip him apart.
Dr. Firestone:	Let yourself get into it.
Mrs. R:	It goes something like this: [angry] Can't he see anything? What's the matter? Is he blind? Can't he see? He always says 'sweet' to you. What's so sweet about you?
	The thoughts quickly turn back on me, but also telling me he's a fool: What an idiot he is to feel that way toward you. [sad] No one has ever felt that way towards you. What's wrong with him?

At this point in the session, Mr. R spoke:

---

*This material was excerpted from an article titled "Voices During Sex: Application of Voice Therapy to Sexuality," by R. W. Firestone, 1990, *Journal of Sex and Marital Therapy*, 16, pp. 258–274, and from the video documentary *Voices in Sex* (Parr, 1990b).

Mr. R: It's interesting that in that incident last night, my immediate reaction was to attack myself. I remember thinking: <u>What happened? Wait a minute. Look, she's fine. She's wet. She's fine. She's okay. She's everything that she should be. It must be you. You'd better make it okay again. You'd better fix it. Move a little faster, move a little harder.</u>

Dr. Firestone (to Mr. R):   What do you do?

Mr. R: Making love becomes impersonal, just mechanical, with me trying to fix things. I immediately take it on myself. The anger goes inside. It starts in on me, instead of toward her. The voice is resigned like: <u>Okay, this is going to happen all the time, because you don't really feel much anyway. Just try to finish it off. At least don't let her know that something's wrong with you, but also don't let her think that there's something wrong with her.</u>

But it's not an angry voice. It's not that angry. It's just calm. <u>Look, this is just the way you are. You've known this about yourself a long time. Why do you think it would be any different now?</u>

Later in the session, Mrs. R recalled other self-critical thoughts:

Mrs. R: I just remembered other voice attacks I usually experience when things are really close between us. Last night when you said I was sweet, it was at the point where I was feeling excited and moving around and I heard, <u>You slut! You dirty, disgusting slut! Girls don't do that!</u> Then the affection wasn't the same anymore.

Dr. Firestone: Do you have any voices about being a sweet person?

Mrs. R: [long pause, sad] It made me sad when you asked me that. I have a voice that says, <u>You're not sweet! You're not any different from us. This isn't you! This isn't how we are!</u> That's definitely my mother's voice.

Following this session, the couple utilized the technique described earlier. If either partner became distracted by unpleasant thoughts or experienced difficulty, they interrupted the sex act to talk and give away these thoughts to each other. In a later session, Mrs. R described the results:

Mrs. R: I remember when we talked about feeling mechanical several weeks ago. When I started having voices and stopped feeling sexual, the most important thing was to just get through the act. But now I feel like the most important thing is to communicate with you. It hasn't felt mechanical in a long time. That's the biggest difference. Sometimes we may not make love, we may stop and talk, but when we go on and make love, it's been nice and I feel much better and much more aware of myself.

It is helpful for partners to understand the origins of their sexual problems in the family context, as Mrs. R was able to do. Identifying specific voice attacks often reveals which parent was most influential in the individual's early life and identity formation, or who had the most significant role in shaping his or her thinking about the opposite sex and sexuality in general. This technique can be effectively incorporated into the practice of traditional sex therapy as described by H. S. Kaplan (1979) and D. E. Scharff & Scharff (1991).

Another voice therapy technique is the basis of an exercise designed to increase partners' tolerance for giving and accepting tender expressions of affection. This exercise consists of simply allowing one partner to do whatever he or she wishes to the other in terms of expressing his or her physical affection, that is, touching, kissing, sexual caressing. During this time, each partner communicates what he or she is experiencing at the moment, revealing his or her voices or reactions.

In the type of verbal communication that takes place while utilizing voice therapy techniques during intimate or sexual situations, partners learn to be more empathic toward each other from sharing their innermost feelings and fears. As a result, they are able to overcome many of their anxieties and self-depreciating attitudes rather than projecting these attitudes on to the other.

Discussion

In analyzing our clinical data, we found that people have both a natural, "clean" orientation to sex as well as an acquired distorted, "dirty" view of sex. The latter can be verbalized in the form of the voice. Many of these voices reveal considerable shame, sadness, and rage toward self and others. In the course of investigating the origins of their voices, most people discovered that their sexual difficulties could be traced to parental and societal attitudes toward sex as well as inappropriate sexual experiences during childhood. Many who reported sexual inhibition due to their feelings of being dirty or having odors uncovered voices that were incorporated during toilet-training procedures.

We found that many sexual problems are based on people's feelings of being unlovable or unworthy of love. Thus, the issue is not one of treating sexual problems, per se, but of helping individuals understand that the roots of their sexual disturbances lie in their defensive postures toward life and their intolerance of being close to another person. By becoming aware of and understanding the part destructive "voices" play in sexual dysfunction, men and women can free themselves of self-defeating, restrictive behavior patterns and significantly improve their sexual relationships.

SUPPLEMENTARY METHODS IN VOICE THERAPY

An understanding of both the internal and external forces that are detrimental to human relationships helped us to conceptualize specialized techniques that lead to positive attitude formation. These methodologies parallel voice therapy techniques and are conducive to people's growth in the context of their most intimate associations. They are based in part on the ethical perspective described in chapter 3, this volume, and on our views regarding the way people could ideally affiliate with one another and express their love.

Teaching Core Attitudes

In therapy with couples, one of the attitudes that we attempt to inspire is an understanding of a tender, loving way to treat one another that would extend outward from the couple relationship to their children, other family members, and friends. This style of relating consists of a noncritical, accepting attitude, a recognition of each person as a separate individual, and a concern and respect for boundaries and priorities. The sexuality and love between two people manifesting these qualities approach a spiritual level and represent an important dimension of the "good life."[3] It manifests itself in simple ways, in a thousand small acts of kindness and consideration, and in behaviors that lead to a deep sharing of life experiences and a sense of kinship and companionship.

Maintaining a satisfying relationship presupposes a nonintrusive posture in relation to the other's values, interests, or behaviors. In behavioral terms, this can mean a simple courtesy such as allowing the other person to finish speaking without interrupting, to more inclusive patterns and styles of relating such as the willingness to bear one's own pain without implicating the other in one's internal conflicts, and giving up efforts to "fix" or change the other.

It is important, however, that in being sensitive to the other's wants and needs, one does not compromise one's own integrity or personal freedom in an effort to maintain harmony. Both partners need to be wary of making fundamental concessions, because these compromises predispose resentment, disharmony, and conflict in the future.

The philosophical approach underlying our methodology provides the opportunity for individuals to learn, on an emotional level, that happiness is a by-product of extending oneself in love and generosity and placing the well-being and happiness of the other on a parallel with one's own priorities. We try to teach couples that genuine love implies finding enjoyment in observing the personal evolution of one's partner, watching him or her grow and flourish in areas even beyond one's personal world. Recognizing that it is gratifying to simply love another, rather than to expect to receive a benefit or reward for one's love, is a vital component in a good relationship.

Developing Sensitivity to One's Partner Through Increasing Listening Skills

The methods we use help people develop a sensitive understanding of their partner's hurts and troubles. Participating in the voice therapy groups makes individuals aware that everybody has suffered to varying degrees in their upbringing, and from this recognition emerge feelings of empathy and a sensitivity to their partner's struggle, as well as to their own.

Revealing Voice Attacks

Individual partners develop the ability to listen to each other with understanding and compassion as a result of their participation in couples voice therapy groups.* We frequently suggest that both partners reveal the negative cognitions toward themselves and about the other in a frank exchange of views; however, we may focus on one partner's individual work while the other listens, as in Natalie's session. We recommend that couples spend up to one-half hour a day engaged in this form of communication. The individuals strive to "give away" their negative attacks in a nonaccusatory style and attempt to not react to the voice statements of the other as personal criticism.[4]

---

*In the group setting, individuals come to gain a broader perspective on their partners as they observe them interact with the other participants. They also learn from the other couples how they have coped with difficulties and resolved their problems.

Use of Free Association

A supplementary technique for couples who have developed maturity and empathy is for each partner to free associate, expressing all of their thoughts, dreams, and fantasies, giving the other a unique perspective on his or her inner life. This process can be structured similarly to the methods used in relationship enhancement programs (Floyd, Markman, Kelly, Blumberg, & Stanley, 1995; J. M. Griffin & Apostal, 1993; Guerney, Guerney, & Cooney, 1985) in which couples learn the roles of "listener" and "expresser" as in client-centered therapy (C. R. Rogers, 1951). Each person, in turn, listens to the entire expression of the other, without intruding remarks, except to occasionally reflect words or phrases to capture the feeling or clarify their meaning. In the last part of the session, they discuss their reactions and insights. This is a structured format that teaches both partners two basic skills: (a) the ability to listen empathically, and (b) self-assertion, the ability to express one's point of view.

Understanding the Dynamics of Projection and Projective Identification

In voice therapy, in the course of exposing their self-attacks, partners learn the specific ways they distort each other and are then able to take back their projections. By exploring the connections between their early experiences in the family and their current interactions with each other, they can learn to distinguish between their distortions and the real characteristics and behaviors manifested by their partner. Identifying distrustful attitudes in terms of negative thoughts directed toward one's partner facilitates this distinction, and individuals come to understand how their interactions are contaminated by the process of defensive projective identification.[5] According to D. E. Scharff and Scharff (1991), in projective identification, the partner who has disowned or expelled a part of him- or herself and perceives it in the love object "so convincingly identifies the part of the self in the external object that the feeling state corresponding to that part of the self is evoked in the . . . spouse" (p. 58).

Disrupting Idealizations of One's Partner and Accepting Ambivalent Feelings

Most people idealize their parents as a primary defense, a process that occurs at the expense of harboring negative attitudes toward self. Because most adults transfer the feelings and attitudes they had toward their parents to significant others, the idealization of the parent is relived with their mates (Firestone, 1985). In our work, we attempt to challenge this idealization process in the service of helping individuals alter their self-concept in a positive direction.

Couples learn to distinguish between the projections and distortions that are a result of the voice process and the realistic perception of their partner's traits, both negative and positive. Individuals also realistically assess their own assets and liabilities. This process leads to an acceptance of ambivalent feelings toward themselves and their partners, and therefore, offers a more stable and honest perspective.

Learning to Formulate and Pursue Personal Goals

In discussing plans for behavioral changes, it is important to teach people the process of organizing their goals in relation to their love objects, of monitoring their actions, and of observing whether these correspond to their stated goals. For example, many people whose stated goal is to improve their relationship continue to interact with their partners in ways they know to be detrimental to the relationship. (See descriptions of such interactions in "Problem- and Solution-Focused Couples Therapies: The MRI and Milwaukee Models" by Shoham, Rohrbaugh, and Patterson, 1995.) On the other hand, when people's actions do correspond to their stated goals, their emotional reactions make sense to them, and their life has direction. Their lack of duplicitousness and sense of integrity also contribute to the building of trust in their relationships.

Lastly, individuals are encouraged to tolerate the anxiety of change rather than alter the situation. As they overcome their resistance to change and begin to alter destructive patterns of interaction, they come to understand how their voices interfere with their progress and lead to acting out behaviors that create distance rather than maintain the gains they have made. Partners learn that by using self-discipline, they can gradually increase their tolerance for intimacy. They discover that the anticipatory anxiety involved in following through on a corrective behavior is often more intense than the emotional response to actually changing one's behavior. If they are persistent, there is therapeutic movement.

CONCLUSION

Voice therapy procedures used in the context of couples or marital therapy help prevent the reliving of negative circumstances that existed in each partner's original family. Ultimately, the most effective psychotherapy for couples involves people challenging their own negative, restrictive thought processes (voices), thereby becoming more individuated and pursuant of their priorities. Fundamental resistance to this lies in the fact that many people are frightened that if they develop a more separate, independent style of relating, they will lose the relationship. They fear that they won't continue to be chosen or that they may no longer choose their partner. Their feelings of insecurity and low self-worth make them cling to the familiar, no matter how negative, and in that service, manipulate and control each other.

However, once the symptoms of a fantasy bond or addictive attachment between two people have been recognized and altered, a new type of relationship becomes a possibility. Individuals can reclaim the territory they lost, not through techniques that support the structure of a fantasy relationship, but through expanding their individual boundaries (Schnarch, 1991).[6] The only hope for the couple as well as for the future of the family is for people to break out of the imprisonment of their defensive self-parenting posture. Freeing themselves from destructive ties and moving toward individuation opens up the possibility for genuine love and intimacy.

ENDNOTES

[1]The material from this section is taken primarily from the *Voice Therapy Training Manual* (Firestone, Firestone, & Catlett, 1997). Used with permission.

[2]*A note of caution:* In clinical studies, it was found that in releasing the accompanying affect, some patients answered the voice dramatically with strong anger. "Yelling back" even at *symbolic* parental figures unleashes feelings of hatred for which one may later feel considerable guilt and anxiety. The therapist and patient must then address this guilt and the voice attacks that accompany it. Although the expression of intense feeling brings the patient some relief, the emotional articulation of voice attacks and answering back does not eliminate the antiself-system. The process of expressing strong emotions in answering back to the voice is still primarily a means to identify the dynamics of the antiself-system which then can be challenged. The therapist helps the patient move slowly and consistently toward his or her personal goals, keeping in mind at all times the patient's ego strength and level of tolerance for anxiety states induced by changing behavior patterns (Firestone, 1997a).

[3]See chapter 18 in *Combating Destructive Thought Processes* (Firestone, 1997a) for an in-depth discussion of various dimensions of "the good life."

[4]A number of marital therapists employ methods that are similar in some respects to voice therapy procedures. See Johnson and Greenberg's (1995) "emotionally focused approach" and Wile's (1995) description of his ego-analytic ap-

proach and the case example wherein the therapist tries to "create a platform from which . . . [the patient] can monitor his negative self-talk, take it into account, appreciate its inevitability, and deal with its negative effects" (p. 116). Several clinician/researchers (Gottman, 1979; Waring, 1988) have formulated treatment methods based on their empirical studies. Their findings showed that relationship satisfaction is correlated with a high ratio of positive self-disclosures and interactions to negative self-disclosures and angry, hostile interactions. Carstensen, Graff, Levenson, and Gottman (1996) asserted that "couples' success in resolving negative issues in relationships predicts marital outcomes better than the frequency with which they share positive emotional experiences" (p. 234). In discussing his goals for marital therapy, Waring (1988) emphasized that "if one could train couples to increase the number of positive or neutral self-references and encourage disclosure in a manner where affect (feeling) and content (thought) were congruent, one might enhance their level of intimacy" (p. 74). The techniques of voice therapy, in combination with the supplemental methods described here, provide an effective means for achieving this goal. By identifying their destructive thoughts that represent negative parental introjects, partners can increase their positive attitudes toward themselves and self-disclose in a manner in which feeling and thought would become more congruent, an important outcome, according to Thomas and Olson (1993).

[5]Ogden (1982) made a distinction between projection and projective identification. In *projection*, "the aspect of the self that is in fantasy expelled is disavowed and attributed to the recipient" whereas in *projective identification*, "the projector subjectively experiences a feeling of oneness with the recipient with regard to the expelled feeling, idea, or self-representation" (p. 34).

The goal of object relations therapy with couples is similar in some respects to that of voice therapy, that is, to encourage the reinternalization of projected material or, in our terms, encouraging the taking back of projections based on the voice. Object relations theorists D. E. Scharff and Scharff (1991) asserted that projective identification is an unconscious process and an important dynamic operating within the dyad. See "Object Relations Theory and Projective Identification in Marriage" in D. E. Scharff & Scharff's (1991) book, *Object Relations Couple Therapy* and "Psychoanalytic Marital Therapy" by J. S. Scharff (1995). In his discussion of projective identification, Zinner (1976) noted that

> the projection of disavowed elements of the self onto the spouse has the effect of charging a marital relationship with conflict that has been transposed from an intrapsychic sphere to an interpersonal one (p. 296). The operation of projective identification within marriage, however, is more than a matter of externalization of disavowed traits. We find that the contents of the projected material contain highly conflicted elements of the spouse's object relations with his or her own family of origin. (p. 297)

Citing case studies described by Dicks (1967), Zinner concluded that "a crucial aspect of the therapeutic work is to encourage the internalization of conflict within each partner in the marriage" (p. 301).

[6]In concluding his book, *Constructing the Sexual Crucible*, David Schnarch (1991) stressed the existential fears aroused by mature sexuality and individuation:

> Existential issues concerning the meaning of life and "the good life" invariably arise in the exploration of sexual potential, touching on spiritual matters (p. 551). We fear transcending ourselves (p. 591). This fear of self-transcendence, which surfaces as fears of loving has several faces: love of self, love of another, and love of life itself. . . . Loving is a self-mutating boundary experience triggered by one's own desire. . . . Love signals our eventual final death. (p. 592)

14

A PILOT STUDY APPLYING VOICE THERAPY WITH FOUR COUPLES: CLINICAL MATERIAL FROM A SERIES OF SPECIALIZED GROUP DISCUSSIONS

An intimate relationship is one in which neither party silences, sacrifices, or betrays the self.

Harriet Lerner (1989, p. 3)

In this chapter, we examine the application of voice therapy techniques in a small pilot study with eight individuals (four couples) who, prior to the study, had been unable to maintain a long-lasting and meaningful intimate relationship. The participants in this series of group discussions were familiar with voice therapy techniques and had taken an active role in ongoing seminars regarding couple relations.[1] In the present study, they focused on identifying, revealing, and analyzing destructive thoughts and attitudes that were causing distress in their current relationships. In the group sessions, they uncovered internalized voices they had not previously recognized or understood. As a result, they gained further insight into defensive behavior patterns that were interfering with the closeness and intimacy they desired. The meetings were videotaped and transcribed for coding purposes, as described in chapter 12.[2]

DESCRIPTION

Participants

Participants in the study included 4 men and 4 women. All were Caucasian and ranged in age from 27 to 52 years of age, with an average age of 38. Three participants, 2 women and 1 man, were previously married (the male participant had divorced twice), and 5 had never been married. The duration of the participants' current relationships ranged from 3 months to 3 years, with a mean of 18 months.

Methods

Seven participants completed the initial version of the *Firestone Voice Scale for Couples* (FVSC) prior to the discussion sessions that took place over a 3-month period. Following these sessions, they again completed the FVSC and the *Marital Satisfaction Inventory—Revised* (MSI–R; Snyder, 1997).[3] At the conclusion of the study, observers and participants filled out a behavioral checklist according to important relationship dimensions (see Exhibits 14.1 and 14.2).[4]

In the group discussions, the participants essentially followed the steps outlined in the previous chapter. They articulated the current problem in their relationship, verbalized their destructive thoughts toward self and others and released the associated angry affect, discussed the resulting insights, and formulated plans for making changes in defensive behaviors based on their destructive thought processes.*

Results

Preliminary results indicated that each partner progressed significantly in being able to examine his or her defensive behavior patterns and modify them. Although participants' scores on the FVSC cannot be generalized because of the small sample, they tend to correspond to two other outcome measures: (a) the authors' and other observers' judgment of improvement; and (b) participants' perceived improvement (see material presented below). Each partner reported constructive changes in terms of happier outlook, more loving responses toward the other, and greater satisfaction in his or her relationship. This substantial improvement lends support to the hypothesis that the maladaptive defensive structure within individual partners is a primary obstacle to achieving intimacy in long-term personal

---

*Each partner verbalized his or her self-attacks and critical attitudes toward the other and discussed the resulting insights while the other listened. As noted in chapter 13, this volume, partners were sensitive and empathic toward each other during this process. They were aware that the tone of their judgmental attitudes toward the other, when expressed in a voice dialogue, was more harsh or cynical than was usually warranted by the situation.

EXHIBIT 14.1
Behavioral Checklist for Partners

How would you describe yourself and your partner on a scale of 1 to 5 along these dimensions?

Nondefensive and open (able to listen to feedback without overreacting/open to new experiences)
Self: 1 2 3 4 5   Partner: 1 2 3 4 5

Respect for other's boundaries
Self: 1 2 3 4 5   Partner: 1 2 3 4 5

Vulnerable (willing to feel sad, acknowledge hurt feelings, etc.)
Self: 1 2 3 4 5   Partner: 1 2 3 4 5

Honest (straightforward, nondeceptive)
Self: 1 2 3 4 5   Partner: 1 2 3 4 5

Physically affectionate
Self: 1 2 3 4 5   Partner: 1 2 3 4 5

Sexuality (satisfied with sexual relationship)
Self: 1 2 3 4 5   Partner: 1 2 3 4 5

Empathic and understanding (lack of distortion of the other)
Self: 1 2 3 4 5   Partner: 1 2 3 4 5

Communication (sense of shared meaning, feel understood)
Self: 1 2 3 4 5   Partner: 1 2 3 4 5

Noncontrolling, nonmanipulative, and nonthreatening
Self: 1 2 3 4 5   Partner: 1 2 3 4 5

How would you rate *yourself* along these dimensions?

Sense of well-being
1 2 3 4 5

Self-confident
1 2 3 4 5
Optimistic
1 2 3 4 5

1 = Does not describe me/does not describe partner; 2 = Describes me on infrequent occasions/ describes partner on infrequent occasions; 3 = Describes how I am some of the time/describes how my partner is some of the time; 4 = Describes how I frequently am/describes how my partner frequently is; 5 = Describes me most or all of the time/describes my partner most or all of the time. © The Glendon Association 1999.

relationships.[5] (See Figures 14.1 to 14.4 for a graphic representation of individual partners' mean scores on the FVSC.)

CASE STUDIES

Couple 1: Elaine and Bruce

Background

In the 3 years since Elaine and Bruce became involved, their relationship had steadily improved, and individually, both appeared to be flour-

EXHIBIT 14.2
Behavioral Checklist for Therapist/Observer

How would you describe each partner on a scale of 1 to 5 in this couple along these dimensions?

Nondefensive and open (able to listen to feedback without overreacting/open to
   new experiences)
Male partner: 1 2 3 4 5   Female partner: 1 2 3 4 5

Respect for other's boundaries
Male partner: 1 2 3 4 5   Female partner: 1 2 3 4 5

Vulnerable (willing to feel sad, acknowledge hurt feelings, etc.)
Male partner: 1 2 3 4 5   Female partner: 1 2 3 4 5

Honest (straightforward, nondeceptive)
Male partner: 1 2 3 4 5   Female partner: 1 2 3 4 5

Physically affectionate
Male partner: 1 2 3 4 5   Female partner: 1 2 3 4 5

Sexuality (reports being satisfied with sexual relationship)
Male partner: 1 2 3 4 5   Female partner: 1 2 3 4 5

Empathic and understanding (lack of distortion of the other)
Male partner: 1 2 3 4 5   Female partner: 1 2 3 4 5

Communication (reports a sense of shared meaning, feels understood)
Male partner: 1 2 3 4 5   Female partner: 1 2 3 4 5

Noncontrolling, nonmanipulative, and nonthreatening
Male partner: 1 2 3 4 5   Female partner: 1 2 3 4 5

Sense of well-being
Male partner: 1 2 3 4 5   Female partner: 1 2 3 4 5
Self-confident
Male partner: 1 2 3 4 5   Female partner: 1 2 3 4 5
Optimistic
Male partner: 1 2 3 4 5   Female partner: 1 2 3 4 5

1 = Does does not describe this person; 2 = Describes how this person is on infrequent occasions; 3 = Describes how this person is some of the time; 4 = Describes how this person frequently is; 5 = Describes how this person is most or all of the time.
© The Glendon Association 1999.

ishing and expanding their lives. Paradoxically, they began to encounter difficulties immediately after an extended vacation during which they both reported feeling especially close to each other. On returning home, Elaine reported that she was no longer attracted to Bruce and felt trapped in the relationship.

Elaine's typical pattern was one of becoming involved in a relationship, then systematically withdrawing while deluding herself with numerous rationalizations for the subsequent break-up. Initially in her relationship with Bruce, she had a similar pattern of becoming distant and then critical toward him, particularly following a meaningful sexual experience. In the couples' seminars, she came to understand and challenge this repetitive style of relating and felt fulfilled and optimistic in the relationship. There-

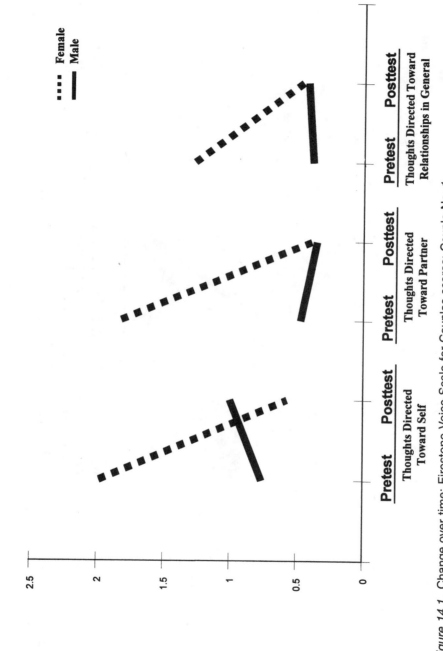

Figure 14.1. Change over time: Firestone Voice Scale for Couples scores: Couple No. 1.
© The Glendon Association.

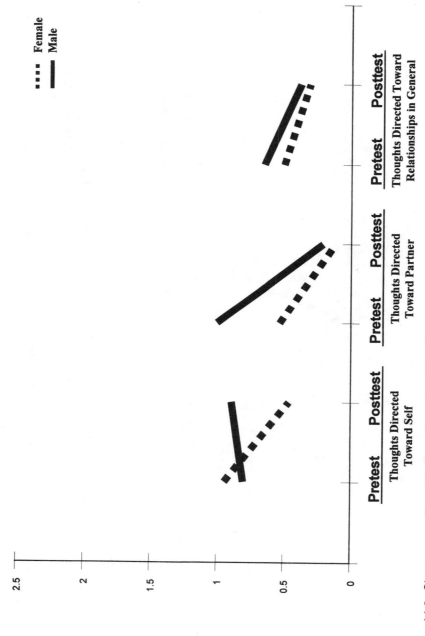

Figure 14.2. Change over time: Firestone Voice Scale for Couples scores: Couple No. 2.
© The Glendon Association.

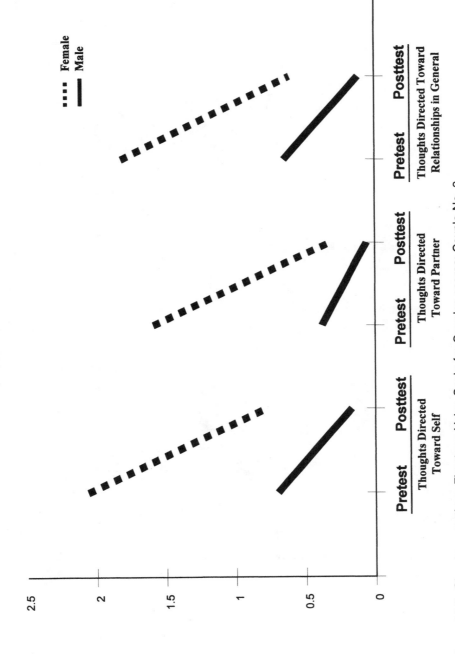

Figure 14.3. Change over time: Firestone Voice Scale for Couples scores: Couple No. 3.
© The Glendon Association.

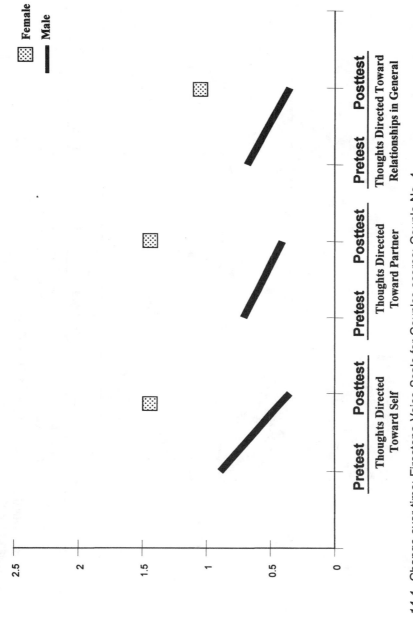

Figure 14.4. Change over time: Firestone Voice Scale for Couples scores: Couple No. 4.
© The Glendon Association.

fore, when she expressed her intention to separate from Bruce in one meeting, the other participants were shocked and disconcerted. (Bruce was not present at this particular meeting.)

> Elaine: I want to talk about this openly because I'm really confused. I feel terrible, so bad, worse than I've felt in a long time. I feel really trapped. I've kept trying to make it work with Bruce, but I don't feel toward him at all like I did a long time ago. Right now I don't have any feelings of wanting to try to go back and make this work. The last time it felt good between us was for only a few days at the beginning of the summer, and then I stopped wanting anything with him. It's gotten worse and worse. I feel like I've got to get away. I just can't stand him any more.

Several participants responded, reminding Elaine of her pattern of rejecting close relationships. The feedback from her friends had the effect of making Elaine even more defensive and argumentative. Although she acknowledged her friends' interpretations regarding her rejecting behavior, she was stubbornly resistant to their suggestions that she explore her feelings further before making her decision.

> Elaine: I know what you're saying is true, that I've done this before, but it's very different this time. I've tried to stay with it, but now I actually hate him. I can't stand to be around him. I feel guilty about leaving him but I know it's the only thing that will give me any relief.

Near the end of the discussion, a woman who knew Elaine well and understood the dynamics of the relationship pointed out an important fact that Elaine had neglected to mention in recounting the events of the summer.

> Tam: I know that during the vacation, Bruce felt so close to you that he had strong feelings of wanting to have a baby with you. I also know how meaningful the issue of having a baby is to you in your life.

> Elaine: [sad] I had forgotten all about that. I had totally forgotten that Bruce talked about those feelings. In fact, I can barely remember what he said to me! Looking back, I remember it made me happy at first, but then I forgot about it completely and started feeling so critical toward him. I can't believe it. It went from Bruce offering me something I had always dreamed of, to me wanting absolutely nothing from him. I completely switched everything around.

Tam's interpretation had an immediate effect on Elaine's emotional state. She experienced feelings of deep sadness, and her attitude toward Bruce and the relationship shifted in a positive direction. This change in perspective appeared to relieve much of her tension and agitation, and she looked forward to telling Bruce about the change in her feelings.

Clinical Material From the Couples' Discussion Groups

1. Formulating the problem. In a subsequent meeting,* Elaine began by revealing her insights into the destructive thought processes that had been triggered by the events of the summer. She felt motivated to try to prevent future regressive trends by further separating the harsh, antagonistic attitudes toward Bruce from her own point of view.

Elaine: I feel anxious at the idea of talking about this, but I feel like it's the right time for me to discuss it. I feel like I'm right in the middle of it. I think this is such an important subject for me, but it's also such a break with my family, my mother, just all my training.

Dr. Firestone: How is it a break?

Elaine: Well, if I just look at my mother's relationship with my father plus any other times that I've seen her after they got divorced, she had so little feeling for anybody but especially for the man in her life, no feeling whatsoever. She had a very casual critical point of view that came out with every word, and I know it's very easy for me to get into her point of view. When I'm in that point of view I've got no feeling for myself and no feeling for you [Bruce] in my life.

Dr. Firestone: How does that work?

Elaine: It could start off with a simple thing like Bruce asking me a casual question. The response in my mind is, "What kind of a stupid question is that?" But it comes out of nowhere. [To Bruce] It's not that I will give you that response, but I'll just be a little colder, and it builds up until finally there's not a thing that you do that's right. I'm critical of your breathing. I'm critical of your walking, your clothes, anything you ask me, and I know in that I've got no feeling for myself and I've got no feeling for you at all. And then I start to attack myself because I know my mother and I know that I'm feeling like her. I know I'm behaving like her.

Dr. Firestone: A couple of weeks ago you really were very much into feeling critical. In fact you were thinking actually of getting out of the relationship. What happened?

---

*The group discussion from which this material was excerpted was part of the series of meetings that comprised the small pilot study, whereas the couples seminar where Elaine initially revealed her desire to leave Bruce occurred prior to the study.

Elaine: What happened was that I was away on vacation during the summer and you [Bruce] had come to join me a couple of times and we had a really nice time. The feelings between us had been sweet and loving and easy, very friendly. There had been a few times when you'd come up to me and you'd give me a hug and say something like "Let's have a baby," or "Let's get married." It was in such a sweet way. The feelings were definitely there.

And then you left the vacation, and I was going be seeing you two to three weeks later. In the course of that time, I was definitely anticipating that things wouldn't be very good between us. I was ready when I came back not to like you that much and not to want anything from you. And it started to make you feel hungry toward me. And then I felt like I had the goods on you because you were wanting something from me but it wasn't what I wanted.

2. *Verbalizing destructive thoughts and releasing the associated affect.* As Elaine continued, she verbalized specific negative attitudes and parental prescriptions that had been compelling her to give up her relationship with Bruce.

Elaine: The voice inside was like, He's just going to eat you alive. He wants something that you don't want. You can't give it to him. There's no way that you're ever going to be able to give it to him. You can't make this thing right.

Dr. Firestone: Try to get into the feeling.

Elaine: He wants so much from you. He's just going to eat you alive. He's going to eat everything out of you. [angry, loud voice] He wants everything and he's so fucking weak that if you don't give it to him he's just going to fall apart. You've just got to pretend that it's right. You've got to pretend that it's right all the time because he's going to fall apart. He can't even handle anything. He can't stand up on his own two feet. You think you can talk to him about this? No, you can't talk to him. You've got to make him feel like everything's going to be okay. You can play him along like a puppet. You can control his every move by what you decide to give to him. And you know what, he's so desperate, he's going to go along with it. He's going to go along with everything that you want.

It is important here to reiterate that in her interactions with Bruce, Elaine had not expressed these negative thoughts out loud; in fact, she was barely aware of them before she revealed them in this voice dialogue. Nevertheless, these thoughts and the associated feelings of hostility had a powerful effect on her behavior, for example, in a diminished level of affection or a sense of not really being there in the situation with Bruce.

> Elaine: I feel very controlled in this, but that's how I feel in the voices. I feel so controlled and so cold. It's like cold as ice. And I've got no feeling at all. And the more that you try to make things better, I feel like you're scrambling to make me happy, and the more that you're doing that, the more angry I am.

At this point in the discussion, Bruce described his reaction to the voices Elaine expressed:

> Dr. Firestone: [to Bruce] How do you feel being exposed to her thoughts now?

> Bruce: It made me very sad because I feel like I like you so much and everything that you described seems right to me. It's very difficult when I feel that confusion. Initially, I think, "What happened?" and I don't quite know what went wrong. Then I start to wonder and I start to ask you some silly questions at that point.

> Dr. Firestone: What kind of questions?

> Bruce: Things like "What do you think the day's going to be like?" or something like that. I want some kind of contact, just to fill up the empty space that I can sense is developing between us immediately. And then I know that I've asked a question that makes you feel irritable and then I get more desperate very quickly.

> Dr. Firestone: So when she pulls away like that, you start to feel really hungry or anxious.

> Bruce: Absolutely.

> Dr. Firestone: And you can't identify anything that really happened between you.

> Bruce: I can't figure out what happened.

> Dr. Firestone: [to Elaine] What do you think accounted for the change from the enjoyable summer to starting to pull away?

> Elaine: The only thing that happened was that I had a really nice time with you [to Bruce]. [sad, tearful]

Dr. Firestone:	Let yourself feel it, it's okay.
Elaine:	I just felt like a sweet woman. I think, especially with the whole subject around having a baby, that it's something that I never, ever considered myself for so many years. I couldn't imagine having a loving child, a sweet child within a loving relationship. Because I think I've always had such a feeling that anything that came out of me would be like a poisonous creature, which so ties in with what I felt about having a baby, that it would just be an unlovable, terrible experience.
Dr. Firestone:	You say that as though you were talking to yourself. Say those thoughts about you.
Elaine:	It's like, What are you thinking of? What in God's name are you thinking of? You know full well what would happen. You know, you know what would come out of you. What are you thinking of? It's disgusting. It's such a disgusting thing. [crying] What are you thinking of? How could you even consider such a thing? And you know what? He's just as bad. He's just as bad. Nothing that came out of him would be any good either. Nothing that came out of you two could be anything!

3. *Discussing insights.*

Elaine:	I think that was the key thing because as soon as I came back I had to get rid of it. I had to get rid of you and me. Obviously it's personal to you because you're in this, but it would happen with any relationship, it would happen with any man, and I think it has happened with every man that I've been involved with. I think that's part of the voices to keep me alone, to keep me living her life. My mother's got nothing in her life.

Elaine went on to recount the sequence of events that helped her get back in touch with her positive feelings toward Bruce. As a result of the feedback she received in the earlier couples' seminar, she had been able to separate out her real point of view from the destructive, internalized view that represented her mother's attitudes.

Dr. Firestone:	What kept you from really just breaking up?
Elaine:	I was hell bent on it. I was desperate. I was panicked and felt that I had to leave because I felt like my whole life was falling apart and that the only way to get back to myself again was to get out of this relationship. But then I talked about it with everybody in that meeting.

Even though they were saying that this is a pattern, "You've done this again and again," in my mind I thought "Yeah, but it's different this time." I felt like this was absolutely different.

But then I think what got me was that so many people who really seem to know me and like me were all saying something that was the opposite of what I was feeling. I felt like if so many friends were telling me something about myself, it was worth listening to. And then, the real turning point in my feelings came when Tam reminded me of Bruce's idea about wanting to have a baby with me, and I felt immediately sad, really sad, and I began to feel more like myself.

Dr. Firestone: It seemed like your friends convinced you of your own point of view as contrasted with your mother's point of view in which you were very much involved. Even though you were angry at first, you began to be realistic in the sense of respecting their opinions, but more than that, you felt that they were on your side, and this strengthened your own point of view. I think the thing that really helped you to turn it around was the insight, the realization that the thought of having a baby had triggered this regression and triggered her point of view or the ascendence of her point of view.

Most people live with a split view of themselves in that they've incorporated into themselves a point of view that's alien and that can't be quite integrated into the personality. This alien point of view is responsible for the kind of thought processes that you went through, and this internalized negative view has a profound effect on a person's actions. Very often you would find yourself in your relationships particularly reenacting your mother's life. It's as though you swallowed her up. Part of that is because when children experience pain and frustration in their development, they tend to identify strongly with the aggressor, that is, the person who is rejecting or hurtful, and they take on that point of view. It has a survival function to do that because instead of being the weak child, now you're identified with the strong adult and it allays your anxiety temporarily. So it's a defense mechanism. But as you defend yourself in that manner, you incorporate a point of view into yourself that's alien.

Most people are operating to a considerable extent on that alien point of view that they've incorporated. I think the people in this group who have been talking about their personal lives and their relationships are pretty aware of how that works and that it controls their life to a large extent because to deviate from that defense mechanism leads to anxiety. So there's a tendency to maintain a kind of neurotic equilibrium at the expense of fulfilling yourself.

I think the fact that you responded to your friends' awareness strengthened your point of view. Also the insight as to the triggering mechanism that scared you and accounted for the regression helped you avoid the potential destruction of the relationship. It's interesting that you've been feeling much better since then and the relationship has really improved. But it would be rather unusual that people would allow anything to come between them and this internalized negative point of view. Most people would tend to break up at that point. It was fortunate that you were involved in these discussions about relationships and were close to your friends and other members enough to look into yourself.

Couple 2: Alan and Carolyn

Background

Alan and Carolyn's relationship has been close and satisfying to both of them until recently. In the discussion, Alan reveals how his decision to change his self-image by losing weight unexpectedly had a negative effect on his attitude toward himself. Surprisingly, instead of making him feel good, the weight loss triggered many self-attacks, which had a profound effect on his appearance and way of relating. Eventually it led to problems in the relationship. Here Alan begins by describing how he felt as a young adolescent.

1. Formulating the problem.

Alan: My story goes back a long way to when I was about 12. I knew I was never going to have a child and I knew I was never going to get married because I just knew that was not a part of me. I was an unlovable person in that way. Based on that way of thinking, I actually spent 8 years with a woman who couldn't ever love a person. So I kept that pattern going on in my life, but by talking with my friends, I started changing a lot of these old images of myself and I ended up going out with a woman who's so different than anything I imagined in my life. And things were really nice for a long long time. For about a year, we were both very affectionate with each other and kind to each other and both very separate too. We had our own lives, and when we did things together, it was meaningful. So, I was pretty happy, to say the least.

Then I started thinking of having a baby. I started thinking about possibly getting married and I still was pretty happy. But then I tried to tackle something that I didn't realize how important it was. I had a very strong identification with my father and his identity was always one of being overweight. He had an addiction with food. He was always 50, 60 pounds overweight, and I always made sure in my adult life that I was a good solid 10–15 pounds overweight. So I decided to tackle that and it brought up an array of feelings. Basically I feel like since that happened a few months ago that I haven't been as close to you [Carolyn] because I've been more like my father. And I feel really bad about that because the one thing I really valued is that I was an individual with you and I was myself. I wasn't him.

Dr. Firestone: It's interesting that you identified this as a big break with your father, to lose that weight. And you didn't anticipate that, according to what you said earlier. It surprised you. But the effect that it had was to stir up a lot of voices attacking you.

2. Verbalizing destructive thoughts.

Alan: Before I lost the weight I felt like a pretty nice person. I felt good about myself. But then I turned against myself. I felt like I was looking for trouble, wanted to get into a fight, was always making people feel bad.

Dr. Firestone: So people do develop until they reach a point where they become anxious. It seems like that's what happened with you. Your whole life had changed for the better. You were successful at work, you were making a lot of money, you had a woman who really liked you and a woman who you were really attracted to and admired.

3. Discussing insights.

Alan: But the key element of that whole thing is that I had my father being proud of me in those areas. He was proud: "Now I have a son I'm proud of. He's making money and he has a great girlfriend." I was making him proud. In that way, I felt like I was a good son. But once I decided to separate from him, which was the weight issue and not look like him anymore, boom.

It's like I had him in my head, just a barrage of stuff coming down.

Dr. Firestone: It made you pull away from Carolyn. It had that effect.

Alan: I'm not sure I would say it made me pull away, I would say that it made me try to push her away. I think I probably tried to push her away more. I just wasn't the same with you and I don't know how to describe it. There's a difference between somebody being relaxed and loving and somebody who's more tense and awkward.

Dr. Firestone: How did you feel during this time?
(to Carolyn)

Carolyn: Well, it's been painful.

Dr. Firestone: How did it seem to change?

1. Formulating the problem.

Carolyn: I noticed that you didn't seem yourself. In relation to the weight, that was never an issue with me. I mean, I felt fine with the way that you looked. I think you're attractive now after losing weight, but you quit talking to me, and I just felt like there was no communication. If I ever asked you more than just "How's it going?" I felt like I was being intrusive. So I felt like there was a barrier there in terms of any kind of communication which I have a hard time with. I just felt your awkwardness and the lack of self-confidence.

Dr. Firestone: You said he didn't look like himself.

Carolyn: Yes. I mean I felt so attracted to you for a whole year and then I quit feeling attracted even though you were thinner.

Dr. Firestone: It seems like when you turned on yourself you didn't
(to Alan) have the appeal that you had just being yourself. That had a big effect.

2. Verbalizing negative thoughts.

Dr. Firestone: So what was your reaction? Were you angry at him?
(to Carolyn)

Carolyn: No, I just feel so hard on myself, so demoralized and the attack on myself is, How did you get yourself into this situation? What are you going to do now? You just can't keep going this way. How did you let yourself become vulnerable in this way?

Dr. Firestone:	You took a chance.
Carolyn:	<u>You took a chance, you let yourself be vulnerable and thank God you didn't let it go further. Just put on the brakes. Thank God, you didn't get pregnant!</u>
Dr. Firestone: (to Alan)	So you succeeded in pushing her away to a considerable extent. So much so that she started thinking these negative thoughts about the relationship. So unless people can break with the incorporated image that's part of a defensive process, they will tend to act out these patterns to the point of disrupting the relationships. That's the tragedy essentially because it was a perfectly good relationship, very rewarding to both of you.

Couple 3: Sheryl and Mark

Background

Sheryl and Mark* were involved for 2 years 7 years ago but were unable to sustain their initial feelings of friendship and attraction. Eventually they separated but remained friends. They began dating again 3 months ago. Their renewed relationship started off well and was close and satisfying, but recently they experienced some problems that were reminiscent of their past relationship.

In the intervening years, both partners had developed personally and had modified many of their defensive behaviors. Sheryl had explored her fears of being vulnerable in an intimate relationship and had traced these fears to early childhood experiences. She had uncovered voices depreciating her as a woman that she recognized as having contributed to the difficulties she and Mark had encountered in the past.

1. Formulating the problem. In this meeting, Sheryl describes her reactions to the affection and intimate feelings that have been developing in the relationship. As she continues, she begins to explore the origins of hostile attitudes toward Mark that emerge at times when he is particularly warm and tender toward her:

Sheryl:	The feeling that I have is that I've always just simply liked you, but I feel like I can't stand it that you're nice to me or that you like me. I feel like I have a mean streak . . .
Dr. Firestone:	In response to his liking you.
Sheryl:	Yes.

---

*See chapter 12, this volume, for a description of Mark's family background and case history.

2. Verbalizing negative thoughts and releasing affect.

Dr. Firestone: What do you tell yourself about the relationship? What are you telling yourself?

Sheryl: It's like, <u>Don't show him anything, don't show him you like him.</u> I tell myself, <u>just don't show it, you'll be such a sucker, you're such a sucker if you show it.</u>

At times when he's really nice, I'll just want to squash him. When he's vulnerable I just want to squash him. I just want to smash him, and it's for no reason except for that he's vulnerable and he's being sweet.

3. Discussing insights.

Sheryl: I've had a million thoughts a day of similarities, of ways I've seen myself feel like my mother and in previous relationships I've acted probably so much like her and I didn't even know it. Every relationship ended basically the same way for me for no reason really, just getting rid of it. And it felt like getting rid of. But I know that that's the point of view like my mother's. I saw her as being a really critical person and she was very critical of my father, very critical of anything about him, and she would be mean to him. She was humiliated to be seen with him when he was sick. He had a brain tumor, and he was probably the most vulnerable then because he was helpless basically. And I think that when he was sick, everything in her personality became like a caricature of her. I think she was like that all the time, but it was magnified then.

Dr. Firestone: How did she act?

Sheryl: There was one time when I went home for the holidays and we were all playing Monopoly, and he was really sick, so he was just watching us and he couldn't really speak, he was losing his physical abilities. So he started drooling and she was disgusted by him, and she said, "Stan, ugh." She was humiliated that he drooled in front of us. And so he went to his room, and I felt so bad for him because there was no kindness in her at all. She was just humiliated, but I feel like sometimes I act like that myself.

Dr. Firestone: So it's almost like a compulsion to reenact those patterns, it's barely under your control.

Sheryl: Yes, it's like that. I thought of the movie, *Alien*, where this thing comes out of my stomach and I'm surprised by it and the things that I say. It's for no reason except to take the pleasure away, the happiness that he might have just from being nice to me. I want to smash that.

4. Formulating plans for behavior change.

Dr. Firestone: So the hope in both the cases [Elaine and Sheryl] is for you to hang in there and to tolerate the anxiety in giving up these defenses, actually in breaking with the imaginary connections that you have with your mothers in that sense and learn to really control that destructive acting out and allow yourself to get a perspective or an empathic view of the person you're with. Basically if you do sweat it out then you'll be able to have more in your life. And it takes a lot of courage to go through that process but it's really worth it.

Sheryl: I feel like it would make me sad too because I would feel a lot. When I'm in that other point of view, I feel big and mean. And when I just let things be, I feel like a soft sweet person.

Dr. Firestone: It's all the difference in the world. And it fits the image that I was saying that we incorporate the person who's hurting us, the prisoner identifies with the guard, essentially. We tend to identify with the very person who's hurting us.

Sheryl: Yes.

Dr. Firestone: And then in that you would feel big as compared with little as the child and even though you might be a very soft, loving person, when you're possessed by that point of view you're acting out destructive behavior.

I thought it would be valuable for men to talk about their defensive behavior. I was thinking how they react to women, how they protect themselves when they're loved or cared for because that would give a perspective.

Mark

Following his involvement with Sheryl several years ago, Mark had begun to challenge his distorted perceptions of men and women. He discovered that these views were based on his observations of his parents' relationship as well as their negative attitudes toward themselves, each other, and the opposite sex. As described in chapter 12, this volume, in verbalizing his self-attacks, Mark recognized that he identified with his father's animosity toward women and had internalized his mother's view of men—and thus of himself—as being harsh and aggressive, and he had attempted to compensate by pleasing women or deferring to them.

3. *Discussing insights.*

Mark: I've seen a continuous pattern in my close relationships of pushing the woman away. I know on one level that I really do want a close relationship, but I don't want to accept the love, I don't want to accept the acknowledgment, I don't want to accept the friendship, I don't want to accept being chosen, and I think I'm very quick to become habitual and to routinize things in a way, but more than that, me pursuing the woman and losing myself I think really pushes things away.

[to Sheryl] I don't want to feel you choosing me. So if I can pursue you, I don't have to stay with that anxiety of you choosing me. And the interesting thing is I haven't been involved in a close relationship for a number of years, and I feel very strong and independent in a very general way. But my tendency is to give that up instantly. I don't think that's happened since we've been seeing each other again but that would be my tendency.

Dr. Firestone: When partners give up their independence, they lose their attractiveness.

Mark: Absolutely. I think that's why I could push Sheryl away so quickly by doing that. I think when we were involved in the past, we both did that. I know I absolutely did that. I gave up interest in other friends, and if you wanted to see me I would drop anyone else in my life to see you. In fact, I would anticipate your desire to see me and drop them before you would even ask. And I lost my old friends and I lost you at the same time. My father, I know, had a very low opinion of himself. And this works into it. I don't want to feel like I'd be the type of man, first of all, the word *man* is the key word here. I don't want to feel like a man. A man can be chosen, a man is strong. I don't want to feel like a man. So, if I pursue you in a desperate way, I'm so much weaker, I'm so much more the type of man that my mother saw men as.

Currently we've talked and I expressed my feeling that being sensitive and expressing tenderness is not the same as being weak. It was very interesting for me because when I said that to Sheryl, I was pissed off. "I don't want you [Sheryl] to interpret my sensitivity or kindness towards you or affection as weakness." And saying that gave me a real sense of myself in a way that I was shocked. I felt so centered after that conversation.

Dr. Firestone: Just listening today it seems like the major deterrent to a good relationship is what we bring to it from the past. The internalized process with which we're critical and self-protective really insulates us. It protects us in a strange way but really limits our lives to the extent that we utilize these defenses. It seems that people are particularly affected by the internalization or the identification with the parent of the same sex, and particularly in close relationships, they mimic the defensive posture of their parents. They feel almost compelled to repeat the same style of relating with their partners that they saw or experienced when they were growing up.

Couple 4: Chris and Jane

Background

For the 2 years that Chris and Jane have been together, they have taken a serious interest in sustaining a close, loving relationship. In the ongoing couples groups, they have developed an understanding of how the defensive patterns that each of them brought to the relationship create distance between them. Jane begins by talking about her awareness of some of these issues:

1. Formulating the problem.

Jane: I know that in learning to be close in our relationship that I've learned a lot about myself. In the beginning of our relationship, it felt easy to feel intimate, you know, feeling you looking at me and feeling your loving me, letting that make me happy. Feeling happy from that, but also believing that I had something to give, that I had love to give and that I'm a sweet woman, that I can make a man feel happy. That's really such a nice feeling.

But a couple of things happened and one was that my life was getting separate even geographically from my mother. At the time you and I were getting closer, I hadn't seen her hardly in about a year. I remember going to L.A. one night and running into her, and I remember feeling how different our lives were. Everything about us was different. I felt loving, and I've seen her throughout her adult life and mine, enter into a nice relationship and then throw it away, time and again with no feeling for what she's doing. And I've seen her get to the point now where it feels like she's given up on love. She might let herself maybe have a sexual relationship, but it's not in a sweet way. It's in a way that I feel is demeaning to her. And so I've seen her throw everything away, and it's painful.

2. Verbalizing destructive thoughts and releasing the associated affect.

Jane: When I saw her that night, it was like a reminder of what I'm made of. That was the feeling, like, You're not any different. This is your family. This is where you come from. You know what I mean. This is what you're made of. What are you trying to do? You know, who are you fooling anyway?

Then in the next month or so, she moved closer to my life again. The thing is I'm so compelled to imitate her and imitating her means throwing my relationship away. That's all it is.

Somewhere I have voices like, Well, what do you need this for? You know, wouldn't it be great if you were just single and you could just go out. I just start having those voices out of nowhere. But that's the way she lives, and I realize that that's her and not me.

Dr. Firestone: You seem very clear as to what's going on. Has it really helped you in the relationship?

3. Discussing insights.

Jane: Yes. I would say that I'm still learning, and I feel like we've managed to still have a lot of sweet times together and intimate times and I think that that wouldn't have lasted. I think I would have definitely talked myself out of our relationship a long time ago if I hadn't known more about myself and about my tendencies.

Dr. Firestone: So there is a way of coping with this—

Jane: Yes.

Dr. Firestone —but it takes courage and it takes sweating through the anxiety and the guilt involved in breaking the negative identifications with one's parents that give a sense of security even though they restrict your life.

Jane: The other thing that I wanted to say is that I know that I'm not as independent or strong as I could be in relation to you [Chris] because I know that I almost never think about how I feel. A lot of the time I'm thinking about how you feel toward me, and it's not an equal way of interacting with you. So if something's off in the relationship, it's me. I'm off. I'm not feeling right. I'm doing something, but I never look to you and think maybe you're not feeling good or something's going on with you. But it's a way I don't want to be because it makes me not independent, gauging myself off of you constantly. Then I hate you in a way.

Dr. Firestone: People use their mates to define them, instead of having an independent view of themselves. That's very destructive and can be very harmful. Chris, I was wondering how you protect yourself.

In this part of the discussion, Chris encounters a new challenge as he explores his defensive reactions to women.

1. *Formulating the problem.*

Chris: It's interesting, there are a number of things I was thinking about along those lines. In relation to the woman in my life, I'm aware of getting defended and like with you Jane, in the beginning I felt very open and very sort of optimistic about my life in general and I wanted to approach this relationship differently than any other relationship that I had been in but at some point, I know that I started to have some of the same kinds of feelings that I'd had in other relationships where I felt more guarded and more sort of self-protective in a way as to not be quite as vulnerable and loving when I would feel that way.

Dr. Firestone: I think your defense tends to be one of seeing yourself as all right and seeing them as flawed, seeing the woman as flawed and that role of being a helper or the "okay" one does really create distance without your even realizing. And it's not that you're very vain about it or that you act that superior or anything like that, but it's subtle. It's a subtle way of protecting yourself. And that fits Jane's fantasy that she's bad, and it sort of works that way.

Chris: I have a very hard time, like a mental block against this, you know what I mean? Against seeing it and, and I'd like to understand it. I sort of understand it intellectually, but I can't see it operating but I guess that's the definition of it. I mean that I have a perspective that is flawed in some way.

Dr. Firestone: It's a built-in protection against extending yourself too far.

Chris: Right.

Dr. Firestone: And being really vulnerable.

Chris: Okay, that I can relate to . . .

Dr. Firestone: That's the form that it takes, just that way of thinking slightly. I know you're not a macho domineering guy. It doesn't come out that way. But it's just sort of a vague tendency—

2. Verbalizing destructive thoughts and releasing the associated affect.

Chris: If I think of it in terms of voices, I would probably say, you know, sort of watch out, be careful, don't fall for that.

Dr. Firestone: Don't let her get the upper hand.

Chris: Don't let her get the upper hand.

Dr. Firestone: So you keep a little bit of the upper hand.

3. Discussing insights.

Chris: Right. I definitely want to feel in control. I'm afraid to feel out of control and to be vulnerable to you [Jane]. I don't trust you, I would say, and I'm afraid I'm going to be hurt or taken advantage of or something.

Dr. Firestone: So it helps you to identify her failings [laughter from Chris and group] to make sure that doesn't happen.

Chris: See, the thing is—I'm very interested in this and my inability to see this but I'm aware in other relationships that I felt specifically critical, but here I'm not as aware of it. I guess I probably would have said that in the other relationships [laughter].

Jane: Partly I'm laughing because this has been a fight between us too, a disagreement, so it's interesting because I know that in this way it hurts us. I think it does hurt the ability for us to talk more as equals and to work things out at times. That's the feeling I have. But it's just interesting. What you're saying makes a lot of sense to me.

Follow-Up Interview

In an interview 2 months after the discussions described above, the partners reported progress, both in terms of experiencing more gratification in their relationships and in an increased sense of independence, self-assurance, and personal growth. In the following sequence, they talk about important modifications they have made in habitual, defensive modes of relating and the impact these changes had on their relationships:

Elaine: Since the last time we talked, I've felt so happy, really happy. I feel like something substantial has changed for me in regard to this subject of having a loving relationship. I feel that I've stopped fighting. I feel like before this, I was so much following my mother's path of keeping everybody at bay, keeping myself on an equilibrium and not giving in to just feeling loving. So now, even if anything comes up between us, it's much easier to talk about it, because I don't have that edge, that sting behind me that's looking for a fight.

Dr. Firestone: What about your plans?

Elaine: The big change is that now we're actively trying to get pregnant, and that's like such a change. That's the biggest change that's happened. I've gone from being terrified of that and from making sure that no relationship got to the point where those feelings would come up to really wanting it, and I've had such a thrilled feeling. I'm excited about my life, excited about you, and excited about that prospect.

Bruce: I feel very, very good. I feel so relaxed and enjoying all my time with you. You're right, I don't feel that fight back from you and it leaves me right now, to tell the truth, thinking about my own life, about what makes me happy.

◆ ◆ ◆

Alan: I feel like I'm really in love with you. We went from drifting apart to being very, very close, as close as ever.

Carolyn: I love the way it feels between us now and I feel really optimistic. I feel like we really did go through a hard time, but it felt worth it, and it meant a lot to me being able to talk with people here. Things aren't always completely smooth, but I feel like we have a better sense of how to talk to each other and be friends and it really helps.

◆ ◆ ◆

Sheryl: I feel like things have grown a lot since we had that last talk, and I do feel a lot closer to you. It's funny, I can still get scared, is what I would say. Even this week,

I recognized a shift in my feelings, to really caring back a lot about you. Instead of just learning how to accept Mark caring about me, I started feeling a deep sense of caring for him too.

Mark: Since we've been talking, I felt really close with you. I've noticed I've felt more grounded in myself, especially revealing some of the issues about ways I would push you away. That seemed to give me some insight, and I learned more about how I would feel desperate toward you and how that worked into the whole situation. A couple of things I noticed, when we were together, and you started feeling sad when we were making love, I felt so close to you. I felt in love with you. I couldn't feel any closer than how I felt at that moment.

Sheryl: For some reason, what's happening is bringing up a lot of sadness in me lately, and I think I'm really resistant to that.

Dr. Firestone: Yes, it's the fear of the sadness. It's ironic that people are afraid of sadness and to feel sadness, when in fact, if they do feel it and let it out, they actually feel better. It's always been puzzling to me. I see it in children, particularly.

Mark: It's followed by closeness and happiness.

Dr. Firestone: Yes, the sadness seems to center people in themselves but people resist it as though it's going to be horrible.

Sheryl: The main thing that happened is that I started feeling a lot, and the sadness was the biggest part of that, and that's when I avoided it.

Dr. Firestone: That's the biggest handicap that people have sexually. Where they would feel sad, they start to tense up and not allow the feelings any more, so they cut off their sexuality. Not being able to tolerate sadness is damaging in almost every area of personal relating.

Chris: Since we've been having these talks, I've felt good with you. [to Jane] What I realize is that I tend to be guarded in a lot of situations, and it comes across as people described it as parental or that sort of controlled kind of tone. But it's really sort of a defended posture that I've had and the more that I've let it down, the more I've been aware of it in intimate situations.

I don't know how to describe it. Vulnerable is the best word I can think of. Where I just am there, experiencing you and what's going on with us, and I feel like it's allowed me to be able to be much more tender and much more expressive of my loving feelings when I feel them.

Jane: The biggest thing that I've noticed is that it's been more equal between us, and that when something feels off, I don't always assume that it's me, that I'm just not close or I'm not okay. But I look at you as a separate person, and I think that maybe I am not feeling myself or that maybe you're distracted or you're not feeling yourself. But that's been a huge change between us, to be able to talk things out.

Chris: One other thing that's been interesting is that you've been more expressive about your feelings towards me and it's a little bit hard to take. [sad] I feel surprised that you like me so much, and I really like it. It makes me sad to say it, but it feels good inside, to feel you feel those feelings towards me and I feel that's really important.

Dr. Firestone: She liked you a lot better after that talk about being condescending. That's had such a big effect. That struck me the most of almost anything, that by giving up a defense, a person can become more and more lovable and it can change the whole relationship. But no one would have thought about that. Chris would not have thought that that was holding Jane back or she wouldn't have thought that. Even though she griped about it, she didn't realize what a barrier that really was. So I think that was a turning point in your relationship. I think from then on, even though difficulties arise, they never get the upper hand any more.

Jane: Yeah, it feels optimistic, not hopeless in some way, like I'm never going to fix myself enough. It feels more like we're dealing with it as friends.

Dr. Firestone: These are funny barriers. It illustrates the point that people's defensive posture pushes the other person away and that's the critical issue in so many relationships.

◆ ◆ ◆

Carolyn: One thing about being in these discussions is that it's added a lot to my life, not just in terms of you [Alan] but I feel a lot toward all the people here, and looking toward the New Year, I feel really excited. It makes my life so much richer feeling a lot toward each person, and what they're struggling with, and I am rooting for everyone. I like sharing the whole process of trying to have more mature relationships.

◆ ◆ ◆

Although the participants came to the discussions originally to improve their relationship within the couple, the significant outcome of this series of meetings has been that each partner has become stronger personally—that is, more centered in him- or herself—and has added new dimensions to his or her personality. As contrasted with many couple therapies where the emphasis is on maintaining the couple relationship, we view the concept of the couple as an abstraction and are concerned with saving the people rather than maintaining the couple or marriage. We perceive each partner's individual defenses as the primary issue that interferes with closeness, and therefore, what we are doing is really treating individuals in a couples' setting. In many ways this form of therapy is as beneficial to the people involved as individual psychotherapy.

In the course of the group discussions, we found that the participants had been living their lives based on destructive thought processes and parental prescriptions rather than on fulfilling their own desires and goals. Once they realized the influence of these early parental introjects, they could begin to identify and challenge the thought processes that were limiting them.

Essentially, the men and women who took part in this brief series of meetings have involved themselves in the process of learning how to love. They are learning to be vulnerable in situations where previously they had been too anxious to protect themselves from the possibility of being hurt again. They have discovered that the most effective way to counter destructive thought patterns is to take risks and alter their defensive behaviors, rather than to manipulate their loved one's feelings to maintain distance through defensive machinations.

In sustaining a loving relationship, one must go "cold turkey," as with any other addiction, and attempt to remain close to one's partner in the face of renewed voice attacks. Through voice therapy, couples can expand their lives by challenging negative images that interfere with giving and accepting love and by experiencing the anxiety aroused in the movement toward closeness and individuation.

ENDNOTES

[1]Although the participants had previous experience with voice therapy methods and were advanced in their understanding of the group process, it seems

reasonable that the methods could be used effectively with clients who have little or no previous experience in psychotherapy. Adapting the techniques to clients in a clinical setting would probably require a longer course of treatment and considerable skill and training on the part of the therapist. See chapter 8, *Voice Therapy Training Manual* (Firestone, Firestone, & Catlett, 1997).

[2]Clinical material from these meetings and the follow-up interview were compiled in a video documentary entitled *Coping With the Fear of Intimacy* (Parr, 1999). The recently completed production is the second in a video series on intimacy.

[3]The initial FVSC consisted of 171 items reflecting destructive thought patterns that are associated with intimate interpersonal relationships. These items were yielded from clinical material, discussion groups with couples, and graduate students studying psychology. Participants endorsed the frequency with which they experienced these thoughts according to a Likert-type scale ranging from 0 (*never*) to 4 (*most of the time*). The FVSC items were sorted into three groups: destructive thoughts about the self, destructive thoughts about the other (partner), and destructive thoughts about relationships in general. The items were evaluated in terms of whether they measured one of the aforementioned groups—a face validity approach. Mean scores were calculated for the three item groupings. The mean is used because there are different numbers of items in each grouping, and additive scores would attribute more weight to those groups with more items and make interpretation more difficult across groups. These groupings will be empirically tested with factor analytic procedures in the future when larger participant samples are available. The MSI–R contains subscales that assess inconsistency, conventionalism, global distress, affective communication, problem-solving communication, aggression, time together, financial disagreement, sexual dissatisfaction, role orientation, and family history of distress in each partner. The MSI–R data were analyzed as prescribed by the manual.

[4]A behavioral checklist was completed by observers and by participants in the study (Exhibits 14.1 and 14.2). The checklist was composed of items derived from dimensions of "Interactions in the Ideal Couple" (see Figure 4.1).

[5]As an example of results, the following trends were noted in the male and female partner's scores (from Couple No. 1) on the FVSC:

The female partner experienced the greatest improvement in the relationship shared by this couple, while the male partner remained stable across most of the FVSC items. In terms of change over time, the female partner made the most dramatic changes in the areas of decreased negative thoughts directed toward the self and thoughts directed toward her partner. Notable change in her attitude toward relationships in general was also evident. The male partner remained relatively stable across the dimensions of self, other (partner), and relationships in general. There was a slight increase in negative thoughts about the self, but the dramatic changes in his partner may have provided this individual with more opportunity to reflect on himself.

15

TRANSFERENCE, THE THERAPEUTIC ALLIANCE, AND LOVE

> The psychotherapeutic alliance is a unique human relationship wherein a devoted and trained person attempts to render assistance to another person by both suspending and extending himself. Nowhere in life is a person listened to, felt, and experienced with such concentrated sharing and emphasis on every aspect of communication.
> R. W. Firestone (1990d, p. 68)

The therapeutic relationship, much like any other relationship, is negatively affected by each individual's projections, distortions, and restricted capacity to tolerate feelings resulting from his or her core patterns of psychological defense. Although both parties involved are limited by defensive reactions based on past experiences that potentially distort their personal interactions, therapy progresses when (a) the therapist is relatively less defended and mature enough to be aware of how his or her defenses operate, (b) the therapist does not behave in a manner that is aggressive or hostile when his or her defense system is threatened by the patient's issues, and (c) the therapist utilizes his or her personal reactions as cues to help the patient.

The term *transference* as originally conceived was restricted to the psychoanalytic process.[1] *Transference phenomenon* refers to the patient's distortion of the therapist based on past feelings and associations. The analysand's projections onto the therapist (who is attempting to act as a blank screen) can then be understood and worked through as a fundamental aspect of the therapeutic interaction. Others have gone on to expand this concept to a broad range of phenomena that applies to all relationships, as in Sullivan's (1954, 1956) concept of "parataxic distortion."[2]

Ideally, in psychotherapy sessions, therapist and patient collaborate in sorting out conscious and unconscious distortions that are operant, transforming their relationship into one that is understandable and workable, a paradigm for other relationships. In an effective therapeutic alliance, working through the transference offers the patient a "corrective emotional experience" (Alexander, 1961). Because the therapist's responses do not correspond to the patient's anticipations based on his or her distortions or projections, the patient gradually adjusts to a more congenial, more constructive emotional environment. The development of the transference relationship and its subsequent resolution have long-lasting effects of modifying the patient's distorted modes of thinking, perceiving, and responding in close relationships outside the office setting.* Because the therapeutic process offers a unique situation in which to be "re-parented," this opportunity for growth must not be limited or interfered with by the therapist's problems or defenses.

Transference and countertransference are important aspects of all personal interactions and are complex psychological phenomena. The attempt to apply empirical research to this level of human experience has been fraught with difficulty (Luborsky & Crits-Christoph, 1998). It is virtually impossible to approach the subject of perceptual and emotional distortion in human relationships in a single chapter as compared with volumes. In this concluding chapter, we discuss the integral role that internal voices play in establishing and maintaining the transference–countertransference process.

CONCEPTUALIZATIONS OF TRANSFERENCE

Psychoanalytic definitions of transference began with Freud's (1912/1958) metaphoric description of the phenomena as "a stereotype plate (or several such) which is constantly repeated—constantly reprinted afresh—in the course of the person's life" (pp. 99–100). In his interpersonal theory of psychotherapy, Sullivan (1953, 1962) expanded on Freud's formulations, emphasizing that current as well as past relationships continuously affect psychological functions. According to Sullivan (1962), there is "nothing other than *the purpose* of the interpersonal situation which distinguishes the psychoanalytic transference relation from other situations of interpersonal intimacy" (p. 283). In a similar vein, Greenson (1965) extended the concept of transference to include the patient's reactions to his or her current experiences with the therapist as well as to the reactivation of his or her needs from the past.

---

*Distortions based on previous experience are part of the transference neurosis that is worked through or resolved during the therapy process. Maintaining these distortions functions to preserve psychological equilibrium and the fantasy bond or pseudoindependent stance of "I don't need anyone," which is a less vulnerable position. The patient keeps trying to prove that it is unrewarding to utilize other people to gratify him- or herself, that it is more rewarding to gratify him- or herself internally.

In a panel discussion at the Evolution of Psychotherapy Conference, Kernberg (1995) defined transference "as the unconscious repetition in the here and now of the pathogenic relationships from the past." He stressed the importance of providing the patient with a "normal object relationship against which the activation of transference appears as a distortion." James Masterson (1995) identified "transference acting out" in patients with borderline disorder and distinguished these behaviors from transference reactions manifested by patients with neurotic disorders. According to Masterson, these patients

> alternatively project on to you the self and object representations. The difference between them and the neurotic patient is that at the time of projection they cannot differentiate between you as therapist and their projection. In other words, there is minimal capacity for therapeutic alliance.

Yalom (1995) expressed views on transference and the therapeutic alliance that diverged from those set forth by Kernberg and other classical psychoanalysts. Specifically, Yalom stressed that

> it is an error to be silent with feelings that you have about the patient. ... I think the therapeutic posture with the patient [is] that we are fellow travelers, we're together, experiencing some of the exigencies of life, we're together facing the existential facts of life. To me, this entails a certain degree of self-disclosure on the part of the therapist.[3]

Object relations theorists conceptualize transference somewhat differently than psychoanalysts or existential theorists. In their discussion of object relations theorists, Horvath and Luborsky (1993) noted that Bibring (Glover et al., 1937) and Bowlby (1988) believed that "the client, as part of the therapy process, develops the capacity to form a positive, need-gratifying relationship with the therapist. This attachment is qualitatively different from those based on early childhood experiences and thus represents a new class of events" (p. 561).

The founder of self psychology, Heinz Kohut (1971), discussed "self-object transferences" that express fixated developmental needs for affirmation and validation.[4] Kohut's emphasis on empathy as a curative factor in the reparative process is similar in many respects to R. D. Laing's (1985) conceptualization of a "transpersonal" space existing between patient and therapist that facilitates therapeutic progress.[5] Laing described a largely nonverbal meeting or coming together of the intrapersonal and transpersonal in the therapeutic encounter. Laing's concept of this type of personal "communion" approximates a truly loving relationship, one that is respectful and sensitive to each individual's sense of well-being, whether it occurs in therapy or in the context of an intimate relationship.

In recent years, a number of studies have been instituted in an effort to explore transference phenomena systematically (Connolly et al., 1996).

For example, Luborsky and Crits-Christoph's (1998) formulations of the core conflictual relationship theme (CCRT) have provided the basis for a series of studies that compared narratives of patients' interpersonal relationships in general with narratives regarding their relationship with the therapist.

Last, there has been considerable disagreement among theorists over what the concept of transference encompasses. One controversy centers on the question as to "whether additional concepts such as therapeutic alliance or real relationship are required to account for the patient's reaction to the therapist" (Piper, Joyce, McCalum, & Azim, 1993, p. 587). According to Horvath and Luborsky (1993), whether transference distortions are part of the therapeutic alliance has been "one of the ongoing controversies in dynamic therapy" (p. 562).[6]

TRANSFERENCE PHENOMENA

There are two basic elements to my conception of transference as it applies to relationships in or outside of the therapy process: (a) simple transfer of feelings based on generalizations from previous object relationships, and (b) projective distortions based on an attempt to disown and objectify internalized voice attacks.

The first situation involves attributing similar personal qualities to new objects based on old associations. For example, if a close relative was warm and caring, a person would tend to react to a new individual who resembles the relative with positive feelings. Conversely, if a person has had a bad experience with a family member, friend, associate, teacher, doctor, or boss, for example, he or she approaches a like individual with negative emotions. In more serious cases, as with persons whose fathers were critical and sadistic toward them, they will tend to misperceive authority figures in the same vein and sometimes generalize to the point of seeing all men as mean. This type of distortion complicates and damages relationships. In the example of the person who grows up perceiving men as hostile based on the transfer of feelings from the prior experience with the father, he or she will tend to react defensively and angrily toward men. This anger and defensiveness will predispose angry responses from new objects, thereby completing the cycle. The original distortion has then become a reality.

This type of transfer is particularly traumatic when it is rigid and refuses to give way to reality testing. Although transference of affects is potentially destructive to satisfying relationships, this is not always the case. Some types of simple transference have positive value in that they aid people in sizing up and evaluating new objects, as for example, when clinicians are able to diagnose and react appropriately and sensitively to patients based on reduced cues from professional experience.

The second element of transference is based on the projection of internalized voices whereby people attempt to externalize their self-attacks. People parent themselves and treat themselves the way they were treated by their parents. This internalization of negative parental attitudes and feelings is not only the basis of people's attitudes and subjective feelings toward themselves but also is the basis of transference projections. This type of transference reaction can be understood dynamically as objectifying self-limiting and self-destructive voices that are part of the self-parenting process. In projecting their introjects onto new relationships, people induce the same feeling reactions in their partners that they experience toward themselves as objects. In order to maintain a sense of equilibrium appropriate to their defenses, people tend to choose others who react in a manner similar to family members, distort them, and even provoke them to duplicate negative associations that confirm their past identity in the family. This process acts as a major barrier to intimacy in personal relationships.

In spite of their stated desire for self-affirmation, people seek confirmation for their negative provisional identity developed in the context of the family. They feel anxious when they are separated from the incorporated conception of self. They experience this separation anxiety both on an interpersonal level when they attempt to give up defenses, and on an existential level, when they more fully experience their freedom and aliveness. The manner in which people limit themselves goes well beyond superego functions and reflects the internalization of destructive voices formed through identification with the aggressor.

Transference distortions operate in other personal relationships as well as in therapeutic relationships. Individuals perceive their voices in their mates, just as patients see them in their therapists. During the formative stages of a close relationship (or in the initial sessions of psychotherapy), people begin to experience their voice attacks as coming from the partner (or in the case of therapy, from the therapist). In both situations, they attempt to externalize their voices and project them onto the other rather than face the division within. When this projection occurs, it induces a complementary reaction in the partner (or therapist) which is similar to projective identification.

There are complex feeling responses being experienced by both parties in the course of a therapy session:

1. Both the therapist and the patient are experiencing conscious and unconscious emotional responses toward one another based on the current interaction itself. For example, people usually react appropriately to hostility, negativity, or critical-

ity with angry or aggressive responses, and they tend to respond to loving emotions and sensitive treatment with positive feelings.

2. Both parties may be projecting or *transferring* feelings from the past into the current situation, thereby distorting the current interaction.

3. The patient and therapist are reacting with *countertransference* feelings to the distortions noted above.

4. Both therapist and patient are being induced by the other to take on the other's internal point of view through *projective identification*. Each person is able to produce feeling states in the other based on transference distortions, and these emotional reactions are more complex than simple countertransference reactions.

My conception of the dynamics involved in projective identification explains how people project their voice attacks and internal emotional states onto each other, thereby eliciting responses that echo contents of their self-destructive thinking. In therapy, patients attempt to externalize their internalized voices, utilizing the therapist as a "container" for painful or disturbing affects associated with the disowned elements of the antiself-system. For example, in one study, Maltsberger and Buie (1989) reported that suicidal patients often induced strong feelings of dislike in therapists. Feelings of aversion produced in the therapists have been found to be a significant prognostic sign of potential suicide in these patients. Psychodynamically, these feelings of antipathy are often elicited, on an unconscious level, in response to suicidal patients' projection of their intense self-hatred and self-destructive voices onto the therapists (Maltsberger & Buie, 1989).

We are concerned with therapists' responses to the disturbing emotions that are often precipitated in them through the process of projective identification. It is vital that therapists not act out their negative responses to the projected material and thereby reinforce their patient's destructive thinking processes. To do so would be to mirror their patients' early environment, thereby reproducing the conditions that originally caused the illness. It is much more important for therapists to recognize alterations in their normal feeling state aroused by these projections and use them to understand voice attacks that the patient may be experiencing.[7]

Essentially, by their responses, therapists are either supporting the patient's destructive voices, or challenging them by helping patients expose self-attacks and take back their projections. Because there is a battle being waged within the patient between the self and the antiself, any communication that supports the negative voice process in the patient can be considered to be a *therapeutic error* because it reinforces a defended, self-attacking posture. On the other hand, therapeutic responses that indicate to the patient that he or she is genuinely seen and accepted, that his real goals and feelings are being acknowledged and supported, will tend to have a positive therapeutic effect. It is important to recognize that this same concept applies to all relationships, particularly those that are more personal and emotionally charged.

Common Fallacies About Transference

In the therapy session, therapist and patient experience a wide range of feelings, thoughts, and fantasies. They relate in ways that are often incorrectly classified by therapists and theorists as transference or countertransference. For example, patients' feelings of love for the therapist are usually characterized as a manifestation of positive transference. This implies that love feelings directed toward parents or other family members are being displaced onto the therapist. This is not necessarily the case. First, there is an assumption that the patient had positive, loving feelings toward his or her parents to project onto the therapist. Second, why would a person in a situation where he or she is respected, listened to, and offered a compassionate helping hand, not respond with loving emotions as an appropriate response to the here and now? Indeed, therapy may provide the first opportunity for some patients to feel loved and to experience or express their loving feelings without interference.

Similarly, why would the therapist who is listened to, respected, loved, and allowed to positively influence the other, not respond with feelings of tenderness as a realistic response? In addition, when the therapist and patient are of the opposite sex and alone in a room together for an extended period of time, engaged in sensitive communication, would they not experience a mutual sexual attraction? Probably no one has ever listened to either the patient or the therapist with this degree of understanding outside the therapy situation. The key issue here is not to identify and classify these responses as transference and countertransference phenomena with negative or pathological connotations, but for therapists to make positive use of this awareness rather than attempt to fill a void in their own emotional needs.[8]

Although a good deal of patients' angry responses relate to projections from the past, it is important to note that not all of a patient's anger or hostility toward the therapist is indicative of negative transference phenomena. It is appropriate for patients to dislike and respond negatively to abrasive, insensitive, or hostile aspects of the therapist's personality. Consider, for example, patients' reactions to the posture of therapeutic neutrality characteristic of psychoanalytic practice, where analysts purposefully attempt to remain purely objective and impersonal. This technique, wherein the therapist attempts to maintain a blank screen as a background for patients' projections, may recapitulate negative aspects of their child-hoods where they were deprived of affective responses on the part of their parents. These patients are being treated by the therapist in the same man-ner they were treated previously by parents who lacked affection, concern, or love for them. This lack of emotional response in the therapy session may have the same destructive impact as the original relationship, and therefore, serve to reinforce neurotic patterns of defense (Binder & Strupp, 1997). When these factors are operant, the patient's anger is an appropriate response to the prevailing environmental conditions.[9]

THE THERAPEUTIC ALLIANCE

Although all forms of psychotherapy challenge defenses and promote behavioral changes that in general lead to positive results, certain char-acteristics of the therapist favor a more successful therapeutic outcome. For example, attitudes of equality and respect for patients and their personal boundaries, rather than responses characterized by manipulation and role-playing are positive factors in establishing an effective therapeutic alliance. Because there is a great deal of controversy in our field and a limited state of empirical knowledge about the most effective methods of psychotherapy, the least the therapist can offer the patient is an honest interaction marked by personal integrity and strength of character.[10]

The same human qualities that are conducive to healthy parenting and close affectional ties between couples and family members are crucial to forming a working alliance that would facilitate progress in psychother-apy.[11] These qualities have a therapeutic effect to the degree that the par-ent, partner, or therapist is open, nondefensive, feelingful, and forthright in his or her approach to life. These positive traits include basic integrity, compassion, capacity for empathy, tolerance of ambivalence, acceptance of feeling, and leadership skills. They are favorable to all types of personal interactions, although there are differences in how they are applied. For example, in a couple or family relationship, individuals attempt to provide gratification to the other to the best of their ability. The therapy situation is different in that the therapist encourages patients to express their prim-itive needs and desires, yet does not gratify them. The appropriate limits and structure of the therapeutic encounter assist patients in working through the frustration of not having their wants gratified, help them to deal effectively with their anger, and in a powerful way, teach them to understand that they possess the necessary strength to cope with frustra-tion, a fact that they had not previously recognized.

A number of specific personality characteristics of the therapist appear to be correlated with the ability to form and sustain an effective therapeutic relationship.[12] As noted, the ideal therapist would be a person of unusual honesty and integrity. This is not simply a matter of trying to tell the truth. The therapist must have developed considerable self-knowledge, recognizing and accepting an objective view of both negative and positive traits in his or her personality (Strupp, 1995).

Therapists need to exhibit strength of character because they serve as role models for their patients in helping them develop into healthy, functioning adults. They must resist regressive trends in their own personalities to be able to foster a feeling of security and trust in their patients. This type of strength derives, in part, from an ability to access and accept one's anger and utilize it effectively when necessary, for example, in confronting a patient's acting out behavior. As a catalyst and facilitator, the therapist needs to be sensitive to the wide range of defensive patterns manifested by the patient and have the strength and courage to help expose and interrupt these patterns.

Effective therapists do not set themselves apart from their patients; rather, they demonstrate through their responses and behaviors how to struggle against destructive forces within the personality and how to live less defensively. They do not try to fit their patients into a particular theoretical framework or model; instead, they attempt to learn from them and gradually develop a unique psychological theory for each individual. They are nonintrusive in their interpretations and suspend judgment regarding the patient's communications, while intuitively searching and exploring the causal relationship between past experience and present malfunction.

In an important sense, the therapist can be seen as a "transitional object" in that he or she provides an authentic relationship for the patient during the transition from depending on self-nourishing processes to seeking and finding satisfaction in genuine relationships in the world outside the office setting. As such, therapists must remain human (be interested and warm as well as direct and responsible), in order to temporarily "hold" or sustain the patient as he or she moves away from sources of fantasy and self-gratification toward real relationships.

Many therapeutic failures can be attributed to limitations imposed on the patient by the therapist's own defense system. Negative personality traits, such as phoniness, narcissism, and hostility, are particularly detrimental or toxic to the patient. In this sense, the key issue in training successful therapists is the selection process.

Candidates for psychotherapy training are drawn primarily from the fields of medicine and clinical psychology. Many medical doctors tend to be parental and act out the doctor–patient dichotomy, whereas people from research or scientific backgrounds tend to be objective and analytical, lacking the feeling dimensions that would make them most likely to offer effective psychotherapy. Because therapists often come from these fields, which emphasize qualities that are antithetical to the development of therapists, many lack sufficient empathy, concern, or intuitive understanding of people and human behavior. Although certain behaviors, attitudes, and qualities can be learned or developed by therapists during training or supervision, these basic elements of personality are resistant to change.[13]

LOVE

The word *love* has become so banalized that to a great extent it has lost a clear sense of meaning. The truth is that mature love (kindness, respect, sensitivity, and affectionate treatment) is not only difficult to find, but is even more difficult to tolerate or accept. Once a person is damaged, he or she formulates defenses that not only preclude getting hurt again, but also ward off loving responses. When an individual has been hurt in past associations, feeling loved and accepted initially brings up anxiety and painfully sad feelings that most people find difficult to endure. Loving relationships often deteriorate into a fantasy bond in which loving feelings are gradually relegated to a fantasy process, while outward behavior between the partners moves in a direction that does not fit any generally acceptable criteria of loving operations. The inner conception that one loves the other without any clear-cut behavioral manifestation becomes a travesty. Internal fantasies of love on the part of one's mate, without the appropriate external behavioral manifestations, have no value for the recipient other than to disturb his or her reality testing.

Love can be operationally defined as those behaviors that enhance the emotional well-being, sense of self, and autonomy of both parties. Whether manifested in a close relationship or in therapy, responses based on love have an overall positive, ameliorative effect on the participants. Mature love manifests itself as appreciation and respect for the true nature of the other and support for his or her personal freedom pursuant to his or her personal goals in life. It goes beyond one's self-interest in the other and perceives one's mate as a separate entity with full rights to an independent existence. In that context, mutuality and shared life experience remain a choice rather than an obligation.

Many people mistake feelings of sexual attraction and sexual pleasure for love and later discover that they have little in common with their mate, whom they chose on the basis of a strong physical attraction. On the other hand, when sexual love persists and is a vital part of a fulfilling long-term relationship, erotic feelings and sexual responses represent an extension of the affection felt by the partners. Indeed, a combination of sexuality and close personal communication represents an ideal in couple relationships.

In summary, there are a number of interesting facts about the nature of love and its significance in people's lives:

1. It is difficult to find individuals who are mature enough emotionally to manifest love on a consistent basis. It is even more problematic to accept love when one does receive it, because being loved challenges core psychological defenses.

2. Survival and healthy psychological functioning do not necessarily require that one be loved. People are programmed during childhood to believe that their future happiness (and even their survival) is dependent on their finding their "one true love" and preserving this love in a long-term, exclusive couple relationship or marriage. This expectation is based on unrealistic notions regarding the nature of love and often leads to disillusionment and misery.

3. Most people are misled in their pursuit of love: They search for a person who will make them whole. These types of relationships, based on compensation for personal inadequacies, are likely to fail. People are more likely to succeed in their quest for love if they strive to develop themselves and attempt to achieve their full potential and seek partners who also manifest strength and independence.

Our approach suggests that by giving up illusions of connection and destructive modes of thinking, men and women can develop the capacity to both offer and accept love. Lastly, when mature love does exist between two people, its expression often approaches the level of a spiritual experience (Chessick, 1992; Schnarch, 1991). Indeed, love is a powerful antidote to the existential despair inherent in the human condition. In this sense, men and women would ideally strive to develop their capacity to give and receive love as a fundamental part of their personal lives. In breaking with defensive programming and pursuing the "good" life, people can maintain feeling for self and others. They can overcome outmoded defensive reactions and exist with others in a manner that contributes to the mental health, life satisfaction, and emotional well-being of all parties.

ENDNOTES

[1]Freud (1905/1953) first described transference in "Fragment of an Analysis of a Case of Hysteria" when he asked, "What are transferences? They are new editions or facsimiles of the impulses and phantasies which are aroused and made conscious during the progress of the analysis; but they have this peculiarity . . . that they replace some earlier person by the person of the physician" (p. 116).

[2]Sullivan (1956) defined "parataxic distortion" as reflecting "undigested experience of the past, things that could not be integrated into a unitary system of

motivation" (p. 200). See Sullivan's (1954) *The Psychiatric Interview* (pp. 23–25) for an example of the concept of parataxic distortion. Jaffe (1991) argued that transference is "operative in all human relationships as a means of regulating tension to keep an optimum distance from the traumatic experience" (p. 503).

[3] In response to Yalom's (1995) criticism of the classical psychoanalytic position, Kernberg (1995) stressed that "Psychotherapy is very much a passionate, committed, honest relationship and transference and countertransference are distortions that interfere, and what analysis does is precisely to analyze those distortions in order to permit that the reality of the relationship help the patient." Others have discussed the implications of self-disclosure by therapists. Ginot (1997) emphasized the significant value of "the contribution that the analyst's self-disclosure may have for the patient's struggle to integrate unconscious aspects of the self" (p. 365).

Regarding the therapist's attempt to remain a "blank screen," Gelso and Carter (1994) noted that "the client . . . will see the therapist, to some extent, in a realistic way . . . even when the therapist tries to hide or make ambiguous his or her self" (p. 298).

[4] Kohut (1971) wrote, "If the optimal transmuting internalization of the idealized self-object is interfered with, then . . . the idealized object is retained as an archaic prestructural object, is revivable in analysis in the cohesive form of the idealizing transference, and the process of reinternalization which was traumatically interrupted in childhood can now be taken up again during the analysis" (p. 106). In addition, constructivists (Mahoney, 1981; Neimeyer, 1993), as well as Guidano and Liotti (1983) and "intersubjective" theorists Stolorow (1997) and Stolorow, Brandchaft, and Atwood (1987) have written about other conceptualizations regarding transference and the therapeutic alliance. These theorists focus on recognizing the "subjective reality of the therapist and its influence on the therapy process" (Solomon & Siegel, 1997, p. 12).

[5] See videotape titled *Existential Therapy*, with speaker Ronald D. Laing, MD, from the 1985 Evolution of Psychotherapy conference. The tape demonstrates this type of transpersonal interaction between Dr. Laing and a young woman diagnosed with schizophrenia.

[6] Several theorists have made a distinction between interactions in therapy that can rightfully be categorized as transference and those that cannot. Greenson (1965) delineated the "working alliance" and the "real relationship" as two types of relationships in therapy that "should not be equated with transference" (p. 164). Horvath and Luborsky (1993) have also clarified the distinction "between the unconscious projections of the client" (i.e., transference) and "working alliance" (p. 563). Also see Gelso and Carter's (1994) definition of a working alliance, a transference configuration, and a "real relationship."

[7] In his chapter "Expressive Uses of the Countertransference," Bollas (1987) discussed appropriate therapeutic responses to a patient's defensive projective identification: "The clinician . . . must function openly as a transformational object. . . . The patient knows something, but has as yet been unable to think

it. The analyst here performs much the same function that the mother did with her infant who could not speak but whose moods, gestures and needs were utterances of some kind that needed maternal perception . . . , reception . . . , transformation into some form of representation, and possibly some resolution" (pp. 234–235).

[8]Kernberg (1997), concerning positive uses of the countertransference, wrote: "The analyst's creativity consists of formulating interpretations in ways that capture the total emotional situation in the transference. Drawing upon his observations of the patient's verbal and nonverbal behavior and of his own countertransference responses, the analyst constructs a metaphor that is specific enough to the present situation to capture it yet open-ended enough to permit the patient to pursue it in unexpected directions" (p. 310). See also Bridges (1994) "Meaning and Management of Attraction: Neglected Areas of Psychotherapy Training and Practice."

[9]The misuse of therapeutic neutrality as a distancing mechanism has come under attack by Miller, Yalom, and others. In her work, Alice Miller (1988/1990, 1990/1991) reproached psychoanalysts for what she refers to as their intellectualized interpretations, lack of understanding of childhood trauma, compartmentalization, and remoteness.

[10]Horvath and Luborsky (1993) noted that psychotherapy research over the past 2 decades has shown that "broadly speaking, different therapies (methodologies) produce similar amounts of therapeutic gains" (p. 563). These findings led to interest in specific elements of the working alliance that might be responsible for a patient's improvement. See Luborsky, Barber, and Beutler's (1993) and Horvath and Symonds' (1991) reviews and meta-analysis of research linking the quality of the alliance to therapy outcome.

[11]Studies investigating variables of the therapeutic alliance have indicated that the "clients' perception of the therapists as accepting and supporting is closely linked with the clients' perception of the appropriateness of technical aspects of treatment and with the therapists' apparent willingness to negotiate treatment goals" (Horvath & Luborsky, 1993, p. 568).

[12]Researchers have investigated a number of therapist variables hypothesized to contribute to the establishment of an effective therapeutic alliance (Beutler & Clarkin, 1990; Beutler, Machado, & Neufeldt, 1994; Bongar & Beutler, 1995; Strupp, 1989). Others (Horvath & Symonds, 1991; Luborsky & Crits-Christoph, 1998) have delineated significant correlations between the patient–therapist alliance and favorable outcomes.

[13]In fact, training may have negative results on therapists' personal characteristics. Researchers have investigated the effects of training on therapist behavior in time-limited dynamic psychotherapy (Henry, Strupp, Butler, Schacht, & Binder, 1993). Results showed that "At the same time therapists were becoming more intellectually sensitized to the importance of in-session dyadic process, they were actually delivering a higher 'toxic dose' of disaffiliative and complex communications. . . . After training, therapists were judged to be less approving and supportive, less optimistic, and more authoritative and defensive [possibly based on a certain anxiety and defensiveness]. . . . We . . . ob-

served that therapists' posttraining interventions seemed somewhat mechanical or ill-timed" (p. 439). See Beutler (1997) for a review of this research and its implications. Horvath and Luborsky (1993) cite Henry and Strupp's (1994) data suggesting that "the therapist's ability to respond accurately to the demands of the therapeutic relationship may be blocked by his or her own relational issues" (Horvath & Luborsky, 1993, p. 569).

REFERENCES

Ainsworth, M. D. S. (1989). Attachments beyond infancy. *American Psychologist, 44*, 709–716.

Ainsworth, M. D. S., Blehar, M. C., Waters, E., & Wall, S. (1978). *Patterns of attachment: A psychological study of the strange situation.* Hillsdale, NJ: Erlbaum.

Alexander, F. (1961). *The scope of psychoanalysis 1921–1961: Selected papers of Franz Alexander.* New York: Basic Books.

Amato, P. R. (1994). Life-span adjustment of children to their parents' divorce. *The future of children: Vol. 4. Children and divorce* (pp. 143–164). Los Altos, CA: Center for the Future of Children.

Anthony, E. J., & Cohler, B. J. (Eds.). (1987). *The invulnerable child.* New York: Guilford Press.

Anthony, S. (1973). *The discovery of death in childhood and after.* Harmondsworth, England: Penguin Education. (Original work published 1971)

Araoz, D. L. (1982). *Hypnosis and sex therapy.* New York: Brunner/Mazel.

Archer, J. (1996). Sex differences in social behavior: Are the social role and evolutionary explanations compatible? *American Psychologist, 51*, 909–917.

Aries, E. (1997). Women and men talking: Are they worlds apart? In M. R. Walsh (Ed.), *Women, men, and gender: Ongoing debates* (pp. 91–100). New Haven, CT: Yale University Press.

Arlow, J. A. (1986). Object concept and object choice. In P. Buckley (Ed.), *Essential papers on object relations* (pp. 127–146). New York: New York University Press.

Bach, G. R., & Deutsch, R. M. (1979). *Stop! You're driving me crazy.* New York: Berkley.

Badinter, E. (1981). *Mother love: Myth and reality: Motherhood in modern history.* New York: Macmillan. (Original work published 1980)

Bakermans-Kranenburg, M. J., & van IJzendoorn, M. H. (1993). A psychometric study of the Adult Attachment Interview: Reliability and discriminant validity. *Developmental Psychology, 29*, 870–879.

Balint, M. (1985). *Primary love and psycho-analytic technique.* London: Maresfield Library. (Original work published 1952)

Bandura, A. (Ed.). (1971). *Psychological modeling: Conflicting theories.* Chicago: Aldine-Atherton.

Bandura, A. (1973). *Aggression: A social learning analysis.* Englewood Cliffs, NJ: Prentice Hall.

Bandura, A. (1977). *Social learning theory.* Englewood Cliffs, NJ: Prentice Hall.

Bandura, A. (1986). *Social foundations of thought and action: A social cognitive theory.* Englewood Cliffs, NJ: Prentice Hall.

Bandura, A., & Walters, R. H. (1963). *Social learning and personality development.* New York: Holt, Rinehart & Winston.

Barglow, P., & Schaefer, M. (1977). A new female psychology? In H. P. Blum (Ed.), *Female psychology: Contemporary psychoanalytic views* (pp. 393–438). New York: International Universities Press.

Bartholomew, K. (1990). Avoidance of intimacy: An attachment perspective. *Journal of Social and Personal Relationships, 7,* 147–178.

Bartholomew, K. (1993). From childhood to adult relationships: Attachment theory and research. In S. Duck (Ed.), *Learning about relationships* (pp. 30–62). Newbury Park, CA: Sage.

Bartholomew, K., & Horowitz, L. M. (1991). Attachment styles among young adults: A test of a four-category model. *Journal of Personality and Social Psychology, 61,* 226–244.

Bateson, G., Jackson, D. D., Haley, J., & Weakland, J. H. (1972). Toward a theory of schizophrenia. In G. Bateson (Ed.), *Steps to an ecology of mind* (pp. 201–227). New York: Ballantine Books. (Original work published 1956)

Batgos, J., & Leadbeater, B. J. (1994). Parental attachment, peer relations, and dysphoria in adolescence. In M. B. Sperling & W. H. Berman (Eds.), *Attachment in adults: Clinical and developmental perspectives* (pp. 155–178). New York: Guilford Press.

Bavelas, J. B. (1983). Situations that lead to disqualification. *Human Communication Research, 9,* 130–145.

Beavers, W. R. (1977). *Psychotherapy and growth: A family systems perspective.* New York: Brunner/Mazel.

Beavers, W. R., & Hampson, R. B. (1990). *Successful families: Assessment and intervention.* New York: Norton.

Beck, A. T. (1978). *Beck Depression Inventory.* San Antonio, TX: Psychological Corporation.

Beck, A. T. (1988). *Love is never enough.* New York: Harper & Row.

Becker, E. (1964). *The revolution in psychiatry: The new understanding of man.* New York: Free Press.

Becker, E. (1975). *Escape from evil.* New York: Free Press.

Beebe, B. (1986). Mother–infant mutual influence and precursors of self- and object representations. In J. Masling (Ed.), *Empirical studies of psychoanalytic theories: Vol. 2* (pp. 27–48). Hillsdale, NJ: Analytic Press.

Belsky, J., & Isabella, R. (1988). Maternal, infant, and social–contextual determinants of attachment security. In J. Belsky & T. Nezworski (Eds.), *Clinical implications of attachment* (pp. 41–94). Hillsdale, NJ: Erlbaum.

Belsky, J., Taylor, D. G., & Rovine, M. (1984). The Pennsylvania Infant and Family Development Project: II. The development of reciprocal interaction in the mother–infant dyad. *Child Development, 55,* 706–717.

Benedek, T. (1970). The psychobiology of pregnancy. In E. J. Anthony & T. Benedek (Eds.), *Parenthood: Its psychology and psychopathology* (pp. 137–151). Boston: Little, Brown.

Benoit, D., Parker, K. C. H., & Zeanah, C. H. (1997). Mothers' representations of their infants assessed prenatally: Stability and association with infants' attachment classifications. *Journal of Child Psychology and Psychiatry, 38*, 307–313.

Bergman, I. (1983). *Scenes from a marriage.* In A. Blair (Trans.), *The marriage scenarios* (pp. 1–202). New York: Pantheon Books. (Original work published 1973)

Berkowitz, L. (1989). Frustration–aggression hypothesis: Examination and reformulation. *Psychological Bulletin, 106*, 59–73.

Beutler, L. E. (1997). The psychotherapist as a neglected variable in psychotherapy: An illustration by reference to the role of therapist experience and training. *Clinical Psychology: Science and Practice, 4*, 44–52.

Beutler, L. E., & Clarkin, J. F. (1990). *Systematic treatment selection: Toward targeted therapeutic interventions.* New York: Brunner/Mazel.

Beutler, L. E., Machado, P. P. P., & Neufeldt, S. (1994). Therapist variables. In S. L. Garfield & A. E. Bergin (Eds.), *Handbook of psychotherapy and behavior change* (4th ed., pp. 229–269). New York: Wiley.

Beyer, S., & Finnegan, A. (1997, August). *The accuracy of gender stereotypes regarding occupations.* Paper presented at the 105th Annual Convention of the American Psychological Association, Chicago.

Binder, J. L., & Strupp, H. H. (1997). "Negative process": A recurrently discovered and underestimated facet of therapeutic process and outcome in the individual psychotherapy of adults. *Clinical Psychology: Science and Practice, 4*, 121–139.

Bloch, D. (1978). *"So the witch won't eat me": Fantasy and the child's fear of infanticide.* New York: Grove Press.

Bloch, D. (1985). The child's fear of infanticide and the primary motive force of defense. *Psychoanalytic Review, 72*, 573–588.

Blum, H. P. (1977). Masochism, the ego ideal, and the psychology of women. In H. P. Blum (Ed.), *Female psychology: Contemporary psychoanalytic views* (pp. 157–191). New York: International Universities Press.

Blum, H. P. (1978). Reconstruction in a case of postpartum depression. *The Psychoanalytic Study of the Child, 33*, 335–362. New Haven, CT: Yale University Press.

Bodin, A. M. (1996). Relationship conflict—verbal and physical: Conceptualizing an inventory for assessing process and content. In F. W. Kaslow (Ed.), *Handbook of relational diagnosis and dysfunctional family patterns* (pp. 371–393). New York: Wiley.

Bollas, C. (1987). *The shadow of the object: Psychoanalysis of the unthought known.* New York: Columbia University Press.

Bolton, F. G., Jr. (1983). *When bonding fails: Clinical assessment of high-risk families.* Beverly Hills, CA: Sage.

Bongar, B., & Beutler, L. E. (Eds.). (1995). *Comprehensive textbook of psychotherapy: Theory and practice.* New York: Oxford University Press.

Bornstein, R. F. (1993). Parental representations and psychopathology: A critical review of the empirical literature. In J. M. Masling & R. F. Bornstein (Eds.), *Psychoanalytic perspectives on psychopathology* (pp. 1–41). Washington, DC: American Psychological Association.

Boszormenyi-Nagy, I., & Spark, G. M. (1984). *Invisible loyalties: Reciprocity in intergenerational family therapy.* New York: Brunner/Mazel.

Bowen, M. (1976). Theory in the practice of psychotherapy. In P. J. Guerin, Jr. (Ed.), *Family therapy: Theory and practice* (pp. 42–90). New York: Gardner Press.

Bowen, M. (1978). *Family therapy in clinical practice.* New York: Jason Aronson.

Bowlby, J. (1973). *Attachment and loss: Vol. II. Separation: Anxiety and anger.* New York: Basic Books.

Bowlby, J. (1979). *The making and breaking of affectional bonds.* London: Tavistock.

Bowlby, J. (1980). *Attachment and loss: Vol. III. Loss: Sadness and depression.* New York: Basic Books.

Bowlby, J. (1982). *Attachment and loss: Vol. I. Attachment* (2nd ed.). New York: Basic Books.

Bowlby, J. (1988). *A secure base: Parent–child attachment and healthy human development.* New York: Basic Books.

Boyd, S. (1982). *Analysis of a unique psychological laboratory.* Unpublished manuscript.

Brazelton, T. B., & Cramer, B. G. (1990). *The earliest relationship: Parents, infants, and the drama of early attachment.* Reading, MA: Addison-Wesley.

Brazelton, T. B., & Yogman, M. W. (Eds.). (1986). *Affective development in infancy.* Norwood, NJ: Ablex.

Brennan, K. A., & Shaver, P. R. (1995). Dimensions of adult attachment, affect regulation, and romantic relationship functioning. *Personality and Social Psychology Bulletin, 21,* 267–283.

Bretherton, I. (1996). Internal working models of attachment relationships as related to resilient coping. In G. G. Noam & K. W. Fischer (Eds.), *Development and vulnerability in close relationships* (pp. 3–27). Mahwah, NJ: Erlbaum.

Bretherton, I., Ridgeway, D., & Cassidy, J. (1990). Assessing internal working models of the attachment relationship. In M. T. Greenberg, D. Cicchetti, & E. M. Cummings (Eds.), *Attachment in the preschool years: Theory, research, and intervention* (pp. 273–308). Chicago: University of Chicago Press.

Bridges, N. A. (1994). Meaning and management of attraction: Neglected areas of psychotherapy training and practice. *Psychotherapy, 31,* 424–433.

Briere, J. N. (1992). *Child abuse trauma: Theory and treatment of the lasting effects.* Newbury Park, CA: Sage.

Brody, S. (1956). *Patterns of mothering: Maternal influence during infancy.* New York: International Universities Press.

Burleson, B. R., Kunkel, A. W., Samter, W., & Werking, K. J. (1996). Men's and women's evaluations of communication skills in personal relationships: When sex differences make a difference—and when they don't. *Journal of Social and Personal Relationships, 13,* 201–224.

Burn, S. M. (1996). *The social psychology of gender.* New York: McGraw-Hill.

Buss, D. M. (1992). Mate preference mechanisms: Consequences for partner choice and intrasexual competition. In J. H. Barkow, L. Cosmides, & J. Tooby (Eds.), *The adapted mind: Evolutionary psychology and the generation of culture* (pp. 249–266). New York: Oxford University Press.

Buss, D. M. (1994). *The evolution of desire: Strategies of human mating.* New York: Basic Books.

Buss, D. M. (1995). Psychological sex differences: Origins through sexual selection. *American Psychologist, 50,* 164–168.

Buss, D. M., & Barnes, M. (1986). Preferences in human mate selection. *Journal of Personality and Social Psychology, 50,* 559–570.

Buss, D. M., Larsen, R. J., & Westen, D. (1996). Sex differences in jealousy: Not gone, not forgotten, and not explained by alternative hypotheses. *Psychological Science, 7,* 373–375.

Buss, D. M., & Schmitt, D. P. (1993). Sexual strategies theory: An evolutionary perspective on human mating. *Psychological Review, 100,* 204–232.

Buunk, B. P., Angleitner, A., Oubaid, V., & Buss, D. M. (1996). Sex differences in jealousy and evolutionary and cultural perspective: Tests from the Netherlands, Germany, and the United States. *Psychological Science, 7,* 359–363.

Canary, D. J., Cupach, W. R., & Messman, S. J. (1995). *Relationship conflict: Conflict in parent–child, friendship, and romantic relationships.* Thousand Oaks, CA: Sage.

Caplan, P. J. (1981). *Between women: Lowering the barriers.* Toronto, Ontario, Canada: Personal Library.

Carstensen, L. L., Graff, J., Levenson, R. W., & Gottman, J. M. (1996). Affect in intimate relationships: The developmental course of marriage. In C. Magai & S. H. McFadden (Eds.), *Handbook of emotion, adult development, and aging* (pp. 227–247). San Diego, CA: Academic Press.

Caspi, A. (1993). Why maladaptive behaviors persist: Sources of continuity and change across the life course. In D. C. Funder, R. D. Parke, C. Tomlinson-Keasey, & K. Widaman (Eds.), *Studying lives through time* (pp. 343–376). Washington, DC: American Psychological Association.

Cassidy, J., & Kobak, R. R. (1988). Avoidance and its relation to other defensive processes. In J. Belsky & T. Nezworski (Eds.), *Clinical implications of attachment* (pp. 300–323). Hillsdale, NJ: Erlbaum.

Chess, S., & Thomas, A. (1987). *Know your child: An authoritative guide for today's parents.* New York: Basic Books.

Chessick, R. D. (1992). On falling in love and creativity. *Journal of the American Academy of Psychoanalysis, 20,* 347–373.

Chisholm, J. S. (1996). The evolutionary ecology of attachment organization. *Human Nature, 7,* 1–38.

Chodorow, N. (1978). *The reproduction of mothering: Psychoanalysis and the sociology of gender*. Berkeley, CA: University of California Press.

Cicchetti, D., & Toth, S. L. (1998). The development of depression in children and adolescents. *American Psychologist, 53*, 221–241.

Cole-Detke, H., & Kobak, R. R. (1996). Attachment processes in eating disorder and depression. *Journal of Consulting and Clinical Psychology, 64*, 282–290.

Colman, W. (1995). Gesture and recognition: An alternative model to projective identification as a basis for couple relationships. In S. Ruszczynski & J. Fisher (Eds.), *Intrusiveness and intimacy in the couple* (pp. 59–73). London: Karnac Books.

Connolly, M. B., Crits-Christoph, P., Demorest, A., Azarian, K., Muenz, L., & Chittams, J. (1996). Varieties of transference patterns in psychotherapy. *Journal of Consulting and Clinical Psychology, 64*, 1213–1221.

Costa, P. T., Jr., & McCrae, R. R. (1985). *The NEO Personality Inventory*. Odessa, FL: Psychological Assessment Resources.

Crittenden, P. M. (1985). Maltreated infants: Vulnerability and resilience. *Journal of Child Psychology and Psychiatry, 26*, 85–96.

Crittenden, P. M. (1995). Attachment and psychopathology. In S. Goldberg, R. Muir, & J. Kerr (Eds.), *Attachment theory: Social, developmental, and clinical perspectives* (pp. 367–406). Hillsdale, NJ: Analytic Press.

Daly, M., & Wilson, M. (1983). *Sex, evolution, and behavior* (2nd ed.). Boston: Willard Grant Press.

Darwin, C. (1958). *On the origin of species by means of natural selection*. New York: New American Library. (Original work published 1859)

Dawson, D. A. (1991). Family structure and children's health and well-being: Data from the 1988 National Health Interview Survey on Child Health. *Journal of Marriage and the Family, 53*, 573–584.

de Jong, M. L. (1992). Attachment, individuation, and risk of suicide in late adolescence. *Journal of Youth and Adolescence, 21*, 357–373.

Deutsch, H. (1944). *The psychology of women: A psychoanalytic interpretation. Vol. 1*. New York: Grune & Stratton.

Dicks, H. V. (1967). *Marital tensions: Clinical studies towards a psychological theory of interaction*. New York: Basic Books.

Dix, C. (1985). *The new mother syndrome: Coping with postpartum stress and depression*. New York: Pocket Books.

Dostoyevsky, F. (1958). *The brothers Karamazov* (D. Magarshack, Trans.). London: Penguin Books. (Original work published 1880)

Duck, S. (Ed.). (1994a). *Dynamics of relationships*. Thousand Oaks, CA: Sage.

Duck, S. (1994b). *Meaningful relationships: Talking, sense, and relating*. Thousand Oaks, CA: Sage.

Dugan, M. N. (1977). Fear of death: The effect of parental behavior and personality upon the behavior and personality of their children. *Dissertation Abstracts International, 38*, 1318A.

Durkheim, E. (1965). *The elementary form of religious life*. New York: Macmillan. (Original work published 1912)

Eagly, A. H. (1995). The science and politics of comparing women and men. *American Psychologist, 50*, 145–158.

Eron, L. D. (1987). The development of aggressive behavior from the perspective of a developing behaviorism. *American Psychologist, 42*, 435–442.

Fairbairn, W. R. D. (1952). *Psychoanalytic studies of the personality*. London: Routledge & Kegan Paul.

Feeney, J. A., & Noller, P. (1990). Attachment style as a predictor of adult romantic relationships. *Journal of Personality and Social Psychology, 58*, 281–291.

Feeney, J. A., Noller, P., & Hanrahan, M. (1994). Assessing adult attachment. In M. B. Sperling & W. H. Berman (Eds.), *Attachment in adults: Clinical and developmental perspectives* (pp. 128–152). New York: Guilford Press.

Fenchel, G. H. (1998a). Introduction. In G. H. Fenchel (Ed.), *The mother–daughter relationship: Echoes through time* (pp. xv–xviii). Northvale, NJ: Jason Aronson.

Fenchel, G. H. (Ed.). (1998b). *The mother–daughter relationship: Echoes through time*. Northvale, NJ: Jason Aronson.

Field, T. (1987). Interaction and attachment in normal and atypical infants. *Journal of Consulting and Clinical Psychology, 55*, 853–859.

Fierman, L. B. (Ed.). (1965). *Effective psychotherapy: The contribution of Hellmuth Kaiser*. New York: Free Press.

Firestone, R. W. (1957). *A concept of the schizophrenic process*. Unpublished doctoral dissertation, University of Denver.

Firestone, R. W. (1984). A concept of the primary fantasy bond: A developmental perspective. *Psychotherapy, 21*, 218–225.

Firestone, R. W. (1985). *The fantasy bond: Structure of psychological defenses*. New York: Human Sciences Press.

Firestone, R. W. (1987a). Destructive effects of the fantasy bond in couple and family relationships. *Psychotherapy, 24*, 233–239.

Firestone, R. W. (1987b). The "voice": The dual nature of guilt reactions. *American Journal of Psychoanalysis, 47*, 210–229.

Firestone, R. W. (1988). *Voice therapy: A psychotherapeutic approach to self-destructive behavior*. New York: Human Sciences Press.

Firestone, R. W. (1990a). The bipolar causality of regression. *American Journal of Psychoanalysis, 50*, 121–135.

Firestone, R. W. (1990b). *Compassionate child-rearing: An in-depth approach to optimal parenting*. New York: Plenum Press.

Firestone, R. W. (1990c). Prescription for psychotherapy. *Psychotherapy, 27*, 627–635.

Firestone, R. W. (1990d). Voice therapy. In J. Zeig & W. Munion (Eds.), *What is psychotherapy? Contemporary perspectives* (pp. 68–74). San Francisco: Jossey-Bass.

Firestone, R. W. (1990e). Voices during sex: Application of voice therapy to sexuality. *Journal of Sex and Marital Therapy, 16*, 258–274.

Firestone, R. W. (1993). The psychodynamics of fantasy, addiction, and addictive attachments. *American Journal of Psychoanalysis, 53*, 335–352.

Firestone, R. W. (1994). A new perspective on the Oedipal complex: A voice therapy session. *Psychotherapy, 31*, 346–349.

Firestone, R. W. (1994). Psychological defenses against death anxiety. In R. A. Neimeyer (Ed.), *Death anxiety handbook: Research, instrumentation, and application* (pp. 217–241). Washington, DC: Taylor & Francis.

Firestone, R.W. (1996). The origins of ethnic strife. *Mind and Human Interaction, 7*, 167–180.

Firestone, R. W. (1997a). *Combating destructive thought processes: Voice therapy and separation theory.* Thousand Oaks, CA: Sage.

Firestone, R. W. (1997b). *Suicide and the inner voice: Risk assessment, treatment, and case management.* Thousand Oaks, CA: Sage.

Firestone, R. W., & Catlett, J. (1989). *Psychological defenses in everyday life.* New York: Human Sciences Press.

Firestone, R. W., & Firestone, L. (1996). *Firestone Assessment of Self-Destructive Thoughts.* San Antonio, TX: Psychological Corporation.

Firestone, R. W., Firestone, L., & Catlett, J. (1997). *Voice therapy training manual.* Unpublished manuscript.

Floyd, F. J., Markman, H. J., Kelly, S., Blumberg, S. L., & Stanley, S. M. (1995). Preventive intervention and relationship enhancement. In N. S. Jacobson & A. S. Gurman (Eds.), *Clinical handbook of couple therapy* (pp. 212–226). New York: Guilford Press.

Fonagy, P. (1998). An attachment theory approach to treatment of the difficult patient. *Bulletin of the Menninger Clinic, 62*, 147–169.

Fonagy, P., Steele, H., & Steele, M. (1991). Maternal representations of attachment during pregnancy predict the organization of infant–mother attachment at one year of age. *Child Development, 62*, 891–905.

Fonagy, P., Steele, M., Steele, H., Leigh, T., Kennedy, R., Mattoon, G., & Target, M. (1995). Attachment, the reflective self, and borderline states: The predictive specificity of the Adult Attachment Interview and pathological emotional development. In S. Goldberg, R. Muir, & J. Kerr (Eds.), *Attachment theory: Social, developmental, and clinical perspectives* (pp. 233–278). Hillsdale, NJ: Analytic Press.

Ford, C. S., & Beach, F. A. (1951). *Patterns of sexual behavior.* New York: Harper.

Foucault, M. (1975). *Discipline and punishment: The birth of the prison.* London: Allen Lane.

Foucault, M. (1980). *Power and knowledge.* Brighton, England: Harvester.

Foucault, M. (1990). *The history of sexuality: Vol. I. An introduction* (R. Hurley, Trans.). New York: Vintage Books.

Fraiberg, S. (1982). Pathological defenses in infancy. *Psychoanalytic Quarterly, 51*, 612–635.

Fraiberg, S., Adelson, E., & Shapiro, V. (1980). Ghosts in the nursery: A psychoanalytic approach to the problems of impaired infant–mother relationships. In S. Fraiberg (Ed.), *Clinical studies in infant mental health: The first year of life* (pp. 164–196). New York: Basic Books.

Freud, S. (1953). Fragment of an analysis of a case of hysteria. In J. Strachey (Ed. and Trans.), *The standard edition of the complete psychological works of Sigmund Freud* (Vol. 7, pp. 1–122). London: Hogarth Press. (Original work published 1905)

Freud, S. (1953). *A general introduction to psychoanalysis* (J. Riviere, Trans.). New York: Permabooks. (Original work published 1924)

Freud, S. (1955). Beyond the pleasure principle. In J. Strachey (Ed. and Trans.), *The standard edition of the complete psychological works of Sigmund Freud* (Vol. 18, pp. 7–64). London: Hogarth Press. (Original work published 1920)

Freud, S. (1958). The dynamics of transference. In J. Strachey (Ed. and Trans.), *The standard edition of the complete psychological works of Sigmund Freud* (Vol. 12, pp. 97–108). London: Hogarth Press. (Original work published 1912)

Freud, S. (1959). An autobiographical study. In J. Strachey (Ed. and Trans.), *The standard edition of the complete psychological works of Sigmund Freud* (Vol. 20, pp. 7–75). London: Hogarth Press. (Original work published 1925)

Freud, S. (1961). The ego and the id. In J. Strachey (Ed. and Trans.), *The standard edition of the complete psychological works of Sigmund Freud* (Vol. 19, pp. 1–66). London: Hogarth Press. (Original work published 1923)

Friday, N. (1973). *My secret garden: Women's sexual fantasies.* New York: Trident Press.

Friday, N. (1975). *Forbidden flowers: More women's sexual fantasies.* New York: Pocket Books.

Friday, N. (1977). *My mother/my self: The daughter's search for identity.* New York: Delacorte Press.

Fromm, E. (1941). *Escape from freedom.* New York: Avon Books.

Fromm, E. (1947). *Man for himself: An inquiry into the psychology of ethics.* New York: Rinehart.

Fromm, E. (1956). *The art of loving.* New York: Bantam Books.

Garbarino, J., & Gilliam, G. (1980). *Understanding abusive families.* Lexington, MA: Lexington Books.

Garbarino, J., Guttman, E., & Seeley, J. W. (1986). *The psychologically battered child.* San Francisco: Jossey-Bass.

Geis, F. L. (1993). Self-fulfilling prophecies: A social psychological view of gender. In A. E. Beall & R. J. Sternberg (Eds.), *The psychology of gender* (pp. 9–54). New York: Guilford Press.

Gelso, C. J., & Carter, J. A. (1994). Components of the psychotherapy relationship: Their interaction and unfolding during treatment. *Journal of Counseling Psychology, 41,* 296–306.

Genevie, L., & Margolies, E. (1987). *The motherhood report: How women feel about being mothers.* New York: Macmillan.

George, C. (1996). A representational perspective of child abuse and prevention: Internal working models of attachment and caregiving. *Child Abuse and Neglect, 20,* 411–424.

George, C., Kaplan, N., & Main, M. (1985). *Adult Attachment Interview.* Unpublished manuscript, University of California, Berkeley.

George, C., & Main, M. (1979). Social interactions of young abused children: Approach, avoidance, and aggression. *Child Development, 50,* 306–318.

George, C., & Solomon, J. (1996). Representational models of relationships: Links between caregiving and attachment. *Infant Mental Health Journal, 17,* 198–216.

Gerall, A. A., Moltz, H., & Ward, I. L. (Eds.). (1992). *Handbook of behavioral neurobiology: Vol. 11. Sexual differentiation.* New York: Plenum Press.

Gilbert, P. (1989). *Human nature and suffering.* Hove, England: Erlbaum.

Gilligan, C. (1982). *In a different voice: Psychological theory and women's development.* Cambridge, MA: Harvard University Press.

Gilligan, C. (1996). The centrality of relationship in human development: A puzzle, some evidence, and theory. In G. G. Noam & K. W. Fischer (Eds.), *Development and vulnerability in close relationships* (pp. 237–261). Mahwah, NJ: Erlbaum.

Ginot, E. (1997). The analyst's use of self, self-disclosure, and enhanced integration. *Psychoanalytic Psychology, 14,* 365–381.

Glaser, B., & Strauss, A. L. (1967). *The discovery of grounded theory: Strategies for qualitative research.* Chicago: Aldine.

Glaser, B., & Strauss, A. L. (1970). Discovery of substantive theory: A basic strategy underlying qualitative research. In W. Filstead (Ed.), *Qualitative methodology* (pp. 288–297). Chicago: Rand McNally.

Glover, E., Fenichel, O., Strachey, J., Bergler, E., Nunberg, H., & Bibring, E. (1937). Symposium on the theory of the therapeutic results of psychoanalysis. *International Journal of Psycho-Analysis, 18,* 125–189.

Goffman, E. (1967). *Interaction ritual.* Garden City, NY: Anchor Press.

Goldberg, C. (1991). *Understanding shame.* Northvale, NJ: Jason Aronson.

Goldberg, C. (1996). *Speaking with the devil: A dialogue with evil.* New York: Penguin Books.

Goldberg, S. (1997). Attachment and childhood behavior problems in normal, at-risk, and clinical samples. In L. Atkinson & K. J. Zucker (Eds.), *Attachment and psychopathology* (pp. 171–195). New York: Guilford Press.

Goleman, D. (1985). *Vital lies, simple truths: The psychology of self-deception.* New York: Simon & Schuster.

Gordon, R. M. (1998). The Medea complex and the parental alienation syndrome:

When mothers damage their daughters' ability to love a man. In G. H. Fenchel (Ed.), *The mother–daughter relationship: Echoes through time* (pp. 207–225). Northvale, NJ: Jason Aronson.

Gottman, J. M. (1979). *Marital interaction: Experimental investigations.* New York: Academic Press.

Gottman, J. M., & Krokoff, L. J. (1989). Marital interaction and satisfaction: A longitudinal view. *Journal of Consulting and Clinical Psychology, 57,* 47–52.

Gove, P. B. (Ed.). (1976). *Webster's third new international dictionary.* Springfield, MA: Merriam-Webster.

Gray, J. (1992). *Men are from Mars: Women are from Venus: A practical guide for improving communication and getting what you want in your relationships.* New York: Harper Collins.

Greenson, R. R. (1965). The working alliance and the transference neurosis. *Psychoanalytic Quarterly, 34,* 155–179.

Greenspan, S. I. (1981). *Psychopathology and adaptation in infancy and early childhood: Principles of clinical diagnosis and preventive intervention.* Madison, CT: International Universities Press.

Greenspan, S. I., & Lieberman, A. F. (1988). A clinical approach to attachment. In J. Belsky & T. Nezworski (Eds.), *Clinical implications of attachment* (pp. 387–424). Hillsdale, NJ: Erlbaum.

Griffin, D. W., & Bartholomew, K. (1994a). The metaphysics of measurement: The case of adult attachment. In K. Bartholomew & D. Perlman (Eds.), *Advances in personal relationships: Vol. 5. Attachment processes in childhood* (pp. 17–52). London: Jessica Kingsley.

Griffin, D. W., & Bartholomew, K. (1994b). Models of the self and other: Fundamental dimensions underlying measures of adult attachment. *Journal of Personality and Social Psychology, 67,* 430–445.

Griffin, J. M., Jr., & Apostal, R. A. (1993). The influence of relationship enhancement training on differentiation of self. *Journal of Marital and Family Therapy, 19,* 267–272.

Grizzle, A. F. (with Proctor, W.) (1988). *Mother love, mother hate: Breaking dependent love patterns in family relationships.* New York: Fawcett Columbine.

Grossmann, K., Fremmer-Bombik, E., Rudolph, J., & Grossmann, K. E. (1988). Maternal attachment representations as related to patterns of infant–mother attachment and maternal care during the first year. In R. A. Hinde & J. Stevenson-Hinde (Eds.), *Relationships within families: Mutual influences* (pp. 241–260). Oxford, England: Clarendon Press.

Guerney, B. G., Jr., Guerney, L., & Cooney, T. (1985). Marital and family problem prevention and enrichment programs. In L. L'Abate (Ed.), *The handbook of family psychology and therapy* (Vol. 11, pp. 1179–1217). Homewood, IL: Dorsey Press.

Guidano, V. F., & Liotti, G. (1983). *Cognitive processes and emotional disorders: A structural approach to psychotherapy.* New York: Guilford Press.

Guntrip, H. (1969). *Schizoid phenomena object-relations and the self*. New York: International Universities Press.

Haft, W. L., & Slade, A. (1989). Affect attunement and maternal attachment: A pilot study. *Infant Mental Health Journal, 10*, 157–172.

Halpern, D. F. (1997). Sex differences in intelligence: Implications for education. *American Psychologist, 52*, 1091–1102.

Hampson, R. B., Hyman, T. L., & Beavers, W. R. (1994). Age-of-recall effects on family-of-origin ratings. *Journal of Marital and Family Therapy, 20*, 61–67.

Hassler, J. H. (1994). Illnesses, failures, losses: Human misery propelling regression, therapy, and growth. In A. Sugarman (Ed.), *Victims of abuse: The emotional impact of child and adult trauma* (pp. 213–222). Madison, CT: International Universities Press.

Havel, V. (1990). *Disturbing the peace: A conversation with Karel Hvizdala* (P. Wilson, Trans.). New York: Knopf.

Hazan, C., & Shaver, P. R. (1987). Romantic love conceptualized as an attachment process. *Journal of Personality and Social Psychology, 52*, 511–524.

Henry, W. P., & Strupp, H. H. (1994). The therapeutic alliance as interpersonal process. In A. O. Horvath & L. S. Greenberg (Eds.), *The working alliance: Theory, research, and practice* (pp. 51–84). New York: Wiley.

Henry, W. P., Strupp, H. H., Butler, S. F., Schacht, T. E., & Binder, J. L. (1993). Effects of training in time-limited dynamic psychotherapy: Changes in therapist behavior. *Journal of Consulting and Clinical Psychology, 61*, 434–440.

Hetherington, E. M., Bridges, M., & Insabella, G. M. (1998). What matters? What does not? Five perspectives on the association between marital transitions and children's adjustment. *American Psychologist, 53*, 167–184.

Hindy, C. G., & Schwarz, J. C. (1994). Anxious romantic attachment in adult relationships. In M. B. Sperling & W. H. Berman (Eds.), *Attachment in adults: Clinical and developmental perspectives* (pp. 179–203). New York: Guilford Press.

Hobbes, T. (1909). *Leviathan*. London: Oxford University Press. (Original work published 1651)

Hoffman, S. I., & Strauss, S. (1985). The development of children's concepts of death. *Death Studies, 9*, 469–482.

Holmes, J. (1995). Something there is that doesn't love a wall: John Bowlby, attachment theory, and psychoanalysis. In S. Goldberg, R. Muir, & J. Kerr (Eds.), *Attachment theory: Social, developmental, and clinical perspectives* (pp. 19–43). Hillsdale, NJ: Analytic Press.

Horowitz, L. M., Rosenberg, S. E., & Bartholomew, K. (1993). Interpersonal problems, attachment styles, and outcome in brief dynamic psychotherapy. *Journal of Consulting and Clinical Psychology, 61*, 549–560.

Horvath, A. O., & Luborsky, L. (1993). The role of the therapeutic alliance in psychotherapy. *Journal of Consulting and Clinical Psychology, 61*, 561–573.

Horvath, A. O., & Symonds, B. D. (1991). Relation between working alliance and outcome in psychotherapy: A meta-analysis. *Journal of Counseling Psychology, 38*, 139–149.

Hudson, L., & Jacot, B. (1995). *Intimate relations: The natural history of desire.* New Haven, CT: Yale University Press.

Humphrey, L. L., & Benjamin, L. S. (1986). Using structural analysis of social behavior to assess critical but elusive family processes. *American Psychologist, 41*, 979–989.

Huxley, A. (1932). *Brave new world.* New York: Harper.

Hyde, J. S., & Plant, E. A. (1995). Magnitude of psychological gender differences: Another side of the story. *American Psychologist, 50*, 159–161.

Ickes, W., Tooke, W., Stinson, L., Baker, V. L., & Bissonnette, V. (1988). Naturalistic social cognition: Intersubjectivity in same-sex dyads. *Journal of Nonverbal Behavior, 12*, 58–84.

Jackson, E. N. (1965). *Telling a child about death.* New York: Hawthorn Books.

Jacobson, E. (1964). *The self and the object world.* London: Hogarth Press.

Jaffe, D. S. (1991). Beyond the what, when, and how of transference: A consideration of the why. *Journal of the American Psychoanalytic Association, 39*, 491–512.

Janov, A. (1970). *The primal scream: Primal therapy: The cure for neurosis.* New York: Putnam.

Johnson, S. M., & Greenberg, L. S. (1995). The emotionally focused approach to problems in adult attachment. In N. S. Jacobson & A. S. Gurman (Eds.), *Clinical handbook of couple therapy* (pp. 121–141). New York: Guilford Press.

Johnston, J. R. (1994). High-conflict divorce. *Future of Children, 4*, 165–182.

Kant, I. (1965). *Critique of pure reason* (N. K. Smith, Trans.). New York: St. Martin's Press. (Original work published 1781)

Kaplan, H. S. (1979). *Disorders of sexual desire and other new concepts and techniques in sex therapy.* New York: Brunner/Mazel.

Kaplan, L. J. (1984). *Adolescence: The farewell to childhood.* New York: Simon & Schuster.

Karpel, M. (1976). Individuation: From fusion to dialogue. *Family Process, 15*, 65–82.

Kaufman, G. (1980). *Shame: The power of caring.* Cambridge, MA: Schenkman.

Kenrick, D. T., Sadalla, E. K., Groth, G., & Trost, M. R. (1990). Evolution, traits, and the stages of human courtship: Qualifying the parental investment model. *Journal of Personality, 58*, 97–116.

Kernberg, O. F. (1980). *Internal world and external reality: Object relations theory applied.* Northvale, NJ: Jason Aronson.

Kernberg, O. F. (Speaker). (1995). *Transference/countertransference* (Cassette Recording No. H260-P5). Phoenix, AZ: Milton H. Erickson Foundation.

Kernberg, O. F. (1997). The nature of interpretation: Intersubjectivity and the third position. *American Journal of Psychoanalysis, 57*, 297–312.

Kerr, M. E., & Bowen, M. (1988). *Family evaluation: An approach based on Bowen theory*. New York: Norton.

Kessler, R. C., McGonagle, K. A., Zhao, S., Nelson, C. B., Hughes, M., Eshleman, S., Wittchen, H., & Kendler, K. S. (1994). Lifetime and 12-month prevalence of DSM–III–R psychiatric disorders in the United States: Results from the National Comorbidity Survey. *Archives of General Psychiatry, 51,* 8–19.

Kestenbaum, R., Farber, E. A., & Sroufe, L. A. (1989). Individual differences in empathy among preschoolers: Relation to attachment history. In W. Damon (Series Ed.) & N. Eisenberg (Vol. Ed.), *New Directions in Child Development: Vol. 44. Empathy and related emotional responses* (pp. 51–64). San Francisco: Jossey-Bass.

Kestenberg, J. S. (1977). Regression and reintegration in pregnancy. In H. P. Blum (Ed.), *Female psychology: Contemporary psychoanalytic views* (pp. 213–250). New York: International Universities Press.

Keys, A., Brozek, J., Henschel, A., Mickelsen, O., & Taylor, H. L. (1950). *The biology of human starvation: Vol. 2.* Minneapolis: University of Minnesota Press.

Kirkpatrick, L. A., & Davis, K. E. (1994). Attachment style, gender, and relationship stability: A longitudinal analysis. *Journal of Personality and Social Psychology, 66,* 502–512.

Klaus, M. H., & Kennell, J. H. (1976). *Maternal–infant bonding.* St. Louis, MO: Mosby.

Klein, M. (1932). *The psycho-analysis of children.* London: Hogarth Press.

Klein, M. (1964). *Contributions to psycho-analysis 1921–1945.* New York: McGraw-Hill. (Original work published 1948)

Kline, C. D., & Newman, I. (1994). Factor structure of the family-of-origin scale: Does this scale measure what its creators say it does? *Journal of Marital and Family Therapy, 20,* 47–52.

Kohut, H. (1971). *The analysis of the self: A systematic approach to the psychoanalytic treatment of narcissistic personality disorders.* New York: International Universities Press.

Kohut, H. (1977). *The restoration of the self.* New York: International Universities Press.

Krasner, L. (1988). Paradigm lost: On a historical/sociological/economic perspective. In D. B. Fishman, F. Rotgers, & C. M. Franks (Eds.), *Paradigms in behavior therapy: Present and promise* (pp. 23–44). New York: Springer.

Kuhn, T. S. (1970). *The structure of scientific revolutions* (2nd ed.). Chicago: University of Chicago Press.

Kunce, L. J., & Shaver, P. R. (1994). An attachment-theoretical approach to caregiving in romantic relationships. In K. Bartholomew & D. Perlman (Eds.), *Advances in personal relationships* (Vol. 5, pp. 205–237). London: Jessica Kingsley.

Lacan, J. (1982). *Feminine sexuality* (J. Rose, Trans.). New York: Norton.

Laing, R. D. (1961). *Self and others.* Harmondsworth, England: Penguin Books.

Laing, R. D. (1967). *The politics of experience*. New York: Ballantine Books.

Laing, R. D. (1976). *The facts of life: An essay in feelings, facts, and fantasy*. New York: Pantheon Books.

Laing, R. D. (1985). *Existential therapy* [Videotape]. Phoenix, AZ: Milton H. Erickson Foundation.

Laing, R. D. (1989). *The challenge of love*. Unpublished manuscript.

Laing, R. D. (1990). Foreword. In R. W. Firestone, *Compassionate child-rearing: An in-depth approach to optimal parenting*. New York: Plenum Press.

Lamb, M. E. (1987). Predictive implications of individual differences in attachment. *Journal of Consulting and Clinical Psychology, 55*, 817–824.

Lasch, C. (1984). *The minimal self: Psychic survival in troubled times*. New York: Norton.

Latty-Mann, H., & Davis, K. E. (1996). Attachment theory and partner choice: Preference and actuality. *Journal of Social and Personal Relationships, 13*, 5–23.

Lavee, Y., & Olson, D. H. (1993). Seven types of marriage: Empirical typology based on ENRICH. *Journal of Marital and Family Therapy, 19*, 325–340.

Lerner, H. (1989). *The dance of intimacy: A woman's guide to courageous acts of change in key relationships*. New York: Harper Perennial.

Levy, D. M. (1943). *Maternal overprotection*. New York: Columbia University Press.

Lewis, H. B. (1971). *Shame and guilt in neurosis*. New York: International Universities Press.

Lieberman, A. F., & Pawl, J. H. (1990). Disorders of attachment and secure base behavior in the second year of life. In M. T. Greenberg, D. Cicchetti, & E. M. Cummings (Eds.), *Attachment in the preschool years: Theory, research, and intervention* (pp. 375–397). Chicago: University of Chicago Press.

Lippman, W. (1955). *Essays in the public philosophy*. Boston: Little, Brown.

Lockard, J. S., & Adams, R. M. (1981). Human serial polygyny: Demographic, reproductive, marital, and divorce data. *Ethology and Sociobiology, 2*, 177–186.

Lore, R. K., & Schultz, L. A. (1993). Control of human aggression: A comparative perspective. *American Psychologist, 48*, 16–25.

Lott, B. (1997). *Cataloging gender differences: Science or politics?* In M. R. Walsh (Ed.), Women, men, and gender: Ongoing debates (pp. 19–23). New Haven, CT: Yale University Press.

Luborsky, L., Barber, J. P., & Beutler, L. E. (Eds.). (1993). Special section: Curative factors in dynamic psychotherapy. *Journal of Consulting and Clinical Psychology, 61*, 539–610.

Luborsky, L., & Crits-Christoph, P. (1998). *Understanding transference: The core conflictual relationship theme method* (2nd ed.). Washington, DC: American Psychological Association.

MacNeil-Lehrer Productions, WNET, WETA. (1987, March 12). *Open door policy? Teen suicide: Fall from grace* (Transcript No. 2989 of the MacNeil/Lehrer NewsHour). New York: Author.

Mahler, M. S. (1979). On symbiotic child psychosis: Genetic, dynamic, and restitutive aspects. In *The selected papers of Margaret S. Mahler, M.D., Vol. 1: Infantile psychosis and early contributions* (pp. 109–129). New York: Jason Aronson. (Original work published 1955)

Mahler, M. S., & McDevitt, J. B. (1968). Observations on adaptation and defense in statu nascendi: Developmental precursors in the first two years of life. *Psychoanalytic Quarterly, 37,* 1–21.

Mahler, M. S., Pine, F., & Bergman, A. (1975). *The psychological birth of the human infant: Symbiosis and individuation.* New York: Basic Books.

Mahoney, M. J. (1981). Clinical psychology and scientific inquiry. *International Journal of Psychology, 16,* 257–274.

Main, M. (1990). Parental aversion to infant-initiated contact is correlated with the parent's own rejecting during childhood: The effects of experience on signals of security with respect to attachment. In K. E. Barnard & T. B. Brazelton (Eds.), *Touch: The foundation of experience* (pp. 461–495). Madison, CT: International Universities Press.

Main, M. (1996). Introduction to the special section on attachment and psychopathology: 2. Overview of the field of attachment. *Journal of Consulting and Clinical Psychology, 64,* 237–243.

Main, M., & Goldwyn, R. (1984). Predicting rejection of her infant from mother's representation of her own experience: Implications for the abuse-abusing intergenerational cycle. *Child Abuse and Neglect, 8,* 203–217.

Main, M., & Hesse, E. (1990). Parents' unresolved traumatic experiences are related to infant disorganized attachment status: Is frightened and/or frightening parental behavior the linking mechanism? In M. T. Greenberg, D. Cicchetti, & E. M. Cummings (Eds.), *Attachment in the preschool years: Theory, research, and intervention* (pp. 161–182). Chicago: University of Chicago Press.

Main, M., Kaplan, N., & Cassidy, J. (1985). Security in infancy, childhood, and adulthood: A move to the level of representation. *Monographs of the Society for Research in Child Development, 50*(1–2), 66–104.

Main, M., & Solomon, J. (1986). Discovery of an insecure-disorganized/disoriented attachment pattern. In T. B. Brazelton & M. W. Yogman (Eds.), *Affective development in infancy* (pp. 95–124). Norwood, NJ: Ablex.

Maltsberger, J. T., & Buie, D. H., Jr. (1989). Common errors in the management of suicidal patients. In D. Jacobs & H. N. Brown (Eds.), *Suicide: Understanding and responding* (pp. 285–294). Madison, CT: International Universities Press.

Maracek, J. (1995). Gender, politics, and psychology's ways of knowing. *American Psychologist, 50,* 162–163.

Marcuse, H. (1966). *Eros and civilization: A philosophical inquiry into Freud.* Boston: Beacon Press. (Original work published 1955)

Maslow, A. H. (1968). *Toward a psychology of being* (2nd ed.). New York: Van Nostrand Reinhold.

Masten, A. S., & Coatsworth, J. D. (1998). The development of competence in favorable and unfavorable environments. *American Psychologist, 53,* 205–220.

Masterson, J. (Speaker). (1995). *Transference/countertransference* (Cassette Recording No. H260-P5). Phoenix, AZ: Milton H. Erickson Foundation.

May, R. (1958). Contributions of existential psychotherapy. In R. May, E. Angel, & H. F. Ellenberger (Eds.), *Existence: A new dimension in psychiatry and psychology* (pp. 37–91). New York: Basic Books.

McCullers, C. (1940). *The heart is a lonely hunter.* New York: Houghton Mifflin.

McFarlane, A. C., & van der Kolk, B. A. (1996a). Conclusions and future directions. In B. A. van der Kolk, A. C. McFarlane, & L. Weisaeth (Eds.), *Traumatic stress: The effects of overwhelming experience on mind, body, and society* (pp. 559–575). New York: Guilford Press.

McFarlane, A. C., & van der Kolk, B. A. (1996b). Trauma and its challenge to society. In B. A. van der Kolk, A. C. McFarlane, & L. Weisaeth (Eds.), *Traumatic stress: The effects of overwhelming experience on mind, body, and society* (pp. 24–46). New York: Guilford Press.

McGrath, E., Keita, G. P., Strickland, B. R., & Russo, N. F. (Eds.). (1990). *Women and depression: Risk factors and treatment issues.* Washington, DC: American Psychological Association.

McIntosh, J. L. (1998, February 28). *U.S.A. suicide: 1995 official data* [Suicide data page: 1995, rev.]. Denver, CO: American Association of Suicidology.

McLoyd, V. C. (1998). Socioeconomic disadvantage and child development. *American Psychologist, 53,* 185–204.

Meltzoff, A. N., & Moore, M. K. (1995). A theory of the role of imitation in the emergence of self. In P. Rochat (Ed.), *The self in infancy: Theory and research* (pp. 73–93). Amsterdam, the Netherlands: Elsevier.

Menninger, K. (1938). *Man against himself.* New York: Harcourt, Brace & World.

Menos, M. D., & Wilson, A. (1998). Affective experiences and levels of self-organization in maternal postpartum depression. *Psychoanalytic Psychology, 15,* 396–419.

Merton, R. K. (1957). *Social structure.* Glencoe, IL: Free Press.

Mickelson, K. D., Kessler, R. C., & Shaver, P. R. (1997). Adult attachment in a nationally representative sample. *Journal of Personality and Social Psychology, 73,* 1092–1106.

Miller, A. (1984). *For your own good: Hidden cruelty in child-rearing and the roots of violence* (H. Hannum & H. Hannum, Trans.; 2nd ed.). New York: Farrar, Straus, & Giroux. (Original work published 1980)

Miller, A. (1990). *Banished knowledge: Facing childhood injuries* (L. Vennewitz, Trans.). New York: Doubleday. (Original work published 1988)

Miller, A. (1991). *Breaking down the wall of silence* (S. Worral, Trans.). New York: Meredian. (Original work published 1990)

Miller, J. B. (1976). *Toward a new psychology of women.* Boston: Beacon Press.

Miller, N. E., & Dollard, J. (1941). *Social learning and imitation.* New Haven, CT: Yale University Press.

Minuchin, S. (1974). *Families and family therapy*. Cambridge, MA: Harvard University Press.

Minuchin, S., Lee, W., & Simon, G. M. (1996). *Mastering family therapy: Journeys of growth and transformation*. New York: Wiley.

Minuchin, S., & Nichols, M. P. (1994). *Family healing: Strategies for hope and understanding*. New York: Simon & Schuster.

Minuchin, S., Rosman, B. L., & Baker, L. (1978). *Psychosomatic families: Anorexia nervosa in context*. Cambridge, MA: Harvard University Press.

Mitchell, R. (1985). *Deception: Perspectives on human and non-human deceit*. New York: State University of New York Press.

Moeller, T. P., Bachmann, G. A., & Moeller, J. R. (1993). The combined effects of physical, sexual, and emotional abuse during childhood: Long-term health consequences for women. *Child Abuse and Neglect, 17*, 623–640.

Moir, A., & Jessel, D. (1989). *Brainsex: The real difference between men and women*. London: Mandarin.

Mollon, P., & Parry, G. (1984). The fragile self: Narcissistic disturbance and the protective function of depression. *British Journal of Medical Psychology, 57*, 137–145.

More, T. (1949). *Utopia* (H. V. S. Ogden, Trans. & Ed.). New York: Appleton-Century-Crofts. (Original work published 1551)

Morrison, A. P. (1989). *Shame: The underside of narcissism*. Hillsdale, NJ: Analytic Press.

Mozdzierz, G. J., Greenblatt, R. L., & Thatcher, A. A. (1985). The kinship and clinical relevance of the double bind to Adlerian theory and practice. *Individual Psychology, 41*, 453–460.

Muller, R. T., Hunter, J. E., & Stollak, G. (1995). The intergenerational transmission of corporal punishment: A comparison of social learning and temperament models. *Child Abuse and Neglect, 19*, 1323–1335.

Murdock, G. P. (1967). *Ethnographic atlas*. Pittsburgh, PA: University of Pittsburgh Press.

Neimeyer, G. J. (1993). The challenge of change: Reflections on constructivist psychotherapy. *Journal of Cognitive Psychotherapy, 7*, 183–194.

Neubauer, P. B. (1986). Reciprocal effects of fathering on parent and child. In G. I. Fogel, F. M. Lane, & R. S. Liebert (Eds.), *The psychology of men: Psychoanalytic perspectives* (pp. 213–228). New Haven, CT: Yale University Press.

Neumann, D. A., Houskamp, B. M., Pollock, V. E., & Briere, J. N. (1996). The long-term sequelae of childhood sexual abuse in women: A meta-analytic review. *Child Maltreatment, 1*, 6–16.

Newton, D. A., & Burgoon, J. K. (1990). Nonverbal conflict behaviors: Functions, strategies, and tactics. In D. D. Cahn (Ed.), *Intimates in conflict: A communication perspective* (pp. 77–104). Hillsdale, NJ: Erlbaum.

Ogden, T. H. (1982). *Projective identification and psychotherapeutic technique*. New York: Jason Aronson.

Okey, J. L. (1992). Human aggression: The etiology of individual differences. *Journal of Humanistic Psychology, 32,* 51–64.

Olson, R. G. (1962). *An introduction to existentialism.* New York: Dover.

Orwell, G. (1954). *Nineteen eighty-four.* Harmondsworth, Middlesex, England: Penguin Books. (Original work published 1949)

Owens, G., Crowell, J. A., Pan, H., Treboux, D., O'Connor, E., & Waters, E. (1995). The prototype hypothesis and the origins of attachment working models: Adult relationships with parents and romantic partners. *Monographs of the Society for Research in Child Development, 60,* 217–232 (Serial No. 244).

Pagels, E. (1988). *Adam, Eve, and the serpent.* New York: Random House.

Palazzoli, M. S., Boscolo, L., Cecchin, G., & Prata, G. (1978). *Paradox and counterparadox: A new model in the therapy of the family in schizophrenic transaction* (E. V. Burt, Trans.). New York: Jason Aronson. (Original work published 1975)

Parin, P. (1978). *Furchte deinen Nächsten wie dich Selbst* [Fear thy neighbor as thyself]. Frankfurt, Germany: Suhrkamp.

Park, J. (1995). *Sons, mothers and other lovers.* London: Abacus.

Parker, G. (1983). *Parental overprotection: A risk factor in psychosocial development.* New York: Grune & Stratton.

Parker, G., Tupling, H., & Brown, L. B. (1979). A parental bonding instrument. *British Journal of Medical Psychology, 52,* 1–10.

Parr, G. (Producer and Director). (1987). *Hunger vs. love: A perspective on parent-child relations* [Videotape]. Santa Barbara, CA: Glendon Association.

Parr, G. (Producer and Director). (1990a). *Sex and society: Everyday abuses to children's emerging sexuality* [Videotape]. Santa Barbara, CA: Glendon Association.

Parr, G. (Producer and Director). (1990b). *Voices in sex* [Videotape]. Santa Barbara, CA: Glendon Association.

Parr, G. (Producer and Director). (1995). *Invisible child abuse* [Videotape]. Santa Barbara, CA: Glendon Association.

Parr, G. (Producer and Director). (1997a). *Exploring relationships* [Videotape]. Santa Barbara, CA: Glendon Association.

Parr, G. (Producer and Director). (1997b). *Fear of intimacy: An examination of withholding behavior patterns* [Videotape]. Santa Barbara, CA: Glendon Association.

Parr, G. (Producer and Director). (1999). *Coping with the fear of intimacy* [Videotape]. Santa Barbara, CA: Glendon Association.

Perris, C., Jacobsson, L., Lindstrom., H., von Knorring, L., & Perris, H. (1980). Development of a new inventory for assessing memories of parental rearing behaviour. *Acta Psychiatrica Scandinavica, 61,* 265–274.

Perry, D. G., Perry, L. C., & Boldizar, J. P. (1990). Learning of aggression. In M. Lewis & S. M. Miller (Eds.), *Handbook of developmental psychopathology* (pp. 135–146). New York: Plenum Press.

Philpot, C. L., Brooks, G. R., Lusterman, D., & Nutt, R. L. (1997). *Bridging separate gender worlds: Why men and women clash and how therapists can bring them together*. Washington, DC: American Psychological Association.

Pianta, R. C., Egeland, B., & Adam, E. K. (1996). Adult attachment classification and self-reported psychiatric symptomatology as assessed by the Minnesota Multiphasic Personality Inventory—2. *Journal of Consulting and Clinical Psychology, 64*, 273–281.

Piper, W. E., Joyce, A. S., McCalum, M., & Azim, H. F. A. (1993). Concentration and correspondence of transference interpretations in short-term psychotherapy. *Journal of Consulting and Clinical Psychology, 61*, 586–595.

Popper, K. R. (1966). *The open society and its enemies: Vol. II. The high tide of prophecy: Hegel, Marx, and the aftermath* (5th ed.). Princeton, NJ: Princeton University Press.

QSR NUD*IST [Computer software]. (1997). Victoria, Australia: Qualitative Solutions and Research.

Radloff, L. S. (1977). The CES–D Scale: A self-report depression scale for research in the general population. *Applied Psychological Measurement, 1*, 385–401.

Rank, O. (1941). *Beyond psychology*. New York: Dover.

Rank, O. (1972). *Will therapy and truth and reality* (J. Taft, Trans.). New York: Knopf. (Original work published 1936)

Rawls, J. (1971). *A theory of justice*. Cambridge, MA: Harvard University Press.

Rheingold, J. C. (1964). *The fear of being a woman: A theory of maternal destructiveness*. New York: Grune & Stratton.

Rheingold, J. C. (1967). *The mother, anxiety, and death: The catastrophic death complex*. Boston: Little, Brown.

Richman, J. (1986). *Family therapy for suicidal people*. New York: Springer.

Ricks, M. H. (1985). The social transmission of parental behavior: Attachment across generations. *Monographs of the Society for Research in Child Development, 50*(1–2), 211–227.

Rilke, R. M. (1984). *Letters to a young poet* (S. Mitchell, Trans.). New York: Vintage Books. (Original work published 1908)

Rogers, C. R. (1951). *Client-centered therapy: Its current practice, implications, and theory*. Boston: Houghton Mifflin.

Rogers, J. R., & Carney, J. V. (1994). Assessing the "modeling effect" in parasuicidal behavior: A comment on Platt (1993). *Crisis, 15*, 83–89.

Rohner, R. P. (1986). *The warmth dimension: Foundations of parental acceptance-rejection theory*. Beverly Hills, CA: Sage.

Rohner, R. P. (1991). *Handbook for the study of parental acceptance and rejection*. Storrs: University of Connecticut.

Rosen, J. N. (1953). *Direct analysis: Selected papers*. New York: Grune & Stratton.

Rosen, K. S., & Rothbaum, F. (1993). Quality of parental caregiving and security of attachment. *Developmental Psychology, 29*, 358–367.

Rosenberg, M. (1979). *Conceiving the self.* New York: Basic Books.

Rosenstein, D. S., & Horowitz, H. A. (1996). Adolescent attachment and psychopathology. *Journal of Consulting and Clinical Psychology, 64,* 244–253.

Rubin, L. B. (1983). *Intimate strangers: Men and women together.* New York: Harper & Row.

Rutter, M. (1997). Clinical implications of attachment concepts: Retrospect and prospect. In L. Atkinson & K. J. Zucker (Eds.), *Attachment and psychopathology* (pp. 17–46). New York: Guilford Press.

Ryan, R. M., Deci, E. L., & Grolnick, W. S. (1986). *Children's perceptions of parental autonomy, support and involvement.* Unpublished manuscript.

Sager, C. J., Kaplan, H. S., Gundlach, R. H., Kremer, M., Lenz, R., & Royce, J. R. (1971). The marriage contract. *Family Process, 8,* 311–326.

Saint Exupery, A. D. (1939). *Wind, sand and stars* (L. Galantiere, Trans.). New York: Reynal & Hitchcock.

Saluter, A. (1996). *Marital status and living arrangements: March 1994* (U.S. Bureau of the Census Series P20-484). Washington, DC: Government Printing Office.

Scarf, M. (1980). *Unfinished business: Pressure points in the lives of women.* Garden City, NY: Doubleday.

Schaefer, E. S. (1965). Children's reports of parental behavior: An inventory. *Child Development, 36,* 413–423.

Scharfe, E., & Bartholomew, K. (1994). Reliability and stability of adult attachment patterns. *Personal Relationships, 1,* 23–43.

Scharff, D. E., & Scharff, J. S. (1991). *Object relations couple therapy.* Northvale, NJ: Jason Aronson.

Scharff, J. S. (1995). Psychoanalytic marital therapy. In N. S. Jacobson & A. S. Gurman (Eds.), *Clinical handbook of couple therapy* (pp. 164–193). New York: Guilford Press.

Schnarch, D. M. (1991). *Constructing the sexual crucible: An integration of sexual and marital therapy.* New York: Norton.

Secunda, V. (1990). *When you and your mother can't be friends: Resolving the most complicated relationship of your life.* New York: Delacorte Press.

Segraves, R. T. (1982). *Marital therapy: A combined psychodynamic-behavioral approach.* New York: Plenum Press.

Seligman, M. E. P. (1975). *Helplessness: On depression, development, and death.* New York: Freeman.

Shaffer, P. (1974). *Equus.* New York: Avon Books.

Sharpsteen, D. J., & Kirkpatrick, L. A. (1997). Romantic jealousy and adult romantic attachment. *Journal of Personality and Social Psychology, 72,* 627–640.

Shaver, P. R. , & Brennan, K. A. (1992). Attachment styles and the "Big Five" personality traits: Their connections with each other and with romantic relationship outcomes. *Personality and Social Psychology Bulletin, 18,* 536–545.

Shaver, P. R., & Clark, C. L. (1994). The psychodynamics of adult romantic attachment. In J. M. Masling & R. F. Bornstein (Eds.), *Empirical perspectives on object relations theory* (pp. 105–156). Washington, DC: American Psychological Association.

Shaver, P. R., Collins, N., & Clark, C. L. (1996). Attachment styles and internal working models of self and relationship partners. In G. J. O. Fletcher & J. Fitness (Eds.), *Knowledge structures in close relationships: A social psychological approach* (pp. 25–61). Mahwah, NJ: Erlbaum.

Shaver, P. R., & Hazan, C. (1993). Adult romantic attachment: Theory and evidence. In D. Perlman & W. Jones (Eds.), *Advances in personal relationships* (Vol. 4, pp. 29–70). London: Jessica Kingsley.

Shengold, L. (1989). *Soul murder: The effects of childhood abuse and deprivation.* New Haven, CT: Yale University Press.

Shengold, L. (1991). A variety of narcissistic pathology stemming from parental weakness. *Psychoanalytic Quarterly, 60,* 86–92.

Shiono, P. H., & Quinn, L. S. (1994). Epidemiology of divorce. In R. E. Behrman (Ed.), *The future of children: Vol. 4. Children and divorce* (pp. 15–28). Los Altos, CA: Center for the Future of Children.

Shoham, V., Rohrbaugh, M., & Patterson, J. (1995). Problem- and solution-focused couple therapies: The MRI and Milwaukee models. In N. S. Jacobson & A. S. Gurman (Eds.), *Clinical handbook of couple therapy* (pp. 142–163). New York: Guilford Press.

Silverman, L. H., Lachmann, F. M., & Milich, R. H. (1982). *The search for oneness.* New York: International Universities Press.

Silverstein, S. (1976). *The missing piece.* New York: Harper Collins.

Simpson, J. A., Rholes, W. S., & Phillips, D. (1996). Conflict in close relationships: An attachment perspective. *Journal of Personality and Social Psychology, 71,* 899–914.

Slavin, M. O., & Kriegman, D. (1992). *The adaptive design of the human psyche: Psychoanalysis, evolutionary biology, and the therapeutic process.* New York: Guilford Press.

Snodgrass, S. E. (1992). Further effects of role versus gender on interpersonal sensitivity. *Journal of Personality and Social Psychology, 62,* 154–158.

Snyder, D. K. (1997). *Marital Satisfaction Inventory, Revised.* Los Angeles, CA: Western Psychological Services.

Solomon, M. F., & Siegel, J. P. (Eds.). (1997). *Countertransference in couples therapy.* New York: Norton.

Speece, M. W., & Brent, S. B. (1984). Children's understanding of death: A review of three components of a death concept. *Child Development, 55,* 1671–1686.

Sperling, M. B., & Berman, W. H. (Eds.). (1994). *Attachment in adults: Clinical and developmental perspectives.* New York: Guilford Press.

Spieker, S. J., & Booth, C. L. (1988). Maternal antecedents of attachment quality. In J. Belsky & T. Nezworski (Eds.), *Clinical implications of attachment* (pp. 95–135). Hillsdale, NJ: Erlbaum.

Spitze, G. (1988). Women's employment and family relations: A review. *Journal of Marriage and the Family, 50,* 595–618.

Sroufe, L. A. (1985). Attachment classification from the perspective of infant–caregiver relationships and infant temperament. *Child Development, 56,* 1–14.

Sroufe, L. A. (1988). The role of infant–caregiver attachment in development. In J. Belsky & T. Nezworski (Eds.), *Clinical implications of attachment* (pp. 18–38). Hillsdale, NJ: Erlbaum.

Steele, H., Steele, M., & Fonagy, P. (1996). Associations among attachment classifications of mothers, fathers, and their infants. *Child Development, 67,* 541–555.

Stern, D. N. (1971). A micro-analysis of mother–infant interaction: Behavior regulating social contact between a mother and her 3-1/2-month-old twins. *Journal of the American Academy of Child Psychiatry, 10,* 501–517.

Stern, D. N. (1985). *The interpersonal world of the infant: A view from psychoanalysis and developmental psychology.* New York: Basic Books.

Stolorow, R. D. (1997). Dynamic, dyadic, intersubjective systems: An evolving paradigm for psychoanalysis. *Psychoanalytic Psychology, 14,* 337–346.

Stolorow, R. D., Brandchaft, B., & Atwood, G. E. (1987). *Psychoanalytic treatment: An intersubjective approach.* Hillsdale, NJ: Analytic Press.

Straus, M. A. (with D. A. Donnelly). (1994). *Beating the devil out of them: Corporal punishment in American families.* New York: Lexington Books.

Strauss, A. L., & Corbin, J. (1990). *Basics of qualitative research.* Newbury Park, CA: Sage.

Strupp, H. H. (1989). Psychotherapy: Can the practitioner learn from the researcher? *American Psychologist, 44,* 717–724.

Strupp, H. H. (1995). The psychotherapist's skills revisited. *Clinical Psychology Science and Practice, 2,* 70–74.

Sullivan, H. S. (1953). *The interpersonal theory of psychiatry.* New York: Norton.

Sullivan, H. S. (1954). *The psychiatric interview.* New York: Norton.

Sullivan, H. S. (1956). *Clinical studies in psychiatry.* New York: Norton.

Sullivan, H. S. (1962). *Schizophrenia as a human process.* New York: Norton.

Symons, D. (1979). *The evolution of human sexuality.* New York: Oxford University Press.

Tannen, D. (1990). *You just don't understand: Women and men in conversation.* London: Virago Books.

Tansey, M. H., & Burke, W. F. (1985). Projective identification and the empathic process. *Contemporary Psychoanalysis, 21,* 42–69.

Tedeschi, J. T., & Felson, R. B. (1994). *Violence, aggression, and coercive actions.* Washington, DC: American Psychological Association.

Thomas, V., & Olson, D. H. (1993). Problem families and the Circumplex Model: Observational assessment using the Clinical Rating Scale (CRS). *Journal of Marital and Family Therapy, 19,* 159–175.

Toynbee, A. J. (1969, April 5). Why and how I work. *Saturday Review*, 22–27, 62.

Trivers, R. L. (1985). *Social evolution*. Boston: Addison-Wesley.

Tronick, E. Z., Cohn, J., & Shea, E. (1986). The transfer of affect between mothers and infants. In T. B. Brazelton & M. W. Yogman (Eds.), *Affective development in infancy* (pp. 11–25). Norwood, NJ: Ablex.

Tucker, W. (1993, October 4). Monogamy and its discontents. *National Review*, 28, 30, 32, 34–38.

Turner, J. (1978). Social categorization and social discrimination in the minimal group paradigm. In H. Tajfel (Ed.), *Differentiation between social groups: Studies in the social psychology of intergroup relations*. London: Academic Press.

U.S. Bureau of the Census. (1992). *Marriage, divorce, and remarriage in the 1990s* (Current Population Reports, P23–180). Washington, DC: Government Printing Office.

van IJzendoorn, M. H. (1995). Adult attachment representations, parental responsiveness, and infant attachment: A meta-analysis on the predictive validity of the Adult Attachment Interview. *Psychological Bulletin, 117*, 387–403.

Wallerstein, J. S., & Blakeslee, S. (1989). *Second chances: Men, women, and children a decade after divorce*. New York: Ticknor & Fields.

Wallerstein, J. S., & Blakeslee, S. (1995). *The good marriage: How and why love lasts*. Boston: Houghton Mifflin.

Wallerstein, J. S., & Corbin, S. B. (1989). Daughters of divorce: Report from a ten-year follow-up. *American Journal of Orthopsychiatry, 59*, 593–604.

Wallerstein, J. S., & Kelly, J. B. (1980). *Surviving the breakup: How children and parents cope with divorce*. New York: Basic Books.

Walsh, M. R. (Ed.). (1997). *Women, men, and gender: Ongoing debates*. New Haven, CT: Yale University Press.

Wang, C., & Daro, D. (1998). *Current trends in child abuse reporting and fatalities: The results of the 1997 annual fifty state survey* (Working Paper No. 808). Chicago: National Committee to Prevent Child Abuse.

Ward, M. J., & Carlson, E. A. (1995). Associations among adult attachment representations, maternal sensitivity, and infant–mother attachment in a sample of adolescent mothers. *Child Development, 66*, 69–79.

Ward, R. A. (1993). Marital happiness and household equity in later life. *Journal of Marriage and the Family, 55*, 427–437.

Waring, E. M. (1988). *Enhancing marital intimacy through facilitating cognitive self-disclosure*. New York: Brunner/Mazel.

Watzlawick, P., Bavelas, J. B., & Jackson, D. D. (1967). *Pragmatics of human communication: A study of interactional patterns, pathologies, and paradoxes*. New York: Norton.

Welldon, E. V. (1988). *Mother, madonna, whore: The idealization and denigration of motherhood*. London: Free Association Books.

Werner, E. E. (1990). Protective factors and individual resilience. In S. J. Meisels

& J. P. Shonkoff (Eds.), *Handbook of early childhood intervention* (pp. 97–116). Cambridge, England: Cambridge University Press.

West, M. L., & Keller, A. E. R. (1991). Parentification of the child: A case study of Bowlby's compulsive care-giving attachment pattern. *American Journal of Psychotherapy, 45,* 425–431.

Wexler, J., & Steidl, J. (1978). Marriage and the capacity to be alone. *Psychiatry, 41,* 72–82.

Wile, D. B. (1981). *Couples therapy: A nontraditional approach.* New York: Wiley.

Wile, D. B. (1995). The ego-analytic approach to couple therapy. In N. S. Jacobson & A. S. Gurman (Eds.), *Clinical handbook of couple therapy* (pp. 91–120). New York: Guilford Press.

Willi, J. (1982). *Couples in collusion: The unconscious dimension in partner relationships* (W. Inayat-Khan & M. Tchorek, Trans.). Claremont, CA: Hunter House. (Original work published 1975)

Wilson, G. (1981). *The Coolidge effect: An evolutionary account of human sexuality.* New York: William Morrow.

Winnicott, D. W. (1965a). Ego-distortion in terms of true and false self. In D. W. Winnicott, *The maturational processes and the facilitating environment: Studies in the theory of emotional development* (pp. 140–152). Madison, CT: International Universities Press. (Original work published 1960)

Winnicott, D. W. (1965b). The theory of the parent–infant relationship. In D. W. Winnicott, *The maturational processes and the facilitating environment: Studies in the theory of emotional development* (pp. 37–55). Madison, CT: International Universities Press. (Original work published 1960)

Winnicott, D. W. (1986). *Home is where we start from: Essays by a psychoanalyst.* New York: Norton.

Wolpe, J. (1969). *The practice of behavior therapy.* New York: Pergamon Press.

Women's International Network News. (1993). The rise in single-parent women-headed families in the US. *Women's International Network News, 19,* 75.

Wright, R. (1994). *The moral animal: Evolutionary psychology and everyday life.* New York: Vintage Books.

Yalom, I. (1980). *Existential psychotherapy.* New York: Basic Books.

Yalom, I. (Speaker). (1995). *Transference/countertransference* (Cassette Recording No. H260-P5). Phoenix, AZ: Milton H. Erickson Foundation.

Zelnick, L., & Buchholz, E. S. (1990). The concept of mental representations in light of recent infant research. *Psychoanalytic Psychology, 7*(1), 29–58.

Zinner, J. (1976). The implications of projective identification for marital interaction. In H. Grunebaum & J. Christ (Eds.), *Contemporary marriage: Structure, dynamics, and therapy* (pp. 293–308). Boston, MA: Little, Brown.

Zuk, G. H., & Zuk, C. V. (1998a). Projection, double bind, and demonic possession: Some common elements in three theories of psychosis. *Contemporary Family Therapy, 20,* 15–23.

Zuk, G. H., & Zuk, C. V. (1998b). When more is better than less: Three theories
of psychosis—Projection, double bind, and possession. *Contemporary Family Therapy, 20,* 3–13.

AUTHOR INDEX

Canary, D. J., 84, 85, 96n
Caplan, P. J., 213
Carlson, E. A., 66
Carney, J. V., 19
Carstensen, L. L., 268n
Carter, J. A., 312n
Caspi, A., 63, 74n
Cassidy, J., 13, 65, 74n
Catlett, J., 215, 267n, 300n
Cecchin, G., 119n
Chess, S., xvin
Chessick, R. D., 311
Chisholm, J. S., 65
Chodorow, N., 205n, 210, 212, 221n
Cicchetti, D., 65
Clark, C. L., 65, 66, 73n, 169, 180n, 223n, 243
Clarkin, J. F., 313n
Coatsworth, J. D., 1998
Cohler, B. J., 116
Cohn, J., 65
Cole-Detke, H., 73n
Collins, N., 66
Colman, W., 90
Connolly, M. B., 303
Cooney, T., 265
Corbin, J., 241
Corbin, S. B., 222n
Costa, P. T., Jr., 244n
Cramer, B. G., 73n
Crits-Christoph, P., 244n, 302, 304, 313n
Crittenden, P. M., 63, 73n
Cupach, W. R., 84

Daly, M., 16, 29n, 30n
Daro, D., 99
Darwin, C., 33
Davis, K. E., 65
Dawson, D. A., 16
Deci, E. L., 31n
de Jong, M. L., 73n
Deutsch, H., 210
Deutsch, R. M., 51n
Dicks, H. V., 268n
Dix, C., 222n
Dollard, J., 51n
Dostoyevsky, F., 55
Duck, S., 85, 90
Dugan, M. N., 114
Durkheim, E., 55

Eagly, A. H., 204n

Egeland, B., 66
Eron, L. D., 51n

Fairbairn, W. R. D., 228
Farber, E. A., 74n
Feeney, J. A., 65
Felson, R. B., 57
Fenchel, G. H., 210
Field, T., 73n
Fierman, L. B., 163, 164
Finnegan, A., 195
Firestone, L., 49, 229, 267n, 300n
Firestone, R. W., 5, 7, 9, 10, 20, 21, 27, 31n, 34, 47, 48, 49, 50, 53, 58, 60, 62, 65, 66, 74n, 88, 91, 95, 101, 102, 103, 104, 106, 108, 119n, 126, 135, 161n, 164, 166, 183, 185, 190, 209, 210, 215, 228, 229, 241, 243n, 248, 258, 260, 265, 267n, 301
Floyd, F. J., 265
Fonagy, P., 13, 65, 74n, 75n
Ford, C. S., 16, 29n
Foucault, M., 55, 72n, 73n
Fraiberg, S., 63
Fremmer-Bombik, E., 74n
Freud, S., 33, 51n, 60, 67, 302, 311n
Friday, N., 210, 213, 223n
Fromm, E., 13, 192n, 222n

Garbarino, J., 71n, 102
Geis, F. L., 194, 195, 203n
Gelso, C. J., 312n
Genevie, L., 212
George, C., 65, 66, 74n
Gerall, A. A., 205n
Gilbert, P., 30n
Gilliam, G., 71n
Gilligan, C., 205n, 207
Ginot, E., 312n
Glaser, B., 241
Glover, E., 303
Goffman, E., 55
Goldberg, C., 46
Goldberg, S., 65
Goldwyn, R., 66
Goleman, D., 30
Gordon, R. M., 222n
Gottman, J. M., 84, 85, 96n, 267n, 268n

Lamb, M. E., 73n
Larsen, R. J., 195
Lasch, C., 33
Latty-Mann, H., 65
Lavee, Y., 244n
Leadbeater, B. J., 73n, 75n
Lee, W., 117
Lerner, H., 271
Levenson, R. W., 268n
Levy, D. M., 120n
Lewis, H. B., 46
Lieberman, A. F., 65
Lindstrom, H., 31n
Liotti, G., 312n
Lippman, W., 54
Lockard, J. S., 30n
Lore, R. K., 51n
Lott, B., 193
Luborsky, L., 244n, 302, 303, 304, 312n,
    313n, 314n
Lusterman, D., 205n

Machado, P. O. O., 313n
Mahler, M. S., 65, 105
Mahoney, M. J., 312n
Main, M., 13, 65, 66, 73n, 74n, 107
Maltsberger, J. T., 306
Marecek, J., 205n
Marcus Aurelius, 227
Marcuse, H., 55, 71n
Margolies, E., 212
Markman, H. J., 265
Maslow, A. H., 47
Masten, A. S., 1998
Masterson, J., 303
May, R., 47
McCalum, M., 304
McCrae, R. R., 244n
McCullers, C., 4
McDevitt, J. B., 65
McFarlane, A. C., 71n
McGrath, E., 221n
McIntosh, J. L., 72, 99
McLoyd, V. C., 116
Meltzoff, A. N., 19
Menninger, K., 51n
Menos, M. D., 222n
Merton, R. K., 56
Messman, S. J., 84
Mickelsen, O., 51n
Mickelson, K. D., 180n
Milich, R. H., 51n

Miller, A., 99, 313n
Miller, J. B., 205n, 207, 208
Miller, N. E., 51n
Minuchin, S., 117, 119n, 120n
Mitchell, R., 30n
Moeller, J. R., 63
Moeller, T. P., 63
Moir, A., 205n
Mollon, P., 192n
Moltz, H., 205n
Moore, M. K., 19
More, T., 54
Morrison, A. P., 46
Mozdzierz, G. J., 19
Muller, R. T., 19
Murdock, G. P., 30n

Neimeyer, G. J., 312n
Neubauer, P. G., 197
Neufeldt, S., 313n
Neumann, D. A., 63
Newman, I., 242
Newton, D. A., 96n
Nichols, M. P., 117
Noller, P., 65
Nutt, R. L., 205n

Ogden, T. H., 268n
Okey, J. L., 51n
Olson, D. H., 244n, 268n
Olson, R. G., 71n
Orwell, G., 54
Oubaid, V., 195
Owens, G., 66, 180n

Pagels, E., 72n
Palazzoli, M. S., 119n
Parin, P., 245
Park, J., 197
Parker, G., 20, 31n, 65, 120n
Parker, K. C. H., 66
Parr, G., 51n, 73n, 135, 192n, 194, 260,
    300n
Parry, G., 192n
Patterson, J., 266
Pawl, J. H., 65
Perris, C., 31n
Perris, H., 31n
Perry, D. G., 19
Perry, L. C., 19

Phillips, D., 65
Philpot, C. L., 205n
Pianta, R. C., 66
Pine, F., 65
Piper, W. E., 304
Plant, E. A., 196, 204n
Plato, 54
Pollock, V. E., 63
Popper, K. R., 70
Prata, G., 119n

Quinn, L. S., 15, 16, 102, 120n

Radloff, L. S., 244n
Rank, O., 171, 222n
Rawls, J., 54
Rheingold, J. C., 212, 213, 214, 222n
Rholes, W. S., 65
Richman, J., 91
Ricks, M. H., 74n
Ridgeway, D., 74n
Rilke, R. M., 77
Rogers, C. R., 265
Rogers, J. R., 19
Rohner, R. P., 104, 161n
Rohrbaugh, M., 266
Rosen, J. N., x
Rosen, K. S., 120n
Rosenberg, M., 244n
Rosenberg, S. E., 243
Rosenstein, D. S., 74n
Rosman, B. L., 120n
Rothbaum, F., 120n
Rovine, M., 120n
Rubin, L. B., 78, 143
Rudolph, J., 74n
Russo, N. F., 221n
Rutter, M., 65
Ryan, R. M., 31n

Sadalla, E. K., 25
Sager, C. J., 242
Saint Exupéry, A. de, 123
Saluter, A., 29n
Samter, W., 204n
Scarf, M., 221n
Schacht, T. E., 313n
Schaefer, E. S., 31n
Schaefer, M., 223n
Scharfe, E., 74n
Scharff, D. E., 262, 265, 268n
Scharff, J. S., 262, 265, 268n

Schmitt, D. P., 25, 29n, 81, 96n
Schnarch, D. M., 78, 86, 267, 268n, 311
Schultz, L. A., 51n
Schwartz, J. C., 74n
Segraves, R. T., 243
Secunda, V., 221n
Seeley, J. W., 102
Seligman, M. E. P., 119n
Shaffer, P., 59
Shapiro, V., 63
Sharpsteen, D. J., 244n
Shaver, P. R., 65, 66, 73n, 169, 180n,
      223n, 243, 244n
Shea, E., 65
Shengold, L., 102, 106
Shiono, P. H., 15, 16, 102, 120n
Shoham, V., 266
Siegel, J. P., 312n
Silverman, L. H., 51n
Silverstein, S., 31n
Simon, G. M., 117
Simpson, J. A., 65
Slade, A., 74
Slavin, M. O., 30n
Snodgrass, S. E., 205n
Snyder, D. K., 205n, 244n, 272
Solomon, J., 66, 73n
Solomon, M. F., 312n
Spark, G. M., 57, 72n
Speece, M. W., 114
Sperling, M. B., 66
Spieker, S. J., 65
Spitze, G., 242
Sroufe, L. A., 74n
Stanley, S. M., 265
Staso, D., 177
Steele, H., 65, 75n
Steele, M., 65, 75n
Steidl, J., 164
Stern, D. N., 65, 74n, 107, 120
Stinson, L., 90
Stollak, G., 19
Stolorow, R. D., 312n
Straus, M. A., 102, 110
Strauss, A. L., 241
Strauss, S., 114
Strickland, B. R., 221n
Strupp, H. H., 308, 309, 313n, 314n
Sullivan, H. S., 301, 302, 311n, 312n
Symonds, B. D., 313n
Symons, D., 25

Tannen, D., 204n
Tansey, M. H., 173

Taylor, D. G., 120n
Taylor, H. L., 51n
Tedeschi, J. T., 57
Thatcher, A. A., 19
Thomas, A., xvin
Thomas, V., 268n
Tooke, W., 90
Toth, S. L., 65
Toynbee, A. J., 3
Trivers, R. L., 25, 30n
Tronick, E. Z., 65, 120n
Trost, M. R., 25
Tucker, W., 30n
Tupling, H., 31n
Turner, J., 55

van der Kolk, B. A., 71n
van IJzendoorn, M. H., 66, 75n
von Knorring, L., 31n

Wall, S., 65
Wallerstein, J. S., 16, 82, 94, 97n, 120n, 222n
Walsh, M. R., 203n, 205n
Walters, R. H., 19, 51n
Wang, C., 99
Ward, I. L., 205n
Ward, M. J., 66

Ward, R. A., 242
Waring, E. M., 243, 267n, 268n
Waters, E., 65
Watzlawick, P., 19, 96n
Weakland, J. H., 19
Welldon, E. V., 65, 210
Werking, K. J., 204n
Werner, E. E., 116
West, M. L., 65
Westen, D., 195
Wexler, J., 164
Wile, D. B., 243, 267n
Willi, J., 64, 172, 233
Wilson, A., 222n
Wilson, G., 96n, 196, 222n
Wilson, M., 16, 29n, 30n
Winnicott, D. W., 99, 101
Wolpe, J., 254
Wright, R., 19, 30n

Yalom, I., 47, 303, 312n
Yogman, M. W., 73n

Zeanah, C. H., 66
Zelnick, L., 179n
Zinner, J., 268n
Zuk, C. V., 19
Zuk, G. H., 19

SUBJECT INDEX

communication
  deception and, 17–20
  fantasy bond and, 165, 174
  gender differences and, 204n
  ideal families and, 113–114
  ideal relationships and, 93–95
  open vs. closed, 113–114
  verbal vs. nonverbal, 85
Compassionate Child-Rearing Parent Education Program, 161n
competition
  compared with jealousy, 241
  fears of, 238–241
conceptual model of relationships, 8–9, 49–50, 64–66
control. *See also* child rearing; manipulative behavior; negative power; withholding
  methods of, 63–64
  sexual withholding and, 188–189
  women's strategies and, 217
Corbin, S. B., 222n
core attitudes, and voice therapy, 263–264
core conflictual relationship theme (CCRT), 244n, 304
core identity, 3–4
core inadequacy assumption, 27–29, 59
couple relationships
  case study of fantasy bond in, 166–175
  case study of inwardness in, 126–140, 144–151
  development of fantasy bond in, 164–166
  early symptoms of fantasy bond in, 165–166
  family relationships and, 102–103
  fear of competition and, 229, 238–241
  form vs. substance and, 166
  hostility toward self and, 229, 230–231
  individual rights and, 56–58
  between opposites, 229, 233–234
  parental attitudes and, 229, 234–238
  reciprocal voices and, 229, 231–233
couples groups, 155–156, 248, 264, 271–300
couples therapy
  components of, 245–247
  group pilot study, 271–300
  therapeutic process in, 247–258
Crits-Christoph, P., 304
Crittenden, P., 73n

Daly, M., 29n
Darwin, C., 33
death, family openness about, 114
death instinct, concept of, 60
decathexis process, 182
deception, 17–20
defenses. *See also* inwardness; self-parenting
  addictions and, 41–44
  aggression and, 44–45
  dimensions of defense process and, 41–46
  fantasy bond as primary defense and, 35–36, 175–176, 177
  ideal couple relationships and, 82–85
  primary defense and, 36
  pseudoaggression and, 45–46
  resistance and, 7
  sexuality and, 41–44
  withholding and, 45–46
defiance, 184
developmental process
  defense system activation in, 9
  ideal family interactions and, 103–115
  men and, 196–200
  negative environmental conditions and, 64–66
  positive and negative attitudes in, 3–4
  relationship failure and, 34–40
  role of the mother and, 210–212
Dicks, H. V., 268n
discipline, constructive, 108–113
distortion, 69
Dix, C., 222n

Eagly, A. H., 204n
emotional hunger
  child development and, 105–108
  love distinguished from, 106–107
  mother–daughter bond and, 210–211
  parental love contrasted with, 106–107
  relationships as based on, 20–21
  secure attachment and, 65–66
  withholding and, 182–183, 210
emotionally focused approach, 267n
empathy, 90–92
Equus (Shaffer play), 59–60
ethics and social systems, 54–58
evolutionary theory
  deception and, 19
  mate selection and, 81–82

existential fears, 5
existential guilt, 5, 47–49
extended families, 116
eye contact, 165

Fairbairn, W. R. D., 228
false beliefs, 58–62, 178. *See also* stereo-
      types
"family projection process," 106
family systems. *See also* ideal family rela-
      tionships
   idealization of, 55
   individual rights and, 56–58
   individuation and, 5–6
   provisional identity and, 67–68
family values, 116–118
fantasy
   of being taken care of, 217
   emotional distance during sex and,
      189–190
   inwardness and, 124, 130–131
fantasy bond. *See also* self-parenting
   adult development of, 164–166
   bond as term and, 74n
   case of, 166–175
   childhood formation of, 9, 35, 163
   in couple relationships, 38–39, 83,
      163–180, 267
   defined, 35
   dissolution of, 149–152
   inwardness and, 124, 138–140
   manifestations of, 168–174
   as primary defense, 9, 35–36, 175–176,
      177
   pseudoindependence and, 38
   psychotherapy and, 39–40, 176–178,
      267
   resistance and, 175–176
   schizophrenia and, 8
   self-parenting process and, 36–37
   social support for formation of, 55–56
   steps for disruption of, 177–178
FAST. *See Firestone Assessment of Self-De-
      structive Thoughts*
feeling release therapy, 7n, 147–149,
      161n
feeling responses
   inwardness and, 124, 135–137
   in therapy sessions, 305–306
Felson, R. B., 57
feminism, 220

Finnegan, A., 195
Firestone, R. W., 301
*Firestone Assessment of Self-Destructive
      Thoughts* (FAST), 49, 229
Firestone Voice Scale for Couples (FVSC),
      272, 273, 300n
Ford, C. S., 29n
Foucault, M., 72n
free association, 265
Freud, S., 33, 51n, 67, 302, 311n
Friday, N., 210, 213, 223n
friendship circle
   couples groups and, 155–156
   dissolution of fantasy bond and, 149–
      152
   feeling release therapy and, 147–149
   general effects of, 157–159
   parenting groups and, 156–157
   voice therapy techniques and, 153–155
   weekend encounters and, 144–147
Fromm, E., 192n
fundamental attribution error, 203n
fusion. *See* fantasy bond; personal iden-
      tity
FVSC. *See Firestone Voice Scale for Cou-
      ples*

Garbarino, J., 71n
Geis, F. L., 194, 195, 203n
Gelso, C. J., 312n
gender, concept of, 203n
Gilbert, P., 30n
Gilliam, G., 71n
Ginot, E., 312n
Gordon, R. M., 222n
Gottman, J. M., 84, 85, 96n, 268n
Graff, J., 268n
gratification, mode of, inwardness and,
      124, 130–131
Gray, J., 204n
Greenson, R. R., 302, 312n
grounded-theory approach, 244n
group marathons, 144–147. *See also* cou-
      ples groups; parenting groups
guilt
   fantasy during sex and, 189–190
   modes of, 46–49
   parental love and, 62
   voice therapy and, 267n
Guntrip, H., 228

Halpern, D. F., 195, 203n
The Heart is a Lonely Hunter (McCullers), 4–5
Henry, W. P., 313n
Hesse, E., 73n
honesty
  extent of dishonesty in relationships, 17–20
  ideal relationships and, 85
  mate selection and, 79
Horvath, A. O., 303, 304, 312n
Hudson, L., 223n
human nature, false assumptions about, 58–62
human rights, and social systems, 54–58
Hunger Versus Love (Parr), 73n
Hyde, J. S., 204n

Ickes, W., 90
ideal couple relationships
  acceptance and, 93
  commmunication and, 93–95
  couple interactions and, 82–95
  empathy and, 90–92
  honesty and, 85
  integrity and, 85
  manipulation and, 92
  nondefensiveness and, 82–85
  ongoing choice and, 92–93
  openness and, 82–85
  physical affection and, 87–90
  respect for boundaries and, 86–87
  sexuality and, 87–90
  shared values and, 93
  understanding and, 90–92
  valuing of the relationship and, 92
ideal family relationships, 99–120. *See also* child rearing
  analogy between good psychotherapy and, 117–118
  couple relationships and, 102–103
  developmental process and, 103
  dimensions of child rearing and, 103–113
  extended families and, 116
  open communications and, 113–114
  purpose of the family and, 100–102
  summary of characteristics of, 115
idealization
  of the family, 55
  of parents, 37, 61–62, 113

of the partner, 169–171, 232, 265–266
ideal systems, concept of, 54
illusory reality, 178
impersonal relating
  inwardness and, 124, 135–137
  sexuality and, 137–138
independence
  in children, 112–113
  in ideal relationships, 86–87
  loss of, and fantasy bond, 171–174
  in women, 22–23
individual rights, 54, 55, 56–58
individuation. *See also* personal identity
  emotional hunger and, 105–106, 108
  family systems and, 5–6
  voice therapy and, 266–267, 299
  women and, 212–214
integrity, 85
internal working models, 74n
inwardness. *See also* self-parenting; withholding
  case study of, 126–140, 144–151
  characteristics of, 124–125
  continuum between outward state and, 125–126
  defined, 123
  feeling release therapy and, 147–149
  group marathons and, 144–147
  remedial procedures and, 143–160
  sociability and, 124, 128–130
  voice therapy techniques and, 152–155
  withholding and, 181
isolation, 124, 128–130. *See also* sociability

Jacot, B., 223n
Jaffe, D. S., 312n
jealousy, 241, 249–251, 254–258
judgmental attitudes, 110–111. *See also* voice

Kaiser, Helmuth, 163, 164
Kaplan, L. J., 221n
Kennell, J. H., 222n
Kenrick, D. T., 31n
Kernberg, O. F., 192n, 303, 312n, 313n
Kerr, M. E., 73n
Kirkpatrick, L. A., 244n
Klaus, M. H., 222n

Kohut, H., 303, 312n
Kriegman, D., 30n
Krokoff, L. J., 84, 85
Kuhn, T. S., 50n
Kunkel, A. W., 204n

Lacan, J., 192
Laing, R. D., 57, 100, 166, 199, 245, 303
Lerner, H., 271
Levenson, R. W., 268n
libidinal object constancy, 192n
Lippman, W., 54
listening skills, 264–265
love. *See also* parental love
    confusion between sex and, 25–27
    continuum of sexual love and, 192n
    distinguished from emotional hunger,
        106–107
    giving and receiving and, 43–44
    myths about, 61, 171, 311
    nature of, 310–311
    state of being in, 77–78, 164
    survival and, 16
    youth and, 77–78
love-food, concept of, 100–102. *See also*
        psychonutritional products
Luborsky, L., 303, 304, 312n

Mahler, M. S., 105–106
Main, M., 73n, 74n, 107
Maltsberger, J. T., 306
manipulative behavior
    childish modes of relating and, 172–
        174
    in children, 111
    family systems and, 172–174
    ideal relationships and, 92
    as pervasive in relationships, 17–20
    psychodynamics of, 62–70
    sexual stereotypes and, 202, 209
    voice therapy and, 249–251
    withholding and, 190, 217
Marecek, J., 205n
Marcus Aurelius, 227
Marcuse, H., 71n
marriage
    family of origin and, 97n
    men and, 218
    polygyny and, 29n

women and, 212–213, 218
Masterson, J., 303
mate selection
    evolutionary theory and, 81–82
    failure to find a mate and, 27–29
    fantasy bond and, 39
    gender differences and, 96n, 195–196,
        217–218
    ideal traits and, 78–81
    negative high-level choices and, 23–25
    rarity of high-level choices in, 21–23
    repetition of the past and, 69
    types of choices and, 21–23
    voice and, 242
McFarlane, A. C., 71n
men
    attributes that contradict stereotypes
        and, 198
    developmental process and, 196–198
    feelings of sexual inadequacy, 199–201
    male vanity and, 201–203, 217
    sexual stereotypes and, 193–196
    short- *vs.* long-term mating and, 96n
merged identity. *See* personal identity
Merton, R. K., 56
Miller, A., 313n
Miller, J. B., 207, 208
Minuchin, S., 120n
Mollon, P., 192n
monogamy. *See* marriage; open *vs.* closed
        relationships; serial monogamy;
        sexuality
mother–daughter bond, 210–216, 223n
Murdock, G. P., 30n

negative attitudes. *See also* voice therapy
    in developmental process, 3–4, 197
    inwardness and, 132
    as key in breakdown of relationships, 9
    mother–daughter bond and, 210–212,
        216
    tendency to maintain, 7
    transference and, 305–307
    voice attacks and, 230–231
negative identity
    anxiety response to love and, 4–5
    assumption of core inadequacy and,
        27–29
    formation of, 3–4
    social forces supporting, 5–6
negative power, 111

negative power (*continued*)
  children and, 183–184
  women and, 207, 215–216, 217
neurotic guilt, 46–47
nondefensiveness, 82–85
nonmanipulative behavior, 92. *See also* manipulative behavior

object relations theory, 268n, 303
obsessive–compulsive patterns, 134–135
Olsen, D. H., 268n
Olson, R. G., 71n
openness, and ideal relationships, 82–85
open *vs.* closed relationships, 88–90
original sin, 27, 60. *See also* core inadequacy assumption

Pagels, E., 72n
parataxic distortion, 301, 311n
Parental Bonding Instrument (PBI), 31n
parental love
  attachment patterns and, 65–66
  clinging children and, 107–108
  concept of love-food and, 100–102
  contrasted with emotional hunger, 106–107
  outward manifestations of, 106–107
  parental ambivalence and, 104–105
  as unconditional, 61–62
parentification, 105
parenting groups, 156–157
Park, J., 197–198
Parker, G., 31n
Parr, G., 73n
Parry, G., 192n
passive-aggression. *See also* withholding
  withholding and, 183–184
  women and, 207–208, 215, 217
PBI. *See* Parental Bonding Instrument
personal identity. *See also* individuation
  inwardness and, 124, 138–140
  loss of sense of, 171–174
  merging of identities and, 124, 138–140
physical affection, and ideal relationships, 87–90
Plant, E. A., 204n
political systems. *See* social systems
polygamy, 29n

Popper, K. R., 70
positive attitudes in developmental process, 3–4
postpartum depression, 214
power. *See also* negative power
  methods of control and, 63–64
  predisposition to insecurity and, 64–66
  psychodynamics of, 62–70
pregnancy, 214, 219
prejudice, 60, 112
primal therapy, 7n
projection, 265, 268n, 305
projective identification, 268n
provisional identity, 4, 67–68, 305
provocation, 69–70
pseudoaggression, 45–46
pseudoindependence, 35, 38, 39–40, 41–44, 163
psychodynamics
  of parental ambivalence, 104–105
  of power in relationships, 62–70
  of voice, 228
  of withholding, 182–185
psychonutritional products, 181. *See also* love-food, concept of
psychotherapy. *See also* therapeutic relationship
  fantasy bond and, 39–40, 176–178
  healthy families and, 117–118
psychotherapy training, 309–310
psychotic children, 105–106
punishment, 109–110

Rank, O., 171
relating. *See also* sexuality
  childish modes of, 172–174
  impersonal modes of, 124, 135–138
  sexual modes of, 187–188, 191
relationship enhancement programs, 265
relationship failure. *See also* fantasy bond
  assumptions about human nature and, 58–62
  couples therapy pilot study and, 271–300
  defensive process and, 41–46
  developmental view of, 34–40
  guilt and, 46–49
  key issues in, 9
relationships. *See also* ideal couple relationships; relationship failure

assumption of core inadequacy and, 27–29

as based on emotional hunger, 20–21

centrality of, 14–15

conflicts of interests in, 218

confusion between sex and love and, 25–27

effects of withholding on, 184–185

extent of dishonesty in, 17–20

false human assumptions and, 58–62

instability of, 15–17

listening skills and, 264–265

mate selection and, 78–82

negative high-level choices and, 23–25

between opposites, 233–234

psychodynamics of power and control in, 62–70

reciprocal voices in, 231–232

repetition of the past in, 69–70

role of voice in, 66–70, 227–244

serial monogamy and, 218

teaching of core attitudes and, 263–264

types of mate-selection choices and, 21–23

repetition compulsion, 67

resistance to change

basis of, 6, 40

close relationships and, 7

fantasy bond and, 175–176

individuation and, 266–267

results of therapy and, 7–8

restrictions

child rearing and, 108–109

sexuality and, 61

Rheingold, J. C., 212, 213, 222n

role models, parents as, 109

Rosman, B. L., 120n

routines, 138–139

Rubin, L. B., 78, 143

rules, 60–61, 108–109

Saint Exupéry, Antoine de, 123

Samter, W., 204n

Schacht, T. E., 313n

Scharff, D. E., 265, 268n

Scharff, J. S., 265, 268n

schizophrenia, 8, 42, 125–126

Schmitt, D. P., 29n, 81, 96n

Schnarch, D. M., 78, 268n

scientific revolutions, 50n

secrecy, 113

secure attachment, 65

self as object, 179n

self-concept, 124, 132. See also negative attitudes; voice

self-denial. See withholding

self-knowledge, 85

self-parenting. See also fantasy bond; inwardness; withholding

pseudoindependence and, 38

relationship failure and, 36–37

self as object and, 179n

voice and, 7, 37

self psychology, 303

self-system, 228

Seligman, M. E. P., 119n

serial monogamy, 218

sex, concept of, 203n

sexism. See stereotypes

sexuality

addictive modes of, 41–44, 187, 188–191

affection-based modes of, 187–188

confusion between love and sex and, 25–27

culture and, 72n

defensive process and, 41–44, 174–175

family openness about, 114

fantasy bond and, 168–169, 174–175

female, 43, 216–220, 223n

ideal relationships and, 87–90

individuation in women and, 212–214

inwardness and, 124, 133, 137–138

mature, 192n, 268n

men's feelings of inadequacy and, 199–201

open vs. closed relationships and, 88–90, 202–203, 217–218

self-gratifying modes of, 41–44, 187, 188–191

sexual fantasies and, 189–190

sexual stereotypes and, 194–195

suppression and, 61

voices that affect sexual relating, 258–259

voice therapy techniques and, 259–263

withholding and, 187–191, 217

Shaffer, P., 59–60

Sharpsteen, D. J., 244n

Shaver, P. R., 73n, 180n

Shengold, L., 106

Silverstein, S., 31n

Slavin, M. O., 30n
Snodgrass, S. E., 205n
Snyder, D. K., 205n
sociability, and inwardness, 124, 128–
    130, 158–159
socialization process, 19, 56–58, 108–113
social systems, 54–56, 54–58, 59
Spark, G. M., 57, 72n
Sroufe, L. A., 74n
Staso, D., 177–178
stereotypes
    child rearing and, 112
    destructive aspects of, 60, 220–221
    of men, 193–196, 198, 200–201, 216
    voice attacks and, 234–235
    of women, 208–209
Stern, D. N., 120
Strupp, H. H., 313n
suicidal trends, 72n, 228, 238–241
Sullivan, H. S., 301, 302, 311n

Tannen, D., 204n
Tansey, M. H., 173
Tedeschi, J. T., 57
therapeutic alliance, 301–302, 304
therapeutic error, 306–307
therapeutic process. *See also* couples ther-
        apy; voice therapy
    components of voice therapy in, 245–
        247
    in couples therapy, 245–269
    patient fears and, 6
    therapist responses and, 306–307
therapeutic relationship
    role of therapist in, 301
    therapeutic alliance and, 301–302,
        308–310
    transference and, 301, 302–308
therapist
    characteristics of, 301, 308–310
    own defenses of, 301, 309
    responses of, 306–307
Thomas, V., 268n
Thomas, W. I., 56
Tooke, W., 90
transference, 301
    conceptualizations of, 302–303
    elements of, 304–308
    fallacies about, 307–308
transference phenomena, 301, 304–308

understanding, 90–92

van der Kolk, B. A., 71n
voice process, 7. *See also* voice therapy
    aggression toward self and, 230–231
    anorexia nervosa and, 221n
    externalization and, 68
    fear of competition and, 238–241
    identification of voices and, 246
    negative core beliefs and, 233–234
    negative thoughts during sex and,
        190–191
    psychodynamics of, 228
    psychological equilibrium in adults
        and, 66–70
    reciprocal voices and, 231–232
    in relationships, 66–70
    as secondary defense, 37
    self-parenting and, 7, 37, 66
    sexual stereotypes and, 194, 201
    suicidal trends and, 228, 238–241
    system of false beliefs and, 177–178
voice therapy (VT) process
    components of, 245–247
    corrective suggestions and, 246–247,
        254–258, 290
    discussion of insights, 246, 252–254,
        281–285, 286–287, 289–290,
        291–292, 293–294, 295
    group pilot study and, 271–300
    problem formulation and, 285–286,
        287, 288, 292–293, 294–295
    projection and, 265
    sexual problems and, 258–263
    verbalization of destructive thoughts,
        246, 249–251, 280–281, 286,
        287–288, 289, 293, 295
voice therapy theory, 228–229
    development of, 152–155
    *Firestone Assessment of Self-Destructive
        Thoughts* and, 229
    group formats and, 155–157
    as laboratory procedure, 242
    purpose of, 161n
    teaching core attitudes and, 263–264

Wallerstein, J. S., 82, 94–95, 97n, 222n
Walsh, M. R., 203n, 205n
Waring, E. M., 268n

Werking, K. J., 204n
Willi, J., 172–173, 233
Wilson, A., 222n
Wilson, G., 96n
Wilson, M., 29n
Winnicott, D. W., 99
withholding
  case study of, 186–187
  as defense against death anxiety, 185–186
  effects on relationships, 184–185
  friendships among women and, 215
  inwardness and, 124, 133–134
  jealousy and, 241
  as manifestation of fantasy bond, 168–169
  patterns in women, 216–217
  psychodynamics of, 182–185
  relationship failure and, 45–46
  sexual relating and, 87–88, 187–191

women
  attraction to other women, 218–219
  changes in attitudes of, 300n
  fear of other women, 214–216
  historical perspective and, 207–208
  individuation and, 212–214
  marriage and, 212–213, 218
  mother–daughter bond and, 209–216
  pregnancy and childbirth and, 214, 219
  role of the mother and, 210–212
  sexuality and, 216–220, 223n

Yalom, I., 303, 312n
youth, and love, 77–78

Zelnick, L., 179n
Zinner, J., 268n

ABOUT THE AUTHORS

Robert W. Firestone, PhD, is affiliated with the Glendon Association in Santa Barbara, California, a nonprofit organization dedicated to the development and dissemination of concepts and practices in psychotherapy. He completed his doctoral dissertation, *A Concept of the Schizophrenic Process*, in 1957 and received his doctorate in clinical psychology from the University of Denver that same year. From 1957 to 1979, he was engaged in the private practice of psychotherapy as a clinical psychologist working with a wide range of patients, amplifying his original ideas on schizophrenia, and applying these concepts to a comprehensive theory of neurosis. In 1979, he joined the Glendon Association, which has made possible a longitudinal study that provided supporting data for his theory and an understanding of the fantasy bond as manifested in normal couples and family relationships. His major works *The Fantasy Bond, Voice Therapy, Compassionate Child-Rearing,* and *Combating Destructive Thought Processes* describe how couples form destructive bonds that impair their psychological functioning and have a damaging effect on their child-rearing practices. His studies of negative thought processes and their associated effect have led to the development of an innovative therapeutic methodology to uncover and contend with aspects of destructive cognition, which was described in *Suicide and the Inner Voice.* In recent years, he has applied his concepts to empirical research and to developing the Firestone Assessment of Self-Destructive Thoughts (FAST), a scale that assesses suicide potential. In addition to his contributions to the mental health field, he serves as a consultant to several large corporations.

Joyce Catlett, MA, author and lecturer, received her BA in psychology from the University of California, Los Angeles in 1969 and her MA in Education from California Lutheran College in 1972. In conjunction with her graduate program, she served a two-year field placement as teacher and

357

child therapist with the Children's Center at Camarillo State Hospital, which led to her certification as a child mental health specialist. Since 1979, she has collaborated with Dr. Robert W. Firestone in writing six books and numerous articles and has coproduced, with Geoff Parr, 35 video documentaries used for training mental health professionals. She is coauthor, with Dr. Firestone, of *Psychological Defenses in Everyday Life*, a book explaining the defensive processes and psychotherapy for lay readers. She has trained instructors in the Compassionate Child-Rearing Parent Education Program, a child abuse prevention model, in six states, Canada, and Costa Rica. She currently lectures and conducts continuing education workshops at universities and mental health facilities throughout the United States and Canada.

DATE DUE

OCT 2 2 2001		
JAN 1 4 2003		
NOV 0 2 2004		

HIGHSMITH #45230

Printed in USA